GHOSTS BEHIND THE SUN:
Splendor, Enigma & Death

"The Mississippi Delta begins in the lobby of The Peabody Hotel and ends on Catfish Row in Vicksburg. The Peabody is the Paris Ritz, the Cairo Shepherd's, the London Savoy of this section. If you stand near its fountain in the middle of the lobby... ultimately you will see everybody who is anybody in the Delta..."
–David Cohn, 1935

"Back in the alley when the games gets fast,
ain't no piece of paper gonna save your ass."
–Lee Baker

GHOSTS BEHIND THE SUN:
Splendor, Enigma & Death

TAV FALCO

MONDO MEMPHIS
Volume One

GHOSTS BEHIND THE SUN: Splendor, Enigma & Death
Mondo Memphis, Volume One
TAV FALCO

ISBN 978-1-84068-181-9
Published by Creation Books, 2011

Cover photo: Gustavo Falco
Other photo credits: "The Singing Brakeman": Alabama Music Hall of Fame; "Memphis and Charleston Railroad Station": Memphis and Shelby County Room, Memphis Public Library; "Slave Collar": The Cabildo Society, Louisiana State Museum; "Antebellum Louisiana: Agrarian Life": http://lsm.crt.state.la.us/cabildo/cab9.htm; "Memphis 1870": U.S. Library of Congress; "Sam Phillips Studio": http://wigowsky.com/images/Elvis/Elvis4.jpg; "Goodwyn Institute", "Bitter Lemon", "Capture of George 'Buster' Putt", "Danny Owens", "Hell Angels in Memphis", and "Art Baldwin": Special Collections, University of Memphis.

To Jim Dickinson
–Godhead, protector, muse, and comrade. His passion for the music of Memphis and all that it touches was ineluctable. Of his presence, we are assured in the abiding words of his self-penned epitaph: *I'm just dead, I'm not gone.*

ACKNOWLEDGEMENTS

Homespun wisdom has taught us that neither cities nor books are built in a day; rather, they are assembled piecemeal, occasionally in short bursts, but, more often, after long, tedious delays...whether due to scheduling conflicts, structural integrity, inclement weather or war; conceived in moments of narcissism, they are mostly the result of quotidian labors and mechanical exercises, which emphasize foundation, symmetry and convention; but despite a legitimate dedication to budget or design, there is the inevitable divagation from the blueprints at hand toward that something which is beyond mere utility or necessity, something capturing the process of the construction itself or, quite possibly, the liminal experience of creating this very *something* out of nothing, until the completed work is not simply a book or a city, but all possible books and all conceivable cities; because architects are authors of space while authors are architects of the word, their respective occupations are much less concerned with writing cities and erecting books than with creating the libraries and pluriverses which surround them.

With this in mind, the authors would like to thank the following people for their insights, equipments and blueprints: Lisa Poggiali, Roy and Karyn Morse, family and friends, James Williamson and Creation Books, Abe Schwab, Alex Chilton, Andrew Hurley, Andy Hummel, Ardent Studios, The Believer, Bernard Lansky, Beverly Sousoulas, Billy Lee Riley, Billy Naylor, Bob Mehr, Bobby Gillespie, Bomb Magazine, Bud Chittom, Rosemary, Wanda, and Bubba Feathers, David Evans, Dean Phillips, Dick Raichelson, Dewitt Jordan, George Klein, Glitterhouse/Stag-O-Lee Records, Guy Maddin, Harold Boone, Hedi El Kholti, Herbie O'Mell, James Cobb, James Dickerson, Jeff Titon, Jennifer Higgie, Jim Cole, Jim Dickinson, Jim Jarmusch, Jim Johnson, Jody Stephens, John Branston, John Fry, Jud and Rose Phillips, Linda Schaefer Yarman, Luce Vigo, Mabon "Teenie" Hodges, Matthew Lassiter, Memphis Public Library, Michael Finger, Mojo Buford, Paul Burlison, Peabody Hotel Memphis, Pete Daniel, Peter Sloterdijk, Roland Janes at Phillips Recording Studio, Richard Rosebrough, Robert Gordon, Ross Johnson, Russell Sugarmon, Sam the Sham, Shirley Richardson, Silky Sullivan, Stanford University's Green Library, Steve Rhea, Terry Manning, Tom Eubanks, University of Memphis Library, Victor Bockris, William Eggleston, Willie and Boo Mitchell.

TABLE OF CONTENTS

PROLOGUE

Upriver from New Orleans, past the ports of Natchez and Vicksburg, looms Memphis – metropolis of the Midsouth and city of murder, necrolatry, and music. Memphis' muse hangs in the air like a crow circling in menacing descent… with sardonic eye winking on the tail draggers below, howling in the night to seduce and repel its prey. It is the song of sex and death sung always in the Delta, and it's the same song with a more baneful lilt sung up in the hills that comes eventually upriver or downriver into Memphis… and lingers in malevolent tones over its bayous and creeks and crossroads. It is the song of earth and sun, of loss and betrayal, of night and sacrifice, of catching the wind off the side of a boxcar, of floating into town on the black wave of a river barge, of drifting on the winding smoke of burning mansions.

Known as the Bluff City, Memphis is built upon the New Madrid fault line – a geological fissure extending a couple hundred miles north and south. It was during the dawn of recorded history that French trappers and fur traders had encamped on the river bluff of what would become the future site of the city, as we know it now. Chronicled in an eyewitness account written by an anonymous Frenchman, a massive, catastrophic earthquake had struck without warning. For three days, the Mississippi river ran backwards and filled a cavernous breach in the earth that the quake had opened – an enormous ravine that became known as Reel Foot Lake. The quake struck with such intensity that it broke windows out of the Capitol building in Washington and rang church bells in Boston. In the words of the Frenchman, "the ground shook for a week thereafter like a freshly killed beef".

Photo: Eugene Baffle 1976

CHAPTER THE FIRST
MIGRATIONS, PLAGUES AND LOST CAUSES

The road to Memphis is a long and unholy one. As a post mortem to the 60s, I pulled the green '50 Ford up to the side screen-door of the decrepit cabin at dawn, opened all its doors and lids and stuffed in junk, old clothes, pots and pans, and art supplies. Just enough room left to squeeze in behind the steering wheel and to work the 4-speed shifter bolted in the floorboard. My partner cranked the starter motor and cast off from the old cabin inherited now by denizens of spiders, snakes, and rodents already snugly at home within its planks and clapboard walls, cozy in the morning chill and warmed by the final embers glowing in the belly of the rustediron woodstove.

The rumble of the twin smitty exhaust pipes sounded muffled as the blue-dot taillights retreated down the gravel road strewn between the ruts with pine needles brown and fragrant. I followed behind on a black and silver Norton motorbike. We hit the main road and by the time we crested Gaylor Mountain – the highest peak on the Arkansas side of the Ozarks – the '48 Mercury flathead motor underneath the hood of the old Ford had come alive breathing the thin, rarefied air through 3-deuces sitting atop Offenhauser intake manifolds. The Norton was flying down the curves swooping past Devil's Den on the right and descending into the foothills of the mountain range that begins at Alma, then around and beyond Fort Smith heading east. By the time the Arkansas River came in sight a reedy, hollow sound was coming out of one exhaust pipe of the Norton. Oil had started pumping out of the left bank of the motor passing a fine but fierce spray from under the head gasket out into the crisp, turbulent air. Running on one cylinder, the engine speed had tapered off to 2700 rpm providing a maximum forward thrust of not more than 40 mph. At Alma the green Ford had already shot by me at 90 mph. The only solution was to stop and add more oil to the tank and then pull in behind a high balling semi-tractor trailer truck and ride in the back draft of its air stream. The drag of the semi pulled me all the way across the Arkansas delta and up Crowley's Ridge, then on to Memphis. Motor oil had now soaked through the sleeve of my motorcycle jacket, penetrated my left engineer boot, and completely drenched the rear wheel of the motorbike, which remained in a constant state of controlled skid. Yet this would not be my first foray into Memphis, nor would it be my last.

First time I came into Memphis was by train. I was working as a brakeman on the Missouri Pacific Railroad. Mostly I was riding fast freights out of Little Rock to Texarkana, Poplar Bluff, and to Memphis. It was a hot summer's day, and the closer we came to the Bluff City, the more the rays of the diurnal orb slanted across the Arkansas Delta and illuminated the dust, coruscated opaque particles, and micro-organisms hovering in the diaphanous atmosphere. The golden light fell like a mantle – palpable and regal – over the farmlands and the sharecroppers' rickety cabins set beside fields or beside a shimmering creek bed. The occasional mansion was wrapped in the same democratic aura of heavenly light as the train rolled past. The air was moist and clement, and people of every age and hue were out on their porches or fishing in ponds, or out riding horses or a mule. Human skin and that of farm animals and wild creatures, and the scales of fish in the streams, were joyous and glowing and at one with the warm iron rails and with the train as it passed over them. Some people stopped to look and to wave. I waved back with my railroad cap from the vestibule of the caboose. The excitement of Memphis was approaching, as if the evening were pregnant and going to give birth to something massive and palpitating. A fecund threshold was looming across which sacrifice of passage was imminent. Then the skyline of the Bluff City appeared on the horizon, and the river at its feet below. Both were brown and moody under the aura of golden dust. While the city seemed planted there, the river ached and twisted and heaved with a sullen torrential rush. On the timber-braced trestle, the train stopped on the Arkansas side positioning the caboose on the hind end high over the swamp below. I beheld Memphis on the bluff as I would never see it again – majestic, lofty, and infused with promise, pleasure, grandeur, and every possibility and human act imaginable. The sun sank behind us as the train rolled inexorably over the Harahan Bridge in full glory.

We pulled into the Missouri Pacific R.R. yards near Lamar and Bellevue Avenues. There was no hotel nearby, so I'd accepted an invitation to stay over at a boarding house off Snowden Circle run by Mae Stover. My high school buddy, Thomas, was staying there while working as a plumber's helper, and had asked if I might care to stay there too when my train was in town. After a robust evening meal of greens and black-eyed peas with the train crew in a diner situated under the MoPac Lamar Ave. overpass, which was uproariously overcrowded with trainmen from the Rock Island, the Frisco, MoPac, and the L&N Lines, I left the joint and headed over to Snowden Circle by foot. In the falling darkness, I walked up to the tall hedges that separated the boarding house from the circular street. Across the front was an old iron fence and gate, and behind it was the porch of the boarding house. It was a tableau as if from a professionally lit stage play at the Orpheum, yet there was only one naked light bulb hanging from the sky blue ceiling of the veranda. There in the half-light was a lumpy woman with ashen hair rocking in a rocking chair and turning the crank of an ice cream churn with the bare toes on one foot while she was chain smoking Pell Mells with her free hand, and with the other hand was holding firm to the arm of the rocker. That was Mae. The pallor of her skin was gray as her hair which was gray as the cigarette ash piled in the ashtray of butts standing on a pedestal beside her rocker. She invited me in and showed me to a small room, more like a proverbial closet off the corridor, furnished with a cot that she rented to working men, most often to railroad men for whom she had an affinity. Her husband had been a career MoPac locomotive engineer until the day he died. They had bought the house together.

Mae was an enterprising woman. Always had been. She was something of a rounder too, in her girlish days. As a teenager, she'd hooked up with Jimmie Rodgers in Meridian. He was a yodeler and guitar player known as the Singing Brakeman. To hear Mae tell it, the two of them did a lot of traveling together around the south and the southwest. Jimmie Rodgers had been a 'boomer' brakeman until TB infected his lungs to the point where he was 'bad ordered' by the railroad. A 'boomer' is a worker who hires himself out to any railroad that will hire him, and he works until he earns a bankroll; then he quits. When that roll of cash is gone, he hires out again on some other railroad. In those days there were many railroad companies, but they didn't like to hire 'boomers' because they were strictly temporary, and one never knew just when they'd quit. So to even get hired, a 'boomer' had to know his job and do it better and faster than regular trainmen, or he had no chance to get the job. When TB ended his railroading career, Jimmie Rodgers took up the guitar and singing for a living. He made out pretty good at his new vocation, and earned such success with record sales and show dates that he became independently wealthy. That first night I met her, Mae had one of his 78s on the turntable playing low behind the screen door:

> *All around the water tank*
> *waiting for a train,*
> *A thousand miles away from home*
> *sleeping in the rain,*
> *I walked up to a brakeman*
> *to ask him for a lousy dime...*

Jimmie Rodgers. Photo: Courtesy of Richard Matteson

The audience of Jimmie Rodgers was immense. People from foreign countries were learning English just to understand lyrics the 'Blue Yodeler' was singing. Before long his disease progressed to the point where he literally sang lying on a cot during his last studio recording sessions. Eventually, Mae would play all of her Jimmie Rodgers records for me.

> *Well, T for Texas*
> *T for Tennessee,*
> *and T for Thelma,*
> *that woman made a wreck out of me...*

In a little railroad terminal/lumber town called Gurdon, about halfway between Little Rock and Texarkana, is where Mae lived with engineman, Stover. This is where Thomas and near where I grew up, and how our families knew Mae. When Mr. Stover bid in a regular engine job in Memphis, they moved there, and Mae opened a café on Bellevue off Lamar that she named Mae's Grill. The eatery was patronized mainly by railroad men, and they served the best tasting cathead biscuits you could find in the Bluff City. Mae was an earthy woman, and fond of a jolly good time. One of her dear friends was from Tupelo, named Gladys, who often came over to Mae's Grill to visit. She'd bring along her son, a wiry little boy named Elvis, because he loved to listen to the jukebox in the café. Many times the boy would jump up on the counter and sing along to country tunes emanating from the jukebox. Mae showed me snapshots of Gladys and little Elvis at her place. Later the black lady responsible for those exquisite cathead biscuits would be hired to cook for special parties at Graceland.

Mae had talents herself. Thomas called them 'gifts'. For instance, Thomas claimed that Mae could read your thoughts. I wasn't so sure, still I always felt a little uneasy around Mae for this reason, and tried to guard my thinking in her presence. I did see her do unusual things that I never saw anyone else do that maybe required special powers, like how she could palm a silver dollar to her forehead and it wouldn't fall off. Then there was the way she could make a silver dollar 'walk' over the back of her fingers. She always wore a simple calico dress and slippers with the backs mashed down under heels that flip-flopped when she walked, like some black women wear. Never did I see her sitting or walking without a Pell Mell burning between her fingers or dangling from her mouth. After the Grill closed, I lost track of Mae and her demimonde on Snowden Circle around the periphery of the Snowden Mansion, but thoughts of her not infrequently cross my mind.

General Nathan Bedford Forrest, C.S.A.

On the Harahan Bridge, entry of the Norton and I to the Bluff City was halted as traffic backed up for miles. Someone was attempting to jump – or had already jumped – from the bridge works into the dark swirling waters of the Mississippi River. I slid off the Norton and looked over the railing into the black torrents searching for some suicidal trace, but there was not the slightest sign of anything human, only the ghastly torrents of the River beckoning to the mortals high above. My gaze drifted upriver and my thoughts began to penetrate the mists 40 miles north of Memphis to the 1st Chickasaw Bluff on the Mississippi. Layers of lives and former events peeled off like leafed pages torn away from a dusty, forgotten book. It was during a rain and mud soaked mid-April in 1864, at not more than 16 years of age, that I joined the ranks of a Confederate Cavalry squadron 1500 strong under the command of Major General Nathan Bedford Forrest. Under the spell of a festive recruitment rally held before the start of the war on the Memphis river bluff, I had succumbed to the florid oratory of Gen. Forrest's elite commanders with their promise of the chance to kill plenty of Yankees. I enlisted on the spot and borrowed a horse from a cousin farmer in Brownsville, who helped me fashion a saber out of garden scythe that I hung from a rope tied around my waist. Although reported to be a six-footer (viewed from the terra firma, anyone appears six feet tall mounted astride a cavalry charger), Gen. Forrest was in actuality a "little bit of a man". He was known to sharpen his saber on both sides and to deliver an astonishing flourish of butchery from horseback not unlike the deliberate pendulum of a swinging razor. With regiments of foot soldiers and rebel sharp shooters with unerring eye, his forces stormed the Federalist-held Fort Pillow catching the 400 white and black Union troops of the Indiana and Iowa regiments in a lethal and unrelenting crossfire. Although hopeless in the face of the assault, the blundering command of the fort refused to surrender and lower the Union flag. After overrunning the fortification, Forrest withdrew toward Jackson but not before having three horses shot out from under him.

The pillage and slaughter went on all night and into the next day perpetrated mainly by stragglers and irregulars who nailed white and black Union troops to logs and set the timbers on fire. They further bayoneted, mutilated, and violated troops who had thrown down their rifles and begged on their knees for mercy. Barrels of whiskey with tin dippers floating on top found inside the fort fanned the flames of savagery to heinous maniacal heights of vengeance, animosity, and murderous ferocity. Next day after the engagement, Forrest ordered a detachment of regulars back into Fort Pillow to restore order. I was attached to this peacekeeping mission (my crude saber was not much good for anything save this type of lowly task). We were instructed to burn all the buildings except the hospital, which Gen. Forrest had ordered fortified with a week's provisions and medicine, and to secure a full day for Union forces to re-enter the fort under a flag of truce to remove and bury their dead, to treat their wounded, and to remove them to waiting steamboats. It seems that the massacre of Fort Pillow has become the atrocity most remembered, scrutinized, and celebrated in the annals of American militarist conflict.

Fort Pillow Massacre, April 12, 1864

The first expedition into Tennessee country that I know of was led by the Spanish conquisidor, Hernando DeSoto in 1540-1541 with an armed force of undetermined size. DeSoto became known for his brilliant horsemanship and for extreme brutality. Yet the Spaniards met their match in a conflict with the Tula Indians near Caddo Valley, Arkansas. At the time, I was little more than a papoose living in a lean-to fabricated with sticks and branches beside the riverbank at the strategic point where the Caddo meets the Ouachita River. Rightly described by DeSoto's secretary, Rodrigo Ranjel, as "the best fighting people that the Christians met with," the Tula practiced cranial deformation, tattooed their faces, and fought with large spears. DeSoto's mission did mark the beginning of recorded history in the region. Other than the French monopoly of the fur trade spreading along the Mississippi from Louisiana to Illinois, nothing much of historical magnitude happened until 200 years later when Jean-Baptiste Le Moyne de Bienville arrived at Fort Prudhomme upon the spot where Memphis now stands. I was there too, in fact. As an aid to sieur Bienville, I'd been given the assignment of tutoring the chiefs of his tribal allies in French, which I had learned as an elementary student under the sisters at the Couvent des Urslines in New Orleans. I witnessed the caprice of his wavering, dilettante personality undermine his campaign to extirpate the Chickasaw Indian nation. It was a mission ill fated due to indecision and protracted delays as much as to the ferocity of the Chickasaw warriors and their blind hatred of the French. Bienville's force of 1400 French and French Canadian troops bolstered by 2400 Indian warriors of mutually militant tribes, ultimately disbanded amid general apathy and tribal infighting combined with endless intoxication that plenty of frontier whisky can induce. Still the human burnings, roastings, live scalpings, quarterings, and cannibalizing of still living human organs reported during the campaign makes the Fort Pillow massacre seem like a genteel garden party.

For sheer unmitigated villainy, I have only to look a little farther back than the War of Rebellion and a little ahead of Bienville's perfumed antics to the origins of the Harp Brothers gang. Two brothers, Micajah and Wiley, known as "Big" Harp and "Little Harp", thought of as the first serial killers, cut a wide swathe through Tennessee and Kentucky. During the Revolutionary War, the Harps sided with the British (as much as such renegades could side with any cause) and fought under Tarleton in 1780. Later they lived with Cherokee and Chickamauga Indians in Nickjack, Kentucky, and fought for 10 years in British-backed Indian raids on white settlements west of the Appalachians. Near Nashville, when Captain James Wood, a local patriot, attempted to intervene in an attempted rape, the Harps shot him dead. They kidnapped his daughter, Susan, and another local girl. Later joined by a minister's daughter, Sally Rice, they became the Harp's wives. During their tenure at Nickjack, the wives gave birth two times, and the Harp brothers murdered the babies. Tipped off just before the Americans raided and exterminated Nickjack, the Harps escaped with their wives.

Then the real killing began. Race, sex, age, nor creed held the slightest compunction for the Harp brothers. Their favored method was to eviscerate the stomach, fill the cavity with stones, and throw the body into a river, not before placing their signature carving on the torso. Just for fun, they often axed the heads of their victims. As whole families lay asleep in their cabins, women would awake to the screams of their infants with their throats slit. Once Big Harp having grown tired of the sobs of another of his baby girls, slung her around and around by her tiny feet bashing her brains out against the trunk of a tree.

Near Memphis, the Harps joined in with the riverboat pirate Samuel Mason, but soon the antics of the sanguinary brothers were too much for even the most grizzled river bandit, and the murderous lot was persuaded to leave. After the mutilation and dismemberment of the 13-year-old son of Revolutionary War veteran, Col. Daniel Trabue, ambushed for a sack of flour, Kentucky Governor Garrard Mason placed a $300 reward on the heads of the Harps. I joined a posse that was sent out for their capture. The first posse chased the Harp clan into a cane field, but let them slip away due to their cowardice. In a second posse that I rode with, we caught up with the fugitives near Morgan County, Tennessee, and a scout named Wilford, drew a bead on Big Harp shooting him off his horse through the back. His head was cut off, taken to what is now Harp's Head Road, and displayed on a pole for passers-by to view the downcast countenance. Little Harp managed to escape the pursuit of our posse, and re-joined Mason and his river pirates. He lived with them for four years, after which Wiley turned up in Natchez carrying the head of Mason in a box. He turned the moldering caput over to the authorities in

The 4th Chickasaw Bluff at Memphis, 1887
(Wood engraving: Charles Graham)

order to collect the reward on it, but Little Harp was recognized, summarily hung, and in turn decapitated. His own head was then impaled alongside the Natchez Trace as a portentous reminder to outlaw brethren. In his dying works, Micajah Harp confessed to 20 murders, probably not counting the babies. Although the figure is thought to be more than 40 murders, Wiley himself is believed to have been responsible for as many more.

It was long after midnight before cars, buses, trucks, and motorcycles were permitted to pass inch by inch over the Arkansas/Mississippi River Bridge and to enter the Bluff City from the West. A dimly orange sun was filtering through the gray dust of downtown as the Norton sputtered by the equestrian statue of Gen. Forrest around which two detachments of enactors sporting wooden rifles had gathered for pre-dawn drill in their jeans and canvas shoes. The drill officers with their potbellies and dirty straw ploughboy hats carried an unsheathed sword crossed on their shoulder. The vagabond officers appeared as stalking specters marching their modest detachments in opposite directions on the dewy grounds surrounding their petrified commander.

Next morning I woke up on a mattress on the floor with a bad case of the cold shakes. Staring up at the lavender ceiling of a humid, over-heated room on Cox Street, not far from the Mid-South Fairgrounds, I tried to figure what had brought it on. Must have been that rusty spoon and the re-used dirty cotton. Randall, my mentor and comrade who had arrived in the Bluff City from Arkansas some months before as a passenger in a '53 Plymouth sedan, termed the condition a 'foreign body reaction'. He spoke with the air of authority having eventually succumbed to such convulsive jitters that wouldn't stop due to the terminal stages of Hepatitis

C. Another wave of convulsive undulations and teeth chattering came before I fell back in a feverish delirium. The lavender of the ceiling was studded with a gestalt of hand-stenciled 5-pointed stars. Night descended and transformed the room into a *grisaille* of bleak subliminal stars.

I was riding with the Wizard of the Saddle on the final raid on his hometown of Memphis. I was the youngest in his detachment of 80 elite cavalry troops who surrounded General Forrest at all times... 19 years old at the time on this moonless April night of 1864. A former slave of General Forrest rode with us, and a former dueling partner of the General, now a liege lord of the commander, rode at our flank. We rode hard out of our encampment near Oxford and reached the outskirts of the Bluff City around midnight. An outpost manned by a half dozen Union infantrymen greeted our approach, but our column of fours rode over them in silence without breaking stride, only the sounds of the saddles and the rattling of sabers in their scabbards, and the melodious syncopations of the horses' hooves were heard crushing the bones of the unfortunate sentries.

Then the main force of Forrest's regiment had split off to destroy a Federal cavalry detachment in the Nonconnah Bottoms south of Memphis in a pitched battle lasting most of the night. Because I rode an unusually fine horse, I was selected to proceed along Hernando Road towards Memphis under the command of the General's brother, Captain Bill Forrest who was riding in the post of honor. We approached an encampment of 90-day-men whose vidette did not challenge us, but some of the sentries asked which command it were. We answered, "Forrest's cavalry". They laughed at us and told us to go to hell. Moving up to the edge of the city, we encountered another federal battery, which we subdued by firing a few shots. Some of the battery men told us there was a regiment of Negroes sleeping in a barracks down in the hollow. We raced down to the Negro barracks. Next morning the papers wrote that around 200 Negro soldiers were killed, but it was too dark for us to keep count.

Arriving in Memphis we entered on DeSoto Street, then rode up Gayoso Alley alongside the bayou to the Gayoso Hotel. We charged through the front doors and filled the rotunda as much as it would hold of us, then dismounted. We had expected to capture Gen. Hurlbert who then was in command of the city, but found only a night clerk and a sole Federal officer. The officer surrendered immediately, but then recanted and proclaimed in pompous manner that he thought he had surrendered to soldiers, but could now see that we were a bunch of damned guerrillas. A boy about my age drew his side arm to kill the officer, but Captain Bill ordered him to stay out if he could not behave himself. Couple of minutes later a shot was fired through the hotel office window that struck the officer right through the temple, and he fell dead on the rotunda floor. No one could see who fired the shot.

We then rode out of the Gayoso rotunda and down to Irving Block, which was being used as a Federal Prison. We attacked the front gates with our rifle butts, but the bars were too strong. Without a battering ram, our efforts to free the prisoners inside were useless. We retreated in a hail of gunfire coming from the upper floors, and rode out of Memphis the same way we came in. On Hernando Road we re-joined Gen. Forrest's forces where they'd had quite a battle with a good many men being killed on both sides, and withdrew across the Nonconnah Bottoms bringing up the rear. Even though Forrest's efforts to capture Gen. Hurlbert had failed, the skirmish undermined the morale and security concerns of the enemy. Strategically the purpose of forcing Union Gen. A. J. Smith to abandon his raid on Mississippi across the then raging torrents of the Tallahatchie River and to return to Memphis was accomplished.

A former plantation owner and slave trader, Forrest had no military training and rose from the rank of private to that of major general. In the aftermath of War of Rebellion Forrest stood opposed to Reconstruction and staunchly against federal occupation. Serving as the first Grand Wizard of the Ku Klux Klan, he became the supreme commander of the Grand Dragons of the Realms. During reconstruction, I remember when the first A.M.E. negro church on Beale Street had established a building fund; the only white person to contribute was Maj. Gen.

FORREST & MAPLES,
SLAVE DEALERS,

87 Adams Street,
Between Second and Third,

MEMPHIS, TENNESSEE,

Have constantly on hand the best selected assortment of

FIELD HANDS, HOUSE SERVANTS & MECHANICS,

at their Negro Mart, to be found in the city. They are daily receiving from Virginia, Kentucky and Missouri, fresh supplies of likely Young Negroes.

Negroes Sold on Commission, and the highest market price always paid for good stock. Their Jail is capable of containing Three Hundred, and for comfort, neatness and safety, is the best arranged of any in the Union. Persons wishing to purchase, are invited to examine their stock before purchasing elsewhere.

They have on hand at present, Fifty likely young Negroes, comprising Field hands, Mechanics, House and Body Servants, &c.

Memphis City Directory entry for Forrest's slave-trading business, 1855-1856

Nathan Bedford Forrest with a donation of $50. That the white and black community lived side by side and was therefore close in a way that has been little understood by Northerners is no mystery. Still matters of racial prejudice and bigotry have hardly been reconciled in the Bluff City, as even the bloodiest of American wars could not resolve.

My flights back into Memphis are not unlike the paradigms of migrations from Mississippi, Arkansas, and Tennessee into the Bluff City since before the Civil War ongoing to the present. Memphis can be thought of connected as much to Mississippi and Arkansas as it is to Tennessee, if not more so. William Faulkner once observed that Mississippi extends from a Memphis hotel room to the Gulf of Mexico. In the aftermath of the "Cession" in 1818 of the lands of the Chickasaw Indian nation, a rush of settlers, speculators, and profiteers began pouring into the area of West Tennessee facing the Mississippi River. Prior to the opening of the Chickasaw lands, an early account – perhaps the earliest – of the settlement on the site of future Memphis was published anonymously in the *Navigator* in 1801. It stated that, "The settlement is thin and composed of what is called the half-breed; that is a mixture of the whites and the Indians, a race of men too indolent to do any permanent good, either for them or society."

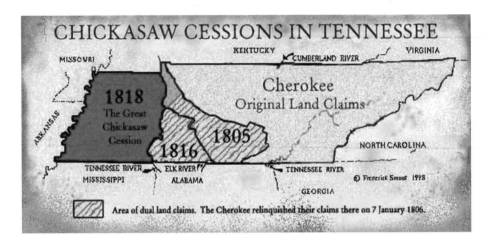

CABIN NOTES:
Thoughts of the multifarious readings with which I had been immersed beside the iron woodstove over wintry cabin nights in Arkansas, continue to pervade my mind. Of the chartering of Memphis, I found that on May 22, 1819, James Overton, James Winchester, and A.B. Carr, land speculating cohorts of Andrew Jackson, had submitted a formal petition to the State Legislature for the creation of Shelby County on a promontory of the 4th bluff of the Chickasaw at the confluence of the Wolf River and the Mississippi. James Winchester, Revolutionary war veteran and brigadier general of the War of 1812, was credited with christening the town: Memphis-On-The-Mississippi, as its namesake on the Nile meant, Place of Good Abode. The city was incorporated by the State Legislature in 1825, and Marcus Brutus Winchester, the son of James Winchester, became its first mayor in 1827, but his popularity soon waned because of his wife's race. She was part Negro, and the Nat Turner Slave Rebellion of 1831 was fresh in the minds of those Southerners who held the greatest animosity for the manumission of slaves.

For 1830 the census read 1,239 inhabitants, and the US. Government agreed to build a Navy Yard at Memphis in 1845. The burgeoning city had now outstripped Nashville as the leading city of Tennessee. The 1850 census counted 8,841 residents, and in this year Memphis became a port of customs because of its commanding position on the Mississippi. Public and private buildings in Memphis were beginning to be built with artesian elements fashioned by European immigrant craftsmen. Favored styles were Federal, Tudor, Italianate, and Greek, Egyptian, Roman and Gothic Revival. During this era of the big side-wheelers, steamboats hastened the transport of King Cotton, the chief moneymaking crop and export of the Mississippi and Arkansas deltas and of the West Tennessee farmlands and hence of the Bluff City, to the open ocean and on to markets in Europe. The Cabildo Society reported that Lady Emmeline Stuart Wortley in 1849 related the night time wonder of "The magnificent 'floating palaces' of steamers, that frequently look like moving mountains of light and flame, so brilliantly are these enormous river-leviathans illuminated, outside and inside." By 1852, only St. Louis and New Orleans outsized the Bluff City as ports on the Mississippi. In this year, an anonymous observer noted that, "The most conspicuous object at Memphis was a brick building, with a very large sign, bearing this disgusting inscription: Bolton, Dickens, & Co. Slave Dealers. It is proper to observe here that no persons are held in greater contempt in the South than professional slave-dealers."

The physician, Thomas Low Nichols, wrote in 1855 that aside from the luxury of ice served on every table in Memphis, "You walk out toward evening, the sky is blue, the air is balm, but a thousand rainbows of gay and flashing colors have broken loose; all negrodom has put on its wonderful attire of finery and come out to take the air. Slavery has its fascinations, and one of these was to see the whole Negro population of a rich city like Memphis out on a Sunday afternoon. The Negroes not only outdo the whites in dress but caricature their manners."

Although at least eight railroad companies were chartered in Tennessee in the 1830s, the geographical problems in penetrating the Blue Ridge Mountains and the financial Panic of 1837 delayed arrival of the steam locomotive to the Bluff City. According to Forest Laws, the building of the Memphis and LaGrange Railroad culminated with the arrival of its locomotive in 1842 by steamboat from Philadelphia, "Amid cheering throngs of Memphians and a marching band, the small, red and green locomotive was hauled to a test course near the LaGrange and Memphis depot. Free rides were offered to all, but officials soon found that no one knew how to operate the steam engine; it was two days before anyone was able to figure out how to run the engine. Once the train was running, Memphians were upset because the train would not move any faster".

Upon completion of the Memphis and Charleston Railroad in 1857, my fellow Memphians had greater cause to raise their glasses in heady celebration. This strategic route connected the Atlantic coast with the Mississippi River establishing Memphis not only as a vital port on the river's north-south axis, but it opened trade links overland across the country all the way east. More than goods and cargo were transported overland, but also various classes of passenger trains carried their customers in newly constructed coaches, the floors of which were invariably slick with the spit of tobacco juice. As a kid in knickers, I rode in the cabin of the locomotive with my granddad Horace, who had started as fireman on wood burning steam engines on the M&C and worked up to rank of engineer. He spent 49 years railroading between Memphis and Corinth, Mississippi. In the early steam days, an engineer fabricated his own steam whistle comprised of a number of flutes or fifes bundled together. Thus each engineer created his own particular melodic tones for his whistle, and was he known and recognized up and down the railroad line by the particular timbre of his steam whistle.

The antebellum age was a period of great awakening when men and women aspired to the American ideal of good manners and personal cleanliness (as bathing had found little favor until then). The style of barbered beards, sideburns, stovepipe hats, and dark frock coats was adopted by men, while corseted ladies with hourglass waistlines, wearing ankle covering petticoats and hoop skirts (foot and leg were forbidden to be seen), and colors equally as dour as the men's, indulged only in the heavy application of perfumes. Ladies as well as gentlemen shared the singular art of chewing tobacco and the dipping of snuff as the most fashionable and habituating of social pastimes. Dancing became a difficult problem in that the only part of the body allowed to be touched during the dance were the elbows. Touching the waist of the lady was strictly forbidden. Further etiquette concerning the body and sexual matters was quite restrictive. Even for married couples, when they did share a bed, a board was placed between them to prevent bodily frottage. So I did not marry, and confined my dancing to Congo Square in New Orleans, and to Beale Street bordellos in Memphis, sporting a beaver top hat and a purple frock coat over gray striped trousers, hung with a silver pocket watch and chain bequeathed by my elder, Horace.

Shelby Dade Foote, the Memphis author of a three-volume history of the Civil War, and father of my running buddy Huggie Foote, once remarked that not a day went by when he was

Memphis and Charleston Railroad Station

not reminded that the fortunes of Memphis and of the South were built upon the backs of black people. During the antebellum period, about a third of the population of the South lived in a condition of chattel slavery. Although cotton was king, prior to the invention of the cotton gin by Eli Whitney, it was not a truly profitable crop. When there was no possibility of ginning the cotton, pickers had to separate the cottonseeds from the fiber by hand. It was a long, tedious, and frustrative ordeal. I picked a lot of cotton growing up on the picayune farm that my granddad Horace lived on, and it was real hard, backbreaking, finger-splitting work. Cotton was fairly easy to grow where we lived, but bad weather and insects could wipe out the crop. Most cotton pickers harvesting the cotton bowls averaged about 150 pounds per day, working from 'can to can': at sunup and at sundown when the sun shown down angularly on discarded bottles and tin cans. If you didn't fill your sack, it was hardly worth a day's work in the fields for a white man. Slaves who did not pick the required quota were routinely whipped raw.

Like on most farms and plantations, Granddad reserved one field for growing corn, which was the essential diet fed to slaves and to livestock. The whole family – men, women, and children, including Granddad when he wasn't railroading – worked side by side with our slaves in the fields. When we weren't working in the fields, our slaves and hired help cultivated gardens and raised livestock, spun and wove cloth, fished the creeks and rivers, and hunted game in the thickets. In our little town near Corinth could be found Renfro's Barber Shop, Austin's Dry Goods, and Wu Fong's groceries. As in most towns down south, there were market and street vendors who were usually Indian or black women plying the same avocation they had practiced back in Africa.

When Lincoln was elected there was panic in the cotton and money markets. Still the sentiment in Memphis in February of 1861 was four to three for union, rather than secession. Yet public opinion shifted as a result of impassioned oratorio, protracted agitation and florid debate in meetings downtown at the Exchange Building and at the Odd Fellows Hall (where the Swedish Nightingale, Jenny Lind had performed, and Edwin Booth had starred in King Lear, Hamlet, and Richard III in 1859). Within six months, due to fallout from countless parades and processions in this climate of political upheaval, there arose amidst whoops of the Rebel Yell a unanimous call for action in support of secession.

As for Memphis' part in the War of Rebellion, the city underwent a summary capitulation in what was essentially a pitched naval battle beneath the river bluff. It was a spectacle witnessed by myself and by most of my fellow denizens of the port city on June 6, 1862. We had ensconced ourselves on the bluff in what turned into a festive picnic atmosphere. There were vendors hawking balloons, sandwiches, and pints of beer and sodas. A ragtag band of flutes and snare drums played marches and gavottes at the shoreline, and little Rebel flags and *visite cartes* of Robert E. Lee were selling like crazy. Less than a proper engagement between nine advancing Union rams and gunboats and the opposing eight Rebel vessels, it was more a contest of naval mayhem, as both sides were without military command. Instead riverboat pilots and engineers were commanding the vessels on each side in a brief, but devastating slaughter of Rebel forces.

John Miller Srodes in command of the Yankee ram boat, Lioness, then steamed into the harbor and demanded surrender from Mayor John Park. Under threat of bombardment of the city, surrender took place in 10 minutes. The city fathers were unaware of Srodes' bluff in that there was no armament aboard the Lioness, only the short arms of its crew of makeshift marines. Even I could see from the shore that there were no canon barrels protruding from the gunnel ports of the Lioness. Despite the tardy entrance of the CSS Arkansas into the fray, the five Federal gunboats warded off its impuissant challenge and kept on steaming downriver toward Vicksburg.

The black smoke from the Yankee steamers spread over the multitude of onlookers on the riverbank like an ominous harbinger of the Lost Cause. Considering that the fleet of Admiral David G. Farragut had already taken the city and port of New Orleans in April, the Battle of Memphis effectively ended Confederate presence on the Mississippi River. However it took six months for the Federal command to realize the strategic importance of its victory on the 4th bluff of the Chickasaw. By the time the Union flag was run up the flagpole of the post office, Memphis had already been cut off earlier in May from the rest of the Confederate states by the Union capture of the railroad terminal at the Siege of Corinth, Mississippi. Still the Bluff City prospered during the two years following its capture as the entrepot of a contraband trade with the Confederacy from which my fellow Memphians profited to the tune of an estimated thirty million dollars.

CABIN NOTES:

In the duplex on Cox St., I lay under the lavender star spangled ceiling of my bedroom and reached for my night table reading, which happened to be a small volume penned in Memphis by the activist, Ida B. Wells. Born into slavery in Holly Springs, Mississippi, she had worked her way through Rust College. When she was 24, she wrote, "I will not begin at this late day by doing what my soul abhors; sugaring men, weak deceitful creatures, with flattery to retain them as escorts or to gratify a revenge." What a charming sentiment. Soon she became co-owner and editor of Free Speech, an anti-segregationist newspaper based on Beale St. When a conductor on the Chesapeake, Ohio & South Western Railroad ordered her to give up her seat on the train, Wells refused to do so. This was 71 years before Rosa Parks refused to give up her bus seat near Montgomery, Alabama. The conductor, with assistance from two other men, had to drag Wells bodily out of the railway coach. Upon her return to Memphis, she sued the railroad and won her case in the local circuit court, but the railroad company appealed to the Supreme Court of Tennessee. In 1887 the Supreme Court justices reversed the lower court's ruling in favor of the railroad.

Ida B. Wells wrote often about the burnings, the lynchings, the tarrings, flayings, beheadings, and quarterings of black men and women in the South. After examining unending reports of lynching attributed to alleged "rape of white women", she concluded that Southerners concocted the rape excuse to adumbrate their intrinsic reason for lynching black men: "black economic progress", which threatened not only the pocketbooks of white Southerners but also their ideas about racial superiority.

In another book, Singing in a Strange Land, *lying on the night table, I thought of a passage where Nick Salvatore wrote, "In the vicinity of Doddsville the Eastland family had its* vast, 2,300-acre plantation, which served as the base of their political power for generations to come. James O. Eastland, who would become one of the country's most powerful defenders of segregation in the United States Senate, was born into this family in 1904. Some months before Eastland's birth, Luther Holbert, a black sharecropper on the family plantation, shot and killed Eastland's Uncle James, who had come to his cabin to threaten him for some unknown conduct involving Holbert's wife. Immediately, both Holberts fled into the swamps, and Delta whites raised a 200-man posse to find them. It took four days. At least three other blacks were murdered in the process, but the Holberts were caught and brought into Doddsville. In a horrific ceremonious burning before an estimated crowd of more than 1,000, each finger was individually chopped off the victims and 'distributed as souvenirs' to the assembled white citizens. Eyes were gouged out with sticks. Before the pyre consumed its victims, a large corkscrew 'bored into the flesh of the man and woman,' tearing out as it was withdrawn by human hands 'big pieces of raw, quivering flesh'."

Little wonder that Beale Street has been the Mecca of Southern society for people of color, a relative safe haven from lynchings and the reaching arm of the KKK. Beale Street, I mused, has represented an oasis of the arts, entertainment, commerce, and cultural confluence where white and black have had the fortuity to intermingle on their own terms. Thus since before the War of Rebellion, Beale St. flourished as an elaborate, yet essential microcosm of black and white worlds overlapping. Yet the practice of miscegenation started not on Congo Square, nor Beale Street, but in Africa. English, French, Dutch, Portuguese, and American slave traders took black concubines on the Guinea coast and mated the females on the slave ships. Many Africans and Europeans were themselves the products of thousands of years of mixing between various African, Asian and Caucasian peoples. My ancestors were the product of inter-marriage along the coasts of Sicily and Calabria where multiracial Mediterranean traders and sailors, as well as the crown of Spain and the agents of Napoleon, had overrun the region for centuries. The Mafia itself began as a force of resistance and protection against these incursions.

Although plantation owners and their minions accounted for only a fraction of the agrarian population, they controlled most of the wealth and political power. In the pre-Civil War South some of most prosperous planters and farmers were free African Americans. When I joined the Cabildo Society of Louisiana I learned about the free black Metoyer family who lived down in the Natchitoches area and had acquired vast holdings of land and slaves. At the height of their affluence, the Metoyers owned more slaves than any other free black family in the United States. This family traced its beginnings to Marie-Thérèze, also known by her African name of Coincoin. The doyen Negress created an empire with her fourteen children on the small plot of land that her white common-law husband, Pierre Metoyer, had left her. I became intrigued with these strata of high-tone African American society. By a process of selective breeding, the Connecticut travel writer Eleanor Early reported, "The French (and to a lesser degree the Spanish) had produced in Santo Domingo an exotically lovely type of woman with straight lithe figures, small hands and feet and exquisitely chiseled features. They were known as Les Sirènes. The Sirènes practiced voodoo and taught it to their daughters, in order to hold, or sometimes to get rid of, their lovers. During the slave uprising in Santo Domingo, the planters fled to Louisiana bringing their mistresses and children with them. It was the daughters of these women and their daughters' daughters who came to be called Quadroons. A Quadroon is a person having one fourth Negro and three fourths white blood. Many of the Quadroons had only one sixty-fourth Negro blood." Miss Early recounted, "The most beautiful woman I ever saw was the colored wife of a Negro diplomat from Haiti, a pale girl with skin like gardenias. I met her at a reception at the President's Palace in Port-au-Prince. Her eyes were the color of Haitian bluebells, which is the shade of delphinium, which is a cross between clear blue and purple. Her mouth was a pomegranate cut in halves, and the wings of her blue-black hair were the wings of a Congo thrush."

The French colonial government at the end of the eighteenth-century registered in Santo Domingo some sixty combinations of white with Negro blood and gave a name to each. In the

American South, the term Quadroon was erroneously used to cover a multitude of combinations. French planters in Santo Domingo had long ago taken the handsomest slaves for their mistresses. The planters were usually aristocrats. The slaves came from what is now French Senegal, and they were a handsome people with silky black hair and straight fine features. Gold Coast Negroes were black and ferocious. Those from French Dahomey were the color of tobacco and a gentle lot.

In Memphis, New Orleans, and Charleston there was theater, opera, concerts, and fancy balls. Eleanor Early maintained, "The most famous and exotic were the Quadroon Balls, where white men met young light-skinned women of color. In these and other southern cities there were organized systems of concubinage. The placer system of New Orleans for example, was a respectable adjunct to the institution of marriage. The placées, *stunningly attractive descendants of mulattoes and whites, were well educated and trained in the arts of casual domesticity. Young bachelors interested in a* placée *could shop at the Quadroon Balls, which were held at the Salle d'Orleans (which later became a convent for Negro nuns) and other places. Some of the best men of the South patronized the system, for it was said the best blood of the South runs in the veins of the slaves. The gentlemen's romantic proclivities were their everlasting concern, and there was no place for romance like a Quadroon Ball. The hostesses were always free women of color who had been the mistresses of white men, and the girls they brought out were always the illegitimate daughters of white men. The purpose of the balls was to display the youth and beauty of the girls in order to find rich protectors for them. Guests without exception were white men. No white woman would have dreamed of attending. No man of questionable color would have dared set foot inside the door. It was a frank and elegant sex mart where bluebloods chose their mistresses with taste and decorum.*

Most of the young gentlemen had mistresses. If they did not, it was a reflection upon their virility. Abstinence was no virtue, and a handsome mistress was as much a mark of social distinction as the possession of fine horses and carriages. The Quadroons were not in any sense prostitutes; they were courtesans and their lovely countenances had dark liquid eyes, lips of coral, and teeth of pearl. Their long raven locks were soft and glossy. They had sylphlike figures, beautifully formed limbs, and exquisite gaits. They practiced subtle and amusing coquettes, and they had the most adorable manners. Many of them were as tenderly and carefully brought up as any white girl, and until they secured a "protector" they were just as virtuous. They were accomplished in music, which they all loved, and in embroidery, which most of them disliked. L'amour was what they were born for, and their mothers before them. It wasn't that the gentlemen were so extraordinarily virile, but that they were everlastingly romantic. Their virility, as a matter of fact, gave them considerable concern. To sustain it, they ate dozens of raw oysters, which were considered a great aphrodisiac. They also took a stimulant made from Spanish flies, dried and powdered and made into a potion. They drank a great deal of champagne and much absinthe.

Among the whites there were marriages de convenance, *and dowries were always the accepted thing. White girls often had less choice in picking a husband than Quadroons did in choosing a lover. Often, of course, there were love affairs,* marriages de la main gauche, *the colored people called them, or left-handed marriages. When a definite arrangement was reached, and a girl was bespoken as a* placée, *her status was a sort of honorable betrothal, and her immediate future was secure. It was customary for the man to buy a small house and present it to the girl. Until the house was completed, he never visited her alone. It was understood that he should support her during such time as they might be together, and make an additional settlement when they separated. If children were born of the affair, there was no question about their support. A Creole gentleman always provided for his sons and daughters. This was the accepted thing, and there were seldom scandals. Arrangements were often made when the man was a youth, and the girl was about sixteen. Although the affairs usually terminated with marriage, there were many aristocratic gentlemen who maintained two households to the day they died. Girls never deserted a "protector" or betrayed him. Sometimes, when their lovers left them, the Quadroons committed suicide.*

Slave Collar c. 1840 – resourceful slaves silenced the bells by stuffing them with mud.

Back at the old cabin in the Arkansas hills, I'd subscribed to various Ebonics magazines. I remember Leone Bennett, Jr. wrote in Ebony that "a deep bond of sympathy developed between the Negro and white indentured servants who formed the bulk of the early population. They fraternized during off-duty hours and consoled themselves with the same strong rum, and in and out of wedlock, they sired a numerous mulatto brood. The aura of incest also hovered over some relationships between Negro sisters, white brothers and white fathers."

A. W. Calhoun suggests that the famous Black Mammy played a central role in the psychological process that led to a fixation on Negro women and the parallel process of compensatory glorification of white women. "Close attention," he surmised, "should be given in the light of modern psychology to the consequences upon white children of constant association with members of the other race.... White babies, for instance, commonly had Negro wet nurses, and it may be wondered whether in view of the psychic importance of the suckling processes there may not have been implanted in the minds of the Southern whites certain peculiar attitudes toward Negro women and whether this possibility may not be a partial explanation of the sex tastes of the men of the Old South."

Another factor in the pattern of miscegenation in the South is the large-scale intermixture of Negro and Indian bloodlines. American Negroes, Melville J. Herskovits wrote, "have mingled with the American Indians on a scale hitherto unrealized." Negro-Indian mixtures began in the colonial period when both groups were held as indentured servants and slaves. In the absence of prohibitions, squaws took black husbands and braves took black wives. Indians were awed by black people. Peter Kalm in the eighteenth century reported, "Indians thought the first Negroes were 'a true breed of Devils', and therefore, they called them Manito for a great while: this word in their language signifies not only God but likewise the Devil." Indian reservations were vast melting pots. Some tribes held Negro slaves with whom they intermarried; other tribes welcomed free Negroes and fugitive slaves who adopted breechcloths and moccasins, married Indians and went on the warpath against the white man. In several notable massacres, Indians killed every white man and spared every Negro. In Alabama, the Creeks spared Negroes in the Fort Mimms Massacre. "The Master of Breath," the Creeks said, "has ordered us not to kill any but white people and half-breeds."

View 1870

Although migration of the freed black man and his poor white counterpart from the rural backwaters, small towns, and plantations continued to pour into Memphis during Reconstruction, the Bluff City served as more of a stepping-stone to the northern regions where lifestyle and culture was far removed from the agrarian peonage of the Old South. They came by railroad coach and boxcar, buckboard wagon, horse, mule, and by foot. Yet, many migrants became beleaguered in Memphis, which represented the anonymity of the big city while still connected to the country ways and manners of the Southern mode of living that they knew so well. Throughout the War of Rebellion, Memphis under Federalist occupation maintained its position as the largest inland cotton market and to this day remains the largest market for hardwood in the country. In the 'interregnum' period that followed, Tennessee Governor William Gannaway Brownlow and his constituency of Radical Republicans, Yankee carpetbaggers, and mercenary scallywags enforced policies of disenfranchisement of former Confederates. After the withdrawal of Union troops in 1877, the Democrats and the Redeemers began to regain control of the South. During this process of Redemption, the Bourbon Democrats typically shut down improved political, educational, economic, and progressive efforts that were afoot despite the corrupt leadership of the Reconstructionists. Suddenly when federally mandated freedoms that came with emancipation ended, the black farmer and the poor white sharecropper found themselves returned to "separate but equal" subjugation by the white planter class and by the white patrician banking establishment. The last Southern black congressman of the post-Reconstruction period retired from his post in 1901, leaving the US Congress composed of entirely white politicians.

The myth of the Lost Cause provided former Confederates and their progeny with memories of the Civil War that sacralized their battle as a holy crusade destined for defeat. Constructing the war as a sacred cause helped Southern whites cope with their grief and maintain authority over blacks and helped create two so-called nations within the United States: one white, one black. After the interregnum, while Memphis festered in its own private hell during the plague of the yellow fever, the black man in the South was hardly better off, and in many ways more persecuted, than in the antebellum era of outright slavery. Thus in the late 1870s there would have been zero migration from the Mississippi and Arkansas Deltas and from Tennessee farmlands to Memphis.

"The King of Terrors continues to snatch victims with fearful rapidity," reported one of my fellow Memphians. "One by one, those who remain in the city and are liable to the monster malady are taken down." Dr. John R. Pierce, U.S. Army Medical Corps reported, "There was no way to protect yourself from it. Even though they knew that it would come in the summer, sometimes it

didn't come. There were some summers where there was very little yellow fever. And then another summer it would come and it would be a scourge of biblical proportions." Dr. Paul Jurgensen, specialist in infectious diseases: "People develop a headache, they develop fever, they develop a back pain. They hurt all over and ache all over. And these symptoms usually last for about 48 to 72 hours. And it's just like having the flu. And then the virus attacks the liver. And when the liver is destroyed, proteins, which are very necessary for proper blood coagulation, are also destroyed." Historian John Tone writes further: "You would bleed from your eyes, from your nose, from your mouth, one of the worst aspects of the disease in its final stages was that you're bleeding internally into your stomach, and then that blood is digested and you end up vomiting it out. It's not a quiet death – you are struggling, you're frantic. Doctors would have to strap their patients down while they watched them die."

From a chronicle related by Gerald M. Capers, Jr.: In 1873 the city found itself in the throes of an epidemic of yellow fever, which took the lives of 2000 of the 5000 inhabitants who contracted the disease. Again in 1878 the fever came, with 5150 deaths in 17,600 cases; and still a third time, the following year, with 600 deaths in 2000 cases. The health of Memphians, situated as they were in the midst of a swampy region inundated annually by the Mississippi, was wretched throughout the nineteenth century; not until 1900 was it known that the mosquito was the cause of much of its perennial sickness. Germs of exotic diseases, brought to New Orleans from Asia, Africa, South America, and the West Indies, soon found their way up the river. Sanitary conditions in Memphis during the seventies were perhaps no better than those of the poorest medieval borough. The water supply, which in ante-bellum days had been the Wolf and the Mississippi, consisted of defective wells and cisterns, supplemented in 1873 by a plant reputed to purify river water. Subject to no inspection of any kind, milk was both diluted and polluted; the Ledger reported an instance of a "live minnow found swimming in one pail". According to the same paper, streets were "huge depots of filth, cavernous Augean stables, with no Tiber to flow through and cleanse them". Avenues, gutters, alleys, front and back yards were full of garbage, refuse, and dead animals that produced a stench which, but for the adaptation peculiar to the olfactory sense, would have driven human life from the town. The whole corporate area with its thousands of 'privy vaults' drained into Gayoso Bayou, a stream once several miles in length, but which in the seventies had for many years been merely a series of stagnant pools, separated by dams of decaying organic matter and human excrement. Travelers pronounced the city the dirtiest in the country; by the close of the decade one-third of the white residents had emigrated.

The amazing extent to which newcomers supplanted the old native stock in the post-fever years is revealed in a census taken in 1918 by the federal bureau of education. Of the 11,871 white parents residing in Memphis forty years after the great epidemic, only 183, less than two per cent had been born there. The populace changed not merely in personnel but also in quality. Among the victims of the three epidemics were thirty-four hundred Catholics, including twenty-four priests and twice as many nuns. Many industrious Germans joined their brethren in St. Louis, and one of their leading clubs in Memphis, the Männerchor, became virtually defunct for lack of members. Of the once numerous German organizations on the bluff, only Germania Hall remains in the twentieth century. It is significant, too, that after the plague the proportion of Negroes increased until by the turn of the century they constituted half of the total population.

In the history of the city, the year 1880 marks a distinct cultural break. It is no wonder, in view of the above statistics, that modern Memphis possesses no aristocracy, no tradition, and little interest in its past. The names of only a few families, like the Topps, McGevneys, Winchesters, McLemores, Trezevants, and Overtons, have appeared consistently in its annals. As the war had disrupted a petit-noblesse in the process of aging, so the fever destroyed a second embryonic aristocracy. If the loss of so many Irish was considered by some a good riddance of undesirables, the diminished scope of the Catholic Church was regrettable, for it had served as a check on rural provincialism. The migration of the Germans was much more serious, since it took from the community an influential group which possessed taste in aesthetic matters as well as sober *commercial judgment. Qualitatively the cost of the fever is not to be reckoned by the number of victims, but by the intelligent and solid citizens it drove elsewhere.*

The old Memphis, with all its filth, was unique; the new city, with all its improvements, was prosaic and in time became a southern Middletown. In losing its filth and some of its notorious viciousness it lost also a certain quality for which paved streets and a sewerage system were by no means complete compensation – that unnamable quality which conspicuously differentiates Boston, Charleston, and New Orleans from Pittsburgh and Kansas City. Once heterogeneous, it became homogeneous and progressive; formerly cosmopolitan, it became hopelessly provincial. Gone were the minority groups necessary to a healthy intellectual atmosphere; and in their places, during the eighties and nineties, came farmers from Mississippi and Tennessee, a simple and virtuous country folk, but stubborn and often unlettered.

From each man was demanded allegiance to four conventional ideals: to an unadulterated Protestant fundamentalism; to a fantastic entity called the Old South; to the principle of white supremacy; and, rather paradoxically, to the Constitution of the United States. The horizontal trade of Memphis suffered as well as the vertical, for northern concerns in search of a location for a single branch office to serve a South that was still moving west chose an inland town in Georgia in preference to a railroad center on the middle Mississippi. Predictions as to what might have been are but the opinion of an individual, whether he be steamboat captain or historian, but it can be suggested with considerable justification that Atlanta owes its present position as the "New York of the South" more to the work of the aedes aegypti *mosquito in Memphis half a century ago than to any other cause.*

Already noon when I rolled out of the sack on Cox St. Upon four or five cranks of the kick-starter, the lusty motor of the Norton grunted under an Aztec sun, then growled to life. The throaty roar emanating from the exhausts presaged impending sacrificial rites in dire palpating tones. The mission today was to get down to Court Square fast as possible to catch the SUN Rhythm Section before their set ended on a makeshift festival stage. The Norton huffed and loafed down the wide boulevards to the downtown grid. Second Street came into view – the thoroughfare bounding Court Square on the east side, with Front Street on the western end over the bluff that slopes down to the river. I opened the throttle on the Norton in a final thrust of speed to hasten my arrival on the southernmost, Madison Avenue side of the Square. I had failed to notice that a thin, single strand of orange nylon cord had been stretched across Madison Avenue at the intersection with 2nd St. by order of the MPD (Memphis Police Department) in an effort to block off entrance to Court Square by the southern approach. The orange cord, invisible to any sort of motorist, caught me under the chin and for a hideous instant I was suspended in mid-air above the speeding Norton. Like in Roadrunner cartoons, I felt like the unfortunate desert coyote, when in the epiphany of a split second Wile E. Coyote realizes that he has been lured off the edge of a precipice in full gallop, and in that moment of self-revelation and shock, his eyes bulge with wry cognition as he drops like a bullet fired into the abyss below. *BAM!* I hit the asphalt. I heard a solid yet muffled concussion and the sound of my helmet bouncing down the pavement like a basketball. The nylon cord had caught the chinstrap of the *casque* and ripped it off my head, while in the process, the buckle of the chinstrap had gouged out an open gash in my throat. Meanwhile, the motorcycle continued on down the street rider-less, until it veered into the curb in a few yards and tumped over on its side.

Next thing I saw was an MPD officer towering over me, as I lay bleeding in the middle of the street. The stalwart officer had only this to say, "Guess you're gonna sue the city, now aren't you boy?" As I struggled to my feet a hot headed colored boy ran up from the crowd of passers-by, apparently over-excited by the sight of blood, and exclaimed in breathless tones, "Hey man, you're really messed up. Look at you, you're tore up bad, real bad!" I had nothing to say to those around me, those who offered not one helping hand, as I retrieved my helmet and stumbled over to the Norton lying on its side in the street. The motor was still running, and

Duplex, 704 S. Cox St. with 1950 Ford V8   Photo: E. Baffle

the back wheel was spinning lazily. I raised the Norton from its restful, supine position and straddled it; then eased the machine off in the direction of Front St. and then right toward St. Joseph's Hospital. The Norton and I rounded the dome of the prayer temple that the comedian Danny Thomas had vowed to build in honor of St. Jude in recompense for deliverance from some dire circumstance, and we – now as one: machine and its rider – coasted into the emergency parking lot. The crash had done little damage to the motorbike; a Norton is practically indestructible, and I left the machine at the farthest edge of the tarmac propped up on its side stand under the glowering sun.

A high-yellow girl still running a strand of floss between her white, perfect teeth to remove fibers of the orange she had just consumed, admitted me in an unconcerned and perfunctory manner to the air-conditioned bliss of the hospital. The bloody wound was washed with antiseptic and taped up, rather than properly sewn shut (as I was just another rider on a donor-cycle), but I was kept overnight for observation due to risk that the afflicted tissues of the pharynx might swell and seal off the windpipe. Under the cooling ventilation and semi-darkness of the hospital room, my thoughts began to drift indolently behind the tranquillizers and pseudo pain relievers the nurses had administered.

By the cart of the honey-skinned gypsy Madame Litha, alluring in her robes of mauve and brocade, I was walking and heard her speaking in low tones about her bottled 'love-drawing' floor wash. The country jakes were scratching their heads over its counter of talismans, Mojo Hands, High John the Conqueroos, and vials of graveyard dust. With the sounds of shoe shine rags popping all around, I passed Pee Wee's Saloon where the big dago bouncer stood taking up most of the front doorway, spitting tobacco juice back over his shoulder in a hit or miss fashion toward the cigar counter spittoon. In passing I caught a glimpse of the endlessly running domino game toward the rear of the mezzanine. Behind the dominoes match in the far backroom was the usual poker game where the sky's the limit, and upstairs the policy racket or numbers game was ever playing out. Pee Wee's had the only pay telephone on Beale St. and the boss, Viriglio Maffei, ran a message service for musicians and jug bands, but I wasn't expecting any phone calls today. Forget that, I thought delicately to myself, I'll step into a posh establishment today, and there's none finer on Beale St. than Jim Canaan's Monarch Saloon, affectionately know on the Stem as the "Castle of Missing Men". An evasion no doubt provoked when encountering the laconic Robert Wilkins with his guitar yesterday singing on the corner of Vance and Main. Wearing his silk vest, canary yellow trousers and patent leather shoes, his Cherokee-African skin shown like a polished nut under a tropical sun, and golden tones were emanating more from his lanky frame as from his vocal cords:

> Goin' to and fro to old Jim Canaan's
> Drinkin' beer, whiskey and sniffin' cocaine
> That's been why I wished I was back at Old Jim Canaan's
> And I wished I was back at Old Jim Canaan's.

A mahogany bar long as a railway coach stretched down one side of the saloon with a burnished brass railing running its entire length. Beveled edge mirrors from the Old World lined each wall, and the banquets were lined with plush purple velvet. Crystal chandeliers hung high, wide, and handsome from the high tin-pressed ceiling casting an ethereal and merry glow over the assembled imbibers. The conversation was fast and easy and the manner relaxed among the regular cast of brown-skinned gamblers, celebrated musicians, riverboat pilots, theater and boxing managers, Beale St. physicians and attorneys, and worthless city hall policy gamers. The revelers sported accoutrements like soft fedoras and homburgs, suede spats, velvet collars and diamond cravat pins, and there were dandified chauffeurs in kid gloves, double breasted charcoal livery, and shiny riding boots. Sporting ladies abounded, and they adorned themselves with silks and feathers, furs and jewels. With powered décolletage, their countenances were fine-featured and affable, and their curves filled up the mirrors all around. Coming from the gambling den upstairs I could hear the salty voice of the teenage songstress, little Memphis Minnie, fingerpicking her big steel-stringed Stella guitar and belting out her version of "Me and My Chauffeur Blues".

> Won't you be my chauffeur,
> Won't you be my chauffeur,
> I wants him to drive me downtown,
> Well he can drive so easy,
> I can't turn him down.

Around dawn after her last set Minnie would rendezvous with her mentor, the youthful Robert Wilkins, in a furnished boudoir they reserved over Earnestine & Hazels sandwich shop at the corner of Main and Calhoun Streets. At the Monarch everyone seems to know everyone else. For recreation, good whiskey, entertainment, fair gaming, and chumming around with friends, I reckon there's no place in the world quite like the Monarch on a Saturday night. What a cozy and intimate part of the world known as the *Stem* – that stretches down on Beale from Main to 4th Street. The theaters, saloons, drug stores, hotels, boarding houses, trolley stops, sandwich shops, barber and beauty parlors of the Stem are all accessible by foot within a few minutes via its sidewalks and alleyways.

Frog was tending bar as usual on Saturdays at the Monarch. His emerald cuff links glittered like the gold in his front teeth as he served me a jigger of rye. I straightened my bow tie, and ascended the stairs. Frog hollered after me over the cracking of pool cues, "You know you ain't going to heaven no how, when you goes up there." Minnie looked lithe and sultry sitting on the discreet little stage holding her big guitar.

Well I wants him to drive me,
Well I wants him to drive me
around the world,
Well he'll be my little boy,
Yes I will be his girl.

Hmmm, those dice even smell lucky tonight. Jesse Manuss was handling the dice horn for the Monarch. A crowd had gathered around the craps table as Jesse shook the leather horn. The tumbling bones inside with the little black eyes made a jolly tinkling sound that fueled the anticipation of everyone. Big Joe Ambrigulio was standing squarely across from Manuss; his pinstriped suit coat hung down in massive drapes like the curtain across the Orpheum stage. His face had transformed from its typically olive shade to a flushed redness, and his huffing and muttering of unspeakable oaths under his breath belied the fact his stack of $50 silver pieces was dwindling lickety-split.

Well I don't want him,
Well I don't want him
To be riding these other girls around,
Well I'm gonna buy me a pistol
And shoot my chauffeur down.

Another dice roll, and snake eyes popped up again. Suddenly the dago grabbed the cuff of Jesse's hand, squinted his eyes and snarled, "Pick up those dice and roll 'em again, dealer – just those two." Jesse's face turned ghostly pale and his eyebrows knitted. He shook the dice in the horn, and then spewed them onto the green felt. Snakes eyes! "Again," bellowed Big Joe. The leather horn rattled again, and the dice poured forth. Snake eyes, again! Like greased lightning, Big Joe drew a stiletto and threw it with pinpoint accuracy through the right hand of Jesse Manus nailing it to the oak table. But Big Joe had forgotten that Jesse was a southpaw, and his left was already on the 45-calibre hogs leg that he drew from under the table. Big Joe reached for the 45 Smith & Weston in his breast pocket, but he was a fraction of a second too late and took the blast from the 44 through the right ventricle of his heart. His knees buckled, but as he sank like the Orpheum curtain coming down on a variety act, he fired bug-eyed and sent a huge hot slug through the carotid artery of Jesse Manus' neck. Blood spewed over the green felt like the spew under the bronze statue of Hebe in the Court Square fountain on a hot day in August. The ladies backed away from the arms of their frozen partners to protect their silks, and Harold Otis, manager of the Monarch, came bounding up the stairs with revolver drawn and shaking in his hand. He spitted instructions under his pencil moustache with the utmost articulation. To the bouncers he said, "Put Big Joe out in the alley, and call Pee Wees and tell Virgilio that the air in the Monarch ain't so good for his boys. Then call Jesse's wife and tell her what happened... that it don't pay off playing with bones that don't belong to the Monarch. Call the undertakers. Have Mr. Holst fix Jesse up looking real nice."

Enough posh entertainment for one evening; believe I'll head over to the Panama Cafe, and grab a bowl of chili and saltine crackers. Then, let's see now... maybe I'll step over to the Palace Theatre for the midnight rambles show. Always amusing to watch the honkys in top hats making clowns of themselves, especially when W. C. Handy with his trumpet and band are onstage at the Palace backing up a revue of silk-hosed, simian high-steppers.

On the narrow bed in St. Josephs I awoke with a strange taste of chili in my mouth... and to the sounds of a breakfast tray being served. A nurse was standing at the foot of my bed sternly urging me to wake up and to breathe deeply. Apparently the danger of closure of the tracheae due a tumescent larynx had passed. Released and at large again on the streets and

Lillian and her plumber Photo: E. Baffle 1978

byways of Memphis, I navigated the Norton back toward the Fairgrounds and to my domicile on Cox St. With the Norton securely docked on the gravel driveway, I sought the refuge of my queen size bed to ease my still aching neck. Through the thin walls of the duplex I could hear the cooing of my hefty and gregarious neighbor, Lillian (once a 'looker' in a 1940s pin-up style) and the gravely tones of her plumber pal and paramour, Bob, engaged in a post-Saturday night beer-soaked clinch. All is well on Cox St. Screw it! I've got to wear this neck brace for another week. Reckon I'll ride the Norton over to see Van Zula Hunt. Got to fix that oil leaking from the crankcase one of these days, too. Van lived in a frame house next to the corner of Fourth and Beale. Around 1929 she recorded "Jelly Sellin' Woman" with Noah Lewis' Jug Band. The ditty became a hit on the race records chittlin' circuit. Sleepy John Estes played guitar and his partner, Hammie Nixon, blew the jug in these impromptu bands. They came from Brownsville north of Memphis. Not long before he died, I remember Sleepy John talking about their hoboing days; he said Hammie never minded carrying his jug and catching boxcars… if the jug was full of whiskey. There's Van sitting in the shade on the front porch in a cotton dress. She still played some gigs with a cathouse piano player, Mose Vinson – an amusing skeletal piano player living off Lauderdale on Trigg Avenue where no white men tread. Once in a while I was invited to back up Van on guitar. She had the pipes, and still sounded just as she did on record in her girlish days. Her high register tonalities needed no microphone.

> *I'm a jelly sellin woman I sell it everyday*
> *I'm a jelly sellin woman I sell it everyday*
> *My jelly's too expensive, you know I can't give it away*
> *I serve jelly, serve it fresh an' cold*
> *I serve jelly, serve it fresh an' cold*
> *Hurry buy my jelly, time for my baker shop to close*

Van Zula Hunt Photo: E. Baffle 1978

Van's daughter was called Sweet Charlene, and she sang like a bird. She started singing in Memphis in the 1940s in the band of Robert Nighthawk. Sometimes we'd all go together with a petite singer and dancer named Little Laura Dukes over to the house of Piano Red and play songs. Little Laura had also worked as a dancer on stage with Robert Nighthawk's band, and she could do a mighty mean grind. Red was a totally bald albino piano player who learned his trade working in the caulk houses off Beale Street. A caulk house was a honky tonk type of place that had a sawdust floor. They had a big barrel of lime in the joint, and they'd spread that lime over the sawdust to hold down the rain of tobacco juice, booze, and other juices that soaked into the sawdust. The lime further helped prevent the stuff from metamorphosing into a noxious moldy life of its own. Red loved to play "Cow Cow Boogie" and Van and Little Laura would sing along merrily. Red would push his rotund belly back from his upright piano, and talk about his hoboing days too. He'd run away from home in Memphis when he was 14, and still today Red was totally on train time. He knew the times and the routes of most every train leaving and coming into the Memphis yards, and could tell you which freight to catch and when to take you wherever: California, Dakotas, Louisiana, anywhere. Then Van would sing her favorite, "The Sunnyland Special", about a streamline passenger train that ran into Memphis over Dyersburg, Tennessee. It was a lonesome tune… about a lover that left her high and dry.

When Red came back to Memphis from riding the rails, he worked as a roustabout on the River, and learned to play his effervescent piano style looking over peoples' shoulders on Beale St. "In the old days on Beale," he said, " you could say it was never nighttime. They just stayed open from dawn to dawn. Everything was lively. You go to playing at 5 o'clock, and play until 4:30 in the morning.

"The Gray Mule, it had a lively bunch. It was kind of crowded, but it was a nice little joint. Had good food in there. They served plenty black-eyed peas and cornbread and baked sweet potatoes. And they would have candied yams and baked ribs, have peach cobbler, apple cobbler or blackberry cobbler. Sell you that dessert for ten cents a little bowl. Or bread pudding. Neck bones and Irish potatoes and beef stew.

"There was all different kinds of places on Beale. Places I played, they were mostly just joints. To tell the truth some of them was just real scallywags joints… but then there was places like the Monarch. It was the classiest. It was the town talk, the Monarch. They're real dressed up, gambling men with diamond rings and suits of clothes. You'd thought it was a preacher or lawyer, the way they dressed them. Some of 'em would dress twice a day."

Red never locked his doors. People in the neighborhood would kill him for sure if they thought he had money, so he left the doors to his house unlocked as a kind of safety precaution. People were always coming and going through the front screen door. Once at one of Red's little house parties, a kid in a t-shirt walked in and sat down in an armchair. He couldn't have been more than 14 years old. He pulled a .32 caliber automatic pistol out of his pants, and began to examine its chamber repeatedly in a ritual of tension inducing alacrity. Then he cocked the trigger, stretched his arm straight out, aimed the pistol right into my face, and asked quizzically, "Now, you want me to shoot you?" Over the protests of the houseguests, the kid put away the weapon.

"I made a $1000 a night playing those tours in Europe, and I don't have one grade of school, no education," Red said. "It's like another world [in Germany]. They're good people. You never hear, like you hear here, vulgar words. They're so lovely to one another." On the night of February 8th, 1982, after he had returned to his house on Walker Avenue from a playing some dates in Europe, Piano Red Williams was bludgeoned to death in his bed with the butt of gun – no doubt by greedy and contemptuous neighbors who figured that Red had some gig money on his person. There was a trail of blood all through the house. He wasn't even worth a bullet to his killers; they just beat him to death with the gun handle. No suspects were taken into custody by the police.

Van Zula told me about playing on the Medicine Shows traveling with the Royal American Circus. She met the blues shouter, Bessie Smith, traveling on that circuit, and they became friends. Van said they made so much money on those shows, that it was scary. They'd accumulate such a huge stash of cash, that they didn't know what to do with it, where to put it, where it hide it. They were traveling too fast to go to a bank, and banks weren't so reliable during those days. Ultimately, she became so uneasy holding huge rolls of cash that she quit Royal American Shows for fear of her life. She returned to Memphis and bought her that little house, a former brothel, at Fourth Street and Beale. Van Zula taught me how to play the one tune that I would ask her to play again and again. It was a modal song called "Mississippi River Blues".

> *Mississippi River so deep and wide,*
> *The man I love,*
> *He's way on the other side.*
> *Well, I can't go across*
> *and I can't go round,*
> *I'd swim the river but*
> *I'm afraid that I might drown.*

CHAPTER THE SECOND
BOSS CRUMP DON'T ALLOW & THE SUBLIME OURO

It was election time and the political rallies around town had turned rabid. Mayor Ed Crump was campaigning hard and heavy for re-election on a reform ticket, swearing to shut down saloons and gambling dens all over town. He had hired Beale Street horn player and orchestra leader W. C. Handy to write a campaign ditty to drive his rallies. Handy was an educated musician and leader of a fashionable orchestra that performed at fancy plantation balls in Mississippi and at high society events in the finest Memphis Hotels. So what he composed for the Crump campaign was not without a soupçon of innuendo and satire. Country blues had become interesting for the young Handy when he saw a trio of blues men appear at one of his engagements in Clarksville, Mississippi. "Fess", short for professor, as he was known among the musicians he played with, was impressed with the musical merits of blues, its crowd-pleasing potential, and above all with the shower of silver dollars that were tossed at the troubadours. In his autobiography Handy wrote, "The boys lay in more money than my nine musicians were being paid for the entire engagement. Then I saw the beauty of primitive music." Based on a good time song, "Mama Don't Allow", Handy wrote "Mr. Crump" (later reworking it as the "Memphis Blues") which, with its jaunty beat and lyrics, ignited the Mayoral campaign across all sectors of society.

> *Mr. Crump doan allow no easy riders here.*
> *We doan care what Mr. Crump doan allow,*
> *We gonna Barrel-house anyhow.*
> *Mr. Crump can go and catch himself some air.*

Early one morning I had just stepped out of Mr. Jim's caulk house, the Nonpareil, on Front Street after downing a nightcap of straight whiskeys doubles. Blithely enroot to the trolley car stop, I stopped cold when I beheld two black Duesenberg touring cars nose into the side alley between Front and 2nd. Appearing behind the side window glass of the second Duesy was the unmistakable wild red quiff of Mayor Crump. At that moment, a long black Ford sedan entered the alley, and out stepped the saloon mogul, Jim Canaan, wearing a straw boater and accompanied by two bodyguards carrying a rather large green leather satchel between them. Canaan rested his shillelagh on the running board of the 2nd Duesy, and spoke in measured tones that I was almost close enough to decipher. The side door opened and Crump personally pulled in the green satchel onto the floorboard, meeting the gaze of Jim Canaan as a grin of victory spread over his reddened features. Jim Canaan spoke to be understood clearly, yet covertly so not to be overheard by eavesdroppers. Their words mattered little on this occasion. Both men knew the measure of the other. Mr. Jim nudged the side door closed with the tip of his knurled shillelagh, and walked away with his two stalwart lieutenants – one white and one black – toward and through the entrance to his joint, which had no doors as it was never closed.

The trolley rolled past and I caught it on the run. At 2nd Street I swung off the back of the car, and walked down to the Ironclad where I intended to sleep most of the day. I eased up the high front steps of the massive, unpainted gray structure that looked more like an ancient hotel or warehouse than what it was: the largest, probably the most inelegant, but surely the most infamous whorehouse this side of New Orleans. Men were known to enter the Ironclad and never be heard from again. With the tarnished doorknocker I struck the secret ritual of taps and pauses that I knew so well, and the huge metal door slid partially open with a rattle. Henry, the cotton-headed porter, older seemingly than the Ironclad itself, greeted me in the half-light of the hall foyer. "Yes, suh. Miss Doney be sleeping in her room. Believe you know where it is." I palmed a silver dollar shaking hands with Henry as I passed. "Thas mighty kind of you, suh," drawled the Stygian hound. Dark cracked paintings in ornate lentiginous frames hung in the draped corridors, which, narrow and circuitous, led to remote passages and hidden chambers. Old timbers creaked and groaned underfoot, as if they'd been nailed down cruelly from planks salvaged from sunken steamboats. The pitted brass trim along the railings, milky alabaster lampshades, and archaic paintings were bartered long ago by riverboat pilots in exchange for favors of the house. Here and there, the flame of a gaslight winked and flirted dimly from wall sconces. Anyway, I could find my way to Doney's room blindfolded. The doors had no numbers, and no locks. It was presumed that if you entered the Ironclad, you knew where you were going. I already knew that if Doney were in her room, a red lace curtain would be hanging in her window toward the upper end of the building, which I could see from the alley off 2nd St. The curtain was red today. If she were occupied, a curtain of blue lace would be hanging.

Her room reeked with the fragrance of patchouli. I closed the door softly, and took off my boots, and then my clothes. An opaque paper shade was pulled down behind the window curtain, and a pale light shrouded the two cane chairs, the mahogany dresser and mirror, and the bedstead of curved ironwork. I slipped under the covers and the slender ginger cake arms of Doney reached for me. Her eyes shone like dying coals; her thatch the color of a brown nut. We slept. A little after sundown, I heard the unmistakable, clipped thud, thud-thud, thud of Jim Canaan's shillelagh on the back staircase. His home was just two alleys over, and he always entered the Ironclad from the rear and methodically climbed the backstairs to the penthouse on the topmost floor. It was well known that Mr. Jim was for many years in love with one of the women of the Ironclad. The lady was seldom seen, and then attired in only the finest tailoring of silk, fur, and feather that New Orleans had to offer. When she did entertain, it was with the most discreet clientele of Memphis. It was thought that one day Mr. Jim would forsake Memphis and retire with his lady to a bungalow in New Orleans where one could live in a civilized fashion without questions being asked. That eventuality would be a long time coming, considering his extended family and household. Although he never married, it was his responsibility to provide an auspicious home, hearth, and educations in the finest schools. Further, his responsibility to the many devoted whites and blacks employed in his dominion of whiskey and gambling was a mandate that Jim Canaan did not take lightly, nor the ongoing fight to maintain the ascendancy and the integrity of his dominion in the underworld of vice in Memphis. Indeed, Mr. Jim was a long way from retiring, and the Ironclad seemed to provide his only solace.

Most of the girls and women of the Ironclad had been taken into that establishment as children abandoned during the scourges of the yellow fever. Doney told me of the grim circumstances of her displacement by the King of Terrors. She was born out of wedlock on a river barge to Harmon Bondurant, a white co-pilot of the steamboat *Luella*, and to its Negro stewardess. Bound between Memphis and the White River in Arkansas, the *Luella* often towed a barge with a little hut built on the stern. Doney grew up on the *Luella* and on her sister ship, the *Amy Hewes*, assigned to menial chores such as dusting out staterooms and emptying chamber pots. Once when Doney was about four years of age, the *Luella* was docked at the wharf in Memphis taking on stores and passengers and off-loading hardwood and bales of cotton. In port she liked to hang around the bow of the boat when the stevedores were loading cargo onboard to listen to the river chants they sang to cadence their heavy lifting.

> *Peckerwood a-peckin' on the schoolhouse door,*
> *Peckerwood a-peckin' on the schoolhouse door,*
> *pecks so hard until his pecker got sore...*

Her pap had warned the crew there was sickness in the town, but the boatmen threw caution to the wind in favor of going ashore to throw their pay at 5-cent shots of saloon whiskey, easy riders, and fast dice games. A few hours before departure, her mother Flora, the mistress of the vessel, fell ill with fever and chills. She was put ashore and two swarthy stevedores were paid 50-cents each to carry her and little Doney in a hand cart up the side of the river bluff to a makeshift quarantine set up in horse stable on Front St. There were no lights in the quarantine, and the steaming August sun filtered through the rough plank walls permitting slices of hot yellow light to permeate the deep shade and to illuminate the miasma of fetid dust floating up from the floor of the stable. Doney remembers the dark figures of the Catholic nuns in their black habits and white collars ministering to the victims of the pestilence. She remembers the moans of despair as the nuns fingered their rosaries, endlessly reiterating their prayers to a silent god, as men, women, and children of all ages lay prostrate upon their cots, or on pallets laid upon the floor, some groaning and gesticulating in the air in the delirium of fever, others gasping the last breaths that rattled in their throats, still others were vomiting up blood mixed with what she thought were coffee grounds. Of the wretches who suffered in the clinic, only a few were Negroes, as this race was not as frequently inflicted with the disease, as were the whites. The majority of those quarantined here were clearly Irish, among them were often a nun or a priest stricken in the final throes of death struggle. Toward sundown was heard the murmuring buzz of mosquitoes hovering over the ghastly tableau. There was nothing to eat save for wrinkled potatoes boiled in river water.

Outside the streets were ankle deep in mud due to the inundation of late summer rain, and the air was putrefied with the stench of countless human bodies, dead animals, and human excrement that were communally dumped together into the brackish pools of what once was Bayou Gayoso. Mules plowed the forlorn streets hauling carts piled high with ashen cadavers. Doney somehow drifted past the pickets stationed gloomily around the stable. She, in her still small intuitive mind, went searching for something she could find to bring to her mother to eat. Some morsel of sustenance. Some fortuitous tuber or frog leg or crust of bread. There was nothing out there except mud and angry dogs and the few shops that were open sold only stale bread and canned meats and fish for high prices. With the last of the pennies from her mother's purse, she bought a flat tin of sardines and a dozen saltine crackers from a leery and cynical merchant at the corner of Vance and 3rd Street. When she once again slipped past the sentries milling around the quarantine, she found Flora was vomiting. Doney opened the tin and ate ravenously as her mother wretched up bloody coffee grounds. Darkness fell. A hush fell over the stables. It was that time again. A merciful time for dying. By morning's dim light, mules and carts were lining up to the big double doors of the stables, as new clients, racked with misery and pain, were huddling into the cavern of gloom. When Doney awoke, her mother was lifeless and her stiff fingers clutched the blanket covering her grotesquely, as if she, in her delirious struggle, had squeezed the last, frozen moment of life itself from the filthy rag. The nuns came with a stretcher and swiftly removed Flora to the waiting mule carts.

Doney was desperate. She slipped past the myopic sentinels again, blinking her eyes in the heat of the white gray light. A feeling of release and nothingness came over her. She walked aimlessly, drifting. Near a rotted wooden sidewalk around Monroe and 2nd St., something wide and billowy floated and wrapped around her. It was the skirt of Hattie, one of the maidens of the night from the Ironclad. Her tan hands reached down, raised the little girl to her feet, and dragged her limp little body by the elbow to the barn-like temple of iniquity looming at the end of the street.

At the Ironclad, Doney resumed her duties pretty much as she had done on the *Luella*. The house served in a sense as an institution of learning and sustenance. Hard times, or good times, the house was always in business, and more often doing better business when the times were hard. She learned social graces and manners, how to read, and learned to write more than her name. She was one of the first to patronize the gothic, pink limestone Cossit Library when it first opened in 1888 on the bluff between Monroe Avenue and Floyd Alley. As the years passed, she learned all the tricks and secrets of the trade in how to please a man, or woman. Along with the other rescued Children of the King of Terrors, Doney, rather than reconciled to any notion of sacrifice, became devoted to the nature of the house and to her existence in offering her modest particle of pleasure in the grand scheme of heaven and earth. On Sunday mornings she attended mass at St. Brigid's, somehow at one and at peace with the black-frocked priests and nuns who conducted the rituals of the altar in clouds of frankincense, uttering the liturgy in Latin and Greek. On these occasions she appeared in a dark dress draped over her lanky body, and with a pure white lace collar about the neck, and a white lace handkerchief pinned atop her closely shorn hair.

She dressed down even further to a simple calico dress when strolling about the town, and eschewed powder and rouge when running practical errands for the house mistress, for primping and the wearing of fine silks, feathers, and furs in daylight was forbidden for so-called, sporting ladies. If one were so brazen, any white woman could order to have the offender horsewhipped on the spot, without question.

Once the tapping of Jim Canaan's shillelagh had ceased on the back staircase, I arose, dressed, and took leave of the Ironclad. Emerging from the side alley, I caught a passing trolley car and debarked on the corner of Union Avenue and 2nd. From there I stepped over to the Peabody Hotel Café to meet the esteemed and genteel Colton Greene at a soirée in honor of his forthcoming retirement from the presidency of the Tennessee Club. Some twenty years ago, seated at a round table in the very same refreshment room of the Peabody Café, Colton Greene became the founder and originator of the gentlemen's club known to be the most discreet and influential in the state. The Tennessee Club was the product of his prescience and his always being there at the right place at the right time with a fertile schema. The Tennessee Club itself was the direct legacy of the clique that Colton Greene had founded and baptized as the Secret Society of the Memphi, and of which he became its first Sublime Ouro.

During the War of Rebellion, Colton Greene had served as a feral cavalry officer, commissioned as a Captain under the command of General Sterling Price. The annals of the Memphi claim, "He dashed into the thick of battle with a brilliant sash around his waist and golden spurs on his heels. A true son of the deep South, he was wholly a part of the culture of his time... a culture which had its roots deep in the chivalry, the gallantry, and social graces of plantation life. To him honor was a sacred thing for which he was prepared to risk his life in the best traditions of the old Code Duello, or in a gallant (hilt reckless) cavalry charge at Pea Ridge, Arkansas. For him the courtly elegance of antebellum social life held a charm never quite to be forgotten. Highly educated, well-traveled, a student and connoisseur of the arts, a linguist who could speak French, German, or Italian with equal fluency, he was always at home in the classic plantation ballroom resplendent with its prismatic chandeliers and elaborate old world furnishings, not to mention its beautifully gowned ladies."

My contacts in the Memphi filled in some more gaps about the mysterious background of Colton Greene, of which he seldom spoke. Captain Greene "had formed an important part of Price's expedition to Mexico immediately after the war where they joined forces with Emperor Maximilian of Austria. Maximilian had apparently promised these valiant officers, who refused to surrender their swords to the victorious Yankees, a sanctuary in Mexico, perhaps even a Confederate government in exile. Whatever the price for their services, it was a poor gamble for Maximilian's government collapsed in October of 1866, and he was subsequently captured by the Republican forces under Juarez and executed on June 19, 1867. General Price returned to his home in Missouri in November of 1866, and one cold winter morning in 1868 Colton Greene rode into Memphis astride a fractious roan stallion, both horse and rider immaculately groomed." Quite a feat as Memphis streets then were nothing more than canals of mud.

Yet to know Colton Greene was to know an individual not only capable of such glamorous minor feats, but one capable of moving mountains.

We are the music-makers,
We are the dreamers of dreams,
And we are the movers and shakers
of the world forever it seems.
                                    –A. W. O'Shaughnessy

When he arrived in the Bluff City, it was a troubled metropole humbled in the aftermath of Federal occupation and oppressed with the onus of Reconstruction. Anyone thought to even remotely fraternize with the military of the occupation was completely ostracized by the other citizens whether of the patrician class, the bourgeoisie, or the immigrant Germans, Irish, and Italians who (outside of the Negro) comprised the labor force. That the city was an odoriferous open sewer, and that the deterioration of the creosote-soaked wooden Nicolson paving blocks spawned mosquito and rodent driven disease, were not the only factors to inhibit the emergence of Memphis as a suzerain on the Mississippi. Taxes were impossible to collect and the local administration was rotten with graft and corruption. Yet emerge it did, fuelled by the entrepreneurial vision and skill of social organization exemplified by genteel super luminaries like Colton Greene. The efflorescence of Memphis was due in large part to his notion to organize a grand Mardi Gras carnival sponsored by the Memphi. Under his leadership – that of a Confederate Brigadier general and an aristocrat on intimate terms with the old families, of a linguist whose fluency endeared him to the European immigrants, of an astute businessman who won allegiance from Southern and Yankee merchants alike – he was able to unite the various groups who had been suspicious of one another and mutually antagonistic. The monumental feat that Colton Green accomplished was to sell the warring factions of Memphis on the idea of a "big party" based on the Mardi Gras of her sister city, New Orleans, predicated on the ineluctable prospect that without the attraction of a grand carnival, their city would continue its slow demise and with it the market for their merchandise, enterprise, and institutions.

When I entered the sequestered salon of the Peabody Café, there already seated at the roundtable were the impeccable Colton Greene, and the assembled leaders and officers of the Secret Order of the Memphi, The Tennessee Club, and the gallant Chickasaw Guards. Standing to lift his glass was Col. M. C. Galloway, former editor of *The Daily Memphis Avalanche*, "Gentlemen it is my honor to toast our esteemed comrade and boon companion, General Colton Greene who had the foresight and initiative to propose the elaborate soirée under the sponsorship of the Memphi that has become known as the Memphis Carnival. The fortuitous celebration that prevented our city from languishing in doldrums of despair and neglect, and that re-established our rank as monarch of the Mississippi, is now the singular event for which the glory and the splendor of Memphis is known from the towering megalopolis of the east to the opulent capitols of the west. Our hats, gentlemen, are off to this native son of the South."

Indeed the *Avalanche* had pressed the holiday flotilla upon a populace eager for merriment and diversion, extolling it as," the event of the year" and proclaiming that "Memphis will be the liveliest, jolliest, and funniest spot on earth". The hosting of the mystic societies and krewes of the Memphi, and the appearance of the pageants and parades of Ulks, Rex Carnivalis (The Lord of Misrule himself), Knights of Pythias, the Knights of Momus and the sidewalk antics of his Court of Mirth, the Cowbellonians, the frolicsome Catfish Brigade, Casino Club, Garrick Club, Deutscher Bruder Band, Memphis Männerchor, Unione Fratellanza, and the rollicking street crowds, were all slavishly reported. The grand parade got under way from the old Charleston Depot, moved down Adams to Second, Second to Market and then to Main Street, and thence past the reviewing stand at the Overton Hotel at the corner of Poplar Avenue. One *Avalanche* reporter mused "no opium eater or hashish swallower ever saw in their magic reveries creatures more fantastic." The elaborate floats carrying the King and Queen of Carnival were drawn through the avenues by mules and by burly Negro field hands and stevedores. The habiliments of the royal court were designed by Monsieur Nonnon, costumer of the Grand Opera House in Paris. Among the Carnival goers comic suits were most popular as well as "dominoes" consisting of black, hooded masquerade cloaks and masks. French gilt, jet, and shell jewelry, spangled tarletons, gimps, and fringes in the brightest and gayest colors were worn along with the latest Paris frivolity. Recognition rosettes, and decorative buds enabled masked revelers to "meet and know each other." Advertised among the *"Novelties de Carnavale"* were bouquets and cut florals that "awaited tender smiles and bright eyes." The *Avalanche* also announced that the traditional finale of the firework displays would form a "magnificent bouquet, respectfully dedicated to the ladies of Memphis by the Tennessee Club," and warned of an interdict against cross-dressing at the carnival.

There were "oyster wars" during carnival. Published advertisements in the Avalanche were hawking "good Baltimore and Norfolk oysters" at specialty prices among "ten-thousand cans of fresh oysters" being offered. Genuine luxury Havana cigars sold at discount and a holiday stock of chewing tobacco, featuring Log Cabin, Gravely, and Bull Durham. Alligator Stove fresh baked, promotional cakes, pies, and bread were distributed to the multitudes along the parade line, and Fleishmann Yeast gave free lunches of "good, hot Vienna rolls". The *Avalanche* advertised the White Collar and the Anchor Lines offer "to Everybody in the United States, the finest steamers in the world, to bring any and all passengers that intend to visit Memphis Mardi Gras Celebration at half fare." By royal mandate all vessels in port were commanded to fly their colors during carnival. Various railroads reduced round trip fares for Carnival "three cents per mile, each way".

Eda Clarke Fain reminded us that, *"The Memphis Daily Appeal* advised celebrants and maskers to 'provide themselves with torches' for the procession, and that weaponry was barred from the carnival ballrooms. Young boys adopted 'big-nosed' masks, and tin horns that were tooted incessantly, producing 'doleful' noises, and stuffed clubs with which to wallop unsuspecting spectators."

Memphi Masquerade Balls and Tableaux at the Greenlaw Opera House were limited to "solely" invited guests mandated to "full evening toilet *en masque de rigueur*". *The Memphis Daily Avalanche* wrote of, "Nymphs in silk and satins. It was a sea of gleaming shoulders, glossy ringlets, and upon heaving bosoms jewels flashed and sparkled." To be Queen of the Memphi Ball was an honor to which every young debutante aspired, for the Queen of the Memphi was also the queen of Memphis social life. Happy are those whom the Queen delights to honor. Every year the Memphi sent out hundreds of beautifully colored invitations to the masked ball to he held on Shrove Tuesday. The name of the sender was not disclosed; only the name Memphi appeared in blazing letters at the top. People who made a serious effort to find out who had mailed the invitation were not invited again. The Memphi was sensitive about its secrecy.

The balls of the military club of the Chickasaw guards were unsurpassed in glamour and excitement. Young ladies from all over the Mid-South covetously desired to be included in these events as well which, as the *Daily Appeal* noted, provided "music as stirring as the harps of heaven and supper tables which were culinary poems." Carnival seemed to recapture some of the old gaiety, the almost forgotten way of life of antebellum times. Memphis opened its doors and conviviality to its invading country cousins and to elite international guests as well.

Lou Leubrie, the indefatigable, mustached impresario of the New Memphis Theater (northeast corner of Jefferson and Third St.) stood and lifted his fine crystal flute of Moët et Chandon: "Today it is impossible to truly evaluate the good that the Memphi and Colton Greene have done for the city of Memphis. Our Carnival celebration's founders have helped to bring about a unity among the townsfolk, which would have been impossible through any other means. More than romanticizing the past, the success of the Memphis Carnival is measured not only by the extraordinary visitation figures that have breathed new life into our economy, but in the cosmopolitan image, social prestige, and renown of our fair city heralded across the nation. Although the purpose of Memphi is ostensibly social, Colton Greene and his lieutenants among us are men of vision, and they applied their vision as an instrument for civic betterment and to form a leadership to clean up the city. Even before the first Mardi Gras was staged, Colton Greene was trying to improve sanitation. He visited and studied the sewage and sanitation system of practically every important city in the country, and deserves full credit for planning our present system of sanitation. A toast of homage, gentlemen, to General Colton Greene – always the mystery man, moving behind the scenes, doing the planning, and picking our leaders."

Standing behind the round table and listening to the toasts and praise from scions of the first families of Memphis, I thought of what Edward King wrote in *The Southern States of North America* in 1875, "The terrible visitation (the yellow fever) did not, however, prevent Memphis from holding her annual Carnival and repeating in the streets, so lately filled with funerals, the gorgeous pageants of the mysterious 'Memphi' such as the Egyptians gazed on 2,000 years before Christ was born, nor the pretty theaters being filled with the echoes of delicious music. The Carnival is now so firmly rooted in the affections of the citizens of Memphis that nothing can unsettle it."

Memphi Priest

Rising from the chair to his full stature with the aid of a simple walking stick of cane, Colton Greene addressed the round table. His sleek white hair and manicured Van Dyke beard graced the cloak of Confederate gray with scarlet velvet lining that he had miraculously resurrected for the occasion. His gaze was level and clear-eyed, and he spoke in modulated tones of a classical stage actor:

"Gentlemen, comrades, and faithful lieutenants. Your tribute this evening commemorating my retirement from the presidency of the Tennessee Club, evokes fondest memories of our years of enterprise and endeavor together. As the first Sublime Ouro of the Memphi, I have seen our organization fill its ranks with the most prominent and influential of Southern society. Since its inception the Memphi has been in every sense of the word a Secret Society and as such so will it ever continue. Our actual membership is small, not more than a hundred, and will remain so to protect the secrecy of our organization and to insure its exclusivity. I have presided over the expansion of the Memphi into the auspicious Tennessee Club. It has been the responsibility of the Memphi to establish and to promote our Memphis

Carnival. No effort has been spared to assure that the designing of the costumes and float motifs was accurate. As you know I made the voyage to Egypt in order that our Mardi Gras would be unequivocally authentic. Soon our Memphis Carnivals were attracting more attention and regard than those of New Orleans and Mobile. Such good things seldom run smoothly. Epidemics of bubonic plague, Asiatic cholera and yellow fever impeded our effort, and one-third of our city's population perished in these epidemics. The plight aroused the sympathy of the entire civilized world. England, France, Germany, India and many other nations, in addition to other sections of this country, poured in contributions to help our stricken city. New York alone sent checks for $43,800. Still, this and all the other contributions were not enough. By January 1879, the city was bankrupt, had surrendered its charter, and became a tax district of the state, losing its corporate identity as a municipality for twelve years. In spite of such formidable obstacles, the city of Memphis has rebounded due to the indomitable efforts and bonhomie of the Memphi and the Tennessee Club and the families they represent: the Overtons, the Hills, the Brinkleys, the Mallorys, Trezevants, and Randolphs. To you this evening, on behalf of the citizens of Memphis, I offer my utmost gratitude for our tremendous success and good fortune."

CABIN NOTES:

The legacy of the Tennessee Club was ongoing. Mayor Crump was a member in good standing and many of his constituents were drawn from its ranks. Yet Boss Crump and his lieutenants also depended heavily on the voter constituency of the underworld of vice and gambling. Although the Red Snapper publicly and loudly vowed to shut down the Nonpareil that Jim Canaan was operating in the Pinch district, they needed kickbacks from racketeers to fund their campaign thrust. The Pinch was a section settled by the Irish running north along the bluff toward the mouth of the Wolf River where it meets the Mississippi. The Pinch district was so named after the Irish, remarkable for their lean and hungry pinch-gut appearance.

Mr. Jim had a fine home on 2nd Street at the beginning of the Pinch around the corner from St. Brigid's Church, which he supported from daily revenue earned by the various saloons and joints that he and his henchmen operated around downtown. Both men were tough as nails and for all the hot-tempered fisticuffs the Red Snapper was known for; Crump could have as well been called the Red Scrapper. Providing the recipient warranted such immediate justice, Jim Canaan too, was known to work a man over in a jiffy with his hand tooled shillelagh. Yet, both the bare-knuckled politician and the whiskey kingpin were high-principled individuals who were capable of an unusual degree of restraint and cunning, and who cultivated practical ideals calculated to assure the success and expansion of their respective organizations at any cost. Crump's ultimate refusal to enforce the prohibition laws of Tennessee would lead to political consequences in that republicans in the state capitol in Nashville eventually had Crump ousted from the mayor's office for failure to comply on this issue. Crump was able to side step this ouster by immediately having one of his cronies step into his job at city hall.

Whether serving as mayor or pulling the strings behind the scenes, Boss Crump would learn how to balance the demands of the black population of Memphis alongside the expectations of poor whites, and how to play both sides against one another when necessary. Thus he succeeded in winning the votes of each sector vital to maintaining the hegemony of his political machine. Banking, financial, educational, and cultural affairs were totally under the grip of city hall. Although he could not be considered a racist and would never speak disparagingly of black people, Edward Hull Crump was born into the planter society of Holly Springs, Mississippi, just south of Memphis in the same community where Ida B. Wells was born into slavery. Without doubt, white supremacy was as central to the thinking of most of planter society as was their reliance on black labor to plant and harvest their lucrative crops.

According to an account penned by a Wayne Dowdy, when Ed Crump was elected to the mayor's office in 1909, "every day was a murder day". Memphians were and still are quick to discharge a pistol or pull a knife at the slightest provocation. In order to prevent the murder of innocent black Memphians, and to curtail racial unrest, the Crump regime established a board of censors to monitor what it considered to be inflammatory and provocative content in the form of movies, books, theater plays and associated media. The city commission established the Board of Censors on the 16th of May, 1911. Insurance executive Lloyd T. Binford was appointed its first director, and would remain in that position for the next four decades. The board was constituted to "prevent the exhibition of immoral, lewd, and lascivious pictures, acts, and performances inimical to public safety, health, morals and welfare."

During the 1920s, Dowdy recounts that Crump built a political organization by connecting neighborhood and civic clubs with reformers and the business class of both the white and the black communities. With this strategy he inaugurated one of the most efficient political machines in American history. Mayor Crump's most influential liaison to the black community was the Beale Street real estate entrepreneur and philanthropist, Robert R. Church, Sr. Knowing very well that without black support his candidates could not have won elections, the alliance forged with Robert Church was instrumental to the Crump machine maintaining both peace and its own supremacy. The 60,000 votes that Crump commanded in Shelby County meant that he was a considerable force in state politics, although such results were not obtained without the use of strong-arm tactics, violence, and intimidation at polling stations across Shelby County. Through his crony, Senator Kenneth McKellar, he aligned himself with the republicans of east Tennessee to spread the control of his political machine across the state. Due to the ravages of the Great Depression, farm workers black and white migrated into Memphis to escape their deplorable existence in the country, creating a tinderbox of racial tensions. Obviously, Crump felt obliged to carefully monitor the image of African-Americans presented in the local media.

Crump Billboard 1950s

During the war years of the 1940s further migrations poured into Memphis as Southerners regardless of race became uprooted. In 1943 the MGM production of Cabin in the Sky, featuring an all-black cast consisting of Lena Horne, Eddie "Rochester" Anderson, and Duke Ellington, was scheduled to show at Loew's State Theatre, which catered to a whites-only audience. The Memphis Board of Censors prohibited the showing of Cabin in the Sky, citing "the necessity of preserving the public peace from outbreaks of violence due to racial prejudices." During this time, Crump and his henchmen aligned themselves with the Dixiecrats, who stood in direct opposition to the proposals of Eleanor Roosevelt. The Dixiecrats also opposed the civil rights agenda of President Harry S. Truman that mandated the end of the whites-only Democratic conventions.

Judge Hamilton in custody March 25, 1944

On March 25, 1944 Harold Preece wrote in the Chicago Defender, *"Dr. Walker is one of those most afraid of Crump's shadow dominating Memphis from the honky-tonks of Vance Street to Crump's real estate office where 2,000,000 Tennesseans of both colors are moved around like pawns on a checkerboard." Not long after this appeared, a half page photograph was published in the* Memphis Commercial Appeal *of a corridor in the Universal Life Insurance Building, the largest black-owned insurance company in the nation. Dr. J. E. Walker was its president and stood at the top of the social pyramid in the black community. The newspaper file photo showed a bewildered secretary standing in the middle of the hall over a large pool of blood oozing from under the door to Dr. Walker's office. A disgruntled former business partner, called Judge Hamilton, had shot the president of Universal Life dead at his desk during business hours.*

The Hoodoo Cartel was a behind-the-scenes phenomenon that poured funds into the coffers of city hall. Voodoo has always been and still is practiced on Beale Street, and maintains a powerful sway over the thoughts and behavior of those who believe in or are unsure of its powers. The purpose of Voodoo is to bring bad luck on the enemy, or to remove bad luck caused by the enemy. The many small businesses and shop keepers who traded in Hoodoo talismans and potions and who laundered money for the local racketeers in vice and prostitution, constituted a potent political voice together with that of the entrenched underworld. Whenever feasible the black vote was covertly manipulated by Hoodoo interests. Suspicious of and aggressively hostile to outside intruders, the Memphis underground was and remains strictly indigenous.

In 1939 the Red Snapper ran again for the office of mayor. Unopposed. Edward J Meeman, editor of the Commercial Appeal, *and lawyer Lucius Burch spoke out vehemently and eloquently against the Crump machine, still no one listened. But why 'step down' to the mayor's office? He already controlled every office in the city, county, and the state. Crump was sworn in; then promptly resigned. Evidentially he wanted to publicly show who was still boss. Prohibition had just ended and along with it the Memphis underground. Local racketeering and the vestiges of the Hoodoo cartel moved off the street and into plush offices. Crump's main supporters had moved on to white-collar crime, that was where the real money was. Crump took it one step further by ordering Beale Street shut down and closed every gin joint, whorehouse, dope peddler, and bootlegger in the city. Thus reorganizing his power base within the age of the new sobriety.*

TIME observed that, "The man who dared the Boss's revivalist anger and self-righteous vituperation was Yale-trained Estes Kefauver of Chattanooga, a hard-working Congressman with a pro labor, New Dealish record. He [Crump] likened Kefauver to 'a pet coon' that turns its head in innocence, 'while its foot is feeling around' for something to filch." The progressive, liberal stance of Kefauver put him in direct competition with Boss Crump when he sought the Democratic nomination for the U.S. Senate in 1948. Crump and his allies accused Kefauver of plotting with the reds and communists. In a televised speech given in Memphis, Kefauver put on a coonskin cap and proclaimed, "I may be a pet coon, but I'm not Boss Crump's pet coon." The Nashville Tennessean, *a liberal newspaper that served as a focal point for anti-Crump sentiment, promoted Kefauver's successful efforts. Kefauver won the Democratic nomination, and his victory marked the beginning of the end for the Crump machine's influence in statewide politics.*

In 1952 Kenneth McKellar, a long time crony of Ed Crump, stood for a seventh term in the US Senate. The Crump/McKellar alliance lasted for decades and along with the "Hoodoo" cartel in Memphis, decided who would get elected, who would get prosecuted, and who would get juicy government contracts on the local and state levels, and in Washington. The often-confrontational yet powerful head of the Senate Appropriations Committee, was opposed for re-nomination by the more progressive Congressman Albert Gore, who defeated McKellar and went on to serve three terms in the Senate. McKellar's defeat marked the end of Boss Crump having any real influence in Tennessee beyond Memphis. A lifelong bachelor, the aging McKellar then retired to his suite at the Gayoso Hotel in Memphis, where he died on October 25, 1957.

This was the period when another native-born Memphian rose to prominence in the nation's capital. Abe Fortas was the son a Jewish cabinetmaker from Great Britain from whom he acquired his love of music, and hence became known as "Fiddling Abe". He attended Yale Law School where he met Carolyn Agger, a cigar-smoking economist, who would become his wife. While teaching at Yale, he met a tall, aggressive Texan, Lyndon Johnson, who became a lifelong friend and staunch supporter. Fortas was appointed Undersecretary of the Interior during the Roosevelt administration, and established an influential law practice in Washington. He managed to play violin in a popular combo in Georgetown on the weekends where Issac Stern was drawn to the charm and personality of the promising advocate who was then beginning to travel in the most influential Washington circles. Fortas represented the author and theorist Owen Lattimore before the Tydings Committee and clashed with Joseph McCarthy during the hearings. When Johnson was elected president, he nominated his longtime friend to the Supreme Court as Associate Justice with the thought that Fortas could expedite his Great Society reform agenda. Abe Fortas was known as a liberal vote and was the architect and author of majority opinions that favored children's rights, that revamped insanity defense criteria, and that ended religiously based creation narratives from public school science curricula.

In Goin' Back to Memphis, James Dickerson tells us that, "After the Kennedy assassination, Fiddling Abe became the second most powerful man in Washington. President Johnson sought his advice on every major domestic issue. He put Fortas in charge of establishing the Warren Commission. It was Fortas who helped draft legislation for the Kennedy Center for the Performing Arts. Fortas projected a complex, dual image. On the one hand, he was a high profile lover of music and culture. On the other hand, he was a cynical, behind-the-scenes power broker, whose services were offered to the highest bidder."

When Earl Warren announced his retirement, President Johnson nominated Fortas for Chief Justice. His nomination was bitterly contested by the Dixiecrats spearheaded by the racist Senator James Eastland of Mississippi, and was further undermined by rampant criticism of the overriding influence that Fortas exerted over White House policy. Under pressure of filibuster, Fortas asked the President to withdraw his nomination. A payoff scandal involving one of his private practice clients resulted in the start of impeachment proceedings that prompted Fiddling Abe to resign his position a justice on the U.S. Supreme Court in 1969.

Crump Tomb Photo: E. Baffle 1975

CHAPTER THE THIRD
STIRRING UP A LITTLE HELL

The L&N station at Binghampton is the first whistle stop out of town heading east toward Nashville. I could see the station from my front porch. What to do today, I wondered? Why not ease over to the farmers' market by the station and pick out of couple of peaches just arrived from Brownsville… maybe grab a paper off the rack at the station to read over a bowl of Cheerios, Pet Milk, and those fresh peaches. I picked up the fruit and tipped into the L&N station. There on the news racks were all these special editions. *Holy Cow!* Headlines in tallest block letters I'd ever seen on the cover of a newspaper: "G-MEN CAPTURE DESPERADO & FUGITIVE WIFE IN MEMPHIS!" "PUBLIC ENEMY No.1 NABBED IN MEMPHIS!" It's Machine Gun Kelly! Brandishing machine guns and sawed-off shotguns, Federal Marshalls, FBI Special Agents, and MPD officers had raided a bungalow in South Memphis near Lamar Ave. and Bellevue just before dawn. Detective Raney crept into the house and got the drop on George Kelly as the shadow of the outlaw preceded him down a corridor. Kelly stepped out of the bathroom in his underwear holding a pistol. Looking down the barrel of the sawed-off shotgun Raney held on him, the bandit dropped his gun and declared, "OK, boys. I've been waiting on you all night". He'd stayed up late reading *Master Detective* magazine. Kathryn, his attractive redheaded wife, was sleeping in a back bedroom. Machine Gun Kelly and Kathryn were red hot. A massive manhunt had been underway for two weeks, as they were charged with the kidnapping of millionaire oilman Charles F. Urschel. At the point of a Thompson submachine gun, the oilman had been abducted from the screened-in porch of his home in Oklahoma City while playing bridge with his wife and friends. Urschel's captors drove to a small farm in Paradise, Texas, where they held him for ransom demanding the astronomical sum of $200,000. Once the ransom was paid and Urschel was released, Kelly and Katherine fled Texas. Not before fleeing the Lone Star state, the couple stashed half of the $200,000 ransom, which had been paid in $20 denominations, in thermos jugs that they buried on neighboring farms and ranches.

They traveled in a 16-cylinder automobile at terrific speed, heavily armed with the latest model .45 caliber machine gun that Kathryn had bought for her husband, plus an array of shotguns and automatic pistols. Kelly had become an expert shot, as Kathryn had coached him to shoot walnuts off fence posts. Early on Kelly earned the sobriquet of "Machine Gun" because he could write his name on a signboard or a bank wall with bullets as easily as he could write it with pen and paper. They even borrowed a 12-year-old girl, Geraldine Arnold, from a friend to pose as Kathryn's daughter during their wild flight across Texas. To alter their identities, Kelly dyed his hair a yellowish blond hue, bristling up in a close-cropped pompadour, and Katherine wore a coquettish wig.

Meanwhile Kathryn penned brazen threat letters to U.S. District Attorney Herbert K. Hyde and Assistant U.S. Attorney General Joseph B. Keenan, promising to either murder or to kidnap every member of their families. The letters bore Kelly's fingerprint and ended with the admonition: *"See you in hell."* FBI director J. Edgar Hoover claimed that it was Kathryn rather than Kelly who had the underworld connections, and the brains, to pull off such audacious capers. The redhead promoted themselves as the most wanted couple in America. Kelly once struck his pulchritudinous wife with a pistol from which she bore a permanent scar, and although the FBI credited Katherine with being clever, they said she was afraid of him.

When the fugitives arrived in Memphis they dismissed "Dimples" Arnold, and went into hiding in the bungalow on Rayner St. in the home of a used-car salesman. The pretty little girl, who masqueraded as the daughter of the nation's most hunted woman, hopped a train alone to Oklahoma City straight into the arms of federal agents, who met the 10:10 Rock Island train from Memphis. Dimples tipped off the Feds and brought the downfall of the marauding outlaws. When asked about Kathryn Kelly, Dimples replied, "She's all right." Kelly was accused of complicity in more heinous crimes: the Union Station massacre of five men at Kansas City, and the slaying of a Chicago policeman who attempted to frustrate the hold-up of Federal Reserve messengers. State Policeman O. P. Ray reported he was almost run down once by a big automobile on the outskirts of Oklahoma City in which Kelly and Charles Arthur "Pretty Boy" Floyd, the notorious Southwestern desperado, were riding.

There is a $10,000 reward for his capture in connection with the kidnapping of Urschel, and a $5000 reward in connection with the Chicago robbery, plus a $5000 reward for the capture of Mrs. Kelly in connection with the kidnapping. But the timing of Kelly and Kathryn was not so good. Gangs during early Prohibition had discovered that kidnapping was a profitable enterprise, until the abduction and murder of flyer Charles Lindbergh's baby. This atrocity that shocked a complacent nation would make kidnapping an extremely risky business and a capital crime. The resulting Lindbergh Law, enacted in 1933, did not bode well for the first gangland kidnapping under the new injunction. J. Edgar Hoover personally took charge of the Urschel case and vowed to bring the "dirty yellow rats" responsible to justice. Obviously the marauders knew the dragnet was closing in and time was running out.

But the *big scoop* that was blasted across the front page of *The Press-Scimitar* stunned most Memphians. City editor, Null Adams, broke the story that Machine Gun Kelly was really *George Kelly Barnes*, who grew up in Memphis the son of a well-to-do insurance agent living in a congenial home at Cowden and Rembert in the staid Central Gardens district of Midtown. He had gone to Idlewild Elementary School, then Central High, never earning a grade higher than "C–". George Kelly attended Mississippi A&M College in Starkville for a spell before he flunked out. It was reported he was in the Army in World War I, went to France, and after his career as a soldier learning to use firearms, was never satisfied to settle down. Barnes came back to Memphis and drifted from job to job – selling used cars, driving a cab with the 784 Taxi Company, even running a goat farm out on Poplar Pike. Soon he discovered the pleasures of easy money, and one day in 1923 he was caught operating a whiskey still out in the boondocks south of town and was sentenced to six months on the county penal farm. Later he surfaced in Santa Fe, New Mexico, where he was arrested for bootlegging and fined $250. Another arrest in Tulsa for smuggling liquor into an Indian reservation sent him to the federal penitentiary at Leavenworth, Kansas, for a three-year term. Upon his release, Kelly learned the finer points about robbery and machine guns from Verne C. Miller, who was then the kingpin of the Kansas City machine gunners.

Nobody here had imagined George Machine Gun Kelly was from Memphis... no public awareness at all. What a gold-plated surprise! I'll catch the next thing smokin' to downtown, I decided. Out on the platform there was a crowd of people waiting. I looked up the signboard; the Dixie Flyer would be steaming by here in three minutes. No need to buy a ticket: this was the last stop on the run from Nashville. I never bought a ticket going downtown because the conductor couldn't put you off the train once it started rolling, but if he recognized you as a chronic dark rider he'd throw you off before the train left the station. Typically, I would have to sneak onboard. In the near distance I heard the steam whistle blowing long and low at the Tillman St. crossing. The lusty black locomotive loomed large coming down the track, its short stack puffing a thick plume of gray and white smoke against the wan September sky. A heavy cloud of dense smoke covered all of Broad Street. Under cover of this lugubrious mantle of railroad smog, I slipped unnoticed onto the second passenger car from the hind end. The six passenger coaches were packed. It was a short run to Union Station – about 14 minutes. I debarked on the Calhoun St. side and walked down to Third St. where I swung onto a passing trolley that would take me past the central police station.

The trolley was packed too, with all kinds of people, many who were carrying Kodaks and folding pocket cameras. I alighted on Poplar Avenue and followed the crowds up to the station. It was a madhouse. Only last year Memphis had been voted the Murder Capitol of the Nation, and the capture of Machine Gun Kelly in the Bluff City seemed to put the icing on the cake. The fugitives were being held in default of $100,000 bond each. In the general rush, crowds of the curious were pushing and shoving into the station to get a glimpse of the bandit and his moll. The police station itself resembled an arsenal. Machine guns were set up. Officers were armed with riot guns or sawed-off shotguns. Newsreel cameramen from Fox, Paramount, and other agencies, had flown into Memphis, eager for just a glimpse of the renegades. When Kathryn appeared in the custody of four police matrons armed with automatic pistols, there was an explosion of flash bulbs. She cheerfully smiled and posed for the cameras. When they escorted Kelly upstairs for mugging and fingerprinting, one officer held a sub-machine gun in the small of his back and another held a long revolver in his side. Now the man who all had come to jail to see – city officials, businessmen, friends of the police as well as the idle curious – was a surprise to most of his visitors. He stood about six feet tall, huskily built about the chest and shoulders. Some remarked that he looked like a prince of a man, apparent in genuineness of his smile. His head was well shaped and his eyes, although small, were wide set in that way which gives the mark of intelligence to a face. "Lend me that machine gun a minute," he jested with a guard. To an officer standing guard with a Tommy gun, "Say, I could use that, but it's a rather old style," Kelly wisecracked, "You should have some of the new guns." Yet he was clearly outraged by the leg shackles placed on him. "Why do they have to put these things on for? Do you think I'm going anywhere, with these guards watching me and these bars?"

The Urschel kidnapping trial was already under way in Oklahoma City, with the other figures involved in the case hauled into the courtroom. Fingered by Department of Justice agents as just "a rat without guts", defense attorney Albert Bates had quipped, "Why haven't these officers caught Kelly? All they can catch is a cold and that's given to them." Now that he was captured, authorities decided to keep the Kellys in Memphis until it was time for them to testify. At Union Station I picked up an afternoon edition with the headline, "KELLY WAS BROKE: George "Machine Gun" Kelly was broke when the officers arrested him this morning at 1408 Rayner. He borrowed a silver quarter from his wife before they parted. She took the money out of her pocketbook, which contained about $15 in bills. As she left the house she collected three packages of cigarettes, saying she smoked two packages a day and would probably need them." With this I felt a little dejected, and a bit disillusioned, but reading on I was impressed with Kelly's braggadocio: "This cell's a bit crowded; hardly room to swing a cat in," Kelly complained to Chief Lee. "Guess it won't make much difference, tho. I won't be here long." Asked why he came to Memphis and if he expected to hide out here, Kelly smiled, tossed a cigarette into the far corner of his cell and replied, "Well, you see it was a case of any old port in a storm, an island would have done. I had no intention of staying in Memphis, just happened thru here on the way somewhere else—had a little business to attend to here." Kathryn was whining, "I don't want to say anything about that guy Kelly, but he got me into this terrible mess and I don't want to have anything more to do with him."

Another article stated that while the Memphis Police Department is being congratulated for the splendid cooperation it gave federal officers in arresting Machine Gun Kelly and his wife, the fact that this extraordinary gunman was captured without a single shot being fired indicates that the Memphis Police are capable of arresting evil doers without shooting them down. How different was the recent police arrest that resulted the shooting of a 17-year-old Negro by Shelby County Deputy Sheriff Phil Armour in Raleigh, as reported by the *Press-Scimitar*. Officers would not have been criticized had they had shot Kelly on the slightest resistance for he is a known desperado. Yet their shooting of a fleeing boy who was unarmed, and whose alleged crime was the theft of a pair of pants, seems hardly justified. Many officers

Machine Gun Kelly under arrest

are too prone to act as judge, jury and executioner. Their motto, "to rightfully arrest, but never to kill unless in self-defense", appears rather inconsistent with their practices.

Charles Urschel, the kidnapping victim himself, testified that he was treated "with consideration" before being released unharmed, but the Kellys were convicted in Oklahoma City and both received life sentences. Kathryn, a beautiful party-girl, was sent to the Women's Federal Prison at Anderson, West Virginia, and claimed she had returned to religion for strength during her imprisonment. George Machine Gun Kelly was ordered to Leavenworth on Oct. 14, 1933. United Press reported that, "The gangster, sentenced to life imprisonment for kidnapping Charles F. Urschel at Oklahoma City, was in high spirits. He spent most of the trip en route from Oklahoma City in the government's armored railroad car writing autographed "wisecracks" on squares of tissue paper which he passed out to newspaper men and officers at stations on the way. All were obscene. The armored car was pushed directly into the prison yard, behind the walls, by a switch engine. Kelly came out, handcuffed, manacled and clanking a leading chain, to change his wrinkled suit for government gray." There he complained, "How the hell did I ever get myself into this fix? I should've stayed with what I knew how to do best – robbing banks." Too tough for Leavenworth, he was transferred to Alcatraz in San Francisco harbor in September 1934. Although he boasted, "they haven't built a prison to hold me," he worked in the prison furniture factory, always with armed guards watching him. At Alcatraz he was nicknamed "Pop-Gun Kelly" by the inmates and was thought not to be as tough as he was cracked up to be. Kelly started out as a Memphis hip pocket bootlegger and became Public Enemy Number One. *Began in Memphis, nabbed in Memphis.* Seventeen years later I read in the paper that Machine Gun Kelly had died in his prison on the date of his 59th birthday. Later on I came across a story by Michael Finger in the *Memphis Flyer*, which read, "Kelly, though confessing to the kidnapping charge, strongly denied taking part in any murders. Ballistics tests proved him right, eventually linking the Chicago policeman's murder and the Kansas City 'massacre' to others." In my handy *Encyclopedia of American Crime*, Carl Sifakis notes, "The fact is that Kelly never fired a shot at anyone and he certainly never killed anyone, is a remarkable statistic for a public enemy dubbed 'Machine Gun'."

It was about 3:00 in the afternoon in Binghampton when rolled slowly out of the bed, and stepped out on the porch. It was a hot ass summer's day. Across the street through the trees I could see a spray truck rolling toward Overton Park, emanating a thick blue/white fog of DDT insecticide aimed to thwart nascent and ubiquitous populations of mosquitoes. Now a second fogging truck passed in the opposite direction. *But what's that sound...?* Above the drone of the fogging nozzle jet, I heard a roar – a distinctive rumbling reverberation of combusting iron and flame. *That's it all right...* the earth shaking sound of twin iron pistons pumping 74 cubic inches of displacement for driving the crankshaft of an Indian Chief motorcycle. It's *him*, that funny fellow Don West tearing around the corner over to Broad Street. First time I saw that Indian, it was parked outside of that farmers union office on Broad, whatever it's called, *Southern Tenant Farmers' Union*, I believe it was. There was that oversized, fender-skirted, low-slung, wicked medieval-looking iron sled propped up on its side stand at a particularly rakish angle. Sure I had to stop and take a real good look at the Tyrannosaurus Rex of a machine. I figured Don West must have heard me coming as well, because he stepped out through the screen door of the office to look me over. The sound *he* heard approaching was the thumping, fire-spitting growl of a sleek black 1929 Norton CS-1 model that was thrusting forward shuddering and smoking between my knees. The 1939 Norton ES model that Che Guevara rode through Bolivia that he called *La Ponderosa* or "the mighty one", was like a piece of farm machinery compared this first Norton of mine. In fact, there was not machine on two *or* on four wheels in Memphis or in the whole state of Tennessee that was faster or more fleet than this howling black and silver rocket. Red could sense that right away about the Norton and invited me next door to Eddy Bob Eddy's Bar & Grill for a 3.2 beer. That was the beginning of some funny times.

The STFU office was at 2545 Broad St. My house was set two streets over, exactly behind, at 2545 Princeton. One block beyond is Summer Avenue, which takes you straight out of Memphis onto Highway 70 and 400 miles east to Nashville. Across from Leahy's Motor Court on Summer Ave. stuck in amongst the strip malls, movie houses, Bar B Q pits, used car lots, root beer stands, beauty salons, drugstores, and gas stations, was situated Memphis Motorcycle Company operated by the Amagliani Bros. They handled Indian and Norton motorcycles exclusively. The allure of this place is another thing that Don West and I had in common: an infatuation with the smell of tire rubber, racing fuels, motor oils, leather saddle bags, and the sounds of the iron barreled motors as they were being fettled and tuned by the Amagliani mechanics. On my Norton, I'd just had the valves ground, the cylinder barrel honed, and new piston rings installed. The machine had metamorphosed into a veritable mile-eating, road scorching daemon hungry for the open road. Over 3.2 beers, Don West seemed to have the right prescription. "Why don't you ride over to Arkansas with me to 'stir up a little of hell'? We'll stop off in Tyronza and pick up some comrades from the STFU local there and then roll up into the foothills of the Ouachita Mountains to Glenwood. That sheriff over in Pike County and his squad of goons are trying to bust up a strike we got going at the roofing plant. The STFU will pay for gas and grub, and there'll be good hospitality and country dances at the Methodist campground." Why not, I thought. Free gas and grub! And country-dances with those pretty Arkansas women.

Riding into Tyronza via West Memphis was fairly flat and uneventful. The town was grim and the folk unsmiling, but the welcome at the STFU hosted by the local dry cleaners was high-spirited and cordial. The ladies were cheery and hospitable and had laid out saltine crackers, spam, and a bowl of fresh purple-hulled peas. The men were also genial, but they were more preoccupied with earnest talk about 'redistribution of the wealth', I think it was, and 'equal justice for the races', 'guaranteed income', marching on Washington, and all kinds of big talk.

Hay Bale, Arkansas Photo: E. Baffle 1975

After a night's rest in the back of the fragrantly prim dry cleaners, we rode our cycles out toward central Arkansas with a contingent of four, and I noticed, rather heavily armed comrades bobbing along behind in a Model B Ford sedan. In addition to the load of firearms aboard the sedan, there were several sacks of flour and corn meal, some tins of lard, and a couple bushels of turnips and sweet potatoes. At breather stops along the way, I learned that Don West was born in Devil's Hollow, Georgia, and that he'd been teaching at the experimental Highlander Folk School over in east Tennessee at Monteagle.

     The Norton and the Indian Chief stretched out into full gallop on the winding roads cut through the valleys and over the verdant hillsides. The air was brisk and cooling as we crested the hilltops and became warm and sultry through the hollows and fertile bottomlands. Dauntless we rode beside the narrow, sunken, yet majestic Caddo River into the slate mining hamlet of Glenwood with our exhaust pipes yowling. Immediately as we approached the "Y" in front of Herd's Company Store, we spotted a submachine gun mounted on a military-type tripod pointed directly toward our approach. It was unmanned. Up on a rise to the left beside the riverbank, stood a lofty, factory structure walled with corrugated aluminum and bristling with metal girder conveyor belts and chutes, and smoke stacks of dirty brick. At its entrance stood another such mounted machine gun, but water-cooled. Also unmanned. The whole dinky town seemed mighty quiet. The one room railroad station was deserted. There was a colored man in a straw hat sitting barefooted at one end of a bench in front of the grocery store, and two white men also wearing sweaty straw hats: one in overalls, and the other in a white shirt, suspenders, and kakis sitting at the other end. They seemed not to pay much attention to our raucous arrival. Fine gray soot lay over everything, gray as the sky.

     The town was deserted for two reasons. Herd's Mill, the roofing granules factory, was closed until Monday due to the present strike. Number two: most everybody who wasn't at home sick with pellagra, measles, or venereal disease, (or with skin so scrofulous they couldn't be seen in public) was down in the campground holler attending a Mount Nebo Tabernacle Church of God in Christ revival meeting. Our STFU contacts were there as well appearing as speakers on the program. As we rode up to the campground with our engines throttled down to a mellow whisper, when we heard the opening strains of the hymn, "We Shall Not Be Moved". We parked in the shade of some black gum trees, and dismounted. Rufus Turnblazer, the local union chief, rose to speak:

"You know what it is to sharecrop the land in eastern Arkansas. Every year that you brought in a crop for the boss man, the further in debt you were obliged to the landowner for rent and to the plantation store for subsistence groceries to feed your family. Then with the New Deal buy-out, the planters kept the federal funds for themselves that Roosevelt had intended to be shared with tenant farmers. Plowing under the cotton crops kept the price of cotton inflated all right, but it prompted the planters to evict every man, woman, and child of you from your homes. Already defeated and exhausted you made this long journey by rail, bus, and mule wagon up in here in these hills to the slate mines of Pike county. Here in Glenwood, we ain't got but two things: Herd's Mill, the Company Store, and the rickety old Herd's Mill miners' bathhouse by the Caddo. We got no school, other than Sunday mornings at this here church, and we got no doctors. The pay from Herd's Mill roofing granules operations and for mining its slate from these hills was no more than $2.00 for a 16-hour shift, and since last year the wages have been cut by 20%. The price of bacon is 15¢ a pound most places in Pike County, but here the only grocery is the Company Store where bacon costs you 40¢ pound. In effect, you are paying the company for the privilege of mining its slate and manufacturing its roofing granules. Last Christmas we saw you walking out from your homes and cabins ragged and barefooted in the snow down to the courthouse grounds to collect the relief rations shipped in by the UMWA and the relief wing of the STFA. There was not even one candy cane to put in a child's Christmas stocking, and nobody could pay the price of Blue Diamond coal to put in your stove to keep warm. If you had a wood axe, and you weren't down with sickness and disease like most of you are, you could chop firewood up on the hill and try to drag it home. During this protracted strike against the slate mining industry, we've seen many of you sink into idleness and drunkenness. We know that some of you, out of hunger and desperation, have formed clandestine gangs to stick up grocery trucks out on the highway. Now we're prey to State Troopers and moonshiners alike. Some of you here today are strikebreakers. I ask that those of you who are upholding the strike to be tolerant of those who feel they have no other choice than to accept the forced labor conditions offered by the company because their children are sick and hungry just like yours. There is no easy answer, no apparent solution, and no remedy other than to hold your course and your direction that you know is righteous, fair and mandated by the almighty. Our representatives are petitioning the legislature in Little Rock, and the office of Governor Futrell. Beyond that there's talk about another hunger march on Washington. Hold your course, friends, brothers and sisters, and our colored and loyal brethren among us. I assure you: *we shall prevail*."

The speech from Rufus Turnblazer was greeted with uproarious applause and whoops and yells. His two little daughters rushed up to his side and took his big hands and swung from them like elfin plumb bobs. Long tables were spread out under the tree limbs, and the country folk were passing around bowls of corn grits, peas, and turnips. The larder of turnips and sweet potatoes that we had brought from the Memphis union office were donations joyously accepted. Dusk was falling and a pink glow fell from over the hilltops onto the proceedings. Don West seemed to be on intimate terms with Turnblazer and his slender, if not frail wife, Ester. They were a cordial couple that introduced us to young and old, white and colored who sat at the table around us. Seems that as guests from Memphis, we were considered something special, and they admitted that there were few visitors to Glenwood since the strike started last October.

After supper someone pulled out a harmonica, then a fiddle appeared, and another one started blowing a Jews harp. The latter was more curious than the others. He must've been one of the musicians with the tent revival because he had bleach blond hair set up in a bouffant, wore mascara, and was naked to the waist. His emaciated ribs were wrapped clear around his body with white adhesive tape – the kind they use in hospitals. Reckon he was a kind of sacrificial goat pledged by one of the faith healers preaching in the tent. Before long we had a real dance going that I'd heard so much about. Those country gals sure know how to lift a leg high. Pretty soon I saw mason jars of white lightning passing around among the celebrants. The moon shone down brightly over the rough tables and on the patch of cleared ground patted smooth by the dancers' feet – most of them barefooted. A yellow glow from a few coal oil lamps set on the tables and hanging from tree limbs cast shadows and silhouettes gyrating rhythmically against the revival tent pitched to the side. Everyone's spirits seemed to rise to a heightened pitch, and couples were pairing off to find some cozy spot in the woods which already seemed alive with those prowling about whose chief purpose in coming to camp meetings was courting. I'd danced with about a half dozen of those barefoot sylphs of the woods, while a number of the men folk had gone off in knots of three and four. THEN of a sudden we heard a god awful thunderous *KA-BLAM BOOM*. The ground shook and quaked under our feet, and the sky lit up with an orange, smoky flash back in the direction of the railroad tracks. It was the kind of back-concussion that made your heart jump up in your throat.

"It's the TRESTLE!" I heard someone yell. Sure enough, the G&FTS (Gurdon and Fort Smith Railroad) trestle over the Caddo River had just been dynamited to high heaven! Rufus Turnblazer jumped up on a bench and ordered, "Everybody just go home. *Don't* go over to that trestle. There's nothing you can do there, but get into trouble. Strike or no strike, there'll be no slate granules shipped out of here for quite a while… but what you can be sure of is that Sheriff Deaton and his posse of hired goons from the county seat in Murfreesboro will be invading Glenwood by noon tomorrow, and probably the state militia right behind them. So go on home. Just go on home." The dance broke up quickly. Don West and I and the other Memphis union boys, made a pallet on the smooth dirt under the revival tent. After the cache of pistols and shotguns was brought in from the sedan, I felt I had better chance to rest easy that night.

Next day was no picnic. Being Sunday, there was a service in the revival tent, so we had to get up early. Mercifully, the service was brief in the wake of the explosion the night before resulting in a mood of uncertainty and a pervasive sense of impending catastrophe about to unfold. Actually, nothing eventful happened, except this creeping uneasiness that amplified in the minds of the townsfolk and undermined any attempt at casual conversation. Monday dawned with no ostensible change. The town was still sooty, and the sky was ever gray. Around noon, Don West walked over to the railroad depot to check if there were any messages from the Memphis office as the telegraph lines ran over the river separately from the now defunct trestle.

Before long, I saw the lanky, dusky frame of Red striding back to the tent with particular intent in his gait. He clutched a sealed telegram in his solid, muscular grip. "Telegram for Rufus from our office on Broad St. Let's get over to his house." Rufus greeted Red and me at the front door of his cabin. Then Red handed him the envelope, "Personal telegram for you, Rufus, from the union regional office in Memphis". Rufus looked at Red kind of funny. "Yeah. What's up?" "Don't know, Rufus. It's sealed," Red replied. The older man took the envelope with steady hands and opened it carefully. As he read the lines, his eyes narrowed and a grim, yet somehow relieved look came over his expression. "It's an advisory that the circuit judge in Memphis has issued an injunction against Herd's Mill re-opening until the strike is negotiated and properly settled. A Federal Marshall is coming over to serve the papers. It's unbelievable… after all these months of petitioning. I'm going over to the front office at Herd's and show this message to the bosses. You can wait here in the house." Red looked surprised, "That's one piece of consequential news, Rufus. We'll go along with you far as the depot and send a confirmation back to the Broad St. office that you got the message."

We marched bareheaded the couple short blocks toward the "Y" and then Red and I peeled off in the direction of the G&FTS R/R depot. The town was dead still. We could hear distinctly the determined footsteps of Rufus Turnblazer receding behind us in the loose gravel they called a street in Glenwood. THEN! The stillness was shattered as we heard the water-cooled open fire in a murderous blast of three-inch shells. The sound was deafening. We turned around and literally froze in our boots, as we saw 60 rounds of automatic machine gun bullets rip through Rufus' body, lifting him clear from the ground and spinning him around in the air before he fell dead weight to the ground. The tremendous force of the blast of high caliber bullets had blown his shoes and socks right off his feet. Most of his left arm was completely sheared away. There was no death rattle, no gasping. Rufus was simply no longer existing. Less, he seemed, than something dead. Nothing more than a piece of roadkill, with a blood-soaked telegram stuck in its disembodied hand. People were already pouring out from nearby houses into the street where Rufus lay. The deserted town was suddenly full of life – and death. Don West charged toward the body, tore off his leather jacket and threw it down over the face and shoulder of Rufus' corpse, and stood there straddling the body.

He wheeled around pointing at everybody and audaciously addressed the mine police and their machine gunners and the onlookers, and the ashen townsfolk. "You see this don't you? You see this man lying dead at my feet: Rufus Turnblazer – a man beloved by every man, woman, and child of this community. He stood up fearlessly for you against the mine bosses and their hired police. Rufus Turnblazer knew that your only real hope lies in your union, in the strength of its numbers, in the power of a single bloc voice to represent you against the closed fist of the company bosses. A voice that has fallen upon deaf ears in government can no longer be ignored by its insistence and its promise of deliverance from oppression, fraud, greed, and the exploitation that you have endured for so long. Our union stands for a guaranteed income and a guaranteed job with a 35-hour workweek, the right to education and medical care, and the right to land for the landless. Rufus Turnblazer was carrying a telegram just now to the front office of Herd's Mill advising that a circuit court judge in Memphis has just placed an injunction against re-opening the mine on Monday, and a federal marshal is on his way here right now to enforce it. He was carrying that telegram, alone, and in a peaceful manner, when the Herd's Mill hired police opened fire on him and shot to pieces an unarmed man in the most brutal and cowardly action imaginable. But we urge you to return to your homes and cabins. There is absolutely nothing more you can do here for Rufus Turnblazer. Now you must do it for yourselves, and you must do it legally. Your union petitioned the federal building in Memphis for the past six months, and now help and justice are finally on its way. You see how the state government has disenfranchised you – the true proletariat, the worker of the soil, the miner in the quarry, the logger in the woods – has disenfranchised you by order of the poll tax that nobody can afford to pay in order to cast your vote. Without the vote you stand no chance of surviving the capitalist mandate and rancor of their corporate minions who control the system in Washington, Little Rock, and right here in Pike County. Right here today in Glenwood, Arkansas, I call for an end to the capitalist mandate! Community Councils like yours here in Glenwood are springing up all across the South, faster than we can organize them. All of you here – white and colored brethren – are certified members and dues paying at 10-cents a month. Likewise union membership is spreading like wildfire across the bottomlands and the hill country of this state and the across the rest of the South. Dynamiting a bridge will solve nothing. The railroad will build a new bridge to replace the destroyed one. The only real change, the only result of lasting consequence must be a fundamental change in the established form of government, ensuring your full participation as registered voters of this so-called democracy. We have been denied full citizenship in America, we are not the partners of industry and agriculture, rather we exist as chattels of the moneyed and corporate capitalist elite. This is *not* a republic; it is an oligarchy. This is *not* the American way. But arm in arm, joined and organized together as one, we shall, in the words of Rufus Turnblazer, prevail over your oppressors who have trod upon your spirit and your livelihood for as long as you can remember. Go on home now. We urge you to go home now, buy nothing, do nothing, sell nothing."

Don "Red" West astride his Indian

At this moment six Ford sedans packed solid with sheriff's deputies came careening in a cloud of dust onto the "Y". Sheriff Royal Deaton and the county judge sitting next to him rode in the lead sedan. Deputies were already out on the running boards of the sedans pointing pistols and rifles indiscriminately. Red looked at me and I looked at him in an instant of recognition, and we both bolted for the revival tent, which was not more than 100-yards away down in the holler. But Sheriff Deaton caught sight of Red and seemed to know exactly who he was – probably from photographs of agitators that were circulated among law enforcement agencies – and he ordered the sedan to keep coming after us. We passed our Memphis comrades on a dead run, who were positioned in among the townsfolk. Over his shoulder Red instructed them to stash their weapons and to blend into the crowd until further notice. Cutting through the trees on side paths, we reached the revival tent and leaped on our cycles. Red cranked over the big Indian, and the motor roared to life. The Norton took two tickles of the carburetor float button, then two prods of the kick starter, and the single-overhead-camshaft racing engine burst into an authoritative growl just as Sheriff Deaton's sedan came sliding around the curve of the two rut gully road towards the tent. Red and I spun out in a cloud of brown dust around the loop of the gully road back up to the "Y". I heard what sounded like bees swarming around my head, and then realized those were deputy sheriffs' bullets flying past. We laid down flat on the fuel tanks of the cycles and cracked the throttles wide open. The sedan of Sheriff Deaton rounded the "Y" on our heels and the bees kept whizzing around. In an instant we were on the Caddo River Road heading south, and the cycles pulled away from the sedans in pursuit like two cannon balls shot from a howitzer. I looked back over my shoulder and saw the chrome headlamps of the police sedans looking like two split peas in the distance. Now in a sudden epiphany I understood why Don West always rode a motorcycle, and one that was stronger than a farm tractor and twice as fast as any police Ford on the highway.

Red and I sped down the Caddo River Road past Antoine where we left Pike County and entered Clark, whereupon we backed off the throttle a bit. Those Arkansas sheriffs didn't have radios in their cars, so having crossed the county line there wasn't much to worry about and we had smooth sailing east across the state. When we got past the St. Francis River in the Arkansas delta not so far from Memphis, Red pulled over at a filling station and bought us a couple of Nehi Grape sodas. I spit the bugs out from between my teeth and cleaned those off my goggles that had stuck there as we were riding the highways through the fields. That's the best tasting Nehi I ever drank, I thought. Red asked me in that Devil's Hollow, Georgia drawl, "How'd you like to stop off here at Parkin with me? We got an eviction of 100 sharecropper families going on over at the Dibble Plantation that we're gonna bust. Gonna be a real 'rookus' going on in there." Whew. "Red, I'll tell you. I'd like nothing more than to ride over to Parkin with you and help bust that eviction, but to be honest, I'm not sure just how much help I'd be. I can get by pretty good at those country dances, but when it comes to a real man-sized job like you're doing, I'm not so sure I'm cut out for it, and I…I really got to get back to Binghampton and get some rest, Red. I don't think I've slept more than two hours since I met you. Anyhow riding those country back roads got the front end riding a little squirrelly on this Norton, and I better take it in to Amagliani and get it tweaked up. See you for a 3.2 beer on Broad St., OK?" That was the last time I ever saw Don West. Never heard his Indian Chief running around Binghampton either. Reckon Don West is out there at some tent meeting, or campground doing the work he was ordained to do, and running faster than anybody else could imagine on some gravel road.

CHAPTER THE FOURTH
BIG DIXIE BRICK CO. AND THE INSECT TRUST

Not long after I had settled into 704 South Cox, I joined forces with my comrade from across the river. The first time I ever saw Randall Lyon was on the 4th floor of Humphrey's Dormitory for freshmen men. He was hanging out in the room of a tall, sandy blond-haired, pock-faced English major who was our upperclassman floor counselor. They both carried canvas book bags and wore loden greens and browns, exuding as they did a bohemian sophistication and an aura of blithe erudition. Randall was the editor of *Prevue*, a literary quarterly published at the University of Arkansas in Fayetteville. He had just returned from a tour of duty with Army Intelligence in Vietnam during that Graham Greene, *Quiet American*, post-French interim phase when there was hardly an awareness of this part of Indochina. Of this, Randall spoke little, coming off like a kind of bohemian 'Manchurian Candidate' on campus. Later the Army had sent him to the Philippines. He'd show snapshots of himself in Bermuda shorts, and his big pear shaped body embraced by a gaggle of Philippine hookers. He had other snaps of stylish Filipino RnR bands dressed in spangles and chisel point Beatle boots that he declared sounded better than the records they covered.

Randall lived in a garret atop an old three-story southern home with an expansive veranda shaded by stately oak trees, now converted to a rooming house. It was situated directly across from Humphrey's Hall, which seemed nicely suited to Randall's predilection for young men. Once I visited him up there in his room. Upon reaching the uppermost floor, a ladder had to be climbed to an opening in the attic floor. Randall was suspended in the half-light, lolling in what appeared to be a sailor's hammock. His face was round and cherubic with a thinly delicate nose. When he rolled in the hammock, the baby fat of his pear belly became exposed under his sweater revealing a Gestalt of blue claw marks, seemingly remnants of bouts of rough sex. Randall was always in a state of angst and dread. That day he was reading a book of poems from Yeats, which he repeatedly threw against the wall in a fury. Often he was heard complaining bitterly how miserable it was to be a "faggot", and how difficult it was to be the friend of someone like him. Not understanding the mysteries of this gender orientation, nor feeling inclined to experimentation in this direction, I simply attempted to cultivate our friendship and collaboration on an aesthetic plane, as he remained my mentor and muse during our association over the next 37 years.

Randall was one of the first to turn on and become psychedelicized, which happened rather quickly. This transformation was, he claimed, an extension of his protracted study into the writings of Carl Jung, Wilhelm Reich, Johannes Kepler, Tycho Brahe, and Paracelsus. He read the entire Bollingen Series of numinous texts. He also ordered plans from the Reichian institute for construction of an Orgone Accumulator, but could never quite get it built. In addition to curt poems and short stories, Randall began, after a deepening psychedelicization, to construct grand collages of particular wit and profound visual irony. He and an accomplice infiltrated the U of A architecture department at one point, and hounded the staff and students into bringing Buckminster Fuller to speak. We screen printed large format posters by hand and posted them all over Fayetteville. This lecture was an astonishing event that surprisingly drew a large and attentive audience to the Chemistry auditorium. Fuller was splendid in a three-piece black suit and with flamboyant gestures expounded on a portmanteau of Dymaxion theories that thrilled and baffled everyone. Upon this success, we persuaded the English Dept. to host readings by Allen Ginsberg. We hand screen-printed posters for this occasion as well, and the Student Union was packed for the appearance of the beatnik bard, and his rendition of the epic *HOWL* was applauded with Parnassian ardor. Ginsberg dubbed Randall's poetry as "modern *freak brain original*".

Randall introduced me to tall swarthy guitarist who'd come to campus from New York carrying a Martin D-28 in one hand and in the other, a stack of Tacoma records in plain white sleeves. He was wearing black suede Beatle boots, big square Raybans with dark green lenses, and his black hair was quiffed, or rather processed, into a smooth stiffened medieval pageboy. His name was Bill Barth, and he was hawking arcane recordings of John Fahey and himself in instrumental, steel-string guitar duets. To this day there has not appeared a more brilliant, more visionary, more deeply haunting, melodic, and aesthetically exquisite guitarist in American music than John Fahey. I finally saw him twenty years later at Folk City in Greenwich Village playing the songs from the album that had become the measure of my guiding aesthetic: *Death Chants, Breakdowns and Military Waltzes* recorded with Bill Barth on second guitar.

Barth thought of himself as a celebrity, although few of us at that time understood why. Sure he had 're-discovered' bluesman Skip James and brought him to new found acclaim at the Newport Folk Festival, but… but once you ever heard Barth sit down with the Martin and attack all six strings with steel finger picks articulating on three fingers, the symphonic deep blues pouring out of that patented wooden box was a revolutionary form of visionary, poetic folk blues that was absolutely mesmerizing. He smoked cigarettes he rolled from a green tobacco that he had stashed in a red tin Prince Albert can with the flip-top. Somehow this and the sheer concentration of his music kept him playing for hours on end, and one could listen to his playing for hours on end.

Some years later I was surprised to meet him in the dressing room of a Panther Burns gig in Amsterdam where he was then living. As a personal challenge, I slept on the floor of his apartment in an effort to learn the versions of "Crow Jane" and "Cypress Grove" that he'd been taught on guitar by Skip James, but Barth was arrogant as ever and stingy with his talent and his licks. It was like, *you play it your way.* Still he managed to show me – when taking breathers from his hash pipe – how to articulate the esoteric modalities and tunings. Before Bill dropped dead coughing at his bong, he made it clear that I had outstayed my welcome, and rightly so after a long summer of diligent euphonic struggle.

Our exit from the halls of academia came after a somewhat abortive production on the main stage of the University Theatre. Randall and I had crafted an adaptation of the 'Ship Wreck' scene from William Burroughs' *Nova Express*. We enlisted talents from the drama department such as the classically inspired, Ron Robran, who stalked around campus in a long black cape left over from a staging of Christopher Marlowe's, *The Jew of Malta*. We had stage sets and paintings constructed by Allen Barber, who had risen to prominence on the east coast and was living in squalid conditions in the married students housing in a failed attempt to earn an MFA.

Dr. Benway was the de facto skipper of the lifeboat, and as his brassiere swung loose, he was wielding a cleaver he'd presciently snatched from the ship's galley as the liner was sinking off the coast of the Azores, and was blithely chopping off the fingers of passengers striving desperately to grasp the edge of the boat and climb out of the shark infested waters. It proved a gruesome spectacle, and the faculty of the theatre department denounced the tableau as an outright defilement of their recently erected theatre complex designed by then internationally pre-eminent New York architect and hometown favorite son, Edward Durell Stone. We had already been walking thin ice in precipitating various unannounced confrontational "Happenings" around the University premises. Impromptu venues such as the Student Union, were afflicted with readings from the texts of Antonin Artaud's, *The Theatre and its Double*. The faculty thought of the oeuvre and theories of Artaud as nothing more than the demented contrivances of an aberrant quack and were quick to condemn any association with the Gallic dramaturgist.

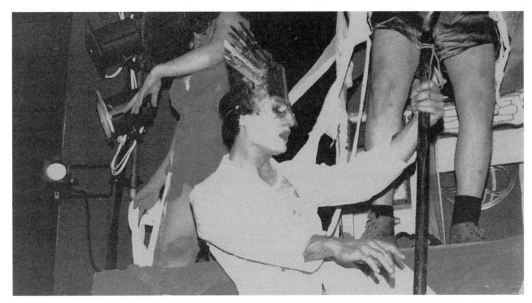

Big Dixie Brick Co. – Studio Theater 1975

In a farewell burst of histrionic art, we staged a Happening just a few yards off campus. It was staged upstairs at the U-Ark Bowl *entr'acte* the gig of a RnR band from Memphis called, Moloch. As Ron Robran had erstwhile hung himself before dinner party guests at his rooming house apartment in his own farewell gesture (Ron always had a true flair for the dramatic), we eschewed the theater dept., and drew our thespians and mimics from the art department instead. We further enlisted the talents of go-go dancers who had come with the band from Memphis. I appeared with a huge EYE painted on my chest, wearing a black top hat with large gold hat band emblazoned with the logo that read: FUCK OFF. We re-produced the shipwreck scene from the University Theatre scenario: with fingers being chopped off as drowning people were clawing madly at the sides of the lifeboat. The finale featured a blond Venus from the art department elevated on an artist model's dais, wrapped only in a full-length mink coat, which she flamboyantly shed at the appointed moment. Chaos broke loose in the steamy room, but at the height of the frenzied ovation, a posse of city police and sheriff's deputies came crushing through the front entrance, somehow tipped off that our so called, and by now notorious, 'mime troupe' was performing in the nude. As the fuzz came in through the front entrance, our troop managed to hightail it out the back door, down the fire escape, and out into the frosty night air of Washington County – some of us never to return.

In Memphis we formed an art-action group we christened Big Dixie Brick Company, after a factory once operated in Pine Bluff, Arkansas, by one of Randall's distant relatives. For Big Dixie, I reincarnated myself as Eugene Baffle – a *nom de guerre* that Randall had invented. Again we decided to steer clear of the legitimate theatre world, and brought in the two go-go dancers from Moloch with whom we'd worked so effectively at the U-Ark Bowl event. Connie Edwards, Marcia Hare, Randall and I were the stalwarts in the troupe. Often a raven-haired, renegade actress actually named Dixie Ashly would join me onstage for a topical routine that we had written together involving the time-honored 'rubber chicken' prop.

At the Studio Theatre on Highland by Memphis State University, Big Dixie appeared *en masque* on a Valentine's Day bill with local troubadour, Keith Sykes. From the saintly midtown sculptor, John McIntire, we had acquired a seeing hand mounted on a long wooden pole, and from St. Vincent de Paul a huge box of pre-worn ladies' shoes. I had found an old mirror dresser and painted it white. Inside its nooks and crannies, I'd stuffed wads of M-80 firecrackers and other small explosives to a central fuse. I removed the mirror from its frame, and mounted in its place an obscure blow up screen-printed image of an incongruous steam locomotive crashing into a Volkswagen. Big Dixie took the stage to the playback of aleatory tonalities of Karlheinz Stockhausen. As Marcia and Connie placed ladies' shoes in the grasp of the Seeing Hand, Randall would stretch the pole connected to the 'Hand' out over the heads of the audience and push shoes up into the faces of the celebrants whilst intoning bizarre incantations. I wore an Italian Futurist-type silver foil mask and a white naval officers jacket that had belonged to my father, but had replaced the buttons with those from a Missouri Pacific Railroad passenger brakeman's uniform. At the height of the onstage antics, I lit the main fuse of the dresser which till then had sit mute left-center stage. The untested, yet explosive cacophonic effect was greater than expected. As the explosives discharged in various corners of the once grand vanity/chiffonier, it actually began to *walk* about the stage propelled by the charge of the smoking explosions. In a cloud of odiferous, purple smog, the trembling thing finally blew itself to pieces to the delight and rage of the assembled crowd.

The Memphis Country Blues Society was organized by Bill Barth, Jim Dickinson, and a cabal of musical provocateurs to host an annual blues festival. They managed to secure the Overton Park Shell for the event. The Shell is an outdoor amphitheatre built in 1936 by the city and the WPA as part of Roosevelt's New Deal. The hillbilly cat himself, EP played one of his first concerts there in 1954 after the release of "That's All Right Mama", and thirteen years later, through maneuvering around city hall, Dickinson and Barth got hold of the venue. Randall Lyon was an essential member of the Country Blues Society, as well as Nick Perls of Yazoo Records, himself a scion of the Perls Gallery in New York. Robert Palmer, a compatriot of Randall's from Little Rock, was also involved in the Society when he was a folkish recorder player. (Later Palmer would marry Harriet Tyson from Holly Springs, a key figure on the publishing scene in Manhattan, and before long Robert found himself entrenched as Pop and Jazz music critic for the *New York Times*. In 1981 he published an influential volume entitled, *Deep Blues*). The sculptor, John McIntire, who looked not unlike his mentor, Khalil Gibran, designed psychoactive woodcut posters for the festivals, which continued on an annual basis till the close of the 60s. Jimmy Crosthwait, actor, puppeteer, and washboard player appeared as a rather cosmic Master of Ceremonies sporting a top hat and louche chimneysweep attire.

The Blues Festivals at the Shell were monumental and their influence enduring. Among the performers was perennial favorite, Furry Lewis who, since he lost his leg in 1916 working on the Illinois Central Railroad, had eked out a living sweeping the streets of Memphis, and playing around town with his guitar. There was Bukka White who'd sung and played his way out of Parchman Farm where he'd been incarcerated on murder charges. Bukka played slide guitar on a steel Dobro with a jack knife on "Aberdeen Mississippi Blues (Cheese and Eggs)" and "Panama Limited Blues". I heard Bukka declare once, "I can't play no wood guitar… I just tear 'em up". There was spiritualized Mississippi Fred McDowell playing "A Dark Cloud Rising" and "Good Morning Little School Girl", and Houston Stackhouse from Rolling Fork, Mississippi, picking electric guitar. Joe Callicott played, and the octogenarian, Nathan Beauregard played solo on electric guitar and sang, "61 Highway" in the eeriest falsetto. Robert Wilkins also performed, now the Reverend Wilkins. He stood singing, "Wish I Was in Heaven Sitting Down" and playing acoustic guitar while his two sons stood on either side of him picking banjo and electric bass. There was Napoleon Strickland and his Fife and Drum Band, Piano Red, Johnny Woods on harp, and Lum Guffin picking and singing "Key to the Highway". Among the white performers were the Jim Dickinson Blues Band, folk artist Sid Selvedge singing solo with acoustic guitar, Grandma Dixie Davis at the piano, and midtown *mauvais garçon* Lee Baker who played lead guitar in a bizarre psychedelic group he'd formed for the occasion. One year Johnny Winter came in from Texas with Willie Dixon on bass fiddle, and hit the stage thrashing a big electric 12-string guitar that blew the first six rows completely out of their seats.

The strangest group to appear on the Blues Festivals was a folk-rock, psychedelic, progressive jazz group called the Insect Trust. Their name came from *Naked Lunch* wherein William Burroughs writes that the world is being held in trust for a race of giant insects. The appellation was bestowed upon the band by Warren Gardner. At the time I was introduced to this quasi-famous beatnik, the robustly handsome, curly black-haired *bon vivant* had walked up briskly to us on the Madison Avenue side of Overton Square, proclaiming a litany about "Red Zoom and the Hobbit". I looked down marveling at the interesting hue of the high-top leather shoes he was wearing, when I realized that he was barefooted – probably for months – and that street dirt and grime had caked his entire foot up to the ankle with a thick fulvous patina. Warren was part of an in-crowd who frequented a small bar called Perception that John McIntire and the photographer, Jim Chappell, had put in a couple doors away from Burkles Bakery, then a cozy eatery on the corner of Overton Square. On the walls of the bar were abstractly figurative, orgasmic murals painted by McIntire, and the atmosphere was cool and slack reflecting the hipness of its bearded and sandaled clientele. Perception was actually a scaled-down, more discreet sequel to a booming coffeehouse, called the Bitter Lemon that Gundy Owens and John McIntire and their coven of artists, musicians, and hipsters had established just east of Overton Square around Union Avenue Extended on the eastern fringe of Midtown.

Once, when I was in town off the Greyhound from Arkansas to attend an early blues festival in the park, I dropped by the Bitter Lemon one stifling afternoon. I was a trifle disappointed as I had chanced upon a snot-nosed RnR band of junior high school kids set up on the floor in front of the coffee bar playing too loudly in view of their meager talent. The room was packed though as the café-goers basked in the innuendo spewing from the puerile minstrels and their salacious posturing. Of more interest was the décor: the walls were covered with antiques and musical instruments, and John had 'psychedelicized' the place with pattern, from floor to ceiling. Some of the clientele were stoned and spaced out just staring at the walls. On my visit to the bathroom I encountered a patron of the coffeehouse putting in a needle somewhere I would *not* want to be putting a needle. I finished off my Suicide, the specialty of the house – a deadly mix of Pepsi, Teem, and grape juice, which fortified me for the long walk back in the heat.

A gathering place for youngsters hungering for new experience is The Bitter Lemon, a rock and roll and folk music club. Billy Wilson, 17, sips coffee and Linda Davidson, 16, samples a "Sanguine Mist" fruit punch. Alcohol is banned in the club.

—*Staff Photos by Charles Nicholas*

Caddy corner across from Burkles was John McIntire's house affectionately know as Beatnik Manor. I was staying there. I'd just had a pair of sandals made to order at a sandal shop that had opened on Beale St., and my feet were aching from walking in them over the roasting pavement, so I didn't get over to the Lemon again to attempt discussing poetry and jazz with the more erudite habitués. Besides on this trip I was enraptured with the charms of a lodger at the Manor on whose floor I was sleeping. Although delightfully unwashed and gritty, her bewitching Joan Baez-esque looks and droll hep talk were endearing. In fact, everything about the Beatnik Manor was gritty, unswept, unventilated, yet convivial and homey. John McIntire, decked out in a different Hawaiian shirt for every day of the week, was a perfect host providing an icebox and a candle stuck in a Chianti bottle for the kitchen table. One night my host Lydia and I had to rescue Randall whom we heard whimpering on the anonymous steps of the house across the street as he sat there whittling at his wrist with a dull razor blade, all in a funk over his fagotry. Randall had plenty of friends and cohorts, was admired for his wit and charm, and seemed to have little cause for loneliness, but he was always impossibly in love with someone in endlessly doomed relationships.

The Solips: Bill Barth, Robert Palmer, Evan Flavell, Nancy Jeffries

The Insect Trust was beginning to draw the attention of an insider clique of aficionados and critics. Their eclectic line-up included Bill Barth on electric guitar; Luke Faust of the Holy Modal Rounders on banjo, fiddle, and harmonica; Trevor Koehler, a jazz saxophonist from New York; Robert Palmer played clarinet, and Nancy Jeffries (reputedly from Oyster Bay) was their spacey, deep-piped singer customarily swathed in black gowns with black flowers popping off the bosom. Placed stage right, the behemoth black and orange Harley-Davidson of a local junkie named Page was a mainstay on every Blues Festival from 1966 to 1970, and the Insect trust played before that at the Shell. Nancy sounded enthralling on a reworking of Skip James's, "Special Rider Blues", but she was absolutely ethereal and otherworldly on an earlier recording effort produced by Chips Moman at American Studios. This was recorded by the forerunner to the Insect Trust; a group that consisted of Bill Barth on guitar, Robert Palmer on recorder, and the singers were Nancy and a young suicidal folk vocalist and guitarist from Berkeley, named Evan Flavell. They called themselves the Solip Singers, and the 7-inch that resulted from those sessions was pure golden, deep country folk blues. Johnny Cash nor Bess Hawes nor Woodie Guthrie couldn't have touched the exquisite darkness of those two tracks: "He Was a Friend of Mine" and "A Woman's Blues". It's astonishing what magic a supremely talented record producer like Chips Moman can draw from a band, and what a lush sonic envelop he can wrap around a recording session.

The Insect Trust was then dividing its time between Hoboken and Memphis. Randall threw the *I Ching* for the band and read their tarot cards. Along with overdosing on psychedelics, faking suicides was a big thing. Trevor was well known as the more spaced-out one of the Trust. Allen Houser, the flugelhorn player, wrote a piece called "Running Wild With Trevor Koehler" that he recorded with his sextet. After going on to play with the Gil Evans Orchestra and with Lou Reed on "Sally Can't Dance", Trevor Koehler stuck his head in the oven in his flat in Hoboken and turned on the gas. This time the phone didn't ring, and no friends came to the door, thus nipping the floret of a promising, if erratic, career, and thoroughly disappointing colleagues and survivors. I remember asking someone in his circle why he'd offed himself and was answered, "Well, Trevor just didn't like the way things were going for him."

Big news around Beatnik Manor was the upcoming show downtown at Ellis Auditorium North Hall featuring Bobby 'Blue' Bland, B.B. King, and Jackie Wilson. Bob Palmer and I got tickets early. Good thing. The hall sold out quickly. Inside the cavernous auditorium, we were hardly surprised to see that we were the only white people present. B.B. opened the show fronting a fashionably dressed band of ace musicians. The Beale Street Blues Boy received a royal hometown welcome. He laid it down and it stayed down. After B.B., an unannounced act followed of young Detroit musicians dressed in futuristically minimal, medium gray suits. The motor city quartet played an instrumental RnB/cool jazz groove that was riveting. Their ultra-cooled, edgy hepness was acknowledged by all. Bob was riveted as well to continual sniffing of his Benzedrex inhalers, buzzing on the propylhexedrine freebase in the cotton rods they contained.

THEN! The curtain rose on Little Boy Blue – Bobby Blue Bland, except Bobby was not so little. The MC in his introductory rave up proclaimed, "Here's the MAN – huh, Bobby BLUE Bland!" and Bobby was no boy either. He was pretty big in fact, high yellow in color, and astonishingly silver throated. Connoisseurs, with whom the auditorium was packed, extol nothing more than the sublime tones of a sissy blues singer. Bobby was raised in the church in Memphis, and he sang divinely with pipes of pure sterling. His voice poured forth full, rich chords like a gospel piano, but in his signature high-register octaves reeking of misery and mistreatment, were the sublime tonalities that brought the audience to their knees. *No one* in the blues can testify trouble and heartache like Bobby Bland. Palmer and I were entranced standing up clapping in time with his velvety beat like everyone else. Rather than a band, Bobby Bland had a complete orchestra seated onstage in three tiers behind him. His musicians were all deep black like the color of their classic matt tuxedos. These were mature artists raising the song of Bobby Bland to swirling heights of ecstatic, harmoniously melancholic wail. If I dropped dead that moment, I knew that I had just witnessed the consummate performance of a lifetime, and would be eternally gratified.

After Bobby Bland there was brief intermission to clear the air more than to take a rest. The curtain raised again, and the fast talking MC appeared before a trendy looking band in short-jacketed, thin lapelled sharkskin suits moving in choreographed steps to rhythms undulating from their instruments. The MC stalked the stage and boisterously hawked the name of Jackie Wilson a hundred times and more. "Are you *READY*? For JACKIE, Jackie WILSON!" A hundred times. The band vamped. The stage lights were lurid; the audience became more and more edgy… then, Jackie Wilson entered stage right wielding a hand-held microphone. The smooth, milk chocolate-skinned star was also dressed in a svelte, short-jacketed sharkskin suit razor lapels and sporting chisel pointed shoes. He belted out, "There's No Pity in the Naked City" in the high-pitched tones that drove the audience completely crazy. Suddenly everyone was standing in their seats clapping and swaying in a heightened emotional frenzy that held them totally wired until the last note was struck. Jackie Wilson got down on one knee. He threw off his jacket, and ripped open the front of his shirt. Every woman in the house was crying, tears streaming down their faces. Time stood still. The bronzed idol, the apotheosis of stardom, laid down on the stage on one elbow and held the mike to his lips intoning his worshippers to sacrifice two maidens. At first his followers resisted, fearful, as another wave of desire and worship saturated the hall. At last two nubile ebony creatures blotting their tears with handkerchiefs, approached the stage with wary steps of trepidation – afraid not of exposure to a grand hall of spectators, but that Jackie might touch them and transubstantiate them into heavenly sylphs. One climbed up the steps on her knees stage left and the other stage right. They crawled across the stage to the center where the bronze avatar laid singing on one elbow. The girls settled beside him with their legs and feet dangling over the apron of the stage as the idol crooned his amorous melodies to each one. Finally he kissed the two girls on the cheek, and they retreated from the stage forever transformed. The curtain came down and up and down on three delirious encores, and as suddenly as he appeared, Jackie Wilson was gone – vanished, immutable, and imperishable into the cosmic haze from whence he came.

During a particularly cold November, Randall and I made a flying trip to the west coast with Marcia Hare in her 1960 Ford Falcon and with a pale gothic acid queen named Margaret on board. On the spur of the moment, we borrowed $50 gas money from a friendly liquor storeowner in the neighborhood. Since the Falcon had no heater, we had to wrap our feet in newspaper to make it through the dire chill of Death Valley at night. The fact that we had just enough chump change to eat snacks from gas station vending machines made it no pleasure cruise. Driving straight through, we made it to Golden Gate Park spaced and wild-eyed. Randall met a kind of psychedelic saint there named, Kent Mont, who had a friend that was an atmospheric physicist adept at concocting discreet batches of LSD 25, for an inner circle of esoteric elite. Later Kent began to send wee glassine envelopes of pure LSD direct from the lab in Berkeley to Randall back at Beatnik Manor. This was hardly the more plebeian manufacture of the hallucinogen being dispersed by diverse renegade chemists under the eponymous rubric of Owsley.

One evening Randall, Bob Palmer, and I walked over to a friend's duplex on Eastmoreland in the Annesdale-Snowden Central Gardens district. A strawberry blonde hipster, a gentle and indolent soul whom we called Rose of Sharon after the character in *Grapes of Wrath*, was the renter of the varnished oak-trimmed old Memphis style rooms. Over the green tiles of the fireplace, hung a broad beveled glass mirror. Randall laid out one of the glassine packets sent from Berkeley onto the smooth surface of a vanity placed against the adjoining wall. In a censer he lit three cones of Mogra incense that produced a blue fog of fragrant vapors wafting about us. He opened the packet and we craned over it with curious anticipation. We each took out a tiny amount of the fine white dust on the end of a tweezers and placed it on the tongue. It was my first time to imbibe such a substance. We waited. After twenty minutes nothing much seemed to be happening. Presently we took a table knife from the kitchen and returned to the packet sitting on the vanity. We each loaded the tip of the knife with a little pile of the white powder, and swallowed that with an impatience measured with trepidation.

After a while a subtle, yet inexplicable alteration in our consciousness became perceptible. We decided to take a walk in the twilight. Stepping off the porch, we headed in the direction of Union Avenue a block over. Suddenly the tiny headlights of approaching cars seemed to loom up to monstrous proportions and pass us with the velocity of a thousand freight trains. One after the other, the cars roared past with a monumentally earth shaking thrust. We became lost in their movement… and decided to find our way back to the apartment. Just off of Union, we were drawn to a darkened house with a deserted porch swing hanging in the stillness. We entered the steps of the porch tentatively and then sat together in the swing. We began swinging… and swinging, and swinging higher, and higher, until we were swinging out over vast dark oceans.

Somehow we navigated the half block back to the duplex marching in single file like the Five Blind Boys of Alabama with a hand on each one's shoulder – except for the leader. Yet none of us knew who was leading our transparent brigade. We sat around the room gazing at an orange table lamp, awestruck by the rhythmic undulation of its translucent paper lampshade.

Randall Lyon Photo: E. Baffle 1969

Randall ignited three more cones and the burning coals of the incense began to breath marvelously in rhythm with the lampshade. By now conversations between us became infused with cosmic import. Thought and words rushed upon our lips with lightning speed and with the inhuman momentum of jet propelled turbines. Every nuance was perceived with multitudinous meanings and profundities. The complete gamut of human emotions was scaled in an instant from the loftiest sentiment to the most basic. In a moment of heightened trajectory, Randall observed that my head had turned into that of a wolf.

There was wide bevel-edged mirror hanging above an armoire. We dared not approach it. When we did, we went together as one to the mirror, and we saw our four faces, but smeared across our visages were transcended expressions of unmitigated insanity – horrifying, yet utterly fascinating. Sometimes there were five heads in the mirror. In ecstatic cognition we tried to articulate the identity of the fifth entity, but it was impossible. We understood everything there was to comprehend in this world and beyond, yet we knew nothing... only the void, the abyss.

After eight hours or so of this sublime communion the intensity and *furore* began to abate. Problem was: an annoying and irritating process of what Randall termed 'Re-entry'. There was an acrimonious edginess we underwent in making ourselves understood while our minds returned to conscious logic and comprehension of language and meaning, as we had once known it. We ended in not liking each other so much during this illogical turmoil and reduction to rational thought, yet we realized why and there was no blame. At dawn we took leave of Rose of Sharon and with wild eyes went our separate ways into the dusty, early light of Memphis while the limbs and branches of trees hung knowingly over our tiny steps of confusion.

Big Dixie got a call one day from Sam the Sham of The Pharaohs fame. Sam had a new single out on MGM Records that he'd written and recorded called "FATE", and he was going to WHBQ-TV to promote it on the George Klein Show. *Mmmm*, I thought. George Klein's *Talent Party* and the WHBQ Cuties – the hottest and slinkiest go-go dancers in the country! Sam had called us because he wanted to try something different, something way-out with the visual treatment for his song. Sam is a thoughtful, creative individual and he's forever trying to reinvent himself. On the show Sam lip-synced the song and did a creepy mime with his hands clutching the air as if he were trying to palpably capture the mythic essence of Fate itself. Although histrionic, in my opinion, his gestures were quite convincing. Big Dixie brought yards and yards of colored scrim fabric that we'd borrowed from McIntire with which we draped the bare TV soundstage. Under the professional studio lighting, the effect was stunning in a spontaneously haphazard way that no ordinary set designer would have dreamed of. For most of the show I wallowed around on the floor wrapped in a nest of clear plastic tubing, while Connie and Marcia evoked their inimitable array of interpretive dance movements, and Randall stood by the coulisse directing the whole business with a baton.

Before the show, we did a 'run-through' of "FATE" in the attic above the apartment Randall was renting on Tutwiler in Midtown – just to block-out the stage actions, and to assuage Sam's sense of professionalism in rehearsing at least once. After we had pestered the tune with a few experimental swatches of mime and movement, we adjourned to Randall's front room and sat on his Persian rug before a blaze roaring in the blue tiled fireplace. Randall popped a big bowl of popcorn, and we set upon it ravenously. Naturally the subject of the Pharaohs came up. "Back in Arkansas," I said, "I remember people talking about, 'Well, if you're going up to Memphis you might see the hearse with Sam the Sham & the Pharaohs riding around town'."

"Yeah…" Sam affirmed, "and I played a 4040 Wurlitzer with a Leslie coupled to it and we didn't have any place to carry it. People didn't want to buy death wagons, but we found one. It was great, it was a Packard. I think it was a '54 Packard or a '52 Packard. It was a Dracula special – it had a high dome. It had a Packard engine, straight eight, and it had the curtains, and back then people had a little more respect for the deceased, the departed, and we could turn the lights on when we were in a hurry and people would get out of the way for us. 'Course we had the organ and the Leslie in the back, and we covered that with a sheet. So we seldom had problems going through towns.

"I fell out of it once, doing about 65 miles an hour. It almost killed me. The side door opened into the wind – they call them suicide doors. It was rattling and it was my turn to sleep in the back, and it was rattling and I sat up and without thinking I reached over to slam it. In a conventional car you can do that; it's not safe, but you can do it without any danger, but going into the wind when I opened the door about an inch, the wind caught it and it just shot me out into the pavement. David Martin was driving at time. He never knew I had fallen out. He drove about a quarter of a mile. And it almost killed me, I mean by the grace of God I… I was doing 65 miles and hour, myself, going down the highway without any brakes. Can you imagine the traffic driving behind a hearse… but all of a sudden you see this hearse and the door flies open and out comes a body! And I had a beard – beards were not that common, and I wore an earring back then, and they were not that common. That was in '62 that happened to me. After David was about a quarter of a mile and come back, and he was in a panic 'cause he had been in another band prior to being in the one we were in and there was a road accident – you know, they're so common among rock 'n' rollers, traveling, trying to get to everythin', but one of the musicians got decapitated. When he ran back and saw me in a pile of hamburger, he just

freaked. I mean I looked with the beard and the hair and the dust from the highway, just really lookin' rough. I looked like the Wolfman in the third stage of the transition. David of course had grey-blue eyes and extra-long eye-teeth and he wore a high top hat – looked like a real undertaker… looked like Dracula. All of a sudden we pull into the hospital, and we were broke, I mean, I couldn't afford to stay in a hospital and I kept telling the doctor, 'We have to be in Memphis tonight.' I said, 'If you will just give me a tetanus shot and some pain pills – I've *got* to go!'

"We played six hours a night, five nights a week, and we didn't start playing until 10 o'clock. We wound up in the clubs that were on their way down or desperate or the ones that other musicians didn't want play because of the bad reputation of not getting paid. But we had come up from Louisiana, where on one occasion a band before we got there had been working and somebody threw a dynamite cap under the bandstand and it blew the microphone stand right through the ceiling. Fortunately nobody was hurt. They were just shocked. We were used to that kind of stuff, so when we got here we were pretty serious. We were always on time; we played 45 minutes to the minute. We were there to take care of business, and my feeling was if you can't do it on a straight head, you can't do it at all. We could play six hours a night without repeating a song – we had that type of repertoire. But, there again, that's another reason they called me the Sham, because on occasion just to break the monotony, I'd just tell the band to kick off a riff and I'd make words up to songs as we went along. That's how 'Wooly Bully' came to be."

"'Wolly Bully' scored a national hit in 1966, I believe."

"Well, '65, but it's the only record that only made it to number two, that after the audit was acknowledged as having been the number one record of 1965. It sold 3-1/2 million copies in the States alone. The Oilers – every time the Oilers make a touchdown in Houston they play it in the stadium. The Chicago Bulls play it; they have a whole production".

"Well, 'Wooly Bully' was recorded, actually, right over here at Phillips Studio, was it not?"

"Yes it was, at Phillips Studio on Madison Avenue. All of this is during the onslaught of the British groups, and we were a part of the retaliation, they call it the American retaliation."

"Bands like the Yardbirds came to Phillips also to record during this period...."

"Uh-huh. We toured with the Yardbirds. We recorded 'Little Red Riding Hood' and it sold a million and a half. Then we had sort of a revue – Sam the Sham & the Pharaohs and the Shamettes. Three lovely young ladies that sang background, and we would come out and we could do a two-hour presentation. The saxophone player in that group, the 'Little Red Riding Hood' group, was Frank Carabetta and he had studied at Juilliard. So he had put the music together and from the first note that was hit, the music did not stop. Precision, you know, we could do that, with steps you know, a show band. We could also stand and just kick it out. If we're gonna be a show group, let's really be a show group – a gold sequined jacket. I mean the first round we wore turbans. If we gonna show time, let's show time.

"There had been times when a song went so well that you just take a deep breath and you say to yourself, 'If I die now, I feel that I've experienced something grand.' You can hang out if you want to, but I've come to the studio for one purpose: that's to get a gold record. Yeah, you can hang out, if you want to be just another garage band. Hey, have at it. Or what I used to say to the band, I says, 'If you wanna hang out, you hang out, but come tomorrow 10 o'clock, you better be standing tall and straight when we hit that first note.' I said, 'Cause we got business to take care of.' And we went into the studio again and recorded Johnny Fuller's 'Haunted House', because we did a thing on television and I put one of the Pharaohs on top of another, put sheet on 'em and made him look like a monster, and we were pantomiming the song 'Haunted House'.

"I don't mind running a risk. I don't like to follow the trend – I like to set it. Forget following the trend. I mean when the Beatles came out, they're great artists and all that... and people thought I was mad, and rightly so probably, because every time any band would go to New York the first thing any news media would ask them was, 'Do you yield to the Beatles?' And when they met us of course the hearse came out to the airplane to pick us up – they had a hearse hired – and so, we got off the plane and the news media said, 'Sam the Sham & the Pharaohs,' says, 'Sam, do you concede to the Beatles?' And I said, 'No.' And my band, I thought they were going to faint, you know... 'Cause, they said later at the hotel, 'Man are you crazy – you're not going to concede to the Beatles?' I said, 'Shucks no, man.' I says, 'They're British. I know where they got their rock 'n' roll, man.' Rock 'n' roll is American music – Chuck Berry, Elvis Presley, you know, Sonny Boy Williamson, all those early people, you know, Little Richard. It wasn't an egotistical thing, because I knew they were a mega-group. It was just, hey, they have their group and I have mine. If anybody can talk you out of your dream, you don't have one. I got a contract with Atlantic Records and I recorded an album that very few people may know about, *Sam Hard and Heavy*, with Duane Allman, the Dixie Flyers..."

"Jim Dickinson is playing with the Dixie Flyers on there?"

"Yes, and Wayne Jackson, Andrew Love... yes, the Memphis Horns. We did 'Going Upstairs' – John Lee Hooker's, and Duane Allman is playing slide on that."

"That album had a lot of influence, and I remember the album cover where you're sitting astride a Triumph motorcycle."

"I rode the Triumph back then, and I didn't ride in a pack. I had made a ride from Memphis to Dallas to Oklahoma then all the way down to Miami. That album cover picture was taken on the side of the road at Ocala.

"I had record company presidents tell me, 'No, no, no Sam, no I don't want to hear that. Bring me another "Wooly Bully". Bring me another "Little Red Riding Hood".' How do you know that this is not that? You see, so I was frustrated. I just backed off and kind of backed completely away. You know, you go through the downgrade, the drugs and the whole thing. What's the whole purpose of it? You know, you're here; you were at the top. Is this all there is...?"

"Makes you wonder if there's life after rock 'n' roll…"

"Well, yeah, definitely. You know, I like to party. I came to a point in the Hollywood Hills where I was on the floor in a heap, and I knew that I was on my way out, and I had some friends that had just died – overdosed. And I remember praying and saying, 'Oh, Sam you just had an emotional situation.' Well, this is what I said: I'm fool enough to try. I love to party and I hear there's going to be a party in eternity that's going to take forever to enjoy, and I don't want to miss it. I've had parties now. We blew back when money was worth a little bit – we blew $9,000 in seven days at the Waldorf Astoria. 50 cases of Piper Heidsieck among other, uh… *sundries*. Now, that's a party. I've had that – but it was all right. But, man if you're talking about a party that's going to last for eternity, you're not going to be tired, you're going to be high. Well, you know, you're not guaranteed the next heartbeat, but I've enjoyed the ones He's given me."

For me personally the TV show was a letdown because there were no WHBQ Cuties. There'd been a format change, and *Talent Party* was now replaced simply by the *George Klein Show*. Still, it was a groove listening to George in the control room after the show talking about high school.

"Well, if you go back to the high schools days, I went to Humes in North Memphis, and I lived right across the street. High school was at 659 N. Manassas; I lived at 636 and I could walk out of my front door and be at the high school in less than 69 seconds. People would come by my house. Elvis and I – we bonded in the 8th grade. It was an 8th grade music class. Elvis moves up from Tupelo. He was a latecomer; I think he joined the class in October or November. We met there. In the 8th grade we had a music class, and the teacher said we're going to do Christmas carols, and Elvis raised his hand and he said, can I bring my guitar to class this week, and being 12 years old in 1948 that wasn't cool. So there were a few laughs in the class and no big deal. So next week Elvis shows up with his guitar and gets up in front of the class and sings two country songs, he sang, 'Old Shep' and 'Cold, Cold Icy Fingers', and I was blown away – subconsciously I was blown away. Obviously, at 12 years old I didn't know what I was going to do, and neither did Elvis, but I was kicking back because all I had ever seen was kids doing athletic things, some children's talent shows… but for a dude to get up with a guitar in front of the class by himself and sing in class where he knew they were going to make a little fun of him – I thought that was really cool, man. So after that we bonded and became friends.

"See Elvis did not live right across the street; he didn't live in the neighborhood. He lived at Lauderdale Courts at that government project. So he'd come out of Humes and go up Jackson and walk down about two miles, and he'd be home. So a lot of times he'd come over and say hello. So you know, your Mom would have cookies and milk and that jazz, and some of the guys would stop by – not just Elvis – but some of the guys on the way from school. At 3:15 when we were let out of school, we all went up to the corner at Jackson and Manassas to a sundry store. It wasn't a drugstore, but a sundry store. You know, they sold cold drinks and cakes and bread and milk and all that jazz. It was like a forerunner of a 7/11 or something, but not as big as 7/11. We'd get up there and shoot the bull, and somebody'd say, let's go home, Bill Gordon's on the air. Bill Gordon was the afternoon jock on WHBQ at that time. He was a really cool dude. He was kind of bizarre. He'd do crazy things. In fact, Dewey Phillips stole a lot from Bill Gordon. Dewey later told me Bill had a little sound he'd make, sounded like a duck. He'd go 'quack, quack'. He'd call him Quacky. He'd talk to Quacky, and Quacky would quack back. Of course it was kind of hokey by today's standards, but it worked then. Dewey borrowed from a lot of people. He borrowed from Groucho Marx. Groucho did a thing on his show he called, 'Tell 'em Groucho sent you', but Dewey picked it up and said, 'tell 'em Phillips sent ya'. Well, it caught on in Memphis. It became a catch phrase, and Dewey was big on catch phrases, but that's where it all started in North Memphis.

"The only guy who did anything musically at that time to come out of that area was Elvis. Later on I think Thomas Wayne was over there. He had a song called, 'Tragedy'. His brother was Luther Perkins (guitarist with Johnny Cash). His name was really Perkins, but he shortened his name for show business reasons. It was Thomas Wayne Perkins. Oh, yea, Manassas High School was a mile and a half, maybe two miles max north of Humes. Hank Crawford over there would play sax, and Isaac Hayes was the biggest thing to come out of there. He was the biggest star ever. He was the Elvis of Manassas High School I guess. But you weren't seeing a lot of clubs and musical stuff in that area at that time. The clubs, you had to be 21, and the clubs were out east like the Silver Slipper, and the Peabody Hotel roof and the Peabody Skyway. Some of those clubs were out on 3rd St. and a few in West Memphis, and there were some honky tonks, but it wasn't the club scene that it later evolved into when Herbie came along and took TJs and ran with it, and Freddie Alfonso had the Thunderbird and Billy Hill had the Manhattan Club. Memphis started to rock because then the 60s move in. What happens is, Memphis really starts happening when Ronnie Millsap moves in and becomes the house band for Herbie Omell at TJs, beside Katz Drugstore in Midtown. Willie Mitchell was at the Manhattan Club on Bellevue. It was Willie Mitchel and his band, the Four Kings. Al Green was an addition to his group and the Bar-Kays came in there with Isaac Hayes, but they were Isaac Hayes and the Do Dads or something like that, and that was at the Manhattan Club.

"When I was only probably about 14 or 15, with some of the older guys, we would hitchhike to West Memphis. That was a crazy trip because that was a long way for a boy from Memphis to hitchhike. How are you going to get home? But we made it. We'd hitchhike over there, and we'd sneak in some of those clubs over there. There was Danny's Club, there was the Cotton Club, and there was Plantation Inn that was where Willie Mitchell was playing, although Willie was playing the Cotton Club, too. There was a lot of great talent in West Memphis at that time for some reason. I guess because of they were probably illegally selling mixed drinks, but Memphis killed all that when they passed the mixed drinks law, and it killed the West Memphis nightclub scene."

What I was curious about was how GK broke into radio, and he started to fill me in:

"Well, I became fascinated with radio, and I got the chance to jump from reporting on high school sports radio to replace Bob Lewis as the gopher for Dewey Phillips, you know someone to help him, a hang out type of guy. Now I knew that I had an OK voice, but I didn't think I had a great voice because back in those days you had the deep throat guys who were really great voices on the air. Well, Dewey would come on the air at nine. See Dewey, he didn't know how to run a control board hardly. He didn't know how to record anything. He was just straight out of the record shop on South Main. At WHBQ they had to teach him all that stuff. Well, they were scared that he was going to tear up the whole radio station at night. So they had a guy babysit him, and that was Dewey's gopher. And from that I'd answer the phone, answer the back door. At that time you could go up and watch a disk jockey do his show. It was a real 'in thing' to do to be able to get in the back door and watch a jock do his show, especially on Dewey who was red hot at night at that time. So I'd screen people at the back door, and I'd let them in. I'd answer the phone. I'd go get Dewey coffee or doughnuts or something.

"Then they told me, you don't have a bad voice, man, and you ought to work on it, you know. So I'd go in there while Dewey was on the air, and I'd get on the tape machine in the other control room and practice. I'd record what I did, and I'd get the other jocks at the station to critique my performance and give me tips cause I never went to radio school. Then all these people started coming up here, man, like Leonard Chess, Jerry Wexler, and all them guys from big record companies. So I got to know them all – Sam Phillips, and everything. We'd hang out after the show, and I'd just listen to everything they said, man. Those guys were cool. Those were the guys who founded, really, rock 'n' roll.

"I kept going to Memphis State and I'd work part time, and I'd go over to Osceola, Arkansas, working at KOSE one summer, and I'd come back and I got a morning show at – at that time it was KWEM, now it's called KWAM, and it was called, 'Jack the Bellboy Show'. I was a weekend guy, and still going to Memphis State trying to get my degree, which eventually

I got. They'd do what they called back in those days, block programming, meaning they'd have R&B in the morning, they'd have country mid-day, middle of the road in the afternoon – something like that, you know. So in the morning they had Jack the Bellboy Show, so the guy that was doing it quit, and I knew the lingo. The guy came to me and said, we're listening to you on the weekend, and you're not bad, you know the lingo. We don't know the records, we don't know the music, we don't know how to talk to these people who like this music. You want to give it a shot? I said, heck yeah.

"Well, I jumped in there and I started doing that morning show, and I was on that morning show about six months, and I get a call from WMC. Bill Grumbles called me; he used to be the program director at WHBQ. Well, he was the general manager, and he said, 'GK, this is Bill Grumbles', and I said, 'Yea, Mr. Grumbles'. 'He said, what are you doing when you get off?' I said, 'Nothing'. Then he said, 'Come by and have coffee with me', and I said OK. I get up there, and he said, 'George', he said, 'have you seen the ratings?' I said, 'No sir. KWEM is such a small station they can't subscribe to the rating service'. He said, 'Did you know that you're number two in the morning in Memphis?' I said, 'What?' He said, 'Yeah, you're number two in the current ratings'. What happened, I caught fire. Rock 'n' roll was just starting to happen. I was playing like Clyde McPhatter and Chuck Berry and Bo Didley and Elvis, and I was playing, you know, all those great acts, the Platters and those guys, and I was talking the talk. I was doing some rhymes. I thought it was cool to do rhymes 'cause I knew I had to do something different. I couldn't be just another guy on the air pitching records. So I was pretty good at rhyming stuff, and I'd say something like this, 'Here's your DJ, the GK, rocking your crazy way on a Monday, got records to play on the turntable, and I got a crazy thing by Mr. Merry, Mr. Chuck Berry,' and I'd do like that, and it caught on. It was a natural thing. I didn't rehearse it; I didn't plan it out, I didn't pre-script it, and the kids would write in, and man, I started getting five letters a day, ten letters a day; I got up to 75 letters a day, and that was huge. The other guys at the station said, 'Why are you getting all that mail?' I said, 'I don't know, man.' I said, 'The show has got hot'.

"Well, anyway, Mr. Grumbles he said, 'George what are they paying you?' I said, 'They're paying me about 75 a week.' He said, 'Would you come over here for 200 a week?' I said, 'Where do I sign?' I said, 'Hell yeah I'd come.' So he said, 'We're going to call it the George Klein Rock 'n' Roll Ballroom,' and he said, 'we're going to feature you on billboards, on commercials on TV, the whole smear.' So I went over there, and I took off like a jet. There were other Top-40 guys in Memphis, but there weren't but two rock 'n' roll jocks in Memphis and that was Dewey and me, and I was in the afternoon, and Dewey was at night with his 'Red, Hot, and Blue Show'. In the afternoon, I'd go hang out with Dewey, and the thing that I'd learned from Dewey was – several things I learned from Dewey: one was, work the street. Get out on that street. Shake hands. Be everywhere. Be at restaurants. Be at bars. Be at hops. Be at ball games. Get noticed, and tell people you're on the air. Build your own audience. I learned also to go by the record distributors and get the records right as they came out. That's one thing Dewey had a secret on, and he had a great ear for music. He wouldn't wait until they got to the record shops and start selling, man, he'd go by the record distributors, and he'd say, OK what's the hottest stuff? I want to play it tonight. See back in those days, we picked our own music. They'd say, Dewey, this new Brook Benton thing just came in, and, man, we're selling it like crazy to the record shops. Well, Dewey would jump on it. 'Aw, ladies and gentlemen, it's old Dewey Phillips at WHBQ, you gotta brand new smash, man. It's gonna be a hit, it's gonna be a hit'. That's the way he talked, and he'd play it, and I learned that from him. Play the hot records first, and so you scooped the other stations cause they were going by the Top 40 list.

"Dewey and I were hot, and all of a sudden I was on there for about a year, and this guy calls me, and I'll never forget what he said. 'GK', he said, 'this is what my father used to tell me. This is harder for me than it is for you.' I said, 'What are you talking about, Stan?' He was the Program Director. 'We don't think this Rock 'n' Roll thing is going to last. We think it's a fad, and you're the only rock show on the station. Everybody else is middle of the road. We're going to have to let you go.' 'Let me go?' He said, 'Yeah.' So they let me go. As fate would have it that very night I ran into Elvis up at WHBQ, and he said, 'Man, why weren't you on the air today?' And I told him, because he'd been coming back and hanging out with me at the radio station in the afternoons, and the kids were going nuts. You know hanging out until he came by. So I told him, and he said, 'What? Rock 'n' Roll's a fad!' He said, 'I'll show 'em how faddish it is.' He said, 'We're gonna hit that road.' I said, 'Where we going, Elvis?' I said, 'What am I gonna do?' He said, 'You're going to be a traveling companion.' 'What am I gonna do?' He said, 'Nothing. Just hang in with me,' and I said, OK, and I said where we going? He said, 'We're going all across America. We're going to the 10 biggest cities. We'll play Philly, Chicago, Detroit, all those big cities.' He said, 'Then we're going to Hollywood to make a movie called, *Jail House Rock*. Get you a bit part in there.' I said, OK. He said, 'Then we're going to Hawaii, and we're going to Canada.' I said, 'Holy shit, Elvis. Let's go. And it was one of the greatest rides I ever took."

"So you went into television a little later, right?"

"Well, the club scene started happening, and these acts, all these hits started rolling out of here. You know, like Sam the Sham cut 'Wooly Bully', and that was the No. 1 record in '65. The Box Tops started happening with Chips Moman. I took the Gentrys over to Chips, and he cut the Gentrys on, 'Keep On Dancing,' which went up the charts to No. 4. Willie Mitchell started happening with Al Green. Then Stax just exploded with just everybody. It was like a miniature Hollywood slash Detroit. Earnie Brasso was in with Freddie Alfonso at the Thunderbird Club. Then they split up, and Earnie had a place called Caesar's, which was the first disco in Memphis, and then Earnie started the Godfathers which was on Overton Square – he and Freddie. Jerry Lee Lewis and his cousin, Linda Gail played the opening night. The Godfather's was happening, and then I got the TV show."

"Yeah. I was there at the Godfather's on opening night," I corroborated, "and I took photographs of Jerry Lee and Linda Gail on stage. Next night I took the finished 8x10 prints backstage to give to Jerry Lee. I could see right away that Jerry Lee was in a real foul, scary mood. He was surrounded by a bunch of hillbillies in straw hats. They were chewing tobacco, and unshaven, and acting like fools around Jerry Lee, goading him on into doing something it seemed like he didn't want to do. I could see that those boys had guns stuffed down in the front of their pants. They kept whispering stuff into Jerry Lee's ears. I think the whole bunch of them were really hopped up on something vicious like yellow jackets or black widows. I started feeling uneasy 'cause I figured they were trying to goad the Killer into shooting me himself. Jerry Lee had already shot his bass player awhile back. Maybe they thought I was going to ask for money for the pictures and wanted to shoot me for that, but I had intended to give the pictures to Jerry Lee in appreciation of his artistry. Every time I ever saw Jerry Lee play he was positively brilliant. A towering artist on stage and on record without exception. So I left my modest gift with the Killer, and bid adieu. The last he said to me was, 'I wouldn't do anything in the world to hurt your feelings, son', and it seemed like he meant it."

GK said, "That's true I'm sure. Well with the TV show what had happened is they had had the dance party show with Wink Martindale, Ron Roanie, and Jay Cook where the kids come out and you get 12 couples from a school, and they dance to records, and they jam, and Coca-Cola sponsors it, and it's a nice little Saturday afternoon show – like American bandstand, a local version. And when I came along, I auditioned. Jay Cook who had the show wasn't into it, so he quit. They auditioned all the jocks at HBQ, and I got it, and I went in, and they said, 'George, we got a problem,' and I said, 'What?' They said, 'We're going to have to eliminate the dancing couples because integration is coming in, and we're scared of what would happen, you know, between the black and white situation on your show.' So I said 'What are we going to do?' They said, 'Well, you've got to play records and be creative.' Said, play records on TV...? So I said, wait a minute. You've got to get more talent in here. So Memphis was exploding with

Jerry Lee Lewis & Linda Gail at The Godfathers Photo: E. Baffle 1975

talent. Shit, I just went and got the Gentrys and the Boxtops and Sam the Sham and put 'em on the show. All of a sudden my show just started exploding, and I worked it into a format. I'd have six girl dancers like the Shindig dancers. They were called the WHBQ Cuties, and then I'd do a star call. I'd pre-record a call with a star, called the Star Line. I'd call somebody in show business and interview them, and then we'd ring the teenagers during the week. Most of the shows I'd have nine acts on. We'd get, you know, Booker T, and Isaac, and Sam and Dave, and all the Stax acts, and Al Green, and Jerry Lee. I started inserting them in my show with a good format and a slick presentation. All of a sudden, the show caught fire, man."

"No doubt."

"Broke a lot of big acts. One cute story was, the acts would come in, and obviously they sounded bad. Not the pro guys, but I knew that I had to have local involvement. So that was the garage band scene, but they didn't call it that back in those days. There were a lot of bands cropping up everywhere. There was a band in North Memphis, a band in South Memphis, a band here, a band there, everywhere. So they all wanted to be on my show with the stars that I was having on. See guys, we can't recreate the sound in a television studio, the sound you get in a recording studio. I said, number one, you're gonna sound bad, not because you're bad, but because you don't have the experience. I said, number two, my people here, my mixer in audio, he don't know beans about rock n roll music, and the studio is not constructed like a recording studio. And so what did we do? I said I'm going to cut a deal with Roland Janes over at Sonic."

"Yeah. He's the best!" I interjected. "Top guitar stylist, engineer, and producer!"

"Roland was a dear friend of mine. Still is today. So I went to Roland. 'Roland,' I said, 'we got to give these young kids a break.' He said, 'what's your idea?' I said, 'When are you downtown?' He said, 'Saturday.' I said, 'OK, for $12 can you let them cut like one side, and can you doctor it up and maybe throw in a little of your own guitar and throw some echo on it and make 'em sound better than they actually sound?' And he said yeah. So I started channeling all these acts to Roland at Sonic on Madison Ave. on Saturday morning, and for $12 Roland would cut 'em. Then they'd go back and listen to their tape on their home tape machine and get it down perfect, and then I'd book 'em on my show as a new up and coming band in Memphis. They would lip sync the tape that Roland had cut for 'em, and they sounded really professional because he mixed it, and you know, put little extra things on it. Maybe played some guitar on it himself and made it sound good, and nobody knew the difference that it was cut in a recording studio. And they started catching fire, garage bands all over town on my show."

This would not be the last dizzying conversation I would have with George Klein. Some years after the demise of Elvis, I encountered George at a bookstore signing for one of Rose Clayton Phillips' editions on the King of RnR. "Well, how's Dr. Nichopolous doing?" I asked the disc jockey.

"Yeah, Dr. Nick, he's still my doctor today. Because of me Dr. Nick became Elvis' doctor. I was the one that channeled him to Elvis. Dr. Nick got the short end of the stick. He's the one who took the fall. He was the good doctor. There was a bad doctor in Vegas, and a bad doctor in Los Angeles, and they were the ones that were giving Elvis – prescribing it because Elvis had a chemical dependency on prescribed medication, and they were giving him that, and Elvis thought it was OK to take it because it was prescribed, but it wasn't. So when Dr. Nick... he'd take the pills that were sent in and intercept them and turn them into placebos. You know what a placebo is? OK, he'd put sugar or salt in those pills, and then that was the best he could do, and then when the fall came, they grabbed Dr. Nick because he was Elvis' doctor, but he was the good doctor. Listen, why did you prescribe all that medication? He said, 'Because I was the doctor for the tour. If the drummer got sick, if the guitar player got sick or a back up singer, I had to get him well.' He said, 'I had to buy all these drugs, and I had to put them in somebody's name, and somebody had to pay for 'em,' he said. So we charged them to Elvis. Soon as we got home we flushed them down the commode. I went on tour with them several times, and I got sick, and I had to go see Nick, and he gave me a shot. I was almost coming down with the flu or something. And you know, he was the good doctor, and he really got ripped bad, man."

"Now Red West, that's Sonny West right?"

"Red and Sonny are cousins. Red is the guy that wrote, uh..."

"*Elvis: What Happened?*"

"Yea, well, he and Dave Hebler and Sonny, they collaborated on that because they were really hurt when Elvis' father fired them. I wasn't happy with the book quite frankly. Red was the only one who was remorseful. They wrote that because they were hurt and scared and they needed some money, and at the same time they were trying to help Elvis, but I still think it was a bad idea, but it's history now. Red came to me, and Red's a real tough guy. He's a street fighter. He was a Golden Gloves guy, college All American football player.

"Athletes and Golden Gloves boxers like the Burnett brothers and the Tiller brothers."

"Yea, he was with those guys. So Red came to me one day at a golf tournament – St. Jude's Golf Tournament, and he said, 'GK, can I talk to you?' And this was about 5 years after Elvis passed away. I said, 'yea, Red,' and we went and talked. He said, 'man, I'm so remorseful about that book. I wish I'd never written that dad gum book. I want to apologize to you, GK, and to all of Elvis's guys,' and he said, 'would you please pass that along,' And I said, 'sure.' All of us accepted his apology."

CHAPTER THE FIFTH
THE FALL OF WEST MEMPHIS
& THE RISE OF CHARLIE FEATHERS

C ABIN NOTES:

In the wake of the Crump city hall clamp down, the Beale Street scene had moved to the joints of West Memphis. At the Plantation Inn the Newborn family composed the house band from 1947 until 1951 led by the father on drums and featuring the electrifying Calvin Newborn, Jr. who taught Ike Turner guitar, and toured with the likes of Count Basie and Howling Wolf. Calvin's prodigy of a brother, Phineas, Jr. played piano and became an internationally celebrated jazz pianist as a recording artist on RCA Victor and Atlantic. After their set the band would pack up and race back to the Flamingo Room just across the river on Hernando Street where drummer Phineas Newborn, Sr. led his 14-piece society orchestra featuring luminaries Hank Crawford, Charles Lloyd, "Honeymoon" Garner, Wanda "Miss Pine" Jones, and including the trumpeter, Gene "Bowlegs" Miller. Bandleaders like Willie Mitchell and Ben Branch followed the Newborns and burned their sensational styles into the collective psyche of a generation of awestruck teenagers who were lucky enough to sneak into the backdoor of the supper club. The band of "Bowlegs" Miller, who had started on Beale St. playing with artists like Ma Rainey and Tuff Greene, also occasioned at the Plantation Inn in addition to the Flamingo Room, Club Handy, Currie's Club Tropicana, the Rosewood, Club Paradise, and the Manhattan Club in Memphis.

For almost five years the house band at the Cotton Club in West Memphis was Clyde Leopard and the Snearly Ranch Boys featuring Warren Smith on vocals. The band included Stan Kessler, future engineer at Sam Phillips Recording Services who later produced Sam the Sham hits; Jim Stewart, a founder of Stax Records; and Barbara Pittman who became a SUN recording artist. Johnny Cash had cut a demo "Rock n Roll Ruby" in the studios of KWEM in West Memphis, and Sam Phillips showed up at the Cotton Club one night and offered Cash and his band a chance to record the tune. Before signing with SUN Records in 1954, Johnny Cash's first radio appearance when he arrived in Memphis was at KWEM Radio. He had his own weekly show with band members Luther Perkins and Marshall Grant. Scotty Moore and Bill Black started their music with a radio appearance on KWEM Radio in 1954, playing with Doug Poindexter as the Starlight Wranglers. A rather green Elvis joined the Starlight Wranglers for one performance before forming his own band with Scotty Moore and Bill Black. In the years from 1947 to 1955, KWEM Radio Station had a pay to play method, generating revenue for radio stations that could not make enough money from conventional advertising sponsors and the spinning of records.

Sonny Boy Williamson had become famous as a leading musician and performer in the Delta while appearing on the King Biscuit Radio Program on KFFA Radio Station in West Helena, Arkansas. Sonny Boy came to West Memphis in 1949 and launched his own live daily KWEM radio program, sponsored by Hadacol Elixer. (They 'had-to-call' it something.) From 1949 to 1950 Sonny Boy invited his friends from around the delta to perform on his program: Howlin' Wolf who was Sonny Boy's brother-in-law, Elmore James, Houston Stackhouse, Robert Nighthawk (King Biscuit regulars), Arthur "Big Boy" Crudup, James Cotton, and Joe Willie Wilkins. Among them was the razor, fuzz-tone guitarist, Pat Hare who recorded 'I'm Gonna Murder My Baby" and brought that prophetic title to consequence in 1962. Joe Hill Louis began his music career with his own KWEM Radio Show in 1949. He moved to the famous Memphis "all black" WDIA Radio Station in the early 50's and replaced B.B. King as the "Pepticon Boy". His one-man-band recorded for SUN and released such tasty titles as "Hydromatic Mama".

Courtesy ACE Records

After that protracted rap with Georgie Klein I got an itch to call up Mojo Buford, a blues harp player that hung out at Mama Beulah's Club on Mississippi Avenue in Memphis, until he migrated to Chicago to form his own group, The Savage Boys. Later Mojo joined the band of Muddy Waters and stayed with the group for ten years.

"How did you meet, Pat Hare – the guitar player," I asked Mojo curiously.

"Well, I met Pat Hare when Muddy Waters hired him. Bobby Blue Bland fired him and then Muddy hired him."

"When was the first time you met him?"

"Oh, man, 60-somethin'."

"What kind of man was he, Mojo?"

"Tragic, gun happy, gun happy..."

"Really? ...Why was that?"

"Bad."

"Did he always have a gun on him?"

"Most all the time."

"Say, did you know Ike Turner?"

"Yeah, I know Ike Turner. I know of him; I don't really know him."

"I just wondered if you know why they called him 'Pistol-whipping Ike'. I saw the Ike and Tina Turner Revue back in 1964 playing outside one afternoon on the lawn at the University of Arkansas. They had a stage set up out there where Tina had to enter from the crowd at one corner and the Ikettes from the opposite corner. Those girls had to tidy themselves up right there by the stage. They were straightening up their hose under their miniskirts and adjusting their wigs and underneath they had hair about a quarter of an inch thick. It was a spectacular show. Ike stood at the center back of the stage by the drummer, looking pitch dark and thin, but ultra-suave in an iridescent blue sharkskin suit. He directed the band with a subtle tip of his guitar neck and by cutting his eyes back and forth among the performers. Ike had a real wicked expression on his face, and his eyes and teeth were super white. Later I met a promoter down in Texas that had worked with Ike a lot. He said Ike was real domineering over the Ikettes. Once a record company junior executive flew in to see them after a gig. He said Ike sat down one Ikette on one side of the boy and another Ikette on the other side of him, and told those girls to start at down at his feet and work their way up to the top of his head."

"I've never heard that before," Mojo chortled.

"Just how did Pat Hare get hooked up with Mojo Buford…?"

"Yeah, Muddy Waters fired him, and me and Jojo, my bass player, went down to Arkansas and brought him up here to Minnesota.

"Why did Muddy fire him?"

"He got tired of his low-down, dirty ways."

"I read that he was unreliable. He wouldn't show up for a gig sometimes."

"No, he showed up, but he was just…couldn't get along with him. I started to knock him out once," Mojo snorted.

"What was it?"

"Alcohol… alcohol problems."

"Were there other demons in there, too?"

"No, he didn't any other demons except alcohol."

"I mean, I've heard nobody else sound like Pat Hare on guitar."

"I know it. He was hard to beat."

"You know, Pat recorded this song for Sam Phillips at Sun 15 years before called, "I'm Gonna Murder my Baby". Now why did that come true in Minnesota? What kind of woman was he involved with?"

"Just womens, period."

"A lot of women or one woman?"

"One woman."

"What was her name?"

"Lillian something. They got along sometimes. In and out, you know."

"Well, why did he shoot her?"

"Well you know, he shot her, and they sent a police investigator over there, and Pat Hare turned around and shot the policeman. He killed him – shot him dead.

"There were rumors that this police investigator was also romantically involved with Lillian. Did you hear about that?"

"No, no. I know the police he killed. He wasn't messin' around with women."

"You knew that man; you knew the policeman. Was he a black man?"

"White man. Pat's old lady was white, too."

"Ah, so Lillian was a white woman."

"Yeah."

"I heard he was kind of a quiet man until he started drinking and then he became belligerent."

"Yeah, he acted a fool. I knew he was gonna get in trouble one way or the other. He was talking about killing *me*."

"Why?"

"'Cause I fired him. Couldn't get along with him... went crazy."

CABIN NOTES:

B.B. King made his very first Radio Appearance anywhere at KWEM Radio in 1949 appearing on the Sonny Boy Williamson show. He got a permanent gig at Miss Annie's Diner on 16th Street in West Memphis for $12.50 a night, 6 days a week, plus room & board. B.B. King recorded "3 O'Clock Blues" a monster R&B hit for Modern Records with the band who appeared with him on KWEM and that band was led by Ike Turner. The hottest tune ever from B.B. King called, "She's Dynamite" was recorded at the same time, but when I saw the King of the Blues at Club Paradise later on – the day he received the key to the city of Memphis from the mayor – he didn't play it. Success can wreak havoc on a good repertoire. Talking to B.B. before his show, I abruptly asked if he had a girlfriend. The regal 'Beale St. Street Blues Boy', as he was still billed on the Club Paradise tri-color posters spotted all over town, replied laconically, "You know, I can't keep a woman. Them lawyers in New York got me playing 365 nights out of the year. I ain't got time for nothing!" That was apparent when the blues boy took the stage that night. He was half asleep and obviously ruffled by the ordeal of waking up under the stage lights shining down relentlessly from the low ceiling of the converted bowling alley.

Howlin' Wolf was the first "colored" artist to have his own daily show on KWEM Radio from 1949-1952. Sam Phillips recorded the Wolf at his SUN studio, a former auto radiator repair shop on Union Avenue at Marshall. The studio was located on high ground – possibly sacred ground at the crossroads of Union Avenue and Marshall, which cuts diagonally across the grid of streets. Marshall Avenue was called Pigeon Roost Road in the nineteenth century, and formerly was the Chickasaw Trail heading east. This was the location Sam Phillips "discovered" in 1949 for his temple of sound. Spirituality seemed to infuse this spot, probably long before the 1950s. Of the Wolf, Sam Phillips spoke to Frank Mills, Jr., "the times I felt it the strongest was a spirituality that came from Howling Wolf once he felt at home. The Wolf had a strong spirituality about him. What we had was a church of the spirit that fed upon itself. It felt so natural and sounded so good that it began to feed upon itself spiritually. It gave people the opportunity to open their book and give what they had inside".

ke Turner first recorded Howlin' Wolf in the KWEM Studios in 1951. The cuts were released on Modern Records. Ike Turner and band, featuring saxophonist Jackie Brenston, recorded at the future SUN Studios that year what is considered the first RnR record, "Rocket 88". The Plantation Inn Band with Phineas Newborn & Calvin Newborn toured with Jackie Brenston after "Rocket 88" became a hit as the "Delta Cats". Junior Parker had his own show on KWEM Radio in 1953. He had been a harmonica student of Sonny Boy Williamson, as had Little Walter, Howlin' Wolf, and James Cotton. Parker recorded "Mystery Train" that was a hit record for Sam Phillips on SUN Records. Another West Memphis harmonica player, James Cotton, had his own KWEM radio program. At the age of 15 he would also be 'discovered' by Sam Phillips and recorded at SUN Records with his guitarist, the aforementioned Pat Auburn Hare, on a number called, "Cotton Crop Blues". Sam Phillips came from a sharecropping family, and had picked cotton himself as had most of the SUN artists. Phillips – the alchemist in his laboratory concocting his experiments with magnetic force fields and radio waves – shared a common background and mentality. He partook of a messianic communion with his cabal of shamanistic music makers, intuitively attuned to their intimate personal chemistries. Around 1954 James Cotton he left West Memphis to join Muddy Waters on the road. Listening to KWEM Radio would inspired another young West Memphis area youth, Albert King, to learn to play and who appeared on KWEM Radio starting in 1952 to promote his "In the Groove Band" at the T-99 Club in Oceola, Arkansas.

A SUN and Mercury Records recording artist, Eddie Bond, played on KWEM Radio and also at Danny's Club in West Memphis. Eddie Bond's guitarist in The Stompers was Reggie Young from around Blytheville, Arkansas, who became one of the most in demand pickers around recording for Elvis, the Bill Black Combo, and on countless Nashville sessions. Reggie picked guitar on over 180 Gold Records. Eddie Bond was quoted on this seminal period by Chris Davis in the Memphis Flyer, *"Johnny Cash might be playing in Bono, Arkansas, and I might be playing in Jonesboro. We would be playing that close together, playing on those drive-in movies. It might be me, Charlie Feathers, Carl Perkins. We played outside on top of the concession stands, you see. That's where we swallowed all of them bugs. There was a running joke about that, you know. We'd be up there playing and somebody would kind of go [hiccup], "Oh no, I've swallowed a bug." Somebody else would ask, "Well, do you want a drink of Coke." And you would say, "Naw, let him walk down. I ain't giving him a ride." There was this place out on Highway 61 called the Hi-Hat, and the people who run it were uppity people – you can just imagine with a name like Hi-Hat. And it was nice, I guess. It had carpet and all. It had a really beautiful bandstand. Well, I had a piano player and a sax, and I was leaning just a little toward pop music. Well, I wanted Elvis so bad because he could sing pop, and I couldn't. Never wanted to, never did. Well, Elvis came down, and he sang with us for a while and he just did a great job for us and gave us a lot of variety. He was dressed in those black pants with a pink stripe and Rose Oil Hair Tonic running down his neck in the back. So this lady at the Hi-Hat, she sat up there looking down her nose at us, and she come up and said, 'If you don't get that slimy looking man off of that stage, I'm going to fire you and the whole band'".*

Eddie Bond was also a DJ heard on the radio along with Dewey Phillips and Sleepy Eyed-John playing this new music. No one was really sure what to name it. "If you moved the dial on the radio just a touch (from WHBQ) you could," according to J. Austin, "have tuned into WHHM and listened to Sleepy Eyed John's 'Hillbilly Hit Parade'. While Dewey Phillips heavily promoted Elvis's "That's All Right Mama" John played the flipside of the Sun 209 single 'Blue Moon of Kentucky'. WHHM broadcasted from West Memphis. Sleepy Eyed-John was not a fan of Sam Phillips or of the releases that came out of SUN recording studio. On the air, he started making disparaging remarks about SUN recordings, musicians and singers. Vernon Presley had to be physically stopped from going to his radio station after one such comment about Elvis's singing, left him fuming. John did and said what he liked on air, often playing a record and ripping it from the turntable halfway through, tossing it into the rubbish bin and then playing something he considered to be more tuneful. John may not have liked what he heard in Elvis, but he knew a good thing when he saw one, and booked him for an appearance at the 'Eagles Nest', a nightclub that he promoted. It was situated at the intersection of Lamar Avenue and Winchester in Memphis, above a swimming pool. Called the 'Clearpool Entertainment Complex', it was owned by the Pieraccini family. John also fronted a western swing band that had a residency at the 'Eagles Nest'. On September 9th 1954, Elvis played with Scotty and Bill on the back of a flatbed truck at The Lamar-Airways Shopping Centre but they were introduced as 'Sleepy Eyed John's Eagles Nest Band'. Johnny Cash mentions him in his autobiography 'CASH', claiming Sleep-eyed John had the looks for stardom as well as the drive.

George Klein was right about how the mixed drinks law killed the West Memphis club scene, but of equal impact was the Carol Feathers murder – something that was completely unique to the time within the white community. On the night of February 20 th 1960, the ninth grader did not come home from the Cotton Club. By her mother's account in the newspaper, Carol frequented the West Memphis club scene, "Carol was a wonderful dancer. Many times they'd clear the floor at the Cotton Club or wherever she was just to let her dance. She could just dance and dance and she would always stay until the place closed at 4:30 in the morning, just dancing." The gorgeous 14 year old with long red hair had been picked up by an old boyfriend, Jerry Blankenship, a former high school basketball star who was seventeen, married with a wife at home nine months pregnant. They drove to an abandoned dog-racing track, which had become a de facto lover's lane just west of the Harahan Bridge. According to Blankenship, the girl teased him, yet rebuffed his advances. "I saw Carol at the Cotton Club," Blankenship said. "I had been drinking a lot. She was with some friends. She had a date. I started talking to her.

She kinda took a shine to me. After her boy friend left we left later about 4 to go for a ride. I went out Dacus Lake Road. She was teasing me. We parked by the dump. Then when I grabbed her, she started fighting. She slapped me and scratched me with her fingernails. When the door came open and we fell out on the ground, I picked up a club. I don't know, I just went out of my head. I hit her a couple of times. I kicked her. Then I dragged her over to a concrete slab, she struggled and I kicked her again and hit her with the club."

Blakenship left her dying body in the dump where she bled out her life's blood on the soiled pages of yesterday's dirty newspapers, magazines, tin cans, and used condoms. When Blankenship was apprehended, the Cotton Club stamp appeared fresh and unmistakable on the back of his hand. From his cell in the Crittenden County jail, he bitterly bemoaned that the Cotton Club was the root cause of this heinous act of murder because he had been permitted to go in there and drink his fill of booze. Much was made of his admission and the attribution of his guilt. Within 48-hours, the Cotton Club and Danny's Club were padlocked by order of the county court. The Cotton Club was permitted to operate, but positively no minors were allowed entrance. Carol Feathers was buried on her 15th birthday.

The leader of the Jesters who recorded, "Cadillac Man" – the last disc issued on SUN – was Jim Dickinson, a piano player and record producer extraordinaire, and spokesman for the Memphis music scene. He recalled, "Blankenship was a high school athlete, a basketball player. He was not a thug at all. Memphis was very regionally divided, and it didn't have any effect on us in East Memphis, other than the fact that you couldn't go to the clubs anymore. They tried to shut it up and box it off as quickly as they could, 'cause it was something that didn't happen. It was ugly when it did happen, though. I mean to beat her to death with a lead pipe or tree limb under the bridge. Still I don't think it had any deterrent effect on the youth culture

Jerry Blankenship at arraignment

whatsoever. Probably scared the crap out of some mothers, but I don't think anybody got the *fear but for the grace of God* feeling from it, 'cause it was that much of an enigma."

Carol Feathers was a cousin of Charlie Feathers, the hic-cupping hillbilly cat who started out on SUN records and always remained true to his cat-daddy style and vision. He grew up near Slayden just over the state line in Mississippi. His wife, Rosemary, came from Ashland a few miles away. They knew each other about eight or nine months before Charlie took her to the altar when he was nineteen. Charlie was a bashful youth, and demurred from playing guitar in Rosemary's presence until after they were married. The first song he played for her was the Carl Smith tune, "I Overlooked an Orchid, While Searching for a Rose." By his daughter Wanda's admission, her father, "hardly had an education – third or fourth grade. Daddy couldn't read at all. If somebody would give him something like a contract, he would look at like you'd think he was reading it, but he couldn't read it." In a sense he may have been better off as an acoustic performer not having that print-stress logic imprinted in his consciousness, for his audial acuity was by far the better developed for the lack of written language orientation. Yet, he knew everything going on in the world of baseball down to the batting averages.

His vocal range was operatic, and his tone exquisitely rich and pure. He could also mimic the sounds and calls of birds and animals faithfully. There's no doubt that Charlie was a smart man, and that he knew exactly what he was after musically. To that quest he was resolute and undeterred, even when the road he travelled went against the grain of the marketplace. Rosemary said that Charlie would go over to KWEM and talk to his brother-in-law, Dick Stewart, who was station manager and who DJing under the moniker "Poor Richard". Charlie's son, Charles Arthur "Bubba" Feathers, says that Stewart became rockabilly star Carl Perkins' manager and was driving the car when it wrecked on the way to Perkins' national TV debut. Stewart had introduced Charlie to Howling Wolf, and it was Wolf who suggested that he go over to SUN Records. From then on, Rosemary remembers that Charlie was down at SUN all the time, but "the credit goes to *Bill* Cantrell and *Quentin Claunch because they were the ones who worked with Charlie, and got him in there (at SUN) to record.* Before Elvis cut anything, he used to come by the house and pick him up in an old pickup when we lived on Pauline Street, and he would go over to Shirley Richardson's house, to the fan club, but that was Charlie's fan club. They would go over there with Charlie's brother or they'd go by SUN. They'd go to the theatre all the time, too, to see Western movies."

Wanda remembers that, "He started trainin' Bubba early". By the time Bubba was fourteen, he was out playing shows on lead guitar with Charlie. Today Bubba Feathers is one of the finest guitar players anywhere, and fronted his own career band at Bad Bob's Vapors Club. Bubba explained, "He wouldn't let me go out and play with other bands and stuff, or play other kinds of music. He didn't let me do that... and he wouldn't go down the road listening to the radio." Wanda said, "I remember when we used to go to my grandmother's there in Ashland. Back then teenagers liked to turn on WHBQ radio station and listen to it. We were not allowed to. Not if Daddy was in the car. Daddy said that's not music. We listened to Daddy's music. That was it. The only time the radio would be turned on was if the Dodgers were playing baseball. I think I was in about the ninth grade and he started wanting me to sing. I guess when he would heard a harmony part, he'd want me to try get that harmony, and he said you need to sing like Sister Rosetta Tharpe – and I'd never heard of that lady before in my life. Daddy didn't practice at home. It was always at Shirley's house at his fan club 'cause that's where he left his equipment. I remember a lot of times whenever he had a record come out he'd come home and say, 'This is gonna be a hit, this is gonna be a hit.' I'd spend the summers down at the farm in Ashland, and grandma would call mother and she'd say, 'Y'all need to come pick her up.' And she'd say, 'Why?' – 'She's in here wearing Charlie's records out.' I was lonesome for home. I wanted to come home. I'd play 'em over and over and over. I never remember him to drink once... no kind of alcohol was in our home the whole time I grew up. And a lot of people, you know, the way Daddy would sing, they'd kind of say, *oh, he's drinks, he's drunk singin' that one,* and he wasn't – that was just him. As he got older, had his lung took out, had a bypass – he could still sing. His voice was still there. But after he had that open-heart surgery in '95 – right after then Daddy started shakin'. His hands would shake and he would not even pick up his guitar, and that wasn't right. As far back as I can remember, every day Daddy had that guitar. He used to pick up his guitar every day. Then he just didn't pick up the guitar no more. He said, 'If I can't play it the way it's supposed to be played, I won't play it at all.' And he was a hell of a rhythm player; he was a really good rhythm man."

A former switchboard operator, Shirley Richardson could talk a blue streak about Charlie Feathers. "And he came over," I asked, "he had his fan club and you were the president of it? And did Elvis have a fan club too? Were you were president of that?"

"Elvis had 'bout two records out when we moved to Memphis in '55, and Charlie brought him over to the house two or three times. Sometimes we'd be there and sometimes we wouldn't. We didn't even lock the doors back in those days usually, because everybody had the keys to the house. We didn't know who was gonna be at the house when we got home, 'cause our friends would drop in. 'Course it was five or six of us girls that lived together in a little guesthouse in the back of the landlady's house. And we all worked at the phone company. As switchboard operator before we had a dial phone, we'd answer the call and we'd say, 'Number, please'. They'd give us a number and we'd put a plug up in the number and ring it by hand. So we would have different hours. Usually somebody was at home most all the time. We'd call up the disc jockeys and they'd play Charlie's song and Elvis's song. Elvis would say, 'Have them play my song.' So we would.

Well, we lived in this little guesthouse and all we had in the living room was a couch and two end tables and a coffee table and a little chair over in the corner and a standing floor light. Then in the dining room we had this little table with two chairs and the little table folded down on each side. We'd push all that aside and that's where the boys would set their instruments up in there. The dining and living room was all together, just an opening like an archway. They would be in the dining room and we'd all be in the living room. We had the doors open, the windows open, and when they started playing and practicing for their shows, well we'd tell all the girls to come over from work, and there'd be 30, 40 people there. They'd be in the streets, on the sidewalk, in the house. One night we had the cops come over there, and it was a big small town then, and all the policemen in that ward, they would call back and say, 'Oh, they're not doing anything but practicing for a show. They'll be through in a little while.' So they didn't bother us no more.

No, we didn't have Elvis's fan club. I worked with the Tankers fan club that Gary Pepper had and his mom. He had cerebral palsy and his mamma, she'd help him with the club and everything, and so I would help them. That's when Mr. Pepper, Gary's daddy, had the guardhouse at Graceland, and he'd just tell us to go on up to the house and make yourself at home. We'd go up there and sit on the porch, walk around the yard and everything. That was in the early days when Elvis first moved out to Graceland. You know, he bought Graceland in '57 – April '57. He moved in, in May. So we'd chase Elvis when Charlie was out on a show and we couldn't go as part of the show and we weren't able to follow, so we'd concentrate on Elvis and start looking for Elvis. Go up to the studio where Dewey played his music from nine to twelve – *Red, Hot, and Blue* – and Dewey would say, 'Oh, he'll be here in a little while, so y'all wait, so he usually comes by before I sign off.' So we'd wait for him, and he'd come in. Of course, Elvis was a loveable guy back then. I don't know the Elvis that they're talkin' about today – all this drugs and stuff. But Elvis was really a nice guy. He had to kiss all of us and I got some sugar like two or three times but he used the French kissing. I didn't like that at all.

"Did Charlie kiss the girls, too?"

"Charlie didn't kiss the girls like Elvis did. Charlie was a hugging person. Oh, I fell for Charlie right away. I mean, he was a nice looking guy, but he was married. So, that was one rule that we didn't break, was going with a married person. Me and Charlie were just really, really close good friends. He was such a sweet guy. Charlie never really had a lot of money, but if he had a nickel it was mine if I need it and if I had a nickel it was his, and he knew that. When we met him he had already recorded a couple of songs: "Peepin' Eyes" and "Defrost Your Heart". He would call us 'Girls'. He never referred to our names – 'The Girls', though. If he's talking to me he'd say, 'Girl, you ought to listen to this song, now.' He'd come over there when he's workin' on a song, 'You got to listen to this song I'm working on'. So he would play the song for me and 'What do you think about it?' I'd say, 'Oh, it sounds real good'."

"Well, I know Charlie always wanted to get a good song. He told me lots of times that the most important thing was a *good* song. You got to start with that."

"Charlie never drank. They have put out that he drank, but Charlie never drank. He was a chain smoker. He almost lit a cigarette off of a cigarette. He was always polite around us. Seemed like he was a timid person and very polite. He never used no foul language around us girls. Never had no liquor in the house. In the summertime, when I'd come out to the country to my cousins that raised tomatoes, I'd bring tomatoes back home. They loved sliced tomatoes and we'd have have bologna sandwiches when they'd come over and we made cold drinks for them. Well, we sat up all night writing cards to the disc jockeys, and Charlie's brother took us down to Mississippi and we'd mail them from different little towns in Mississippi. If we seen a tower down there, a radio station, we'd take the record in there if Charlie just had a record put out. We listened to Sleepy-Eyed John – played a lot of country songs, and to Poor Richard, but Dewey Phillips had to be our favorite DJ, because we never went to a studio. It was just a room in the Chisca Hotel that he'd invite us all in, probably six or eight girls. He was always very nice to us and made us feel welcome. He was a character and his favorite saying was, 'Anybody wants to buy a duck?' and 'Tell him Daddy-O-Dewey Phillips sent 'em'. Yeah, and 'Anybody wants to buy a fur-lined mousetrap? A flock of them just flew over that time.' He would say on the radio.

In those days you could just walk in the studio and hand the disc jockey a record and they would put it right on the turntable and play it. Today it has to go through all kinds of channels – I guess it has to be on *Billboard* and probably has to sell a million copies before they will play it. But back in those days Dewey could do anything and he did. Everyone I knew was listening to Dewey. One night he told us if they was listening, come down on Main Street and blow the horn, and he almost got fired. His show was at night and it was called *Red, Hot and Blue*. I guess he wanted to see how many listeners he had, so one night around 8:30 he told everyone that was listening to him on the radio to honk their horn at nine p.m. About 8:45 cars were lined up in front of the studio, blocking traffic on Main Street for blocks. At the stroke of nine, horns sounded throughout the city. Various police chiefs called Dewey to remind him the city had an anti-noise ordinance he was violating. But his whoops and hollers, his mother-in-law jokes, his Dizzy Dean impressions, and his gulf of good humor made him the number one disc jockey for a very long time. Dewey was the first D.J. to play the music of black artists to an almost all-white audience.

Roy Orbison was in town in March of 1956. He just got out of high school; he was 19 years old. I'm sure it was the song "Ooby Dooby" that he recorded at SUN that was his first record. So Charlie knew where they were staying and we all went out to the motel and got him out of the motel and he followed us back to the house. We partied all night 'til about four or five o'clock in the morning. I took pictures of the little guys when they did a show in Greenwood, Mississippi, on a flatbed truck in a football field – pictures of Roy Orbison and his first real band. Sure he was bashful, very bashful. He was just a little bashful kid back then. Charlie was acquainted with all those guys down at SUN, because he was at SUN just about every day. Charlie's music was more important than money. He didn't get no money all his life for his music. You know, he wrote "I Forgot to Remember to Forget" with Stan Kessler. So he didn't get nothing for that, either. That was the first number one million dollar million seller. They say "Heartbreak Hotel" was, but it was not. It was "I Forgot to Remember to Forget" - was on the *Billboard* charts for 43 weeks at number one 'cause I've got a thing from *Top Tunes* here from 1956. We'd go out with Charlie to record songs - when he recorded "Tongue-Tied Jill" out at Meteor on Chelsea. And we went out there and listened to them 'bout all night recording those two songs for that record. That's when Sam Phillips wouldn't record the song. He put it aside because by that time I guess Elvis had come along or Carl Perkins or somebody like that, and he worked for them. He'd seen the talent in them; he just put Charlie aside. He figured, well, Charlie'll be here; these guys probably won't. They'll probably go on. Like I've told 'em before, if it hadn't been for Sam, would none of 'em be known. Sam was operatin' on a shoestring, too. He had everything ah, still owed for, all the equipment and everything. And he just recorded over tapes that would be really valuable today, because he couldn't go out and buy tapes every time they recorded.

Every September we'd all get together and go out to the MidSouth Fair, about 10 or 12 of us. We'd run into Johnny Cash and his wife and two little girls. He'd be walking down the midway and we'd stop, talk to them - just going about our business. They were just like local people, you know, they wasn't no stars, they were just people that we knew.

Charlie told me that when he was really young, about nine years old, he got his first guitar. He learned to play it from this Obie Patterson, and he spoke proudly of this man and always went down to Mississippi and visit with him. He was a black guy. Playin' blues – he played blues music, you know. Charlie said he always listened to Bill Monroe and the Bluegrass Boys. He went to see Bill Monroe when he was about seven years old, he said, and still remembers it. But when Charlie started out he sounded like Hank, Sr. and if he weren't so stubborn – you know, Charlie was stubborn – if he weren't so stubborn, and listened to Sam, and went that direction – 'cause Charlie was real skinny and he favored Hank, Sr., and Hank Sr. just died in January of '53. If Charlie had stuck with that, he would've probably been better off, done better, you know. But you couldn't talk to Charlie about nothing but rockabilly, rockabilly – that's all he wanted to play. So Charlie was more or less at first doin' the country western. That's what Sam wanted him to stick with, but he wanted the rockabilly. He wanted to play the rockabilly. So him and Sam would butt heads about that and Sam wouldn't record for him. That's why he went over to Meteor.

They used to play on weekends - Friday and Saturday night at places, at different clubs, over in Newport, Arkansas. That's where Narvel Felts met him, over in Newport. He'd heard about him so he went down to the – I think it was called the B & B Club. Jerry Lee played there, too. Charlie was really more popular back in those days than Elvis was. They didn't really catch on to Elvis, you know. They was breakin' his records. They wouldn't play his records for a long time, 'cause they said he was makin' the young kids go wild. So Elvis had a hard time gettin' started, I guess. They didn't even want to play his records, you know. I think that Elvis should've come back and got back in touch with us and come back to his old friends. He'd probably still be living today. We wouldn't have been after his money or nothing. But I went to the movies with Elvis, you know, with the group and went to the skatin' rink and went out to the fairgrounds with him. He always spoke to me by name. We'd be walking out the theater side by side and he'd say, 'Hi Shirley, how're you doing?' I'd say, 'I'm fine, Elvis.' So, he was just a nice guy, too; was just really nice. Him and Charlie was real good friends... but I think Elvis, if he would've come back home and got back in touch with the old bunch again, like I said, he probably would still be living. He wouldn't have got in those drugs and stuff. 'Course I know it wasn't hard drugs. People keep saying hard drugs. I say, naw, it was prescription drugs. I saw everybody thinkin' – drugs and probably an addict. I'm an addict, too, 'cause I'm taking drugs: takin' high blood pressure medicine and cholesterol.

I imagine there was 20, 40 or 50 of us in the fan club; most of us were local. We had the little cards. My brother-in-law worked at Murdock Printing and he printed my cards for nothing. But Charlie – the two boys – that picture was all three of 'em in the band on the card. So we would take those cards and they would fill 'em out. I think we charged, like, three dollars a year or five dollars a year, or somethin' like that, for the stamps. Well, we'd send 'em pictures and we'd send 'em schedules when Charlie would be playin'. When we started going to the shows in Mississippi and Arkansas and around where Charlie played, we got a few girls that would join the club from Arkansas and Mississippi and around. When we would see him he would play the rockabilly and lot of his songs that he had written. Like, he did sing, "Defrost Your Heart". He sung other people's songs, too. He loved Bill Monroe, and he loved Eddie Arnold. Later on in the Seventies we went on up to Detroit, he played up there on November 11th in 1978. He said, 'This is for Shirley Richardson' and it was "The Day I Started Loving You Again".

When Charlie got in bad health and his insurance run out, Bob McCarver – that's Jerry Lee's ex-father-in-law – would book benefit shows for Charlie."

"Yeah, I went to one of those benefits at Bad Bob's. Charlie was in a wheelchair that night. Dennis Quaid was up there onstage acting like a buffoon, dressed up like the Killer from his role in the movie they were filming, "Great Ball of Fire", but when Jerry Lee hit the stage that night, he destroyed the place."

"Well, Charlie said the three boys he could always depend was Charlie Rich, Jerry Lee Lewis, and Narvel Felts. See, they would draw the crowds when they held those benefit shows for Charlie. I was in the office with him and Charlie Rich before Charlie Rich went on, and took pictures of them. I've got pictures with Jerry Lee. I used to run into him, playin' in these little clubs around Memphis."

"Yeah, I used to see him once in a while late at night down at Hernando's Hideaway, just with the house band like around three in the morning."

"We thought well apparently he was a silent partner with the Hideaway, because he'd come in there when the boys took a break. Bubba played down there, too, Bubba Feathers. When he would take a break, well Jerry Lee would get up there and start playin' the piano and he'd play about two hours. Well, the boys didn't care because that'd give 'em rest a long time. Well we'd stay there 'til they locked the doors. We were the last ones would leave. Walkin' in, we'd sit at that table at the right side there, about six girls.

Of course, Charlie wrote – I guess Charlie wrote about 300 songs, maybe more. I'd go over to his house when he lived over there off of Lamar Avenue, and he had his equipment set up in one of the rooms back there, one of the bedrooms. We'd go back there and he'd want me to listen to some of the songs he was working on. Well it looked big to me; it was big speakers and everything, like they use in them clubs, and those reel-to-reel tapes. He'd meet me after I got off work up there at the Kettle on Lamar. We'd sit there and drink about 50 cups of coffee and talk about the Fifties. I said, 'Charlie, you know what?' I said, 'All these guys that's not known now, usually when they pass away they'll get known. I guess that's when you'll get known is after you pass.' He said, 'I guess so... I guess you're right, girl.' And I'm really happy for 'em – Rosemary, you know - 'cause she worked hard supportin' the family all those years while he was doing his music and not gettin' nothin' for it. He would sing in a recorder and I think Rosemary would write it down. Jerry played the lead guitar and Jody Chastain played the upright bass and steel guitar with Charlie on live shows. Jerry Huffman worked for the government and he was going to college, too. Jerry worked at night, and he went to sleep in the daytime, and Charlie would go over there, get in the middle of the bed, slap his face, and make him wake up. He had an idea for a song and he'd sing it to Jerry and Jerry would write it down. That's why they usually put all of their names on the songs, because they did it together. So that was the fair thing to do. When Rosemary and me went up to see Jody, it was about a month before Jody passed away. He was tellin' me that a lot of the songs that Charlie had wrote with me in mind. I never knew that before and I come back home and listened to the songs and I think, *Lord have mercy*, it does like that one "Too Much Alike" had to be wrote for me, 'cause Rosemary always said, 'You and Charlie are just too much alike'. I mean, Charlie – we could start talking and I could finish his sentence or he could finish mine; it was weird.

I guess Rosemary and them told you about Eddie Bonds bookin' them up there in

Knoxville. I think gasoline was about 15 cents a gallon back then. So they got up there and Eddie Bonds was bad about not payin' the boys. After the show the boys asked for the money and he said, 'I'll pay you when I get back to Memphis.' And they said, 'Well, we need the money now. We don't have any gas in the car; we gotta get some gas.' He give them seven dollars to get back to Memphis. They said every time they come to a hill, 'We get to a hill and we'd just turn the car off and push it down the hill,' and they rolled into Memphis empty on gas.

Charlie was a mamma's boy. He loved his mamma, and she spoiled him rotten. There's six of them boys and then one girl. The girl married Poor Little Richard, Jim Stewart that was on the radio, and he also drove the car on shows for Carl Perkins. He was drivin' the car when he went to sleep and run off the road and almost killed Carl Perkins. Well it did kill Carl Perkins' brother. He didn't die right away; he lived about eight months, but the wreck is what caused his death. Carl was out of commission for a long time, for several years. They didn't think he'd get back to singing again. Carl had just started out, and they claimed that would be the end of his music career. I think that's the reason Elvis recorded "Blue Suede Shoes". Well, Carl had recorded "Blue Suede Shoes" too, but his record didn't sell like it did when Elvis recorded it. Ralph Emery – I watched the TV show one night when Carl was on there and Ralph Emery asked him if he was he jealous of or resented Elvis's recording it. He said, 'Oh no, man – he retired me. I can retire after Elvis recorded "Blue Suede Shoes" for me.'

I probably had more records of Charlie than Charlie had. You would think he would have every record he made, but he didn't. Wanda paid $500 for one of his records off eBay. That song he sung of Eddie Arnold's was "I'll Hold You in My Heart". That's the song he always sung. Eddie Arnold said Charlie done a better job on it than he does. I'm thinkin' that Charlie was named after Charles Arthur Lindbergh, Jr. because he had got kidnapped the year that Charlie was born. He got kidnapped in the early part of '32 and Charlie as born June the 12th of '32 after the little child got kidnapped. So they named him Charles Arthur Lindbergh Feathers."

It was a jaunt going out to Charlie's house - a claustrophobic low, brick structure way out at Lamar and Winchester behind the Rebel Inn Motel where he lived with wife Rosemary and their progeny Bubba, Wanda, and myopic Ricky the youngest. The old Chevy that didn't run was parked in the weeds out front. Many mornings I'd find Charlie sitting up in his front room chain-smoking Viceroys, left alone with a big pan of cat-head biscuits Rosemary had freshly baked and laid out on the kitchen table before she trundled off to the factory to turn in a day's work. With sententious ease Charlie would play songs for me on an antiquated 8-track tape cartridge player of the type that was once installed in automobiles. Of particular interest to him was a number he'd been experimenting with for years, *I'm Gonna Dig Myself A Hole,* an anti-war/anti-draft conscription ditty composed by bluesman Arthur Crudup. Charlie's treatments were hiccupping masterstrokes of dramaturgic proportions. He expounded with grand oratorical justification on his obsession for recording that song. Like most of Indian descent, he could incant pyrotechnic squeals and hoots and as aforementioned could mimic the calls and utterances of the creatures of the forest and the swamps.

Charlie was driving a dump truck part time for a gravel company, and at night he was gambling away his wages in shuffle board games at a joint called the RACK around the corner off Lamar. Once I brought out a friend's 1936 Harley-Davidson VLD for him to ride. He was delighted, and said that he used to ride one just like it that had belonged to his older brother. Eventually Charlie's legs gave out due to advanced stages of diabetes, and he pretty much stayed home except for an occasional shuffle board tournaments at the RACK or a trip to Bad Bob's Vapors Club to watch Bubba leading the house band. Still Charlie would pull out his acoustic Martin guitar from under the couch to pick and strum along to "One Hand Loose" while watching a Dodgers baseball game on TV. During commercial breaks would come the inevitable re-telling of his story about how Vernon was not Elvis' daddy, claiming his real father was an albino Negro....

By the time I met Charlie he was ridiculed as a quack in certain quarters of the

Charlie Feathers on VLD Photo: E. Baffle 1986

professional music establishment in Memphis due to his outspoken demeanor on stage denouncing sound technicians and musicians alike. Point is: Charlie knew exactly the sound he was after, and he knew just how brilliant he *could* sound when conditions were optimum. After all, when a flatcar load of PA equipment and amplification gear was stacked up on stage, and trained, technologically encumbered sound engineers were darting around like smug laboratory technicians, why can they not produce a simple effect like a pleasing Echo? Sure Charlie was hotheaded, afraid of nothing and nobody. The only sense of intimidation that he ever felt was, I conjecture to think, connected to his relationship with his mentor Sam Phillips. Yet when Charlie Feathers came out on stage he invariably captured the audience on the very first note and held them in the palm of his hand till the finish with sparks of charisma shooting off his body 90-miles in all directions. He never played loudly, but his voice had the power and vocal range of Pavarotti. He'd confide to me, 'Now you gotta scare'em a little. You know, the audience. You gotta scare'em just a little.' And 'Now if you ain't doin' somethin' different... different from anybody else, you ain't doin' nothin' at all.' It took me a long time to come to the realization that by 'different' Charlie did not mean wildly frenetic antics on stage. He meant something else.

As a kid he first learned guitar playing from tenant farming blues artists like Obie Peterson, whose wife babysat him, and growing up with David "Junior" Kimbrough around in the same neighborhood. I'd seen Junior once in a memorable appearance at the Orpheum Theatre at Main and Beale on a bill with the big band Bar Kays and the almost as big and more highly amplified, Son Seals Blues Band. Junior came out on the grand stage alone between the larger acts, and stood swaying, rooted to center stage picking a huge hollow-body electric guitar slung over his cotton picker's barrel chest. He played a snaking, drone rendition of "Tramp" that

Phillips Recording Studio Photo: E. Baffle c. 1980

sounded like he was singing "TRAM… way out on the TRAM" and coming off far more hypnotic and erotic than the Lowell Fulson buttermilk version or the Bar Kays live review.

A rumor got around that some rockabilly reunion sessions going on down at Phillips Studio with just about everybody that mattered: Paul Burlison, Doug Poindexter, Charlie Feathers, Roland Janes, Malcolm Yellvington, Glenn Honeycutt, Marcus Van Story, Sonny Burgess, James Van Eaton, Stan Kessler, Smoochy Smith. I slid onto the Norton and rode down to the studio under a blazing afternoon sun. From sales generated off of "Raunchy", the Bill Justice instrumental hit, Phillips Recording Studios was built in 1958 in a California Tropical Moderne style at 639 Madison Avenue. The new studio was situated just a couple blocks away from the converted radiator garage original SUN studio on Union. This new temple of audial recording boasted two studios, a triangular echo chamber, split-level angular architecture, tangerine and aquamarine décor, a Japanese rock garden, private upstairs glitter bar, and shag-carpeted offices. The entire facility was permeated with the singular odor of mortified rubber cabling. On the walls hung galleries of gold records and awards. In the coolness of the lobby across from the kidney shaped Formica reception desk puffing Viceroys, was Charlie Feathers wearing a powder-blue leisure suit whilst relaxing on a Naugahyde couch. One afternoon not so long before, I had encountered Sam Phillips himself sitting on the other side of the boomerang reception desk attired in a polo shirt. With the eyes of an alchemical wizard, the gaze of Sam Phillips seemed to look right through you to your innermost secrets.

Today Charlie appeared to be in an expansive and amicable mood as we listened to velvety vocals pumping through the ubiquitous studio speakers. Between recording takes we held our own rockabilly pow-wow.

"When you started who were you listening to mostly, Charlie?"

"Well, there was a group called Bill Monroe and the Bluegrass Boys and they had some guys with them – I believe called, Jam Up and Honey, something like that, two white guys paint their face black – and I liked them and they were going around in tents – put up a big tent – and they did it in Holly Springs. 'Course we lived out in the country; so we went and see 'em… and then after that Hank Williams."

"So you and Junior Kimbrough grew up near Holly Springs, Mississippi."

"Well most of the black people, we'd just meet them out around what they called picnics. We lived in a place right across a road out there in a big long house. Out across the field there, across the road they used to have a picnic every year called, Rossville Picnic. People picking their guitars, just sitting down there, and they'd get to dancing in the road. I used to stand across the road there and listen to them and watch them. Then I come to Memphis and I used to go with my brother-in-law, he was on a radio station over there in West Memphis – KWEM – and he had an all-girl band. Now he was a disc jockey over there, and later he come to WMPS and he was there for several years. My sister, she was in this girl band. I used to tune ol' guitar down all the time in an open tuning. Yeah, that's the way I started off rapping on the guitar and singing. Oh, and I just come up here and Sam's in the studio; wasn't nobody in there but him, and Mary. We'd sit around up there and talk, me and Sam. That went on for a year or so at 706 Union. Yeah and then I had some things in mind, but I never did get 'em to come off to song. Me and Scotty and Bill, we cut on 'em up there. Then Sam did the thing on Elvis. I met Elvis over in a park over on Mosby Street, and I think he was living down at Lauderdale Courts at that time. He come out there in the park. I was going with a girl out over there, so I'd take my guitar and we'd sit out there in the park and strum it. Well, he asked me something about this studio, and I said well, I go up there. Next thing you know Elvis is over there. He come over there and he cut a dub with Sam. Then next thing you know, Sam called him back in and cut a record. Then Sam wanted me to cut a country record. That's what he wanted me to cut. Man, I ain't wrote no country songs. Didn't know nothing about it hardly. Two guys named Bill Cantrell and Quentin Claunch, they wrote a thing for a guy named Bud Deckerman, and they came back to show it to Sam and Sam turned it down. A song called, "Daydreaming". I think

Johnny Newman covered it when it come out on Meteor Records.

"That was a competitive label in town wasn't it, Meteor Records?"

"Yeah, Les Bihari learnt Sam all the know-how about the business. Sam knows that. Yeah, he knew how to make money in the business. He's the one set up all these racks and things and commence to selling records. Sure did. Anyhow, I kept hanging around there. Bill and Quentin came back by and they had a song and Sam kinda put me with them and said me to do the song, called, "I've Been Deceived", and I had one called, "Peepin' Eyes". We worked it up and cut it. That's with a fiddle and everything. I wasn't used to hearing no fiddle at all, man."

"So hillbilly music wasn't something that you paid a lot of attention to, other than...."

"Down in this area you didn't. Bluegrass, as for feelin' – everybody's got a little feeling for bluegrass, boy, 'cuz it was the first music come over here. Then Elvis got it mixed up, they got bluegrass all mixed up with the cotton-patch blues, and I don't know what they called it. Sam didn't know what to call it. He says, 'I just let them call it whatever they want to call it.' Somehow or another, years later, you come to hear rockabilly. I would truthfully say the first records that Elvis cut was rockabilly. They didn't have no drums on 'em – nothing. It had the speed of the bluegrass and the bass slapped a little bit and Scotty thumb picked a little bit like Chet Atkins. They made mistakes on it now, but it still sounded different and it was good. White people related to it and the black people did too when he put that slappin' on the bass in there. Yeah, like "That's All Right (Mama)" and "Blue Moon of Kentucky". Absolutely. Well, then, lot of people think it took right off, but it didn't. It didn't. Sam, sometime a month go by, wouldn't sell but 25 records. That's on Elvis, now. Then eventually, get a little more, a little more, and a little more.

We had so many sessions up there, boy I'm telling you right now...stuff; we just roll the tape all the time, cuttin', putting down ideas and things. Some of it wasn't any good at all; most of 'em wasn't. But you take them things and daydream on it a week or two, a month or so, you probably come up with a song out of 'em, see. And that was the idea, right there – a good song, man. Aw, man – I'm telling you right now.

A lot of people don't know how Elvis was singing. He wasn't singing like what they heard him on the records. Lawd have mercy, no! Sure did now. He was an amateur from word go. He wasn't just *that way*. Sam and them *made* him that way, right there in the studio. Absolutely. In that studio, you just couldn't cut country, man. The rockabilly sound, I would say, it was just there. I played a lot with the black people and their music, the cotton-patch blues, is my first love – of music... still today. I hear it and I just grew up around that, myself. Even Sam and them could hear it, and it was coming from the country, too; it wasn't coming from the city. Now, go out on a show – a show's a different thing than a record, see. You gotta make them love what you done on that record. If you fail doing that now... and fortunately Elvis had both of them: they loved him on the show and they loved him on the record.

Well, if I'd a stayed there with Les Bihari... I was just telling a guy in there that's where I made my biggest mistake. But the musicians with me, 'Oh, man he's so-and-so'. Well he knew the business 'cuz he showed Sam, taught Sam a lot about the business, and he come from out from Beverly Hills. They were Jews, but they knew this business. They knew how to sell records, man. They're still sellin' records. Cut B.B. King on a lil' ol' recorder. Yeah, and there's some wonderful things happening... there's still some wonderful things happening right here in Memphis again, before it's over with. It will definitely come back. Now, I might not be around to see it, but it will come back. And it will be basically just Memphis music like it always was.

Now it's a lot of 'em here, a lot of the studios don't know how to record people. They don't. Was sittin' here a while ago and I mentioned to Roland [Janes], you just gotta have your place here and you there and you there and you stay there, now until we get what we want. And that's the way it is down here in Memphis. You stay in them spots and you work until you get what you want, until he gets it on the board. You gotta get it down here on the floor, and some of 'ems not... the musicians not talented enough to get it right off, but they'll stay in there and work 'till they get it. And when they get it, it just blows them fine musicians' mind, 'cuz they can't quite get the tone... they just can't pick it like they did because they can't get the *feel* that they get. Yeah, I never did hear nobody play a guitar like Luther Perkins. *Nobody.* Carl Perkins got with Cash after that and tried. Naw-aw – too *progress.* Luther, he worked. He didn't know much, but boy he stood right there and he just thumped it and thumped it until it sound good. He wouldn't say nothing. He thumped that son-of-a-gun until it sounded good, man. "Cry, Cry, Cry" and "Hey Porter", was his first record. Well, my brother-in-law broke the record on WMPS. I took him up there; he couldn't get in no other way. I called Dick Stewart, took Johnny Cash up there, and he thanks me today for it. And he got to playing this record, and he booked Johnny and them on some shows with me at that time. They were kinda sad, but people was listening and they bought his record, 'cuz they just stand out there and look at you just like, *Well, you're supposed to like it.* You know, that's kind of the way it was. And they were liking it, but they just didn't make no sound. They just stood there; they didn't clap and tilt their head – nothing. Kinda made me wanna go outside until it was all over. No, people wondered about it. *What is that now? I never heard nothing like that before.* Then they go buy the record – see if it's so. *See, did it really sound like that?* On the record, he had the sound there and the tone; it was there.

"Well, how did Mr. Phillips develop this slapback technique? Did he use this on Johnny Cash, and on your records and Elvis' records?"

"Oh, yeah – and he used it on Johnny Cash, no doubt about it. Yes, sir, he used it. Well, it was done with two mics – *two mics.* That's what a lot of people mess up on, now. They get one mic and try to get it all comin' in over there, over that. It won't do it. It won't *never* get it – not the way they got it. Singing right *between* two mics. One mic's a basic sound just like Bing Crosby and them used to record when there was no slapback or nothin', and you could stand there and you had to say your words just so-so and not too low and not too loud because the needle will jump into the red. Now you put slapback on it, on that racked-up side, it takes the *edge* off of it a little bit. And you can kind of ad-lib a little like Elvis did. Sam was bad about getting too much of it on there. Now, he was. Too damn much echo on there. And you could very easily do it, too."

"What were these live shows like, that you and Johnny Cash and Elvis and the others would play – were you able to get a kind of echo on stage for your vocals?"

"Of course, I was just doing them country songs. That's all I did out there, with them. 'Cause I had to do what I recorded. Now Elvis... Scotty Moore got an old machine and put that on top of his amp. He got it from Germany. He had a tape rolling in it, and plugged the vocal mic through that and into the PA system, if they had one. Elvis sang through that and man, it sounded just like he was in the studio. He sung through that thing on many a night. He'd go out there and say a word or two and just blow the people's minds. They never heard nothing like it. They think something done come down from space, man. And that's what made Elvis. Well, what they heard... it wasn't nothing like Elvis' normal voice sounded. The minute he said, '*Weeell*' – something like that – it'd jump right out at 'em, see. Everybody else on the show walked out, with a normal voice, 'Well', like you done hit a dead note, you know. He could hit a *bad* note and it would go out there then so quick and fast, it'd sound good when it got to them. Now, that's what made Elvis. Then he changed. See, Elvis wasn't Elvis when he... Elvis I knew died in '55 – last part of '55. Because they went to RCA... and they didn't know. Sam cut a thing on Carl, "Blue Suede Shoes" and RCA thought for a while that they done got the wrong artist. They sure did now. They didn't know what that slapback was. Jack Clement came in up there doing recording for Sam for a while. He come in wantin' the echo chamber. There wasn't no damn echo chamber in there, man."

"So those RCA engineers were really searching for that echo, themselves, too?"

"Hey – a lot of 'em *still* searching for it! Trying to get that tight-up sound and that voice that said, '*Yeeeeah*', right there at you. It goes out so wide, and yet, not so wide, and you can sing hard and puff the mic a little bit, and it wouldn't jump so far in the red. That effect kept the gain back down, because people were beginning to raise hell about needles going into the red. You put that record on a jukebox – it would outdo any damn record you put on there. Any record that RCA and them could put out, or anybody else put out. 'Cause it was raw music, and his voice sounded so pretty out there, man. You take right here, today. Right here in this studio. I guaran-damn-tee ain't but one person can walk down here and get that slapback sound. That's Sam Phillips – *himself*. Now he don't show these boys nothing. He let them get in and work and get what you can get yourself. 'Cause he feels like everything's changed. But I believe it – I truly believe that – I know that. I did a thing one time, a song that Elvis was fixing to record – they done worked up it with Carl Perkins when he and Sam got in a little argument – called, "We're Getting Closer to Being Apart". I did this thing for a boy, down at NBC Studio in Houston, Texas. Even Stan [Kessler] heard it. He said that's close as he ever heard to that slapback. Now Stan heard it, heard the slapback up there, but he wasn't familiar with how it was got. Now, first thing I know Stan had a studio. He had a slapback *machine* in there, man. And that machine is good, but it's just not… here's the difference, when we started getting these super reverbs, they had a "Y" echo thing in 'em.

"Yeah, a spring reverb – a spring in there to vibrate."

"Right. That's what the echo they're getting today sounds like. Now, you get the other real, true slapback – comes through the board, and the tape rolling there. You set it 7-1/2, or 3-3/4 rpm if you want to. Aw, man – ain't nothin' touch it. And you're gettin' a dead voice, just like he sounds. Just like he's cuttin' – not even, you know, with echo chamber, or nothin'. You got that voice on there, too. Then you touch it with the other one with the slapback – just barely touch it. Say, *this is a singing son-of-a-bitch. Where'd he come from?* That's true. I have yet to really cut a rockabilly sound like I… like I know. "We're Getting Closer to Being Apart", you listen to that. It was two mics, singing right in the middle. It sounds *good*… it does! Bass, guitar, and a rhythm guitar… and set 'em up on the mic right. Get your slapback right, in a small room, and buddy, I'm gonna tell you: don't nothing sound empty. The whole room's full – the sound goes right into the mics. You could use brushes on a snare drum. See, playing rockabilly, if you keep slapping that bass, and drum with sticks, it's going to collide together. It's never going to come off. It'd be a big mushy sound. Now I've tried that too, and it don't come off. All these young ones… they can't even play brushes. I have to just be satisfied with whatever they can do. A lot of them get up there and think they're playin' rockabilly… they start off just lying. Now, they can get louder, maybe, but it don't have the dynamics in it. That's what makes the people listen. That's what's in bluegrass. That's what Bill Monroe has makes people listen at him. And they got one mic on the stage, and the Dobro and the banjo, and they all use that one mic, taking turns at it. But them two mics for slapback, you gotta stand right there, though, boy. Can't be nothin' movin' but the lip movement. Now, you move them all you want to. Now if you move one way or the other, that mic will pick up more, you see."

"You've been supportive of musicians around Memphis, new bands coming along. You've come down and played with 'em. I've seen you on a lot of shows – and independent little shows around town – working with new artists, new rock 'n' roll kids coming along. You've come out with your son, Bubba Feathers – one of the best guitar players I've ever heard – and your whole your family come to these shows."

"Bubba just loves music, man. He's been playing it since he was 12 and 13. He came in and won a contest out there at Bad Bob's, one time. Well he played all over the world with us, three different times. Then he's been playing down at Greenville, Mississippi, at Ramada Inn, and they broke all kind of records down there. They played there five and a half years. He just got tired playin' down there. They called him back, wanting him – 'Naw,' he said, 'I want to stay at home some now."

"What about your first band Charlie Feathers and the Musical Warriors…?"

"That was the fiddle and the pop rhythm and bass, and steel. Stan Kessler played steel guitar in that band. See we played all around with Elvis on his first tour. Like, Huntsville,

Alabama, and Tupelo – his home ground there – and Camden, Arkansas; Little Rock, Arkansas... man, I played over there so much, me and Elvis and Johnny Cash, and all of them. Every time we look up we's going to Arkansas. Jimmy Haggard up there in Blytheville had a radio station. That thing'd reach out, man. You could pick it up going down Main Street in Nashville. It really boomed out. He booked a lot of artists up there. Man, every time you look up you think you're on the one road coming back toward Memphis, but you'd be on another one, thinking it looked like that."

"Was Jerry Lee Lewis on them, or he came a little later than those early shows?"

"Naw, Jerry wasn't even born then. I thought I met Jerry Lee up here, and he said, 'Naw,' he told me. He said, 'Naw, I met you in another place.' 'Where's it at?' He said, 'Down in Louisiana.' He said, 'You played down there one night at...' someplace and I do remember after him sayin' it: some guy played piano and sang out there before we came on, and that was Jerry Lee. Then I met him on back when we went out to Millington one night and played a show. Then we went to Jackson... man, Johnny Burnette and Dorsey Burnette and Jerry Lee and Ace Cannon. Carl Perkins came to the show up there – he wasn't even on the bill. That's where I lost my plaque I got from Nashville – the one for, "I Forgot to Remember To Forget". The man, he was promotin' the show and he was runnin' it on TV, and that afternoon, before the show come into town, he had a wreck out there, killed his self, and he had all that material in there with him. "Song of the Year" plaque, just like the one on the wall out there. That's where I lost mine at."

"What did Dewey Phillips do in terms of promotion for all of you?"

"Aah, now let me show you somethin' here, now, a guy named Sleepy Eyed John – he broke Elvis, you know, on a little ol' station, WHHM. It wouldn't reach out of Memphis, but it busted Elvis so hot here man, it was pitiful. Booked him out at the Eagle's Nest, kept him out there and around little places here. Then, he got to arguing with Sam, 'bout some guy that sing out there with him; they did western swing. Wanted to record it and Sam just didn't think that he could. But, maybe he couldn't do that type music up there, you know. It takes a lot doing western swing. Well, then he begin to say things against Sam, 'Ah, he don't know what he's doin' – how to record a record none'. He kinda quit playin' Elvis's records, and then Sam went to Dewey Phillips, got him playin' it. Now this is true. Then, after that, Dewey would pick up every record, play 'em, and Bob Neil on WMPS, and they were bookin' us all. I knew Dewey well. I went to see him when he went to Little Rock. He didn't go over too good over there, at all. Not at all."

"It's a different ball game over there in Little Rock isn't it, than in Memphis?"

"Sure is – a different town. Little Rock is just like Nashville: Nashville is Nashville and Memphis is Memphis. We come from right here in the Delta, man, and that kinda music couldn't happen nowhere else but right in here. These other people, they tickle me to death. Sometimes I sit and laugh about it. Doin' this music here, man. They just could not do this music. I've seen some of these people from up North and from overseas and everywhere doin' the music – they can't do it. They don't have that accent or somethin'. It's not there, man. A guy used to bring these Elvis singers by the house, and I say, 'Tell you what, sing me a little bit of, "That's All Right (Mama)", or somethin' like that.' Aw man, they couldn't get up there on that and get it. They just couldn't get it. They'd get out on another key and naw, forget it, man. These first five songs Sam cut on him. Small sound, but the world was huntin' for it before it even got there. I mean, they were going *wild* for it before Sam and them could get the record out. Sam didn't want to send out it to them, and them not pay for it. You know, he had to figure out a way to get it there and them payin' for it. They were waitin' on 'em records so much. Then here come over Hank Snow, down talkin' about Elvis, blowin' these guys off. Man, he spoke bad about Elvis when Elvis first went up there to Nashville. Introduced him, 'Here's a boy singing on a Bill Monroe song...' Didn't say give him a hand or nothin'. Elvis walked out of there so scared, he didn't know what to do."

"On the Grand Ole Opry…?"

"Yeah, man. Total scared. Told Scotty he's gonna do one; told Bill Black he's gonna do different one. He started off on… man, when he opened up he started off, *Blue Moon…* that bass started working – man, them people about tore the house down. I say, there's a new train done roll in here now, man, I'll tell you that.

"But he wasn't accepted at Grand Ole Opry, he had to go to Louisiana…"

"Yeah, he was accepted by the people. He wasn't accepted by the people that *run* the Grand Ole Opry. I was right up there when they called him back the second time. He told 'em… he said, 'Buddy,' he said, 'I'll tell you what,' – and done busted *big*, man, down in Louisiana and everywhere else, too – he said, 'You call me again and I'm going to come up there and buy the *whooole* Opry, and throw the key in the sea.' I'm glad he did! He sure did! We were sitting up there one night talking, boy, and that happened."

"You put out a record a couple of years ago on the Electra label, produced by Ben Vaughan – one of your biggest fans – and everyone around here, everybody I've met was really surprised and glad to see this new album come out."

"Yeah, but hell, they wouldn't let me do… I couldn't do what I wanted. Ben Vaughan and them. And everything I done there with him, *Oh man that's good, that's good*. It wasn't nothing but a bunch of crap. See, I know this, man. They ain't foolin' me."

"How about this new single you've done here, "I'm Gonna Dig Myself a Hole?"

"I'd liked to have got with it. Didn't quite, but I'd liked to. I shouted at these two boys too fast, too quick. I should have sat down and went through it and worked it out with them, but I shot it to 'em too quick, man. They didn't know which way they were going, or what. I knew where I was going, but they wasn't sure, and it shows. Yeah, picked the hell out of it. You couldn't get nobody else to sound, do, no better. But, had they worked it out… maybe. But they didn't; these boys didn't work nothing out. And I started singing – here it is man, and it's gone."

"Well, it's got a real happening, spontaneous feel. It's got a great tone. The performance is magnificent."

"Yeah, see – I felt that way. I can feel that way and the rest of the musicians don't, and it don't mean nothin'. I hear these things, man, but I'm scared to tempt 'em… on account of the musicians. I'm telling you what, God loves the truth. Even down here cuttin' up with Ben Vaughan and them. I heard other things, man, but the whole band's gotta go with you and you gotta show them what you're doing. And you don't have time to do that, 'cause man, it takes a lot of time to show them what you're doing. That guy's gotta sing it and that guy's gotta live and breathe it, playin' it."

"The difference it seems between your records and ones that are manufactured in the studio is that yours are *created* in the studio."

CHAPTER THE SIXTH
GHOSTS BEHIND THE SUN

Over by the Coke machine in the hallway, I ran into Billy Lee Riley, and I had to ask him how he got from Arkansas to SUN. In a slow affable drawl he replied, "I actually grew up in Osceola. That was where most of my young days were spent – in Osceola, Arkansas. It's right in the delta, big cotton country down there, and at the time I was living there – we were living on a plantation – and it was all farmers, cotton farmers. The black blues was very prominent there, and of course that's my roots. That's why I sing the way I do, is because I was raised in that era of the blues. T99… the Rebel Club was there back during the '50s. It was a big club. I didn't know anything about the clubs when I was a child, but I did listen to a lot of good blues. The interpretation of blues is what I call, honest music; that's the way I term it. The only place that we got to hear that type of music was like on weekends they would gather at homes – their houses – and sit on the front porch, back porch, and play the guitars and harmonicas. There was no shows – they didn't do any shows. I don't remember at all seeing a black musical show back in those days. Now, we did see a lot of traveling country shows come through. A lot of them back then would come into town and set up a tent and have a country show. But, as far as the blues, the only place that I could hear the blues was either walking by some of the old blues beer joints or else on the front porches of their houses themselves, during the weekends. That's the honest, that's what I'm saying, that's the honest music, and that is where I learned to play guitar, and play and sing that type of music. I sort of put it all together – the country and the blues.

"Once I got to Memphis I started playing music in a club with Jack Clement and that group. He had a studio on Fernwood and he asked me if I wanted to come over and do a session, and I did, and Roland Janes was there. We did a couple of sides and he brought them to Sam Phillips's SUN. I wasn't that familiar with SUN Records at the time and he brought it over there and made some kind of deal with Sam, and that's how I wound up on the SUN label. Not something that I planned. Well, Roland, the way we met, was through Jack Clement and that session. He was the first musician, the first member of the Little Green Men that I did meet, and he was on the very first records that we did. He and I became friends and he helped me get the rest of the group together, and Roland Janes gets credit for bringing in 'Flyin' Saucers Rock 'n' Roll'. That is where the name Little Green Men came from, and I think that was tagged by Sam Phillips. The Little Green Men were James Van Eaton on drums, Marvin Pepper on bass, and Roland Janes on guitar.

"As far as the Sun sound is concerned, I think that our sound is the one that really created that. Roland Janes, J.M., and I – us three were on most everything that came out of that studio over there, and either one or two of us individually was on practically everything. Like, J.M. played practically all of the drum work over there – with of course me, Jerry Lewis, Charlie Rich, Bill Justice, Johnny Cash. And then later on the piano player that we had, Jimmy Wilson, he played on all the Johnny Cash; so anything that was a keyboard he got the job. And of course Roland was the guitar player at the time, so he was on practically everything, and I played guitar a little bit – not as much as Roland, but I played – and I managed to get in on quite a few of them myself. So the SUN sound as far as I'm concerned was the Little Green Men. They have tried and tried to recreate that in a lot of places. They've never been able to do that. That is one sound – between Roland, J.M., and me – that's one sound that has never been duplicated. They just can't do it, because we did it how we *felt* it. It was a thing coming directly from us – it wasn't something we were trying to sound like or trying to play like this guy or over play somebody."

"You were playing in a way that I've only heard people in jazz relate to each other and in certain blues groups, how they key-off of each other and are actually heard answering and responding to each other in the context of a song."

"We had a lot of fun, and a lot of times we had problems and we'd argue sometimes, but basically we were there to do a job and we got the job done, and it turned out great. Sometimes we'd be in the studio for three or four hours; sometimes we'd be there all night. But regardless, when we finished there was a product that came out of our sessions that was *good*. Why it happened like it did is because at that time what we were doing was more or less at an experimental stage. We were new to it, the music was new, and we were really new. I mean, half the time I didn't know what we were doing. Most of it was experimental, but we knew once we got into a good sound. We knew when we had something going, and we knew we were going to come out with something.

"We played everywhere from what they call the 'back of a truck' for an opening for some store. We played tops of drive-in movie concession stands, we played theaters, we played nightclubs, we played… you name it. If it paid anything at all, a little bit, we were there. It was sometimes hectic: sometimes we would get paid, most of the time we wouldn't get paid. Half the time we would go out on a job, finish the job, and whoever was supposed to pay us would be gone by the time we finished and there was no money in it. A lot of the shows we played, like go to a club and play for what we called, 'the door', and the admission, or part of the admission price. I remember nights where it would cost a dollar to come in, each person, and maybe we would have two dollars in there some nights. But most of the time we had good crowds, and we had a lot of fun doing what we were doing.

"There were also what they called package shows in those days with other artists like maybe the Johnny Burnett Trio, Rock 'n' Roll Trio as they called it, or some of the other artists on the labels. We traveled quite a bit with the SUN package, with Johnny Cash in local and southern regions. Johnny Cash, Jerry Lee Lewis, Carl Perkins, Roy Orbison, and Warren Smith, and occasionally there would be other artists like, well, Ferlin Husky, Hank Snow, and people like that from the country part of the business – they would mix because Johnny Cash was country. Basically he was country with a touch of the SUN thing.

"Well, when I went out on stage, I was so insecure that I had to act crazy to keep people interested in what I was doing instead of what I was saying and singing. I was very insecure at the time, and what I did was just go out on stage and do a wild show and hope for the best. And it worked. It really worked. And the band was hot, and we had the greatest band, I guess, anywhere around here. In most of the package shows we wound up backing every artist on there. If they didn't have a band of their own, we did all the backing work on it. Songs like 'Red Hot' were great for the stage show because we could get out there and put on a show with that. And we still do – I still do those songs and I still do 'em the same way back in the '50s. I still go crazy. I go out on stage and act like a fool."

Sitting in the front office, was Jud Phillips, Jr., son of the great SUN records promoter, Jud, Sr. I ducked in to escape the smoke filled hallway. There with him was Rose Clayton, the ravishing, strawberry blonde-haired authoress and daughter of the motion picture pioneer and national news service cameraman, John William McAfee. Rose, soon to be Rose Clayton Phillips, is a chic, mature woman upon whose attractive features the bloom of youth ever resides. Jud, Jr.'s gracious mother, Dean Phillips, the full time secretary and accountant at the studio, was present as well. Her son carries the robust six-foot stature of his father and walks with the same determined gait. Jud, Jr. possesses that unmistakable Phillips' family mien and countenance with the penetrating, yet amiable blue-green eyes. He also happens to be the proud owner of the complete Amos and Andy Show TV series. I asked Dean from where she had migrated to the Bluff City, hoping to might peel away another layer of the enigmatic chimera that is Memphis and its supernal music.

Billy Lee Riley & Tav Falco Photo: Judy Peiser 1998

"Florence, Alabama. The Tri-Cities, its all in that area, south of the state line from Tennessee. That's where Jud and Sam were from – out there in the country around Florence."

"So you grew up around music?"

"Yeah, music was a real part of my life."

"Which church were you a member of?"

"In Florence, I was a Baptist. It was the Highland Baptist Church in Florence, Alabama. And I was always active in the choir. I played piano for my mother and dad. They were in a quartet. My feet wouldn't touch the floor from the bench. A radio station there, WLAY; it's still there, and we had a radio show on Sundays.

"Your husband and his brother played instruments?"

"Actually", Jud, Jr. interjected, "Sam, believe it or not, played tuba in the high school band."

"He played drums too," Dean added, "and he was a drum major of the high school band."

"But Sam's first love was always radio," Jud, Jr. said. "To the day he died, that was it."

"Then I moved to Florence to go to the Teacher's College," Dean said.

"Was that an easy transition for you to come to Memphis?"

"Well, it was just me and Jud right after we married. Yeah, me and Jud and Sam came to Memphis. Then it was Sam and his wife, Becky and Knox was a tiny baby. North Waldron… we didn't live in the big house. There was a little bitty house in the back. It was built almost like a garage. There were two apartments there. Sam and Becky had one and we had one. We had to walk down a stairway to get down to the ground level. We washed our clothes in the bathtub, and then we'd go outside and hang them out and then bring them back up. The stairway was very dark and very narrow, and there was about a 40 watt bulb at the top of that stairway. Knox was just a little fella; he was crawling. And Jud and I would be on the road working with the quartet and we'd come in and Knox would know we were there. There was a little hall between our apartments and Becky would try to keep him quiet when we would come in at 3 or 4 o'clock in the morning. But Knox would come and peck on the door and one of us would have to let him in. He was crazy about his uncle Jud. He'd come in and he wouldn't let us sleep.

"Didn't you meet Sam before you met Jud?"

"Oh, yeah."

"They were doing radio in Florence before they came up here," Jud, Jr. said. "And live radio was a huge deal in the 40s."

"Yes it was. Sam was an announcer on the show and Becky was an announcer. And Becky's sister was an announcer. Jud did announce some. When we were in Florence he had an early morning radio program. Sam came first to Memphis and before the studio he worked for WREC for Hoyt Wooten. He announced. And at that time the radio wasn't on 24 hours a day. They had a sign off time at night, and Sam was the sign-off man. He had the late shift and signed off the station every night. When we came down here to Memphis, we had organized our gospel quartet, and we were traveling. When we had night shows, sometimes we'd get back in and wouldn't have time to go back to the apartment. We'd get in at 5 o'clock in the morning and we'd have an early morning radio show and we wouldn't have time to go across town. So we'd just park in front of the Peabody Hotel, put down the seats and take a nap.

"Bill Gaither and Gloria, his wife, used to write a lot of gospel music. He's got a lot of people on his TV show now that were in our group: Jake Hess, Hovie Lister, The Goodwin Family – they all used to sing with our bunch. Jake Hess and Hovie Lister started The Statesmen out of Atlanta, one of the biggest gospel groups of all time. We had a guy named Cat Freeman in our group. He was from Sand Mountain in Alabama. He was a tenor. He sang with us and then he went to the Blackwood Brothers. The Blackwood Brothers are famous now. The Blackwood Brothers were on a lot of the programs we were on."

"The Jordanaires came later, right?"

"Yeah, the Jordanaires. We knew all of them and did shows with them. Jud was traveling everywhere with the gospel quartet and that's how he started promoting rock 'n roll. He knew who the people in all of those little cities were, and they knew him because he had already been there. And that's when people asked, 'How did they distribute all of those rock 'n' roll records?' It was him calling up favors from all of these people he'd known racking up points in all of these cities, playing in the gyms and the churches and colleges. Plus, Jud's dad was like Jud was. He never met a stranger, you know. He was real personable. So he knew like every person in town. When they had Charlie Rich or Jerry Lee or Elvis, he would go back to these towns, and it was all the same people and radio stations. They didn't have different stations for every format back then. They had a gospel show and a pop music show.

"There was such a big sense of community back then and the church was a big part of the community," Rose said.

"It was the center of the community," affirmed Dean. "I think a lot of people don't get that connection. They talk about Elvis' connection to gospel music but I don't think they get that the *label* had that too, because at one time there were three partners at SUN Records – Jud, Sam and Jim Bullock whose background in gospel, and is what helped to get that music played. I don't know if you've heard any of the real old Southern gospel records, but they had introductions on them, and Jud would be the one to introduce them. This was on the recording so you'd hear it when you played the record. In fact the SUN gospel that came out on Bear Family a few years ago, it had a song by Sam on it, didn't it? Sam did a song on it and so did George Klein. They had the label called SUN SPOT. It wasn't connected to SUN Records. They had the Sun Spot Quartet, and then they had the Jolly Boys Quartet. That was on WREC. They talk about the blues music and the country music but for all of these little towns the basis of SUN Records was not blues or country that helped start rock 'n' roll, but it was the gospel.

"Jud caught hell for some of that music later on because he had been in there singing gospel, and now he was bringing in this devil's music. They always talk about the blues, but it was also that Southern Baptist church. And it wasn't just Mississippi and Arkansas and Memphis. It was also Kentucky, Alabama, and Georgia. It was the culture of the church and the values that it instilled in people that was the basis for this. That's why when the lyrics started

Jud Phillips, Sr. (in uniform) & Dean w/Quartet - Hattiesburg, Mississippi 1951

changing and the beat started changing and the dancing started changing, people started to ban it."

"Before there were clubs people would go to the live radio shows," Rose said. "I know that a lot of people that worked downtown would go to WMPS. It was right at Monroe and Main Street. The Blackwood Brothers had a gospel show, and people would take their sack lunches and go see them. Tammy Wynette was one of them. She worked for the beauty shop down there, and she would go watch them. We'd try to be down there at 4 o'clock in the afternoon when they had the afternoon radio shows. They had one down at the Goodwyn Institute Auditorium downtown at Second and Madison Avenue called, Saturday Night Jamboree. Elvis would go there a lot around 1953 and play. I saw him there many times. Paul Burlison was there. I think that's where I met Paul. People don't understand there wasn't TV back in those days for people to gear performances to. Before Elvis nobody really cared. You had to go see these people live. There was Chuck Berry, James Brown, Jackie Wilson – the black entertainers actually moved around. Like Porter Wagoner, the white performers, were stiff as a board. You have to remember these people were recording on radio and they had to stand still in front of the microphone. You couldn't move around because you'd distort the sound. So when you went down to see people live at the clubs on Beale Street, like Elvis did, people were drinking… and one thing Memphis had that other people didn't have was, Memphis people danced to music. Some other cities people didn't dance to music. Early on performers in

Nashville would tell me that they loved to go to Memphis because people danced to our music. People here appreciated the groove and they would get up and dance. In Nashville people would listen to songs and they'd sit there stiff. So people would love to come to Memphis to perform, like at the Overton Park Shell, because people would get up and dance. And you didn't have to have a dance floor in Memphis to dance. Anywhere you could stand, you could dance. And if there wasn't enough room between the benches, you'd stand up on the benches."

"The other connection," Jud, Jr. pointed out, "especially in the black Pentecostal churches, pretty much any black church, is they are very animated in the services when they're inspired, and this carried over into other venues. They will not hesitate to get up and show their emotions."

"There were three churches in our area that were like full gospel churches. There were three within walking distance because we walked everywhere in the 50s you know. We would sit on the bridge out there and listen to the gospel music. One of the things that we loved was the beat from all the clapping. We used to listen to the black gospel shows on Sunday and listening to these R&B shows at night, but on Sunday there was only gospel on the radio – the black gospel and the white gospel, which was mainly preaching. So we listened to the black gospel. And that's how we got into R&B music was through the black gospel shows. There was still a beat to the black gospel music with the hand clapping even though they weren't dancing. It was joyous music," Rose maintained. "It wasn't all that straight-laced, stuffy stuff."

"When Jerry Lee would come over the house he would always go straight to the piano," Jud, Jr. recalled. "He and mom would sit there and play piano together. Actually that was the same piano that Jerry did the first run through of "Whole Lotta a Shakin" for Dad at the house. Charlie Rich used to do the same thing. Charlie Rich used to come and audition his songs at the house."

"They wanted Jud's opinion. Charlie Rich would be out performing somewhere and we were in Florence. And he'd come back through there after his show on Saturday night. He'd come and he'd sleep in his car. He wouldn't call the house early. He'd be down on Main Street, and he'd call. Jud wouldn't be up, but I would. And he'd say 'What time does Jud get up? I slept in the car last night and I wanted to come by and play a ditty, a little ditty I'm working on.' And he'd come by the house and play the ditty he was working on. Nobody else had heard it yet. He wanted Jud's opinion. And that's when we had a bird, and it drove him nuts. He was doing his little whistling and carrying on when Charlie was playing. One time Charlie said, 'Me or that bird – one of us has got to go.'"

"That bird spoke a lot," Jud, Jr. narrated. "Dad had bought him from Red Pierce who had had a bar, and this bird was at the bar for several years. And there were all those drunks sitting giving him incredible phrases. We had to cover him up anytime anyone came over. I don't even want to repeat all of the things he would say. He had an incredible vocabulary. We'll leave it at that."

"The Memphis Recording Service was started primarily for those people would often record things for posterity, like weddings or the eulogy at funerals. *We record anything, anywhere, anytime.* That was the motto of the business. And the other part, the music, came along as a natural thing to record these people. They were rental clients. They would remote to the weddings or whatever and then come back and burn acetate discs for them. So usually people would come in to rent the facility. These early musicians like B.B. King and Howlin' Wolf, they were recorded and released through a connection with Leonard Chess in Chicago. So those things like 'Rocket 88' were licensed in a deal," Jud Jr. explained.

"But this is where he got fascinated with sound. He would go out live and record these big bands that would come through and play. Sam was a genius of sound. When he built that studio he was just so far ahead of his time. That's where he said he got the idea of rock 'n' roll. He said he would notice when the big band would play and they would have a solo and they would step out, just three or four instruments, and everybody would get real quiet and sometimes they would stop dancing and listen to the little solo part and then applaud and go back to dancing. And he thought, *Wow, if that little part was so intense, that's all you need.* That's when he told me he first got into music," Rose revealed. "Before that, he was just interested in radio and recording."

"What people don't realize is that this was a two-man operation. Sam was as good as anybody in the studio and Jud was better than anybody on the road. He could promote; he was the best promoter. He and Sam were a good team. Anybody in the business back at that time would tell you the same thing," Dean affirmed.

"Sam knew all of the peculiarities of sound and the dynamics of a room. But another thing he knew was when to get out of the way." Rose construed. "They could encourage a person to get the best sound that they could get. Waylon Jennings told me one time that usually a producer wants you to be yourself so much that it comes off contrived. So it ended being not your best. The thing they did was making you so comfortable with yourself. Jud had a way of doing that to artists when they were onstage so that they could get things out of people live just like Sam could in the studio. They could get people comfortable enough with whom they were, and help them realize how they were unique without trying to make them be like anybody else. They helped you be comfortable with that even if everybody else said it sucked. Many places I've read, and I've heard from Jud and Dean, how much Jud believed in Jerry Lee and Elvis, and everybody said how much more he believed in Elvis than Sam did as far as the potential. You've just got to get Elvis comfortable with what he's singing and he could sing anything. Let him find what he wants to sing and let him do it until he gets it right. That was a characteristic I saw in both of them. They made people feel good about themselves. There were no preconceived notions about any standard you had to meet. Because of that, they brought out the best. I think that's why Jud could find this talent because he could find those people who had that courage. Most people talk about how different Sam and Jud were because they have really different personalities but that was the thread I saw between them. I think how wonderful it must have been to be a musical artist in a time when nobody was doing what you did and to have somebody tell you that what was in your soul, and what you were expressing in your music was great… and that they were going to help you find an audience for this."

"They would go into a big organization, a big publishing house, and Sam would go in, go the president of the company, talk to him a long time and leave. Jud would go in, and at that time the elevator would have elevator operators… and Jud would go in and talk to them. He would go and take the counter girls and their boyfriends out to dinner that night and make friends with them. He would go up to anybody, didn't matter," said Dean.

"Being the people person that he was," said Jud, Jr., "he would go in and establish good feelings about SUN Records because he was the ambassador, he was taking care of the little guys, he was really pushing it. Even when he was not on the road, when a SUN record came in, it was looked at. It was that branding, that association; it was a good feeling. There was a positive spin about a new SUN record."

"One release of Jerry Lee's was not doing anything, so Jud called Dick Clark. He knew all of the top people but he did not ignore the lower echelon. Anyway, he got with Dick Clark and those people and they worked up a deal with Beechnut Chewing Gum, it was one of the biggest records they ever had with Jerry called, "Breathless". If you saved so many Beechnut wrappers and sent them in you'd get a free record. They worked out that deal and it sold more records than you could imagine. I think that was the first corporate interactive advertisement for an artist," Jud, Jr. surmised. "They were doing things with Dick Clark that had never been done before. The thing is people would never forget him because he was so flamboyant. He would make it a point to know everybody in the room before he left. He knew Jack Dempsey and Jimmy Durante, too. One of the first things he did was travel with the black artists because in those days there were no hotels for black people to stay in. And with the black artists, not only did they not have hotels, but they didn't have restaurants where they could go in and get something to eat in the South. So Jud knew people in these little towns that he could get food for the guys. He'd take Rufus Thomas, Bobby Bland, B.B. King, Jackie Brenston, Ike Turner and take care of them on the road. They'd have to get them on the road for people to see them so they'd want to buy the records. Well in '53, he created the first tour bus out of a school bus and people said he was crazy. He would pull up at the record distributorships and he'd have a steward on the bus with a white dinner jacket and tie serving drinks and hors d'oeuvres."

"You remember when they opened Phillips Studio, not SUN. When that building opened, they had a big party. Everything was out on the roof. They had pink champagne and everything. One of the biggest distributors – I think it was from Chicago – anyway it was owned by two black guys. And they could have bought out a lot of these people down here that were so snooty with them. They could have bought them out with their petty cash. All of these distributors were invited and it was a big deal. We were going to have this party on the roof and then they made reservations at some restaurants afterwards. Anyway, these guys could have bought the restaurant, but those people wouldn't even let the black distributors come in. There was a big bunch of them stopping them at the door. So Jud and I went out and got the keys from Buster Williams to his office. He had a real nice office at his Plastic Products record pressing plant, and we called and had it catered – a party just for us at Buster Williams' office," Dean said, "and we just had dinner with them."

"That was one of the big innovations back when they had black artists that needed to go somewhere to play, when they couldn't get them in there, couldn't get food for them and they couldn't get accommodations. That management started with SUN before Elvis and Johnny Cash. They were a good partnership because Jud understood these guys and so did Sam, because they were from a little town in Alabama and they came to the big city. There were all these artists who were coming from Arkansas, from Louisiana, from Mississippi and these were guys that understood and said it's going to be okay. It didn't take a lot for people to be happy in those days. You were happy if you got good food and something to wear that you looked decent in and you had a car where you could get around. The needs were very basic in those days. What's interesting about all of these people, other than the Rock 'n' Roll Trio, was that they were all from someplace else. So when people talk about Memphis music, this is just where the recording studio was. These aren't Memphis people doing this. They wanted to establish the sound early on. Like Carl Perkins was the first writer, both the music and the lyrics. Elvis didn't do that. Jerry Lee didn't do it. The artists that were here that created Memphis music, they really got it from other artists who brought their style here. So that's why people claim that Memphis created this music out of nothing," Rose contended. "It was a melting pot, what every individual had to offer, knowing again that there weren't any standards or framework because you had people from everywhere. Nobody was trained – no one read music. They were just making it up as they went along - same with Jud trying to figure out all the stuff about publishing. Nobody had publishing companies outside of CBS or RCA. So there they are making up an industry."

"Learning the industry from the Bihari Brothers?" I asked.

"They learned distribution from the Schwarz Brothers, from Heilicher which was in Minneapolis, and Sid Talmadge in Los Angeles. Stan Lewis was the distributor in New Orleans; he had Jewel and Paula Records. Big conglomerates like RCA had their own distribution. Rose said something that was very important that I don't want to get lost: that Carl was the first one to come in with his vocal abilities, musical abilities, *and* his songs. Now in the 50s you were on the backside of phasing out what's called Tin Pan Alley, where there were people called writers and that's all that they did. They'd just get wind of somebody and they'd write for them whether it was a big band or solo artist signed to RCA or Capitol or Decca. This was the beginning of the end for the big song because then it was okay for somebody to write their own song."

"Johnny Bragg from The Prisonaires was in the penitentiary at Nashville. Jud went up there a lot and I went with him," Dean recollected. "He showed me where the electric chair was. Anyway Johnny Bragg and the Prisonaires did 'Walking in the Rain'. Didn't Johnny Bragg have like three lifetime sentences? At least. And he was in prison there. The first thing he did was 'Walking in the Rain' and it was doing pretty good. Jud would tell how well it was doing and he'd say 'You know what, Mr. Jud, I've got a great future in this record business, don't I?' With three life sentences in prison! The Prisonnaires were just playing locally in the prisons, and Jud would go up there a lot of times because he knew the warden. Johnny Bragg, I hadn't seen him for forty years, he came down to Memphis a while back, and I walked up to him and said 'You don't remember me but…' and he said, 'Oh I do. I couldn't ever forget you,' and he hugged me. I'd changed a lot, but he had too. He got pardoned before he died. They would go out and make money on shows they would let them do, and then they would put it in the prison fund so they could buy things for the prisoners. They came down to Memphis to record. They came on the bus with a bunch of guards. I was in the studio when they recorded. The guards were standing around. But everything went just fine."

"There was the period of time when the artists began transitioning from Memphis to Nashville, and I remember Carl Perkins telling me the difference between SUN Records and going to Nashville. The first thing he noticed was that it stopped being fun and started being business. He said going over to SUN was just like going over to somebody's house. You could bring a pint and sit there and record as long as it took to get it right. Nobody criticized you or told you how to do anything. The most that Sam would say was 'Why don't you try this again?' or 'Why don't you try it that way?' 'That was working well.' But when he went to Nashville, the first thing he remembered was that it was like a business. When SUN was totally gone, as Carl told me, that's when it all got citified. I asked him what he meant by 'citified' and he said, 'You know like a business with rules. Before then it was like a big family.' I think that was something that, even after SUN, at Phillips Recording and at Stax and at Hi, there was still that simpler community, that camaraderie with the musicians because they were still unschooled, and everybody would just sit there until they got it right," Rose said, "and contribute what they could unselfishly. At least for a while, until Stax was taken over by CBS, they still had this sense of creating something. Let's create a sound – something that feels good. Now they had that at Muscle Shoals, too. The musicians at Muscle Shoals were more sophisticated. They had, like Dean, gone to college and studied music in school. They had developed their craft. But the people at SUN weren't."

"Charlie Rich was the most trained musician at SUN," Jud, Jr. disclosed. "Even after Sun folded, there was still that feeling of community that Memphis music had that still was at Muscle Shoals. When people went down there to record they were still trying to recapture that kind of sound. It was the last stronghold to do it, because everybody else wanted to make it slick and professional. But at Muscle Shoals they still had that feeling of wanting to create a record. Of course there were several studios down there – Fame, Ric Hall, all of them. And that was the next layer of it before it was all gone. Naturally people want to get more professional, naturally people want to learn their craft, naturally you want to grow and polish, and it was just a place in time that was what it was. It went on to be something else. If you look at that, Ric Hall, Buddy Killen and myself all went to the same high school. Buddy was in the music business, he was producing, but he got into publishing and he built one of the biggest publishing companies in the history of the business, Tree International. He's another one that learned on the fly. He learned as he went."

"You did engineering and producing, too Jud?" I asked.

"Mostly engineering. I did a lot of commercials, a lot of Hanna-Barbara music tracks for their cartoons. I went out to LA and got started on a small label called Dimension. Then I was hired as the first studio engineer of a studio called The Sound Factory. In about a three-year period I had 50 chart records, as an engineer.

"We remodeled here about '67/'68. All those acoustics that are in there now, we did most of the labor along with two other carpenters – like all the drum booths. Putting all the burlap over the fiberglass, this itched to death 'til we got used to that. Another thing about that building you may or may not know is that the building is as acoustically sound proof as the studio itself. Its outer wall is 12-inch concrete blocks. There is a 6-inch air lock and then there's another full 12-inch block wall on a separate foundation and not touching, so it is unbelievably soundproof. 'Lonely Weekends' is one of the hit records recorded in there, and 'Third Rate Romance'. Jerry Jeff Walker's original 'Mr. Bo Jangels was cut here, and all Sam the Sham's records were cut here. Robert Plant has come in there and done a lot of stuff on his own. Most of Jerry Lee's *Last Man Standing* was cut through there over a period of time.

"There are no parallel walls in the studio", Jud explained. "Down at the end of the hall there is something that people much younger than me would never know anything about. It's a legitimate echo chamber with all sorts of configurations with three speakers that you can use to send the signal. There are two or three different microphones that you can use in different patterns. So how you send the signal in there is faster than it falls and it just bounces with all the different angles. You got a choice between your send and your return as to which mic returns or which speakers send. Nobody has a live chamber now. Only thing most of these guys know is when they see a button on there that says 'echo' and they turn it. In studio B is one of the very first AG 440 8-tracks."

"I think one of the things that made Stax records have such a great sound was that the studio was a movie theater, and they had those big speakers. The motion picture sound came out of them. When I was growing up we used to go in there and watch the movies on Saturday afternoon at the Capital Theater," Rose said.

"Well, what about Colonel Tom Parker?" I inquired.

"There are different kinds of promotion. There is promotion that is genuine and caring and getting out there and doing things, and then you got your carnival barkers," Jud, Jr. replied. "Where you buy the ticket and that's the last they care about seeing you. And Colonel Tom was a carnival barker. It was just the art of the deal."

"With Jud, I think he really wanted an artist to get out, and in his heart he wanted to support the artist and to know what they were about to experience – the whole thing. With Colonel Parker it was like a game," Rose augured. "I remember one of the things that he did was out at the old Fairgrounds. He was going to let the people come in and park. It was a free concert, and everybody sat there on their cars watching the free concert. It was free, but on the way out it said, *Two Dollars to Park*. But you were already fenced in!

"We got ourselves a hotel and Dad rushed over to this park out of town where there was supposed to be a matinee. We got over there and there wasn't anybody there, and Dad said, 'Well I thought this was supposed to be a big event.' And Colonel Tom said, 'Well I haven't got the people here yet. Just go back and then I'll call with you when we're ready.' And Dad said, 'Tom, it doesn't work this way. This is news here.' And the Colonel said 'Ah, hell. It ain't news 'til I say it's news. I'll get them there. It was just his way of doing things. He'd have the National Guard come out for crowd patrol before he got the crowd. And he'd say 'Well, you got to time it. If you get the crowd there before crowd control, then you're going to have a big mess.'

"He was fun. Colonel Parker was fun," Rose insisted. "Colonel Tom had that house out in Palm Springs, and he decided that he was going to rent it out for corporate retreats. So he invites me out there to spend the weekend to see the house, and he wants me to write it up in a magazine. Colonel Parker calls our hotel and said to me, 'You've come on the right weekend. I'm moving to Las Vegas, and I'm selling everything. You can buy anything you want.' And I said, "Yeah, like I've got enough money to buy anything I want?' He said, 'Well, who else is there?' Greg, the magazine manager was out there, so he said, 'Let me talk to Greg.' And I heard him say, 'You what?! How much?! Ah hell man, I'm not going to pay you that.' He gets off the phone and he says, 'He wants me to buy back the piano I gave him!' Then Colonel Tom calls back in a little bit and he says, 'I'm going to give you a tip…you remember those Burma-Shave signs that used to be out on the highway? Well, I tell you what to do. You know the Peabody's got that famous parade of ducks in the lobby. You need to get the Peabody duck signs going from the airport to the Peabody Hotel.' I said, 'Well, that's really not our market, the Burma-Shave crowd.' He said, 'you know, I think you guys need to lighten up a little bit.' Colonel Parker's style was just very corny, not into the polish. And a lot of people were critical because they thought it made Elvis' image too much of a carnival. The Colonel was always thinking promotion. He was another person that was trying to kick off an industry. And there was all this negative publicity about how much he took of Elvis' salary. People didn't realize how much he did for Elvis though. He did everything for all phases of his career. So instead of having five people were working for him, he had Colonel Parker. Even though Elvis had RCA and the William Morris Agency, Colonel Parker coordinated everything with the label. He was the wheel and they were the spokes. He made all of the decisions."

"I've heard he made some decisions that kept away some of the best directors in Hollywood?" I interjected.

"Well that's a whole different thing: working to make Elvis a movie star. I'm not saying he didn't make some big mistakes. But Elvis did have a number one record 30 years after he died. So Col. Tom did know something about branding and creating an image. That's what he knew how to do. There are a lot of dubious things that he could have done better, that he didn't. He knew branding before other people knew what branding really was. Elvis respected the fact that he had his best interests at heart and knowing where his market was and keeping him on top. After he got back from the army, I think Elvis thought his career was over. So when the Colonel made decisions he didn't really like, he was still loyal. It goes back to the cultural values we were talking about. People in our generation were fiercely loyal. They're loyal to a fault. I think that was one of Elvis' biggest problems, he was loyal to a fault. You make a commitment with somebody and then you honor it. And often you honor it for life when you shouldn't. I think he got locked into the Colonel and that was that."

"I think there were two occasions when people around Elvis were trying to get him to break with the Colonel. And Elvis told them no. It was the deal he made and he was sticking with it," Jud, Jr. affirmed.

"That was the difference between Jud and the Colonel," Rose added. "Jud was quick to say, 'You need somebody else. This is who you need to bring in to help.' He knew what his limitations were, and Colonel Parker wanted to do it all. Jud saw himself as somebody who organized a team because he wanted the artist to do well, even if he didn't make as much. He knew when he was out of his league. He knew when it was time to sell SUN. He knew when it was time that he couldn't go any further with it. And the Colonel didn't have that attitude.

"It got to be such a joke about the Colonel creating the news. I remember when I was in college and Elvis got back from the army for the press conference, and Dad called me at the payphone down in the lobby at Memphis State. He said, 'Well the Colonel just called. Elvis is getting ready for the press conference.' When I was home, he would call either Mother or me to tell Dad, 'He better head on that way'…and that was always a big joke for him because he would always come last because Dad covered the national news and everybody else covered local. He was the card-carrying cameraman for ABC, CBS and NBC, and he was a freelancer. And so whoever would call him first would get the story.

"What were the places as a teenager you went to – and the places that were off limits?""I guess from the time I was in junior high, when you're old enough to go somewhere by yourself, about twelve years old then… it's about the time children really get into radio and music and everything. We were too young to date in those days, so you had to go everywhere as a group. So the things that were to do: there were ballgames, nobody much went to baseball or basketball games in those days. It was football. Skating rinks were a big thing, more so than bowling. People tried that for a while but it didn't catch on. I think people liked skating because you didn't have to concentrate as much, and you could just go wild and carry on. We would have dances at the high school auditorium, and that's where the local bands would come play. In the afternoons, the big things to do were to go up to the radio stations. It was up at Hotel

Chisca at WHBQ.

"So we'd go up so we could see the artist interviewed. Most of the kids couldn't go and see them where they played, but we could see them be interviewed. I met Dewey Phillips playing records at Kress variety store downtown across the street from Goldsmith's. There was a Dance Party with Wink Martindale that was later when the TV stations happened. Then on the weekends in summer, we would go to the Black & White department store on Main St. where they would have emceed events like "Queen for a Day". We'd go to Clearpool, that's where the Eagle's Nest was. Elvis would perform out there. People didn't have a lot of swimming pools like they do now, and they didn't have them at the community center. But some community centers in town had large ones. This was after the polio scare so they closed a lot of the local pools and opened a few larger ones like at Clearpool out at Winchester and Lamar, so they could control the health issue.

"Schools were so diversified back in the '50s. It was the culture of the time. You had the girls' Catholic schools, the boys' Catholic schools, the Jewish schools. Southside High School was for people who became firemen or policemen. You had Central High, which was where people went if they were going to go to college. You had Tech High School, which was where you went if you were going into radio or electronics, or auto repair, and Humes, which is where Elvis went, was for people who became factory workers. There was a purpose for every high school. Then you had Mann private, which was where guys went if they played in a band and had to have a flexible schedule. This was the cool place, where rowdy people went like Charlie Feathers, Rodney Smith, and all these super-cool people. They were really dropouts."

"Charlie Feathers was in the rowdy crowd?"

"He was in that crowd. He was just weird I thought. That was just my feeling. One of the things we used to get into trouble for was sneaking into drive-ins in the trunk. People didn't date and go out a lot in '58 was because most of the people didn't have cars. You would have to go two or three or four couples at a time to pay for the gas. We'd go to like Leonard's Drive-In and turn up the speakers and dance outside. The drive-ins you had were The Jungle Gardens, Gilley's, Ray's, and Leonard's. The Jungle Garden was interesting because it really was for an older crowd. They were into brown bagging and making out. When you drove up, there were hedges like six feet high. There were hedges all around the place and tree arbors were in there. It was a parking lot, I don't remember it being paved, I think it was dirt, but there were trees all over. The big thing in those days was not drinking beer. It was drinking Coca-Cola with whiskey in it. So the girls would put the whiskey in their purse, they would go in there, and then you could put the alcohol in your Coke. So the Jungle Garden was pretty risqué. You didn't want people to see you go to the Jungle Garden. People would talk about you. You'd get a reputation. And the police would cruise around there.

"There weren't a lot of places that would stay open late at night. There was a supper club called The Silver Slipper that was a real neat place, too that would get the older crowd. Before they had liquor by the drink, people would go to the liquor store or the bootlegger or whatever. If somebody were old enough to get the alcohol and be able to get a car and be able to sneak it in somewhere, then they'd be real popular. Like The Jungle Garden was a younger crowd right on the edge. Like Parkway, twelve miles out, was the city limits. That's where the Silver Slipper was. Early on it was a group mentality. Then they had the Overton Park Shell, which was the family entertainment place for music. When Elvis played the shell, July 30, 1954, we happened to be out there."

The session broke for a few minutes in Studio A. While they were taking a breather, I thought I'd slip in the control room to see what Roland Janes was doing behind the board... and try pestering him with my insatiable probing.

"Roland, you came here from Brookings, Arkansas, right?"

"That's right," replied Roland as he was spinning off a tape onto an imposing Ampex 2-track machine. "It's a small town in northeast Arkansas."

"That's a couple hundred miles from Memphis, then."

"About 125."

"And then you went north and grew up in St. Louis?"

"That's right." While the massive tape reel was spinning indolently in real time, Roland tilted way back in his sprung office chair and folded small, nimble hands over his ample girth.

"During the early part of the Second World War, a lot of families moved to the city to work in the factories, etc., and my family did that. So consequently I ended up in St. Louis, Missouri – which was about 250 miles north."

"What drew you to Memphis?"

"I really don't know. I don't remember having a particular reason for it. I guess it was some kind of spiritual guidance, but I really can't say. I don't really know how I ended up in Memphis. I came here before I enlisted in the service and I liked it so well when I got out of the service, I returned to Memphis."

"How has Memphis changed?"

"Well, primarily in size. It was basically a really nice, big country town, and now it's actually growing into a metropolitan city."

"Was there really music in the air when you first came to Memphis?"

"Music was in the air, very much so I think, throughout the South, but really in Memphis. The beginning of my music career, as much as of a career as I've had, was through Jack Clement, who was a musician-singer-songwriter himself, and he had decided to become involved in production. So at the point that I met him he was involved in producing a record on Billy Lee Riley and he asked me if I would like to get involved, and I naturally did. That was the beginning of it. That was sometime in 1956."

"Did a band called The Spitfires come out of this association?"

"Well, that came later on. The Spitfires, that was a one-record artist deal. That was actually the Little Green Men in disguise. We did that from time to time – we'd cut a session and maybe get it released under a different name. Primarily that was Jimmy Van Eaton, Billy Lee Riley, myself, Martin Willis, and the basic Little Green Men band. In reality, my first love was country music and the early 50s pop music. And by that I mean Les Paul, Patti Page – that kind of a thing. So when we got involved in cutting rock 'n' roll records I had to come up with some kind of style that was more fitting, rather than the more or less country-style that I played. So I developed that sort of a style, and it's been very good to me."

"You played guitar with Bill Justis, and you played the major guitar part on the Bill Justis hit, 'Raunchy'."

"Well, Bill Justis was what we referred to a 'schooled musician', and most of us were not. We learned the hard way, so to speak, and by experience. But Bill was a schooled musician. He was also a very talented man; he was a great arranger. He did arrangements for other big band orchestra leaders, and he had his own big band and they played jazz or whatever – they played many styles of music. He was really a well-known person in the South when he went to work for SUN Records cutting rock 'n' roll records, which was totally foreign to him at the time. I was fortunate to work on several record dates with Bill and travel some with him on the road. But, it was kind of an unusual combination: basic country musicians and rock 'n' roll musicians and the big band jazz influence. His regular guitar player was a fella named Sid Manker, who was a great guitarist. When we traveled, it was basically just the three of us, Sid and myself and Bill, and we used house musicians. Now, in his regular big band he had probably 12, 15, 20 people, just depended. But the traveling we did was for the rock 'n' roll-type shows, and we used house musicians."

"So he had a double life, in a sense, playing rock 'n' roll shows on the road and then doing his big band performance in country clubs and proms and things like this?"

"He did. He later went into arranging – like in Hollywood he arranged music for several movies and for a lot of hit records by Dean Martin and Frank Sinatra and people like that."

"You played with Jerry Lee Lewis, too."

"He came to Memphis to try to make records, and in the process of doing that we did cut tapes on Jerry Lee. While he was waiting for the record to come out, he worked some as a staff musician in the studio and he worked some jobs with us, with the Little Green Men, but he wasn't a regular in our band. He worked on a couple of things with Carl Perkins, Hayden Thompson, and a few other artists. I worked on most of Jerry's records for the first several years that he was on SUN, and as did J. M. Van Eaton and as did Billy Riley. We, as a band, we developed into kind of the staff band, and we worked behind a lot of the artists. Lot of the artists had their own band; lot of them didn't. Some of them, they would use maybe one or all of us along with their band. With Jerry Lee, from the very beginning, Jimmy Van Eaton and I worked on all of his records, just about. I did work on the road with Jerry for a little while. I think we all kind of came from a similar background so we kind of knew – we could almost read each other's mind. Jerry could look at Jimmy Van Eaton and Jimmy could kinda tell what Jerry was going to do next, and he would play something to complement that and Jerry may do something to complement what Jimmy did, and then I fell in the middle there somewhere. You can tell by the endings on some of those records, everybody was trying to get in the last lick. But it was very loose and very exciting and a lot of fun."

"Well, it's this loose, dynamic feel that people admire and I think that's, well, missing in a lot of the music that's being made today. Some of the musicians working now look back to this music and they hear this looseness, this abandon, this communication between musicians and wonder themselves, *how can we get this?*"

"Well, it's very difficult to get it today because the recording is done differently today. Then everything was done live – the vocal, everything – because we didn't have multi-track recording in those days. Everything was done on mono. We had to get it right, on the spot. At the same time, the people recording us like Jack Clement and Sam Phillips, they had the vision to allow us the freedom of doing it the way we felt. And we'd do it over and over until we got it right, or the way that it was acceptable. They just allowed us to have fun with it, and I don't think that happens today. Everybody kinda relies on fixin' it in the mix, so to speak. You know, go ahead and get through with it and then fix it later. Probably if we tried to cut some records like some other people are cuttin' today we would be as unsuccessful as they are trying to accomplish what we did. So it's an attitude and I think it's relative to the era and the people you were working with. You can never recapture anything exactly the way it was... and maybe you shouldn't. I don't know.

"Now on a live show our intention was to play it the same way as the record, but we weren't hung up on that type of thing. Our live performances were just like our studio performances. We were determined to enjoy what we were doing, and the people would get into the act, and we may do it totally different than the record. We may do it three or four times as long, or if it wasn't happening maybe even shorten it. Everything was spontaneous – the live performances and the recording – in those days. I think that's kind of missing today. Everything's too orchestrated and it's fun to look at, but there's something missing in today's performances. I think it's a lot more exciting to just not know what's going to happen next."

"There's a rumor that Jerry Lee Lewis never did more than two takes on any song in the studio."

"Well, that's not necessarily true. The majority of our recordings were done in a very few takes and especially the good ones, the ones that really happened. There were a few things that we probably tried too hard on, and those generally didn't do as well. It seems with Jerry Lee that you either got it or you didn't, pretty quick. But the majority of his records were one, two, or three take recordings and some of the things that maybe didn't get released at all, or maybe didn't do as well, were some of things we worked the hardest on. I think the main ingredient was to just *have fun* doing it, and Jerry Lee was great at that. When he came to the studio, Jerry would just start playing a song. No one knew what he was going to play or anything, we just fell in behind him and tried to complement what he was doing. I think he was the real leader, and he's so spontaneous. We just happened to feel his music well enough to be able fall in behind him and complement what he was doing and get away with it. It was all fun."

"What do you think about his ability as an interpreter and stylist?"

"I think he's the absolute greatest in the world that I've ever worked with, and probably the greatest that anybody ever has. I think the man never really realized just how talented he was. I think he could have done anything that he wanted to do, musically. I think he, himself, never realized just how wonderfully talented he is."

"Over at the Fairgrounds awhile back Jerry Lee was playing an afternoon show on some festival, and I was off to the side of the stage talking with Myra Gale, Jerry's third. Frankly I was surprised to see her there, but she's still a *huge* fan. After the gig, Tarp, that crazy drummer in Jerry's band, said everybody was getting together over at Jerry Lee's offices, and invited me to drop by. Jerry had rented an office suite in a little strip mall near downtown just south of Union Avenue and Manassas, so I rode down there on my motorbike. The rooms were already crowded with loyal fans, festival hangers-on, and a smattering of high-heeled socialites with their beaus in tow. After some time waiting, Jerry Lee and his entourage of running dogs finally arrived. When Jerry entered the room, he stopped, looked at everyone cross-eyed and said, *I'm gonna shoot the first son of a bitch that moves!* Then he ambled over to his desk and sat down. His henchmen gathered around him. 'J.W. listen,' he said, 'go out to the Caddy and bring in the Thompson.' J.W. reappeared toting a Thompson submachine gun, and placed it on the desk in front of Jerry. As soon as Jerry picked up the gun, everybody hit the floor. Jerry Lee proceeded to spray all four walls and the ceiling in a wide swathe of roaring gunfire that discharged about 900 rounds of smoking .45 caliber bullets. It only lasted about 45 seconds, but apparently the dentist next door had a few bullets come zinging through the thin walls of his office, and called the police. When a couple MPD officers arrived, Jerry Lee was still seated at his desk with his arms folded staring glibly over the machine gun that lay before him. The lawmen looked at each other, then at Jerry and said, 'Now Jerry you're gonna have to behave yourself, or next time we get a call about this, we're gonna have to take that pop-gun away from you.' Jerry Lee didn't blink an eye, the officers left, and the party resumed. But that day on stage and *every* time I've seen him, I've been absolutely floored. I think he's magnificent."

"He interprets a song better than just about anybody. Working on the road with Jerry, we worked a lot of package deals. Shows then that there would be 18, 20 acts on it, and the biggest names in the business like Buddy Holly, Jackie Wilson, Chuck Berry, the Everly Brothers, on and on and on. After the show was over, Jerry would sit down at the piano and start playin' and singin', and all these stars would gather around and just idolize him. That's how incredible he was. It used to amaze me. I mean, I've never seen anyone that could top him."

"I used to go out to Hernando's Hideaway real late on Monday nights, 'cause on the weekends the cigarette smoke was so dense in there it would burn out your eyes in two minutes. Well, Jerry would come out unannounced and sit in with the house band – Robert Tinsley and the Southern Knights. Maybe there would be six people in the club, and he'd play to each one of us."

"Oh yeah. Jerry is a very unique person. He'll play just as hard for six people as he will for a hundred thousand. Money was never really the object with Jerry. He just truly loves music – as much or more than anyone I've ever known. And he loves people. Jerry Lee Lewis is really a great, great person. He's so much greater than people realize. There're two sides of Jerry. I happen to know the really good side."

"You had a fabulous song called, "Mountain of Love" that you…"

"Yeah. Eventually I kind of got tired of working on the road and I decided to settle back down and try to get into production work. Consequently, Billy Riley and myself and a friend of ours named Vaughan formed a record label, and one of our early recordings was called, 'Mountain of Love', which was a tremendous hit by an artist, Harold Norman. That was on our

Hernando's Hideaway Photo: E. Baffle c. 1979

own label called, Rita Records."

"Did you work on a recording of 'White Silver Sands' at one time?"

"Yes I did, as a sideman. The artist was a gentleman by the name of Dave Gardner, who actually was a stand-up comedian, but he also sang as part of his nightclub act. Some people here in Memphis formed a label called O.J. Records and he was one of their artists. One of the songs we recorded was 'White Silver Sands', which turned out to be a standard."

"I remember growing up how popular Brother Dave Gardner was as a comedian in the South – terribly funny and *everybody* loved his kinky humor."

"Well, he became really well known and cut several hit comedy albums, for RCA, I believe, but this was after "White Silver Sands.""

"Later, you started your own recording studio, Sonic. In fact, this was the first recording studio I ever walked into in my life. You were recording a blues artist, Johnny Woods, that day."

"I opened a little studio and I did business primarily with newcomers and people that maybe didn't have a whole lot of money to spend. It was kind of a stepping-stone – a first step recording experience for a lot of people. A lot of people did their absolutely first recording in that studio. I was in that studio for 12 years, and I had a lot of great times in there. Cut a few chart records, and got a lot of people headed off, hopefully, in the right direction in the music business."

"That was up the street on Madison Avenue at Belvedere. Did you record the hit song 'Scratchy' there, with Travis Womack?"

"Yes, Travis is a great guitarist. He is now the music director for Little Richard's band. He was, like 16 years old and the fastest guitar player I'd ever seen – a great guitar player, and a good little singer. I took a likin' to Travis. I really admired his ability, and we did cut a chart record called 'Scratchy'. It was an instrumental record. And I think Travis was 16 at the time."

Jud Phillips, Sr. Photo: Jud Phillips, Jr. 1961

"What was it like working with the team of Sam Phillips and Jud Phillips?"

"Well, it was a wonderful experience. I owe everything that I know in the music business to those two gentlemen. They're both great in their own right. Sam was the producing part of the team and Jud was the promotion, and he was beyond all doubt the greatest promotion man in the world. I used to marvel at his work. He had a *large* part in the success story of SUN Records. A lot larger than many people realize. Jud had the same charisma and charm in the promotion area that Jerry Lee had as a musician. I've seen Jud gather around him some people that had the name for being great promotion men, or great radio people or whatever, and always Jud would be in the center stage. They would be gathered around him, just hanging on every word, just as I would. He just had a charisma and a charm that nobody else had. I think one of his great secrets was the fact that he loved everybody. He didn't talk to just the top people, he talked to the smallest person all the way up to the largest person within an organization. He spoke and felt equally about all of them, I mean, the same. Like, if he went into a record distributor, he was as friendly to the person working on the desk as he was to the person that owned the company. What he said you could believe. He was totally honest in his dealings with them and if he told you something, you knew you could count on it. And everyone just loved him. This included people like Steve Allen, Dick Clark, everybody. Everybody loved Jud."

"What in your mind distinguishes Memphis music from other music centers like Nashville or Los Angele?"

"Of course Los Angeles and Nashville both are highly successful, we know about their success. I think Memphis was a more loose location. The music is less inhibited, as are the musicians. I think that's the basic difference. I think Nashville and Hollywood are more business-as-usual. In Memphis you never know what to expect."

"The way I hear it there's a certain rawness in a lot of Memphis music, yet a refined and lazy sound, a little behind the beat – it's not forced, but has an unbridled power and an uninhibited quality that's pleasing at the same time. It sounds like a meeting of heightened harmonies and contrasting rhythms, you might say."

"I think you've answered your own question better than I could answer it."

The reunion sessions seemed to be not only a concentrated effort in recording the elusive spirit of an primal era, but seemed to be evolving into a quest for origins, and how things happened the way they did. Sitting at the piano bench on the floor of Studio A was Rose alongside Paul Burlison, guitarist of the Rock 'n' Roll Trio. Paul and I had a common interest beyond music, a compulsion, in fact, in our attraction to Ford Thunderbirds. One day Paul had invited me out to his house in South Memphis, to show me his '59 model black T-Bird with red interior that he used to drive to gigs. The beast was parked in the weeds in front of his shop, even in its dereliction still looking sleek and rakish. Knowing the inquisitive nature of Rose exceeded even my own, I edged closer to overhear their conversation.

"Now exactly where did you move to...?"

"We moved onto Jefferson St., right there at Jefferson and Dunlap – a few blocks just east and north from Phillips Studio.

"So, what was it like...?"

"Yeah, well I'll tell you, it was different, completely different back in '37. Back then, you walk down Main Street on Saturdays and it'd just be so full you just could hardly walk down the street; so many people would be walking down Main Street. Mr. Peanut used to walk up and down in front of the Peanut place and you'd get peanut samples, and he had this great big ol' peanut-looking hat on his head. Mr. Crump would be always walkin' up and down the street up there shakin' hands with people and tippin' his hat to the ladies and pattin' the babies on the cheeks. I remember that they had this ham bar there they called the Orange Bar. They had the best ham sandwiches and the best orange juice that I've put my mouth on, I guess. 'Cause I didn't get much along about that time, so to get one of those sandwiches was really a treat. It was right next to the Strand Theater. We'd walk all the way uptown just to go to the Strand on Saturdays. We had to cut the grass all morning with a push mower – no motor – a *push* mower. My brothers and I would cut the grass, and my mother would give us a quarter a piece so we could go uptown and go up to the Strand Theater and see two features, a serial, and two or three cartoons. It'd be after dark when we got home.

"What serials...?"

"Yeah...*Deadwood Dick* and *Dick Tracy*, *Green Hornet* with Kato, and later *Red Rider*. *Deadwood Dick* was one of my favorites. You had to go every week to see what happened, you know – *to be continued next week*. So all the kids would sit down in the front; always sit in the front, eat popcorn, throw it at each other. It was fun. It was completely different back in those days than it is now, because the black and white situation was just completely different, too."

"You ever been down on Beale Street back then?"

"Yeah, went down there a lot. I went down there a lot because they had a lot of guitars down in the pawnshops. I'd walk down there and look at the guitars and go in and this one particular guy would let me sit back there and play 'em. I'd sit back there for a long time playing the guitars. Beale Street was just full of black people. Both sides of the street were packed full then. Mostly just blacks, not many whites. Pantaze drug store was on the corner, ol' fruit market was on one corner. Home of the Blues was there, and right down the street in the alley was an old shoeshine stand – one of those double deckers where you sit up real high and they'd shine your shoes. The little jug bands were on every corner down through there. They'd play with the old jug and the stick and the string bass and washboards and stuff. Memphis Minnie would run up and down Beale Street playin' on every corner. Just work on this corner for a while and then move down the street playin' for the hat, you know. A cup, metal cup – they'd pass that cup around. You could smell fish fryin' and everybody was enjoyin' themselves and having a good time. Back in those days the crime wasn't anything like it is now. We'd go up there, stay 'til 10, 11:00 at night – we're just kids – and walk home. I would never, ever once be approached by anybody, never was threatened, or anything, back in those days."

"Do you remember going in the Home of the Blues record store?"

"Yeah, I used to go in there and play the blues. It was the only time I could hear blues. I couldn't take 'em home with me because some of the words were too suggestive back in those days, but I'd go in there and play 'em and listen to 'em. My mom wouldn't let me bring 'em home with me, but I'd go in and listen to 'em. I liked all the old blues, what we called *cocktail blues* back then – Muddy Waters and them. Of course I met Howlin' Wolf later on, but this was early. Before that there was a lot of jazz back then, like band stuff – kind of a mixture between Memphis and New Orleans-type stuff. It was soundin' good to me. 'Course I never listened to the words much, most of the time I just listened to the music. You'd walk in there...there'd be a long counter. They had records sittin' all around there with a little turntable. They did have some booths sittin' back in the back. I'd always sit right there at the far end of the counter and looked at the guy that worked there and I'd pick out something that I that want to hear and I could put it on this little turntable."

"Where did you get your first guitar, Paul?"

"I was ten. I bought it down on Beale in a pawnshop. I had a hole in my Sunday shoes and my mother gave me two dollars. You could get a good pair of shoes for $1.98. She gave me about two dollars to go downtown to get me a pair of shoes. So I walked uptown and went down Beale. Saw this little guitar hangin' up in the window there on a string and it had five dollars marked on it. I kept lookin' at that guitar and lookin' at it. So I went in the store and asked, 'Can I see that guitar?' He said, 'Sure'. So he took it down. He told me, 'Go over there behind that counter if you want to play it. Sit down over there and play it.' I played that thing for a long time. I must've sat for an hour. I didn't know how to play – my grandmother taught me two or three chords and I could play that, but that's about all. But the strings was up past the neck 'bout 3/4 of an inch. I said, 'I'll give you two dollars for the guitar.' He said, 'Oh, no kid, can't do that, at least four.' I said, 'I don't have but two bucks,' and he said, 'Well, pay me back two dollars. Go home, get two dollars, and come on back. I'll sell you the guitar for two more bucks.' I said, 'I can't do that. Listen, I'm spending my shoe money, now.' He said, 'You mean, your mamma gave you money to buy shoes and you're buyin' a guitar?' I said, 'That's right.' He said, 'She gonna tear your britches up when you get home.' I said, 'Yes, she probably will. I'm not gonna tell her right away. I'm gonna wait until it's the right time.' So he said, 'Well I still can't take two dollars for the guitar. I just can't do it.' I said, 'OK, I'm sorry, that's all I got.'

"So I walked out of the store and started up the street toward Main, and I went way up the street, and I heard a man; he came out on the sidewalk and he said, 'Hey kid, come here.' I went back down there and he said, 'You really want that guitar, don't you?' I said, 'More than anything.' He said, 'I will let you have it for two dollars, but I'm not gonna give you a case with it, is that OK?' – 'I don't care. I just want the guitar.'

"I took it home with me. It was an old Stella guitar. I kept that thing up on top of the house, I did. I'd throw it up on the house and hid it up there when my mother and dad was both working. My sister knew I had it, 'cause she was home during the day. When they would go to work, I'd get it out and play it around the house. She had some records and I'd put them on – 78 records and play 'em. Take my fingers and slow 'em down so I could hear what the record's doin'. Now we got delay, you push them back, start, stop, pause, and everything. Back then we didn't have anything to go by. No fuzztone, no effect boxes, no nothing. So we just had to listen what was on that record and it was goin' so fast, you had to slow it down to listen, even to the guitar. So I took my finger and drag it 'til I hear it. I'd hear something, and I'd play a track, figure it out – pull it down again. It took forever to learn it. But she got mad at me a couple of weeks after that. Told my daddy, my sister did, told my daddy – told my mamma, and my mamma told me, 'I'm gonna tell your daddy when he comes home, now. He'll probably give you a spanking.' I says, 'Well, if he has to, he has to, 'cause I wanted that guitar'. But when he came home that afternoon, he just said, 'You know, things are really tough right now.' This was during the Depression. He said, 'I'm surprised that you took that money and then didn't buy new shoes.' I said, 'I pushed cardboard in the bottom of my shoe, in the inside. That'll last me for a while, Dad. I keep putting cardboard in there.' It had a little round hole in it. So I said, 'But I keep 'em polished.' He said, 'if you want that thing that bad, I want you to learn to play it.' I said, 'I will.' So the next day when he came home from work I could play on one string the old song, 'I'm Just Here to get my Baby out of Jail' – *yes warden, I'm just gonna get my baby* – and he used to hum it and sing that song, my dad did. So I really knew that song.

"What year was that?'

"That was about '41, '42, 'cause the first song I started picking out was 'The Marine's Hymn'. That's the first song, besides 'I'm Just Here to Get my Baby'…"

"Did you go up to the shows?'

"Lightnin' Chance and Mike Roberts had a good band… a lot of time playin' upright bass that had a snare drum head mounted on it, and he'd play like Bill Black and slap the bass. But they would brush or hit that thing at the same time, just a thing like a drumhead on his bass. His name was Lightnin' Chance. He was from Love, Mississippi. Tony Censiola was playing accordion. Sonny James was playin' fiddle over there. He had different guests all the time. I used to go up there to the radio and listen to 'em a lot. They had a place there for people to sit and watch while it was broadcast live. Same with Al Burns, Bobby Knight, a blind fella, and he was on WMC along about that time, and Gene Steele was on WMC, the singing salesman."

"Do you think Elvis ever went up there?'

"Now he went to an Eddie Arnold show one night before he ever recorded – I saw him at the south side of the Cook Convention Center. My wife and I was goin' up the steps, and Elvis was comin' down the steps. He had been up in the balcony to the Eddie Arnold show, but

Goodwyn Institute

he was by his self. 'Cause I was workin' at Crown Electric Co. and he was at Crown so I knew him. We just spoke. You know as we walked by, just spoke, but that's all. I hadn't actually been introduced to him. I was what they called at that time a journeyman electrician, where I was working with my tools, out on a job. You didn't go in the shop. So you just out there on the job; what they call a gang bunch. I'd be out there workin' on a new school and we'd run out of material. When we needed some material, we would call the shop. Then they would get Elvis to bring it out to the job in that little pickup truck. So one day I had to go in the shop for something, so when I was in there, well he's back there in the back putting up stock. He swept the floor and put up stock and unloaded trucks when it come in with material, and he'd have orders: several different jobs going at the one time. Everybody had to go through that as an apprentice to learn the material and everything. They would do that to be an apprentice or an electrician, to learn the material – couplers, connectors, conduit, and stuff. So I had to go in the shop one day and I heard this guitar, back there in the back, playin'. So I stuck my head in the door and he's sittin' up on a table back there playin' his guitar. Sittin' back there playin' chords, you know, and singin'. So I walk back and I says, 'Sounds pretty good'. But he wasn't doing tight stuff like he did later. He was just sittin' back there doing some country song. He just said, 'Thanks', but he's kind of shy back then; he was really kind of shy. I just knew they called him Elvis, and I knew he was trainin' to be an apprentice. And after you become apprentice, in four years you become an electrician."

"Did you ever go to the Goodwyn shows – the Goodwyn revues? That was mainly WDIA..."

"I played on WDIA, back in the '40s. I played out there before it was black, when it was still white. Tommy Cogbill played out there."

"And Dewey Phillips was on back then, right?"

"Dewey was on WHBQ at the Chisca Hotel in the early '50s. Yeah, we'd go up there and talk to him. Oh, he was always talkin' about Falstaff Beer and about Leonard's Bar-B-Q. He said that *Falstaff Beer is so good, if you can't drink it, you freeze it and eat it.* He's always talkin' about like *y'all goin' out to Leonard's... I'm comin' out there after a while.* We'd all go out there to Leonard's Drive-In and they had speakers out there. We used to get out there, and bop on the concrete with the speakers goin' on while we was waitin' on the barbecues and stuff to come out. We'd get out there and that music was playin' and a whole bunch of kids would be out there dancin' and boppin' right there under the canopy, where the barbecue pits were. And the speakers would be playin' big band, sometimes. What I remember is that 'Flip Flop and Fly' that Big Joe Turner had out, and Clarence 'Frogman' Henry."

"How did you get started with the Rock 'n' Roll Trio?"

"We were playin' clubs around Memphis: Hernando's Hideaway, the Rodeo Club, Shadowlawn up at Oakland, Tennessee – old Shadowlawn Club. Scotty Moore played up there with us some, and they played with Johnny Dorsey at Shadowlawn the night that Dorsey had a big fight up there and got stabbed. I was sick with the flu and I didn't go that night. So Scotty and Bill run off and left that night. They got in the car and took off, and Johnny had to break a bottle and cut some guys to get Dorsey out of there and into the car and get out of there. That place was tough."

"It must have been tough, 'cause they were Golden Gloves fighters."

"All three of us. Five years, I've boxed along with either one of 'em. I fought five years. Johnny Burnette didn't do but one or two years, Dorsey Burnette boxed four. I was defending champion in Memphis three years in a row."

"I remember boxing was big..."

"Oh, it was... that coliseum was full for them City Championships. They was packed. And it was just full of smoke, too. Boy, you couldn't breathe in all the smoke. But we was playin' clubs around Memphis. We was workin' during the day, Dorsey and I as electricians, and Johnny Burnette was collectin' cars. He worked for Murdock, the separation corporation, and would pull the cars in when they wouldn't pay for 'em. Had an old crowbar in the back of his car, and he'd come get me on Saturdays to go with him 'cause it was in bad neighborhoods."

"So what was a bad neighborhood in those days?"

"Run-down areas... usually is just a lot of drinkin' goin' on. There wasn't too many drugs around, Benzedrine and Dexedrine 'bout the strongest things in those days. There might've been a little pot around. I'm talkin' about early '50s now. I knew one kid, a musician that was on drugs. That was the only ones I knew in Memphis. He was a good pianist, I mean, very good playing jazz so he must've been on heroin."

"Benzedrine and Dexedrine were pretty common. We would take them in college to stay up," Rose recalled.

"Yeah, we did it to stay awake at night, 'cause we was drivin' from town to town every night."

"Were they hard to get in those days?"

"No, manager got them for us. He'd get us a jar full. And I'd come home and they're in the suitcase, like the way you put your socks up there, and I'd flush 'em down the commode. I just didn't want the kids to get a hold of them. And when I'd go back to New York City, he'd give us another jar – all we wanted. But he didn't want us to get killed, either. He wanted us to keep drivin'. He's getting that 10%. And GAC, who we were signed with – we signed with the same one that Carl Perkins signed with, General Artists Corporation – they booked all of them from the Mason Dixon Line up. And William Morris Agency had everything on their side. I'm talkin' about they was two biggest bookin' agencies in the country at that time. Now there was small ones like Bob Neil that was bookin' people. Everybody was playin' a different town seven nights a week. That's what they call one-nighters. And we were playin' like, Memphis tonight, and Nashville the next night, Cincinnati the next, you know, a different town every night. So we had to drive, and most of the time we would get away from that town real late. Sometimes we'd go out to eat and everything after the shows was over. Sit around and talk and we'd be gettin' away real late. By the time you get to the next town it was almost daylight. Then you had to go down for rehearsals or sound check at three or four o'clock in the afternoon. So, then you had to play the show at night, and same ol' routine. We'd play the same show every time. I lost 12 pounds and was tired all the time. 'Cause you had to get on stage, and on stage you make everybody think you're having the best time of your life. And we'd just smile and laugh until we get in that car and then we'd start growling, *you're too close. Don't touch me*."

"What kind of car did you have back then?"

"1949 Ford. That was what we went to New York City in. We bought an Oldsmobile convertible, after we signed with Coral Records. That's what we traveled in until we got a Cadillac. It was long and wide, too."

Under the weight of such exhaustive dialogues, I slipped out of the reunion sessions at Phillips studio and guided the Norton back to Cox Street and the serenity of Midtown. Next afternoon, I dropped by Jud, Jr.'s office at the Holiday Inn Rivermont by the river, and Rose and I decided to drive my '64 T-Bird over to Lansky's Men's Shop on Beale St. While I was poking around the shop looking over Tom Jones shirts and tight sharkskin pants, Rose was conversing with Bernard Lansky:

"In the heyday, in the Forties and Fifties when we first started out down on Beale Street we did Army surplus, and then we went into the men's clothing business. What we did, was we went into high fashion menswear, really. What you'd call ethnic clothes. The white and the black at that time, Bobby 'Blue' Bland, Rufus Thomas, B.B. King, rock 'n' roll groups, a lot white entertainers would come down, like Elvis Presley, Roy Orbison, Jerry Lee Lewis, Carl Perkins, Warren Smith, Gene Simmons, Billy Riley. At that time Elvis was an usher at Lowe's State Theatre on Main Street. He used to walk around the corner on his coffee break. Not knowing who Elvis was, I'd invite him in. I said, 'Let me show you around'. 'I don't have no money', he said, 'but when I get rich I'll buy you out.' 'No, don't buy me out, just buy from me.' As time went by, he made recordings, couple of records, and started getting big and kept on coming in. We were bringing in something fresh all the time. Fresh merchandise back then, we were going to market all the time. We used to go to California, New York and we used to look for something no one else had, something different. We used to bring all this merchandise back. A lot of these guys were coming in here that were goin' all over the country in rock 'n' roll groups and things like that. They'd want stage clothes – want something different."

"Somebody told me that another key to your success is that you extended credit to people before other people did."

"Elvis was one of the first."

"One of the guys told me that Elvis had a black leather jacket in those days that he got from Lansky's, and said it was a real expensive jacket and nobody else had one."

"In fact I saw it; it was the only one made. It was a sample that no one else had. I bought it and I said, *this is mine*, and not only that, I bought a gold lamé coat – I had it made. I told this company, I said, *you make this up*. That was his gold lamé outfit that he had that I had made for him, and he wore it on a lot of shows. Elvis was a dynamite young man. Not only was he a big customer, he was a PR man for us all over the country. Ask him where he gets his clothes: from Lansky down on Beale Street. From then on we were doing a fantastic job. He helped out tremendously, fantastically. A really nice guy – real gentleman, nice as he can be.

"Seems like I remember there were some coats that had Lansky Brothers on the back…athletic coats?"

"No that was Tri-State Boxing. We used to have down at Chelsea Park down on Beale Street boxing and whoever won the fights; we used to give them jackets. Tri-State Champion with Lansky on the back of 'em, and we used to take 'em out for steak dinner, which was fantastic, and word got out that we took care of these young kids."

"So how long did Elvis shop at Lansky's?"

"Elvis shopped here until he died… I put his first suit on him; I put his last suit on him."

"What was the last suit?"

"White suit. Put his last suit on him, shirt and tie. Put a white tie on him."

"How did Elvis change over the years? Did you see him change a great deal?"

"When his mother died, that's when he really had a problem. Well, you never know about him, 'cause he's on the road all the time. Everybody's got problems, you know, touring all the time. A dynamite guy though. Years ago when he sold a million records for RCA Victor, they gave him a three-wheeled Messerschmitt, a German car. One day he come up to the store and I was in the back and he said – he always called me Mr. Lansky – 'Where's Mr. Lansky?' I always tell Elvis, I'd say, 'Elvis, Mr. Lansky is my dad. I'm Bernard.' He'd laugh. He said, 'Come on…I've got something to show you.' We went outside, and it was a beautiful burgundy with black trim, bubble top, German Messerschmitt. And I laughed; I said, 'Elvis, when you get through with it, that's mine.' He laughed, and he walked out. 30 days later, I had it – I still got that car. I got it in a warehouse. I don't let nobody see it.

"Tell me about the Superfly."

"I got a lot of stuff from that period – all pink leather. Superfly was a movie, *Super Fly*, with the big collar with the leather topcoats. They had these big black pants. Elvis used to take all of his leather coats and put all mink collars on them. In fact, some of them are still in the airplane. Not only that, he used to buy hats. Play cops and robbers and things…"

"You go out to Graceland?"

"Went out there anytime I got ready, but I didn't like to bother him, because I knew he was busy. A lot of times he's up all night and he'd sleep all day. A lot of times he used to come out, say, *we gonna be out to the Fairgrounds; come on now, we're gonna be out there…* You know, when he was first starting out. This was something like a kid with a new toy… *Come on out*, and I said, 'Naw'. He had all these…fellas, or whatever you call these young men who were with him. I knew I wasn't going to follow behind them.

"Johnny Cash, I made him a Prince Albert coat. He wanted something different. That Prince Albert coat was dynamite. His wife, June Carter Cash; she come in. You know what she wanted? She wanted a men's button-down shirt. She got a button-down shirt, men's oxford. That's what she liked to wear…"

"Was there anything else in particular that Elvis liked to wear?"

"White half boots they used to wear."

"Yeah, his whole entourage had that."

"That's right, you'd buy one and you'd have to buy for all of them. What's good for one is good for the other. He set the pace. We knew what the trend would be, because if you put it on Elvis it's got to be fantastic. He was our fashion show. When he brought Priscilla back… when Priscilla first came to Memphis, she came up to the store. She didn't have any money, and so we had some beautiful coats – waist-length coats we had, we're selling – and she put one on layaway for him, for Christmas. She got it out of layaway for him."

"I know that you dealt with a lot of stars, is there anything that was, like, totally different with Elvis, in your mind, like as to why he made it big?"

"Elvis had the right man. With Sam Phillips and Bob Neal, they knew they couldn't go any further with him. They sold out to Colonel Parker. Colonel Parker was a real merchant; he was a real merchandiser. He was a dynamite guy. To be a merchandiser you know how to present your people, just like we do in our merchandise, like we do in our clothing business. We know what to put up; we know what to put on sale. We know what to hold back; we know what to put out. And Colonel Parker, he was a promoter, from his heart. People tell me if it wasn't for Colonel Parker, he wouldn't have had nothing. Colonel Parker knew when to pull and he knew

Beale Street Photo: E. Baffle c. 1973

when to push. He knew when to hold 'em and he knew when to let 'em go. He did not burn Elvis out, 'cause Elvis burned himself out, because he never would listen. Colonel Parker was like a father. Colonel Parker was sharp. He was a real sharp promoter. You can learn from people like him. Every time I seen him we'd always sit and talk. He had shows going on up at the Claridge Hotel. We used to see it all the time, the Billy Vaughan Show. He knew what was happening. He knew what to do. Timing is the most important thing and he had the timing, and not only had timing, he had the people in his hand. He knew what he could do and whom he could sell Elvis to. And he didn't *sell* Elvis for no potato chips, he sold him for big money – big money."

We walked out of Lansky's with a white shirt in a Carnaby Street style trimmed with ruffles all around the collar and on the cuffs, and a pair of tight iridescent blue trousers. I still wanted to get a white boater's cap, so we walked down Beale a few doors to Schwab's Dry

Goods where I'd seen the caps before. Schwab's motto was, *if you can't find it at Schwab's, you're better off without it.* We passed over the voodoo and talismans counter, and stepped down into the cap and glove department. One of the black sales ladies greeted us, 'May I help y'all find sonthin'?' 'Well, I'm looking for a boaters cap...' 'Right over heah, suh.' While I got busy trying on caps, the proprietor came up to us. I knew him, but Rose knew him better and they started talking about the old days... naturally, because everything in Schwab's, although new and old retail stock, evoked an era of the past.

"My grandfather's name was Abraham. I just took the *h* off of it. I'm third generation. I'm Abram Schwab. They call me Abe most of the time, and the family's been on this street since 1876. However, before that, my great-grandfather occupied this building in 1860. Abraham Schwab came over about 1868. He was born 1852. He was 16 years old, came from Alsace, France. Strasbourg area is where he came from. On Beale Street, most of the shops were Jewish, couple Italians. If you read the names on the buildings, you'll see Epstein's, Lansky's, Schwab's. From Main Street to the river was wholesale houses. That goes back to the time of boats. Warehousing was as near to the river as could be, and then the wholesale houses was as near to the river as they could be, basically. Then this was retail up in here. You came to town by boat, they bought as much as they could wholesale first, then had to buy retail what they couldn't get wholesale. They worked their way on up the street.

"The next block I called the fun block. That's where all the men was going anyway. Beale Street was kind of, I call it an escape street – leave all your troubles away from here. You get paid Friday night, Saturday come down here and have one hell of a big time, 'til your money runs out. You had picture shows, you had restaurants, there was something here for everybody. They came from the country, and some who'd come by boat, later on even came by wagons and cars. They didn't get to town like today, driving anywhere you want to. They only went to town maybe once or twice a year, in the fall of the year or the spring of the year. It was a trip just to get to Memphis. Anything less than a 100 miles would be a big trip, and so just coming to town was quite an event.

"Beale Street was laid out about 1840. This was South Memphis. They were looking for the boat traffic. City of Randolph was north of Memphis. Memphis, South Memphis, Fort Pickering, and all of it was trying to get the river traffic. Memphis kind of won out and South Memphis became a part of Memphis in 1850. Beale Street was the main shopping area at this period of time, I'd say, and remained pretty good until the yellow fever hit. Then Memphis was abandoned. My great-grandpa died in 1873. A lot of families died in the yellow fever, and everybody left Memphis. Either you died or you left Memphis – you had a choice. Memphis ceased to exist.

"It came back, I'm saying like the 1890s. They cleaned Memphis up quite a bit, put in this new sewer system and just overhauled the city when the people came back. Memphis had three epidemics, in '73, '78, and another one. You leave home the first time, come back; leave home the second time, you may come back; the third time, give it back to the Indians, we're through with Memphis. Main Street originally was a wholesale and manufacturing street. Then it became a retail street, a high priced retail street. Beale Street became – I call low-end merchandise. You had pawnshops down here, you had second-hand stores down here, we were down here, Lansky's, Greener's Department Store was on the other corner, and this was your low-end priced merchandise. You're goin' out tonight, you want a nice dress, you go to Main Street to get it. But also you need a dress just to wear around the house, a work dress, you come down here to get that.

"Basically, the customers were a mixture: integrated, blacks and white both. In the segregation period of that time, your black restaurants were down here, your black theaters were down here. 1922, you've got half blacks and half white in here. Only thing that was segregated was restaurants, theaters, and nightclubs; like that, social things. Memphis was integrated; I guess that's what I'm saying. On Beale Street you had black doctors and dentists. There were 18 of them within two or three blocks of here. There were pawnshops: Davidson's, Nathan's, Sonny Epstein's, Safferston's, American Loans, Uncle Sam's, Cohen's. There used to be a record store, Home of the Blues, run by Ruben Cherry.

"When riverboats come to town, it lent itself to gambling. On the boat there was gambling and it was kind of competing against the street. Part of that scene was back of our store: was a big wagon yard, a parking lot for wagons. Because the wagon is open you couldn't lock anything in. You'd come in with your husband, wife, and children and you're shopping. Somebody has to stay at the wagon, someone to take packages back to the wagon, and someone had to keep shopping, and so with good prices here you bought a lot of stuff, and you had your cotton money… when you sold the cotton. Somebody had to stay at the wagon. Now, there's more than a 100 people out there at the wagons. Pretty soon somebody hears a pair of dice rolling. Well, you get in a dice game. This is perpetual gambling going on in this lot, you might say. Then there's heat back there and they'd barbecue, cook back there and like that. They'd spend the entire day there.

"Behind about where this park right is over there were the theaters: the Old Daisy, then they had the New Daisy, and they had another one, too, that's where the Midnight Rambles were, the Palace Theater. And the shows were black shows, black stage shows, rather risqué. The white folks came too because it's a black show. So it had Midnight Rambles when only whites could go, and that didn't start 'til midnight. They had the same show for the whites, and this was Friday night and Saturday night. In the '30s, '40s, you didn't get a show 'til midnight, then you got out around 2:30 or 3:00 and you went to Johnny Mills, who sold barbecue, and spent the rest of the evening at Johnny Mills eating barbecue, and left the street at daylight. It's hard to understand in the black area that a black man can't go to a white show, and black can't go to a black show when they had the Rambles. The Main Street theaters all had sections for black. Orpheum Theater had a box office on Main Street and a box office on Beale. The box office on Beale was for the blacks only, and the front box office was the whites only. I think Warner Brothers had a similar arrangement. That lasted 'till around '54.

"Now the whites couldn't go into a black establishment or a joint, unless somebody slipped you in. Elvis would slip in, into these black establishments. By law it's illegal, but nobody really cared anything about it one way or the other, 'cause it was fun to sneak around. Everything's better if you sneak around. Street musicians, they're not beggars, but they sit out there and play musical instruments and they expect you to throw a penny or a nickel or a dime or something into their hat. They would sit between every building – right there is the no man's land. Between the two businesses is a space, and they'd sit in that space on a Coca-Cola case or box like that and they'd play. Then you had what I called pick-up bands – some folks sitting there playing the harmonica, another'd be coming over with the Jew's harp and they'd be playing. They don't know each other; they'd just play together. Pretty soon have a little band going. What he'd do is try to raise enough money to buy some wine; so soon he'd get enough money to get a little wine or beer. He goes into one of the cafés or joints, and then he sits there and plays. That's his work; he's earning money playing. It's not a beggar; he's entertaining. You get tired of sitting in that restaurant, then you go to another, and a whole crowd follows him. His entourage follows to the next restaurant, and that's the way they would operate. They were not necessarily big name people, but it kind of gave them a start. They were living on the street. There were beggars on the street, but the musicians are not begging, they were performing.

"I was raised on the street. I'm part of the street. People, like they say, I'm gonna go to Beale Street… not really a street, they're talking about an attitude. Yeah, *I'm gonna raise hell*, I mean, that's, *I'm gonna get drunk*. And what they do, they come in here and they just got their money, and they get my uncle: hold my money from me, and he'd take five dollars out of his money because he's gonna blow that five dollars. On Monday he'd come back, get the rest of it. He'd know he's gonna get it back; he knows this. But that's the way the system works. Beale Street made its own laws, its own system. During the day different people were in the store. In the mornings, in the daytime, country people – people from the country, outside of Memphis – come and shopped. In the early evenings, about four, six, a little later on, you had the workers downtown who were going back home, and they'd shop after work, shop and go home. They had a night crowd and night clubbers and wine drinkers, all like that, all night long. You had three changes of people.

"Busy was September, October, November, December. That's cotton money. The farmers, the landowners, the workers – all of them farm people. They get in the end of the year money to buy seeds and fertilizer to plant the cotton. If they got a little extra money, they steal a little bit out and shop for Easter time. Then they work all summer; they have no money, no income. Very little…butter and eggs is about all what they can do. They don't really come to town too much. Then in September when they start picking cotton, picking all this September, the first bales goes to pay off the debt to the bank, to pay off the borrowed money. Then the rest of this money, they sell the cotton and it's their money. They pick in good weather; they don't pick Sunday – they pick the rest of the time. Sunday they go to church.

"On the first rainy day, cold rainy day in September, this store would be packed with people. They can't work the fields and they got money and here they come, and this is their big shopping. They get their cotton money and then they'll meter it on out to Christmas time. This lifestyle they had, the cotton money, the bale money, selling their cotton, was what the mother and the children and the girls and the boys and the grandmom and the grandpa all worked for…and so they all shared in this cotton money. Everybody got something out of it. Also, they got paid for picking the cotton. Little children, they got paid for taking water out to 'em in the fields, or for taking food out to 'em, or to pick up the loose cotton. The kid may have 25 cents that he earned in a week's time. That's the hardest money to get out of anybody's hand is a child worker that earned 25 cents. He's gonna spread it as far as he can. It gave him pride in that it's his money. Now the family money, the mother and the father control that. Like they bought him shoes; they bought him pants. But this 25 cents, that's his money. He can buy a toy, he can buy candy, he can spend it. I'll say that was good training for the children, because it taught them the value of money. You worked a week and get something ain't nobody can take it away from you. The parent bought him shoes. That was an easy sale; that was easy, 'cause you're gonna get a pair of shoes. This lady used to work this shoe parlor. She knew all the families, and she had a stack of shoes this high. Three foot high of shoes: the old man shoes, the mother shoes, the children shoes, the baby shoes; had them all stacked there. She loved doing that. Just kind of showing off how much she sold. And there's competition between our clerks and the clerks in other stores. A little lying' going on too, and in fact how much they'd sold – it didn't make any difference; it was just talk, just talk. She'd say well, Annie down the street, she didn't sell but $50 today and I done sold $60 and….

"They used to sell a cheap wine down here. I think it was when they drove wine off the barrel, the big kegs, what's left in the bottom, you buy that, 35 cents a quart. It's the trace…sold on the street, 'cause it's cheap wine. There were several liquor stores on the street when prohibition ended. Liquor store was one on the corner up here, one in the middle of the block, and one in the next block and a lot of liquor stores."

"So what killed Beale Street? When did that happen?"

"Alright, the shopping centers: they built the shopping centers, and to build up their business they told you: *you don't have to go to Main Street to shop, you come to the shopping center*. The same stores what're on Main Street had stores in the shopping center. They hurt downtown. It wasn't intentional, but that's what happened as downtown lost the white customers going to the shopping centers. The black customers, basically, were on Beale Street. They started catering to them on Main Street, which pulled our customers away from us. This was in the '50s and the '60s. About the same time in the '60s, Walter Simmons – I think I got the right name – who was director of the Memphis Housing Authority, envisioned restoration of Beale Street. It was famous, world famous, and he wanted to restore it, repair the buildings, and these buildings get old and need repairing. He started the wheels turning. Government is slow, even at their best, to get the laws passed, and he passed away before it actually came about. The ones that took over from him didn't have the feeling that he had for Beale Street. So they would say, let's just eliminate Beale Street; just get rid of it. They started buying up the property here; threw the people out. First thing they do is move everybody out of the second floors. The second floor was doctor's office, dentist office, living quarters, insurance, uh – little offices…and they devastated the street. We were the only thing left here and Lansky. They just boarded the buildings up and walked away from it. The street was torn up in the process. A year and a half, the street was gone."

"So when did you have the record department?"

"From the '20s. My father operated the records. He ran the record department, and he was a violinist. He enjoyed music."

"So did you all have the same kind of music as the Home of the Blues, or did you have…?"

"Home of the Blues came in after. We sold race records. Race records are blues, and they called them race records with the colored. We sold blues records, as on Blue Bird label put out by RCA Victor. Had a separate label for the black artists, and Victor was the white artists, basically. We sold blues records. I don't know this for a fact, but I'd say we were the biggest dealer in town for that kind of record.

"You had your beer joints; they all had jukeboxes in them. No blues was played on the radio as today. There were only white stations. They only place that they could hear black music was if they bought the record here or heard it in the jukeboxes on the street. Many of them couldn't read, didn't care to read, and maybe he's sitting in a beer joint and record is playing, and we'll say that's number three. Well, he likes it, so he comes down here, 'I want number three.' 'What?' 'Number three.' 'What are you talking about?' 'Number three on the jukebox.' I have no idea what number three is! 'Go back and get the waitress to write down the name, then come back here, with it written on a napkin.' "Cat Blues", number three.' Well, now we know it. That's number three, but then next week, they service the jukebox once a week, they change the records; put on a new one…and what was three is now number seven. So, we keep up with the stuff like that. Then the first blues that was played on the radio was played by us. During the wartime in the '40s newspaper space was cut down because they couldn't get the newsprint. That limited us to how much advertising we could do. So we had a radio show called Blues Time, 4:15 to 4:30 on WHBQ. We had to give them our records. We'd give them 25 records every Monday, and they'd play those records during the week. They'd bring them back Monday and we'd give them 25 other records, or different or the same, whatever. This was at 4:15. Most houses had maids in them, and there's one radio in the living room. Therein was a problem. They wanted to hear the blues on the radio, and they can't go in the living room to listen to it. So they'd turn on the radio and go to the back of the house and they'd listen to the show. This is WHBQ and we were appealing to the black trade on this show. In radio they sell the spot in front of the show or behind the show that ties it in with the show, in a sense. So WHBQ started getting a black listenership with our show. They could sell the space in front or behind us to Royal Crown or black cosmetics. It built up quite a bit of the black listenership in this period of time.

"Then around '47 we got back to normal after wartime, and WDIA came on at that time catering to the black business. So WHBQ started losing what they'd built up, and so they hired Dewey Phillips. Daddy-O Dewey. He was controversial, oh – he was controversial. They tried to shut him up. He was something else, Daddy-O Dewey. He had *Red, Hot, & Blue* show ten to midnight. He was the record salesman at Grant's, at Gayoso. He sold the same records we sold. We were competitors. Home of the Blues came in about that same time. This became the hotspot of all the records, between us, Home of the Blues, and Grant's. Dewey shopped all three places. Competition generates business…and Dewey Phillips came on to build up this black listenership. Up until then disc jockeys played a record, then they'd play another record, and then a commercial. Dewey – uh-uh, he'd have a commercial, like, go to Schwab's and buy ladies' shoes for $1.98. But he would read it: *Go to Schwab's, get ladies' shoes for $1.98, but go down to Greener's, they got the same thing for 98 cents.* That's my competitor! I'm paying for his time and he sends them to my competitor! Okay, he'd come back on: *Greener's got boy's shirts for 98 cents, but Schwab's got the same thing for 50 cents; go down to Schwab's and get them.* On the air he would say this. My God, the guy's crazy. They couldn't control him. He did what he wanted to do.

"Every day the postman would bring deejay records that they sent out, promotional records. We used to get them; we were on the mailing list. Everyday we'd get a stack of records this high, and the secretary thought this was all worthless trash. The secretary takes them and goes to the garbage bin, throws them in there. Nobody wants them; ain't nobody listening to them. Uh-uh, Dewey listens to every record. He hears one that's different, he takes it and hides it way in the back somewhere, behind something, for about a week. Everybody'd get rid of their copy, and he comes out with this new hit, and he's got the only copy in the city limits. He had to do it to show you what's new, 'cause other disc jockeys, they're not gonna take the trouble to do it. Dewey. I don't think he was a musician, but he liked music. He could hear music. He'd be walking down the street, like at 1:00 at night – and he'd get off at 12:00. 1:00 at night. He's crazy. He hears some sound up some dark stairway in an alley. He goes up there! Dewey, he's not trying to do anything, he just hears that music. He was uncontrollable. You couldn't control him. But he had such a following; they couldn't get rid of him, either. Poppa ain't gonna let you listen to any show. For that period of time it was pretty rough. So you had to take the radio under the bed covers, let me tell you, and hide and listen to Dewey's show. He was something. He'd say anything. He'd say stuff that's illegal to say, not improper, but illegal. It didn't make a difference to him.

"But, he played Elvis' record eight times every night. Elvis, Jerry Lee Lewis – there was about six of them that came out – Roy Orbison came out about the same time. Dewey liked Elvis. He promoted Elvis. The early SUN records of Elvis were only sold in this area, but nobody'd ever heard of Elvis."

"So there was more jukebox music in the joints than there was live entertainment? Most of the musicians were on the street?"

"Yeah, the only place that had live music, I would guess, was like, Club Handy – these sort of dancehalls, clubs, like that, but mainly it was the jukeboxes. Everyplace had a jukebox in there. Also, you had people who were told that you come to Memphis and get jobs. You come to Memphis – there ain't no jobs. And singing the blues is when you feel down and you're so low down that if you laid down on the sidewalk and people just stepped on you, you wouldn't bother to pick yourself up. Then you can sing the blues. Now, they'd get up in the stairwells, back in between the buildings. This used to be a living quarters up here. There's a little door on it and to the hall to upstairs. They'd sit up there in these stairwells and they'd play their music. Now remember entertainment is not necessary. You have to eat, but you don't have to have entertainment. So there's no money spent on entertainment out in the country. At the crossroads is a grocery store and a juke joint and maybe a filling station, and maybe something else, a retail store. The Jew had a retail store. Anyway, they didn't have any money for entertainment, so entertainment has to be no expense. They'd dance in these beer joints. On the weekend they'd just walk to town, and so everything they have is makeshift, and that was the way the entertainment was."

"What about the minstrels?"

"Yeah, costume shows, dancin', there would be vaudeville. Now vaudeville was a circuit, and the way the circuit works, you sign on for 40 weeks and you travel all the different theaters in the circuit. Then you're off; your contract's run out. You take a vacation. So then they make up a new show of all these people that are off for 12 weeks. All the same acts that played a year earlier, but they change them around. Put a juggler with a dancer, or this or that – a new act. Then you work around the circuit. This was part of the circuit, part of the black circuit. There would be a stage show and movie.

"Lansky's – Guy Bernard – opened up across the street right after wartime, '46, '47. These boys worked hard. See 'em working 'til 11:00 at night, every day. There's nothing more cutthroat than selling men's work clothes, seriously. They worked hard and they weren't making no money. So then they got the idea of putting in these men's pink shoes, purple hats. We think the boys don't know what they're doing. They're gonna lose what money they've earned with all this baloney. So, when all this stuff kinda got going, then Elvis comes along and sees all these jumpsuits with the turned-up collar, and this is all Lansky's baloney. So Elvis was their best customer. Elvis was on the street every day, being fitted or they're showing him some new cloth they got, or whatever. Every time Elvis gets an outfit, when he's entertaining, then all the rest of his entourage has to have matching outfits. So they need six suits made out of this cloth to match with Elvis' jumpsuit. George Klein, my wife used to baby-sit him when she was a young girl, and George Klein's mother and my wife's mother were very good friends, card playin'. All right, you have to understand, Jewish women play cards on Saturday night. They're the meanest bunch of women you have ever seen. Every Saturday night it's the same thing all over again. Anyway, Mrs. Klein was a good friend of my wife's and we took something over to their house, and Mrs. Klein showed my wife George's suits: a hundred and fifty of them, on a rack. All paid for by Elvis. If Elvis comes out in a pink suit, George comes out with a pink suit on. He'd say, Elvis decides he wants a green, then I get the green. He had to complement Elvis, which is stage business. All this came out of Lansky Brothers. They did very well – wound up with four stores. They were very shrewd fellas. They knew what they were doing. Beale Street has always set styles."

We stepped out of Schwab's in style. I'd found a white boater's cap – the kind yachtsmen wear – with "Memphis Belle" inscribed on the visor in fancy gold lettering. Rose and I nosed the Thunderbird toward the Rivermont as the sun was setting on the river bluff and sunbeams were bouncing on the waves rippling toward us from the Arkansas side.

CHAPTER THE SEVENTH
FREEDOM RIDE

Once I overheard entertainer Rufus Thomas backstage at some outdoor show in Memphis throw down derisively, "Well, you know Sam Phillips had that *white thing*". Yet without doubt the efforts of the brothers, Sam and Jud Phillips, working out of the Bible-Buckle of the South, did more than most to break down color barriers on jukeboxes, on the airwaves, and on concert stages up to the dawn of the Civil Rights Movement.

One steamy day in July, the daughter of a modern architect who was a member in good standing invited me for the one and only time to the University Club. It was like a country club, *sans* golf links, situated at the entrance of the Annesdale-Snowden central gardens district. White-jacketed waiters served cocktails as we lounged at a shady linen-covered table under the spreading limbs of venerable oak trees. There appeared a dashing young gentleman of light color in a three-piece gray suit. This was unusual because the University Club had a Caucasian only policy. Even Jews were not permitted other than as member-invited guests. My friend waved to this charismatic apparition. He approached and was introduced as newly appointed Judge Russell Sugarmon. I asked if he were an habitué of the University Club, and Judge Sugarmon replied, "the only reason I've come back here is to see what it looked like when I wasn't waiting tables… curiosity, because I was working here when I was a student. These clubs can go their own way as far as I'm concerned. I have no interest and have had no interest in clubs for social whatever." Surely he was the only black person present other than those carrying silver trays of mint juleps. I too was curious… about his take on the Bluff City as a native son, how his family came to be established here, and how he became a judge. However I did not have the opportunity to delve further into the origins of Judge Sugarmon that carefree afternoon at the University Club.

It was some years later that I happened to run into Judge Sugarmon at the annual Martin Luther King memorial downtown in the parking lot of the Lorraine Motel. After the ceremonies I approached him and invited him for a coffee up the street at the Arcade restaurant. Seated in the leatherette booth toward the rear of the café, I enquired, "As we happen to be here, Judge Sugarmon, positioned across from the Central Station, do you see Memphis as a kind of gateway between New Orleans and northern destinations?"

"Well, people were coming up to Memphis leaving the cotton fields. This was the first stop on the way to Chicago. On the East Coast they went up the Atlantic seaboard to New York and here they went up the Mississippi River, then up to Chicago. This was a way station, but a lot of people settled here. This city was the cotton capital of the world, because all the cotton raised in this area came in from farms in east and west Tennessee, eastern Arkansas, Mississippi, and Alabama. The bulk of that cotton harvest came to Memphis and was put on steamboats up to Illinois and freight lines to St. Louis. So we had a lot of dockworkers, people who loaded and unloaded riverboats. The black population would go out and pick cotton in the seasons so they could live and exist. You know, the second-class citizens. So there was quite a bit of cultural identity here as a result of that, and there was enough of an economic base so you could eke out a living.

"My father was an illegitimate child of an octoroon and some guy from Chicago. He wouldn't talk to us about it. That was a no-no in those days. He lived on a farm in Gunnison, Mississippi, and my mother, her father was Chinese and her mother was American Indian and black. My father, you couldn't tell he was black if you saw him. He used to get beat up, 'cause when he was going to school – the black school – he stood out. So a local white grocer had a store called the Pig Jaw and had hired my father to sweep it out and dust. He told him, you need to go to Memphis and try to find a job there. So they moved to Memphis. This is in the late '20s. Through an acquaintance from Gunnison, he got hired by a bank. What they hired him to do was travel to Mississippi. The banks were foreclosing farms all over the South and the banks owned most of the farmland. They would take over control of acreage, and they had to send him down to look it over and come back and tell them what he thought it was worth. He spent the best part of his life appraising farmland for this bank. That went on for a long time while he studied, and he became a real estate broker. He and one other guy out there were the only two licensed black real estate brokers in the city.

"When I was born there was a streetcar line that ran right down Walker Avenue past Lamar Avenue and College, and the car stopped next to the corner. My mother had me raised to be a gentleman. So anytime a lady dropped something, you pick it up for her. I was about eleven and I was waiting at the trolley stop, and some white lady was there. She was looking for something in her purse, and she dropped a dime. I went to pick it up for her and she slapped my hand, 'Don't you touch that, nigger.' I jumped back and went and told mother. She said, 'Oh…anybody like that, just leave them alone.' That was my first personal experience with the race issue. You know, at that age we hadn't recognized that there was a social and cultural difference being made.

"They wouldn't let me go down to Beale Street until I was in high school. It could be a pretty rough place. I saw a knife fight down there, one time: two guys standing there just slashing each other with switchblades… but they did have a lot of music. We lived around the area of Lemoyne College. There were a lot of professional offices though, on Beale Street and in that entire area. At night there was entertainment, but in the daytime there were banks and doctors. My father made money for first time with bank sales, and then he got stock in Tri-State Bank on Beale St.

"When I was in high school I went to a private Lutheran co-operative school right across the street, grades one through eight. It was headed by a German woman who came down from, I think, Minnesota. She had a three-room schoolhouse – it was three rooms in the church parsonage. They only had three teachers and nobody else, and so you couldn't go outside, 'cause there were no fences and no supervision. So you had to stay inside. When we were in class, if we were being taught – it's three grades in one room – the kids in the other two grades had three options. We could either sit or be quiet, we could sit and read, or we could take a nap. She had a library so we always took a book and we all learned to read. We became avid readers by the time we were in the eighth grade. She had a 15-volume edition of somebody who traveled in the Napoleonic campaign, and I read all 15 volumes. It was incredible; she had all the Greek classics. You could go to another world through a book. It enlarged our lives tremendously just sitting there with those books. When we went to high school, there were two high schools for blacks: Booker T. Washington and Manassas on the other side of town. So, Maxine Smith was there, Ben Hooks was there, and A. W. Willis. We had some teachers, when there was nobody around that would snitch, who would talk about black history and Christmas, Hanukkah, and all that sort of thing. We got history behind closed doors. My algebra teacher was a guy named Booker T. Jones. His son was Jones with Booker T. and the M.G.s that later on was one of the Stax groups.

"When we finished high school, three of my classmates and I went to Morehouse in Atlanta, and we made the dean's list. In those days the skyline of Atlanta was not like it is now and you could see Stone Mountain if you went to the bell tower at Grace Hall, which was the first building built on the campus. It was old so it had been condemned, but because of World War II, the city had let them use the lower floors, but they said keep people out of the bell tower, it's not safe. Well, we would sneak up to the bell tower, and from the bell tower you could see Stone Mountain. When the *Constitution* wrote an article that the Klan was having a rally that weekend, we went up there to watch them burn crosses. We could see the crosses burning when they did it on Stone Mountain. It was like a cross floating up in the air. But we made the dean's list and went there to celebrate, and we chipped in and we had enough for a fifth of scotch. I think it was about $2.98 or something like that. And we got exposed. We got found out and put out.

"So that morning we each had a letter on our door saying come to my office and pick up your ticket home, while the students and the faculty decides upon the appropriate punishment for y'all. So I just packed my bags and went and got my envelope and my ticket and went home. I showed my father that expulsion from Morehouse, only after I had gotten my degree from Rutgers. Martin King was a sophomore, there, my first year at Morehouse. I met him, but we weren't chummy or anything, just one of the people on the campus. He always had a book with him. He was focused. I went to Rutgers, I finished in 3-1/2 years, but I wouldn't get my diploma 'til June that year. So I just stayed up there until the end of the year. I had applied to Harvard. I had applied to about three or four law schools, and I got a response. I made a pretty good mark on the little aptitude test. I was feeling pretty good about it until I got to Harvard – it was a 94.5 or something – I didn't meet anybody in three years that made less than that. But anyway, the first question was: Why do you want to be a lawyer? I said because I do not like my hometown and I went on to describe segregation. I guess that's what made them decide to give me a shot. I got a letter almost immediately accepting me.

"At the time, a desegregation suit had been filed against the University of Tennessee's Law School. It had been sent to trial, but it hadn't been tried. When I got home I got to thinking about it. I had been 'student exempt' through law school, and so I owed three years of national service to the military. I called the draft board and I gave them my registration number, and I asked, 'When am I likely to be called up to meet my obligation?' And they said, 'Let me check. Let me call back.' So, 'Oh, about 2-1/2 years.' I said, 'My goodness, I just finished law school and I got to sit 2-1/2 years before I can do anything? I want to get started. Can I get moved up?' The guy said, 'Can you what?' I think the Korean War was on the way, and I said, 'Yeah, I mean, I don't want to sit around doing nothing, waiting for 2-1/2 years. Can you help move me up?' The guy said, 'I don't know, we've never even thought about that. Nobody's ever asked us.' I said, 'Can you find out?' 'I'll see what we can do.' He got interested in the idea. He called back about two weeks later and said, 'Well, we found a guy who's due to go in in August and he'd be willing to swap.' I said, 'Tell him you got a deal.' So I went in and I took this guy's place in the rotation. I went in August and I got out of law school at the end of May and I went in the army. Later I finished Harvard Law School.

"The University of Tennessee Law School comes in as an adjunct in getting to Harvard, because while I was at home trying to get my draft status worked out, they had been sued. So I sent my law aptitude test and a copy of my admission letter to the UT Law School admissions office, along with my transcript. And I told them that I was a graduate of Booker T. Washington high school in Memphis, so they knew I was African-American and that I had been admitted to Harvard Law School. But my family didn't have the resources for me to go there, 'cause I said that I couldn't work while I went to law school. It just wasn't clear that would be possible given their reputation as a rigorous experience. I said since my credentials are acceptable to Harvard, I believe they should satisfy your requirements. Please send me an application. At that point they wrote me back and said you will hear from the commissioner of education: congratulations, we wish all of our young citizens fulfillment of their educational goals.

"Then the letter from the commissioner of education said, how much does it cost to go to Harvard? And they paid for my tuition, transportation, and fees. So that solution kept UT from working on the case. They paid my way. I didn't realize that was going to happen. I just wanted to see what their reaction was. But I didn't go to UT Law; I merely sent an application. I mean, I don't know if it was UT Law or the State of Tennessee. Some Southern states had some kind of fund. I never knew about it. They didn't publicize it. But there was a medical school that educated black doctors in Tennessee; there was a veterinary school in Alabama that trained black veterinarians. Several of the states had unique colleges where you could get certain professional training, and if the state you were in didn't have it they would send you to the state that did and under their agreement; they would treat those students as home students for that particular state for purposes of qualifying for whatever educational cash benefits they were allowed. So to keep me from going to UT, they were prepared to send me to Harvard. I didn't even know that was the basis for which they sent me there. I'm theorizing now. I just know that program existed. All the commissioner of education asked, 'How much does it cost...?' That was an unintended consequence. Maxine Smith at UT, it's the same thing. She had written them and they paid her way for a graduate degree at Mount Juliet. She went to the top language school in the country, got a Master's in French.

"While in high school we all talked about going away and getting some education to come back and get involved. That's what I did, that's what A. W. Willis did; that's what Maxine Smith did; that's what Ben Hooks did. We went away and we came home... to segregation. The Crump administration was unique in the country. Crump was from some county in Mississippi not far from Memphis. He came to Memphis about 1904 and ran for a clerk's office and he won. He ran for mayor time after time. So until he died, nobody ever beat that machine. The basis of his control was he realized the black population was about a third or so of the city. There was a minimal school system started, and he kept the school system going. But whether or not your particular school got any support and decent teacher's pay, depended upon the results of whatever election was going on at the time as far as whether that school system's population supported the Crump ticket. We all started taking interest in politics when our teachers used to explain to us why they had to support the Crump machine. We all understood. We didn't get textbooks; we didn't get money for lunches unless the political line was followed. That was an early lesson about what mattered: was whether you had power over your destiny politically. If your district didn't support that ticket you could forget about new textbooks. You got second-hand textbooks. Booker T. got 'em from Central High. We had books there with Central stamped in them. The teachers could forget about raises. The principal couldn't get the right improvements. So the school system structure was his vehicle for control in the black wards, which worked successfully. He had control of the black vote and a strong influence on about 20% of the white vote, and with that he controlled the city. The black vote was about a third of the population, and that gave him a little bit over 50%. That's what he needed. Nobody ever tried to challenge him for a long time."

"What about the law firm of Burch, Porter, and Johnson, and Edward J. Meeman – editor at the *Press-Scimitar*?"

"The Crump machine had their critics... 30 or 40 percent of the population was consistently against him, but 30% didn't win an election. There was also an opposing group of people: among them Jesse Turner with a black insurance company here; it was Universal Life, which is one of largest black insurance companies in the country."

"It was quite a jolt," I interjected, "when the chairman of the board of Universal Life Insurance Co. and founder of the Tri-State Bank on Beale St. was shot dead in his office downtown on Linden Avenue. His confessed slayer was a former business associate called Judge W. Hamilton, who claimed to have murdered Dr. Walker in seeking revenge against an old grudge. On a visit to his office a year before, Hamilton broke a walking cane over the shoulder of Dr. Walker. He continued to threaten his life on a number of occasions, but the CEO, a self-made man who had been born on a tenant farm, just laughed it off. The fact that Hamilton had suffered carbon monoxide poisoning earlier in life and was considered to be 'mentally off' could have been good reason to take him seriously. Apparently, Judge Hamilton took himself seriously enough to make an appointment with Dr. Walker at 8:30 in the morning and cheerfully blast a hole through his aorta with a .38 caliber revolver.

Mayor Orgill spoke praise of Dr. Walker and cited his tragic passing as a great loss to this community. I believe Judge W. Hamilton died three years later incarcerated within the walls of the Central State Hospital for the Criminally Insane."

"Well, Universal Life had a clerical staff that had pretty decent jobs and they used to let the clerical staff – the ones who were working with us as NAACP volunteers – stay after work and use the typewriters… and they raised money, anything they could get done. We had boycotts. We always had voter registration, 'cause we recognized at the time of Crump that the black votes could vote for themselves and not the machine. Edmund Orgill, he was part of an enlightened group here – that minority white group. When I first got home they were communicating that they would set up a rendezvous somewhere outside of the newspaper purview because they told us we need to keep this quiet 'cause if they find out that we're working with colored folks we won't win. If we can't get in the office, we can't help. It was sort of a secret force. We got to the point where there were two white votes for every black vote. So we had a city council, commission form of government. We decided that if any time one of the incumbents decided not to run, we'd watch it, and if they wound up with several white candidates, if there were two white candidates of equal voter attraction and one black, it was a horse race – a third, a third, a third – and we had a shot.

"Well, the biggest commission seat was public works. They had the biggest, I think 1700 employees at the time. The Commissioner there was a man named Henry Loeb and he had won that seat with black support. Then almost immediately after he won it, he announced that he planned to run for mayor at the end of his council seat term. So we started planning. They decided I should be a candidate for that seat. Ben Hooks was gonna run for Juvenile Court, and Bishop Bunton was a Baptist minister who ran for school board. When it started out it wound up with seven white candidates. So I got in the race, and the *Press-Scimitar* ran an article twice spelling out the odds, the math, and saying with seven white candidates, Sugarmon was a lock unless some of them withdrew. The reporter was named Clark Porteous and I called him and I said, 'You know, we thought you were amenable to colored folk, answering their cause, and here you are just like a peckerwood Paul Revere.' He never spoke to me again."

"Even Henry Loeb, who became Mayor Loeb, had courted the black vote and had promised certain things, changed and became…"

"Loeb said that he thought actually of dropping that race after people were talking about the odds of me winning with the white vote split up like it was. He said that I should withdraw for the benefit of the community. So the reporters asked me what I thought about that. I said, 'Well, I think that the voters are going to be voting on who's best qualified to perform their job.' I said, 'I don't think the voters of Memphis are going to react that way. Is that the way he feels?' He was a member of an – in some quarters – unpopular minority, too; he was Jewish. I said that's why he says that because of his race, you know, but I have more faith in the people than he does."

"I know his son very well, Henry, Jr. He showed me pictures of his dad riding a Harley-Davidson motorcycle on the road from Memphis to New Haven when he was a student at Yale. During the Sanitation Workers Strike crisis, Henry, Jr. said his father kept a sawed-off shotgun in his desk drawer."

"A couple of his friends called, Jewish friends, and said, "But he married a country club beauty queen," and I said, "Well, who's *not* Jewish."

"When you came back from the Korean War…"

"When you say Korean War, I was inducted into the army when it was going on and I was in 1st Cavalry Division Headquarters Company, which was stationed, when I got there in Japan. And I *loved* my tour in Japan."

"Well, when you came back to Memphis the political climate here was affected by the symbiosis between Memphis and the political regime in Washington, was it not? What do you know about the influence of Senator Kenneth McKellar during this period?"

"K. D. McKellar was a Crump man. There was a sheriff right outside of Chattanooga who had a machine and the two of them between 'em had the major weight in the Democratic Party structure. He was hated by all the other Democratic candidates in the state. Crump took care of his candidates in the state. All I know about K. D. McKellar was you wanted something done by him, you saw Crump not McKellar. We never did have any direct relationship with him, because there was no point. Estes Kefauver was the first one we backed. We worked for him, and we helped his run across the state. That was the beginning of a statewide political organization, with the Kefauver campaign. That campaign was the November election in '59. The '59 election in Memphis was the one that galvanized the black vote in the city. That was the one I ran for public works and Ben Hooks ran for juvenile court. So we had the church organizations behind us, we had the Eastern Stars and the Masons behind us. All over west Tennessee there were, you know, Masonic clubs and Eastern Star clubs. We split our vote and we would look at the returns and checked them. We sent those stats out to every county in the state which had more than a 15% black population and that was 52 counties. They were all west of the river except for..."

"West of the Tennessee River...?"

"Yeah, we met at Fisk one Saturday, and told people send 'em to as many beautician lists, barber lists, teacher lists, anything we could get by race and sent letters like that. I guess we sent two or three thousand of them all over the state. And so we'll be in Nashville at Fisk University to discuss what we ought to do. When we got there, there were bunches of people from every county that we mailed letters to. In one day we formed the Tennessee Voter's Council: 52 counties – east Tennessee, middle Tennessee, west Tennessee – and that was the vehicle through which the black vote was cast for a decade. Then Kefauver had a heart attack and died.

"When Frank Clement won the governor's seat, he invited the leadership of the Voter's Council to Nashville and he had a room in a hotel reserved, a table and hors d'oeuvres and stuff and he had three tables up on the stage with a secretary behind each one with a Steno pad. He said, 'I want you all to know that Frank Clement never forgets his friends, and I know all of you have probably somebody you want us to consider for employment, as we will...' We said, 'Governor, that's not quite what we had in mind.' He said, 'Well, what do you mean?' So Vivian Henderson stood up and he says this is a study of Tennessee government. It shows minority employment and we want you to take this and we want you to let us know how you can change these figures. We haven't got anybody to recommend, we just want to see you start filling in some blanks. We got huge areas of government in which there are no black employees, and we can assure you that you all can find somebody who's competent for a lot of those positions. But he hadn't done much of that when he ran again, so he got beat. Then A. W. Willis got elected as state Senator and I was seated in the House. A. W. and I flipped a coin to decide who'd run for the House or the Senate."

"Didn't you have an office on Vance Avenue with a couple of other attorneys after you were Representative?"

"Hooks, Willis, & Sugarmon opened up down on Vance. That was the office I was in until we set up the interracial law firm."

"Well, in the Sixties you represented civil rights cases, I believe, from the territory north of Jackson, Mississippi, up to Memphis."

"That was our area of responsibility during the Freedom Summer. That was the summer when kids from all over the country volunteered to go to Mississippi and Alabama on voter registration campaigns. Anticipating trouble with the local sheriffs, the NAACP agreed that they would have a headquarters based in Memphis for everything going on from the state line down to a line just north of Jackson. They had an office in Jackson from that line north of Jackson down to the Gulf. Lawyers and students came from all over the country and volunteered."

"Do you think the Freedom Rides and the sit-ins in Mississippi and Tennessee in the early Sixties were an effective method of targeting segregation in an everyday context, as opposed to going through legalist, political devices?"

"Let me give you a predicate for that. During the '59 campaign John Seigenthaler, Sr. was a reporter for *The Tennessean* Nashville daily, and he came to Memphis looking at the '59 campaign and he became friends with me and with A. W. Willis and with Ben Hooks. When the Freedom Rides started in 1961 he got hit on the head with a lead pipe in Montgomery trying rescue Susan Wilbur, a Freedom Rider who was being chased by an angry mob. We went down there and got off the bus, and they had pictures of him with his head wrapped in bandages. He and Bob Kennedy were very close. We had gone to Washington right after Kennedy got elected and Seigenthaler was Bobby's executive administrator in Justice. He had arranged a meeting for us with Robert Kennedy, who met us, and he said he wished to thank us for the effort we had done for his brother in Shelby County, because we had reversed the black vote. It had been 60% Republican four years earlier. We made it 60% bigger than that for Democratic campaign that year. Kennedy didn't get Tennessee, but they checked every black precinct in Shelby County. We carried every one of them. Well then he said, 'If the rest of your people down there would vote like you all, then you would have very little problem. So you need to tell them to go home and get off their asses and register to vote.' But he had no understanding. A couple people got killed later. Then when Seigenthaler got hit on the head I called the office up there and I said, 'Give me the Attorney General.' I said, 'Well, give the Attorney General a message.' He said, 'What?' I told him the story: 'The Attorney General told us to get off our asses, tell him,' I said, 'we're off our asses.' That's when they finally realized that it wasn't just a matter of not wanting to vote. Hey, you could get killed for trying to vote in some of those places. Not in Shelby County. Shelby County was unique, I think, across the South, where black voting was accepted as universal."

"Well, the black vote was also a problem during those days because in the Democratic primary only white people were allowed to vote."

"Everywhere but Shelby County, Tennessee. The next county to us had people run off the plantations when they tried to vote. They had Tent City in Fayette County and they had a Tent City in Haywood County. I used to go up there to try to get people out of jail and that sort of thing."

"Trying to get people out of jail who attempted to vote?"

"Yeah, they'd go over there and try to register to vote and they'd put them all off sharecropping. They were living out on a pasture in tents in those two counties. So Robert Kennedy had no idea the degree to which, and the viciousness with which, the 'blacks don't vote regimes' were enforced across the South. For example, the SNCC organizer, Fannie Lou Hamer from down in Ruleville, Mississippi, in the Democratic convention in Atlantic City, which was after the assassination of Jack Kennedy, she testified in front of the Democratic Convention's Credentials Committee, and we were given the Freedom Democratic Party delegation. They had run a parallel delegate election to the convention across Alabama & Mississippi. Fannie Lou Hamer testified before the rules committee for about three days. This was an uneducated black woman. For three days, she told them, that they had stripped her, and whipped her until they gave out, then another deputy whipped her until he gave out, and kept her handcuffed to a cell, in a cell block, and left her there for about five days. She said the sheriff finally came in and he says, 'Look Fannie, I'm tired of this crap. Now, you sign a paper admitting the Communists hired you to organize the niggers here, and if you don't we're going to drop you in the river.' Yeah, but those days, you didn't know whether he meant it or not. And so she said she prayed and she cried and she cried and she prayed, and she said that next morning the handcuffs were hurting her arm so bad that she said to herself, *if you's gonna die, you might as well die for something*. But that type of thing was going on."

"It was like a battleground."

"It was a struggle for power and the vote was the power. I mean we understood why they didn't want us to vote. I didn't blame them, hell, they were trying to hang on to their wealth and we wanted to get it. We were at the point where you know *this life is no life…* it was sort of semi being alive. You couldn't be a human being under those circumstances. Some students sat-in at a Rexall Drugstore over in Somerville, Tennessee, and they got arrested. Maxine Smith called and said you all need to go up there. Jim Larson had a church here and he was a proponent of redemption through 'creative suffering'. Ben Hooks' wife had just got a brand new white Plymouth station wagon, and Jim, Benny, A. W. Willis, and I drove that over there. So we get up there and it looks like a movie set: pick-up trucks, and bob trucks and wagons. It was dusk so people lighted up pitchforks to see by. Fortunately the kids were in a jail that had been built by the WPA in '38 or '39, and it had solid iron bars, was fire proof, and was like a fort. So we said it was best for them to stay in there for the time being. The General Sessions Judge named Paul Summers was there with the sheriff and we had a bondsman meeting us who was already standing right next to the sheriff. He made bonds in that county for people who were bootlegging – bootlegging was a big industry in the rural parts of the South. There was a deputy sheriff and one policeman. They were holding the mob back over the sidewalk in front of the jail. The bondsman looked around and said, 'Wait a minute before you all say one word. I'm gonna make one thing clear,' and he turned to the sheriff and said, 'How long have you known me, Sheriff?' He said, 'Why?' He repeated, 'How long have you known me? Just answer the question.' Sheriff said, 'Oh, 10 or 15 years. Why?' Bondsman said, 'In all those years, have I ever lied to you?' He said, 'No.' He said, 'I'm gonna tell you something, and I ain't lying.' He says, 'You see all those peoples?' He said, 'Yes, I do.' The bondsman said, 'If they come after me, they're getting *you* 'cause I ain't letting you go!' He had the sheriff by the gun belt – he just had him by the gun belt holding him.

"So they let us in and we talked to the kids. We said, 'Well, it's kind of messy out there. It would be better if we got you out in the morning 'cause it might be a lot of hassle otherwise.' And they were not upset at all. They said, *okay, that's fine.* They understood. By the nature of that jail, it was the safest place for us to leave them. So we got back in our car. The sheriff told the policemen to escort us, and we were to follow behind. So we get to the city exit, and the policeman rolled his window down and said, 'Keep straight that way to Shelby County. This is as far as I go,' and he rolled his window back up and lit a cigarette. Here we are driving down this road and it curves and A. W. looked around and said, 'Oh look at all those cars following us. This looks like a funeral.' And the Reverend Hooks he looks and said, 'What the hell do you say at a time like this?' So we drive a little further, and A. W. asks Jim, 'Jim, you've been preaching to all those creative sufferers, do you think we ought to stop and let them beat the bum out of us?' Jim didn't pause a second, he said, 'Creative suffering requires witnesses. No witnesses back there. Drive faster.' We were more comfortable in Jim's spiritual leadership after that scene.

"We passed a car on the right side of the road and as we got to the front of it, there was a *crack!* It sounded like someone had just gouged a groove right across the windshield. He fired, but waited an instant little too late. So the angle wasn't right to break the glass. You could put your finger down through that slit and you could smell the gunpowder. You know how playing football you get used to the reaction time and the game slows down. When the bullets hit it seemed like we were ducked down for years. Benny was ducked down like that driving… they couldn't see anybody in the car, but we couldn't see *out.* I said, 'Benny, how can you see?' He says, 'I can't, but I can feel the shoulder.' We drove on blindly a few more miles, I don't know how long, but it seemed like a week or two. Then we raised up and drove the car back into the middle of the road. We were lucky there wasn't a car we'd run into out there on that gravel shoulder, but we didn't. Finally we got back to Memphis, but with a pattern of fresh bullet holes blasted in the new Plymouth."

"Well, speaking of Mississippi, how influential was Senator James Eastland in keeping the federal government from intervening during those times?"

"Yeah, well I'm saying, we just regarded him as…one of the enemy."

"Do you think Mayor Henry Loeb was ultimately responsible for much of the conflict in Memphis during the Sixties, or was he simply a point man in a much larger state and regional move against desegregation by organizations like the White Citizens Council?"

"I was never impressed with him as a person… he wasn't capable of anything but an attitude. His attitude was negative, and his family was wealthy. He had no need to work. He held jobs, including the mayor's office, but I don't ascribe to him the worst involvement in the segregationist movement on his own at all. All he worked from was attitude."

"So he just represented a constituency. Whatever he felt was the prevailing mentality, he would react to that."

"No, he reacted to segregation through racial prejudice. That was his attitude; that's the way he was. I don't think he reacted to the constituency; he reacted to his beliefs."

"So you feel like he embodied racial prejudice?"

"Well, that's a complicated way of saying he was a racist."

"I mean, he *was* educated, he should have understood racial equality is an inalienable right guaranteed in our constitution. Of course President Bush went to Yale, too… which in the end justifies very little. I think everyone could have expected a lot more positive leadership from Mayor Loeb than what came out with his handling of the sanitation workers' strike… to see how the whole thing played so tragically out under his stewardship."

"He was just being himself. He was being a jerk."

"So he had an aggressive, belligerent type personality to go with it? That's rather unexpected for an educated Jew, in my opinion."

"Well, you know, he had a strong personality. He overcame education. My hope is that what happened with Congressman Steve Cohen in the last Congressional district election here proves that we're advancing on *issues* rather than racial lines. He is Jewish; he was in the state Senate for maybe 12 or 15 years, and during that time he worked consistently on trying to sort out the Board of Education. He worked on animal rights things and all kinds of progressive agendas. I think that he is one of the most effective congressmen that I've seen around here in my lifetime.

"In his active first term there was a black woman, who had worked for Congressman Harold Ford. She came to town from Alabama or somewhere, but she had about $300,000 available for a campaign. I don't know of anybody who starts out with no history, no face in politics who could get that kind of money, but she had it. She got beat, and next time Steve was running, and she ran again. The district this time is almost 70% black, his district. He won with 80% of the black vote. I think that means our folks learned that race is not the issue now. The issue is record and platform, and he made it possible for every family in Tennessee to get their kid a college education because of that lottery financing the scholarships. Our folks knew it.

"I had retired from the bench and gotten involved in politics again, and I was with one of the workers putting up signs in yards in a low-income district, a black district. I'm putting out in the county these board plywood signs, and this woman was sitting on a front porch in a rocking chair across the street from where we're putting up a sign. She saw us and she says, 'Oh, you're all in politics? I got a question.' So I went over there and she came out with this campaign piece, and she said, 'I used to respect this guy and I don't know what's wrong with him now.' It wasn't about Steve; it was about a black lawyer who was endorsing this woman running against him. The ticket, the only thing she had was her race. Then she said, 'He's gonna back this woman against Steve Cohen? And after what he did?' This woman, she was just an average, old lady, black. I said, 'Lady… God, you made my day; we were worried.' She said, 'I already voted for Steve.' Obviously she knew where her interest lay. So I'm hoping that maybe our folk have grown up. I imagine the white vote here now is the minority and a lot of them are very uncomfortable. I'm uncomfortable too, but the vote for Steve Cohen was a positive thing in terms of race being a minimal issue in that campaign based on the issues involved. He got an 80% vote. I mean, that represents an enlightened evaluation of what matters. Maybe that can spread because Steve, he's active and he's around and his value to the community is appreciated, black and white. Maybe other people can do that same thing. I don't know. I think we're in the process of learning how this is supposed to work. If it works out, I don't know, but at least we got this far."

CABIN NOTES:

Lying down here in the bed on Cox St. with a pain in the neck from reading, I lapsed into a reverie of my last audience with 60s civil rights compatriot, Charles Sudduth. Jr. It was down in Hollandale, Mississippi, on a Sunday afternoon sitting on his front porch. As he was talking around the still disquieting specter of the Ku Klux Klan, Charles recounted his first encounter with the KKK and the ordeal of Coon-on-a-Log.

"Well, when I was about 10 years old, advertising flyers appeared in our town. Notices also appeared in the local paper and on the radio as well. It was announced that there was to be a Coon-on-a-Log contest at the dam on Kelly Drew Alexander's plantation on such and such a day. Black people were also referred to as "coons" by the Klansmen. As it was no more than a few yards from our house, I walked over there with my dog on his leash on that day. The contest was a great festival for the Ku Klux Klansmen who brought their coonhounds to participate in the contest. Some of them I knew, but most were strangers to me. They were the filthiest people I had ever seen; they were so dirty that it scared me. They appeared to have been mutant ghouls dredged up from a fetid swamp, or pulled from some muddy cave.

"A huge boar raccoon was chained by its neck to a log that was floated in the water above Mr. Alexander's dam. One by one the Klansmen turned their hounds loose on the raccoon to see whose dog could pull him off the log. Raccoons are not aggressive; they will usually run and hide from an attacker. The only way to make them fight is to chain them so that they have no choice but to stand and fight. A raccoon is extremely dexterous and can at times drown a coonhound but there was always a Klansman standing nearby chest-deep in the water ready to pull the 'coon off the dog before that happened.

"At the end of the contest it was announced that there would be a second contest held for the winners of the first contest. Such contests were the favorite sport of the Klansmen and were carried out in many places in Mississippi. The women and children were then instructed to leave the area and the Klansmen were invited to gather on the other side of the dam for the second contest. A hallmark characteristic of the Klansmen was their cruelty to animals; they thought nothing of killing pets, livestock or wildlife and encouraged their children to do the same. A favorite terror tactic was to kill the dog or cat of a civil rights worker to leave it on his doorstep or hang it on his gate. But their cruelty to black people was almost beyond description.

"The next morning I walked back to the dam and there I observed a pile of intestines floating on top of the water but some time elapsed before I learned what happened at the second contest. At that contest a black man was chained to another log and it was floated in the creek, then one by one the Klansmen turned their coonhounds on him until they ripped open his chest and tore out the entrails and organs then left the body to float down the creek."

"How did you get to know other Klansmen as you were growing up, Charles?"

"When I was about 12 or 13 years old, Mr. Patterson, a neighbor down the street carried me to meetings of the Ku Klux Klan. They showed me their secret handshake and taught me their secret code words. I remember the Confederate cigarette lighters handed out by their Exalted Cyclops, Kelly Drew Alexander. He was deacon in the Baptist church, Colonel on the staff of Governor Ross Barnett, and a lawyer in the Mississippi Bar Association. Alexander was also head of the Washington County draft board local #82. The cigarette lighters had the battle flag of the Confederacy on one side and the portrait of an aged Confederate soldier wielding a saber on the other side with a caption underneath that read "FORGET HELL" and it played the tune Dixie when the lid was flipped.

"Mr. Patterson was the accountant for the Torrey Woods Plantation at Murphy where black people were lynched by the Klansmen. Torrey Woods Senior and Torrey Woods Junior together *were the wealthiest planters in the town. All the Pattersons and Woodses were members of the Ku Klux Klan/Baptist church. The Klansmen wore Confederate uniforms in our local pageants and parades. They perceived themselves as Confederate soldiers, operating as guerrillas behind enemy lines sworn to use guile, terrorism, infiltration, and dissimulation to drive out the Federal Government and destroy federal institutions. Like all Klansmen, Mr. Alexander hated the Federal Government with a passion that was venomous. Mr. Alexander said that Klansmen were entitled to do anything...lie, steal, cheat, rob, commit murder, do absolutely anything to get the Federal Government out of Mississippi.*

"Everyone is aware of the unmitigated hatred that Klansmen/Baptists held for Catholics, Jews and Jehovah's Witnesses, but few are aware that they hated black religions even more, despite the fact that many black people called themselves Baptists. Other than tearing down a school built by the Federal Government, Klansmen loved nothing more than burning down a black church. While the white school was at least physically designed to be able to impart the semblance of an education, the black school, in contrast, appeared to be some sort of a warehouse. It had no playground equipment, no shade trees, no room for activities or sports, no gymnasium. It looked like a medium security prison set in a cotton field and surrounded with barbed wire; the only visible plumbing was a ditch along the front. This was all justified under the program of 'separate but equal'.

The Arcola Chief-of-Police also attended the Klan meetings. Ace Matthews was an honored person in Washington County for it was he who murdered those three poor black people and dangled their carcasses from the bridge in the middle of the dirty little town of Arcola, Mississippi. Hundreds if not thousands of Mississippians journeyed to the town of Arcola to gawk at and mock and glorify in that spectacular crime against humanity. No rational man could talk to Ace Matthews for he was an incoherent, psychopathic barbarian. He would shout and rant and rave and point his pistol in any direction just like the dangerous hoodlum that he was. White people in Washington County were so proud of Ace Matthews that they let him ride their children around town in his police car and run black people off the road.

"A few years later Byron Dela Beckwith was bragging all over the state of having murdered Medgar Evers; he boasted endlessly how he shot Medgar in the back but was always careful – or not so carefull – not to put his admission in direct words. In 1965 my roommate at Delta State College at Cleveland, Mississippi, went to a rally for Beckwith and returned as white as a sheet. When asked what happened, the Ohioan gasped out, 'My God! He publicly admitted killing Medgar Evers! What kind of people are you?' The Congress of Racial Equality sent two white civil rights workers to our town in June of 1964. One was a Charles Carpenter from Wyoming. They were such friendly and well-educated boys only a couple years older than myself, and it was an honor to help them in their activities of leafleting, talking to people and in their demonstrations. In truth, it was black people who fought and gained their civil rights... there was very little that white civil rights workers could do. About the only thing we could do was to be polite, friendly, respectful, and try to persuade white people not to kill them. The two civil rights workers were provided with lodging by a black lady in her own home, and for white people to live in a black home was regarded as one of the greatest of all imaginable crimes. The Mayor of Hollandale, J. W. Fore, approached the two boys and advised them that 'you cannot live in the Negro section of town and register voters.'

"The CORE workers served out their three month stint, then escaped Mississippi but the black lady who befriended them had no such luck. In May of 1973 Mayor Fore and four other men caught Mrs. Daisy Savage and her 11-year-old grandson fishing near Steele Bayou at the Yazoo Wildlife Refuge, a few miles outside of town. They stoned both of them to death with the riprap limestone chunks that lined the banks, stuffed their bodies back into their car then pushed it into the bayou. No one was ever charged with these murders. This is the only public record that exists of it. Daisy was the finest and bravest woman in the entire town. Mayor Fore was always detectable by sound, if not by sight, as his voice rang out above all others when they sang

'Bringing in the Sheaves' in the choir at the First Baptist Church.

"*The hierarchy of the Ku Klux Klan is drawn exclusively from the hierarchy of the white Southern Baptist church; their Kleagles, Exalted Cyclopses, Grand Wizards, etc., were all deacons. Persons suspected of atheism were regarded as double-criminals. Nearly every lawyer, judge and bailiff in the state was a contributor to or member of the Ku Klux Klan as the Klansmen regarded jurisprudence as their exclusive domain. Law degrees and judgeships were handed out like candy to the most vicious and ignorant louts that could be found, which is how most came to obtain their law degree as law for the Klansmen was only a case study of how to evade federal law.*

"*Many people think of racism whenever they hear the word Klansman but they were far more than just racists: their hatred of women was almost as great as their hatred of black people. If you ever see a woman in Mississippi who has a black eye or bruises on her arms or scratches on her face or missing teeth or unexplained absences at work or hear her husband yell at her in public, you can mark it down that woman is married to a Klansman. They beat the hell out of their wives. Wherever you find a strong Ku Klux Klan, you will also find a house of prostitution just around the corner. Although they have no respect for women whatsoever, they will quickly raise a lynch party for any outsider even slightly suspected of looking at one of their white women.*

"*The Klansmen were all expert moon shiners and bootleggers, and produced more illicit whiskey than all the major distilleries put together. It was the Ku Klux Klan and the Southern Baptist Church who in the 1920s disfigured the simple beauty of the US Constitution with their 18th amendment (Prohibition). The only amendment that ever had to be repealed by a second amendment. They stayed drunk six days a week, went to their Baptist revivals on Sunday to roll on the floor, 'get religion' and to swear off alcohol forever, then were right back at it again on Monday morning. Prohibition for the Klansmen was only a method of eliminating their competition from the commercial distilleries. Some authorities claim that the largest cash crop in Mississippi today is marijuana production and one can believe that these operations are carried out by Klansmen. They are the only ones with the land resources, agricultural and distribution expertise as well as the knowledge of who to bribe and who not to bribe. Mississippi police officials frequently intercept South Americans smuggling marijuana through the state but they NEVER apprehend local growers of the state's largest cash crop.*

"*Whenever the Klan had a black person they wished to punish without actually killing him, they would take him to Merlin Jones who would beat him nearly to death with a black leather bullwhip. Merlin Jones was also the chief bootlegger in our town and openly supplied both moonshine and name brand whiskey to the town's thirsty citizens as well as to two black juke joints across the tracks. Merlin had a whiskey store/tavern on Highway 61 and he kept several illegal one-armed bandit slot machines in a back room. Directly across the road he owned a diner and a run-down motel consisting of about six rooms where he supplied both black and white prostitutes to the Klansmen and traveling salesmen. Organized crime was totally controlled by members of the Ku Klux Klan. All of the Joneses were members of the Ku Klux Klan and the First Baptist church. The niche occupied by the Mafia dons in New York and Chicago was the same niche occupied by Klan leaders in Mississippi but with a greater degree of malevolence and intolerance. The Mafia was primarily concerned with their own members; Baptists tried to control everything from the flow of liquor to the thought patterns of the entire society.*

"*The Klansmen were notoriously intolerant to anyone who would flaunt their social mores yet they themselves had not the least qualm of breaking them. The greatest of all the Baptists' taboos, sexual contact between white and black, was smirked at when it came to their own members breaking them. Merlin Jones had in addition to his white wife and white children, a second, black wife by whom he had more children. Jones openly divided his time between the two wives.*

"*The infrastructure of the Ku Klux Klan was largely broken up by the FBI in the late 1970s and early 1980s after the demise of J. Edgar Hoover. The Ku Klux Klan is no longer a unified, formal organization with a recognizable office or telephone number but it is still a powerful force." Charles voice had the assurance of one who knows, and its mellow tones began to fade in and out as I rolled over to reach for the half full tumbler of soothing Bourbon on the night table. Always a pleasure, I thought, talking with a true son of the South.*

CHAPTER THE EIGHTH
HOP HEAD RAMPAGE

"If you're going from Heaven to Hell, you have to go through Memphis."
–Overheard in the Memphis airport

On May 28, 1962, Eddie Bond lost all hope for the career of his baritone-throated protégé as the prison doors closed shut upon Hi Records recording artist, Tommy Ray Tucker. Bond had been grooming him for stardom under contract since the little singer was 17-years-old. Got him on the Louisiana Hayride, recorded him on the Feathers tune, "Lovin' Lil", and promoted Tucker's crowning achievement – high-tone, ultra lush production of Jack Clement's monster country rocker, "Miller's Cave". Tucker had been singing nightly at a joint on 61 Highway in South Memphis called the Little Black Book. He drank a few beers during his set, and polished off a few swigs of whiskey and Coke with customers before he left the club early one starry night. Alone he headed north to town behind the wheel of a powerful 1957 Oldsmobile V8. He must have been pushing the Olds pretty hard when he rammed the rear of a 1960 Chevrolet ahead of him, smashing and igniting its gas tank into an exploding ball of flame. The impact pushed the flaming Chevy and its occupants – a man and his wife knocked unconscious – into the path of an oncoming station wagon that met it head-on in a disastrous fire-drenched collision. Driving the doomed wagon, was a successful attorney and civic leader, US Navy WWII veteran, and winner of numerous Jaycees' awards including "Outstanding Young Man of the Year" of 1955. At his side was his attractive wife, seven months pregnant, and mother of their six children. They were returning to Coro Lake from an evening at Front Street Theater and an after-party at the Rathskeller near Court Square.

The left front tire had been blown off the rim, but Tucker kept plowing the Oldsmobile onward at formidable speed. Running on the rim of the front wheel, firey blue-white metallic sparks were scorching the street as he shot passed three youths leaving the roadside Hi-Hat Club at what they estimated to be 70 to 80 mph. They could see the car had been involved in a crash, and they jumped in their car and chased the apparition in hot pursuit, but it wasn't easy keeping up with the Olds as it was swerving all over the road with tires screaming. Finally Tucker turned off near Mallory and Third St. He brought the fuming behemoth to a standstill, and stumbled out of the car apparently unhurt, but inebriated. The kids pulled up behind, and demanded his car keys until they could summon the police as it was evident he was running away from something... not knowing that Tucker had left four people burned to a crisp in the middle of Highway 61. Strangely a carload of youth drove up all dressed in maroon sweaters with the same letter "S" patched on the front. They challenged the two boys and girl over the car keys, and a fight ensued. Meanwhile a Cadillac appeared driven by the shapely brunette owner of the Junkers Club who had dropped by the Little Black Book to talk to the singer about appearing at a Halloween party at her club. As Tucker had left the club early, she missed him, and followed him here... after passing the conflagration of smoldering metal and charred bodies in the middle of the road. Tucker sullenly climbed in the Caddy and was driven to a girlfriend's house in Midtown where officers from the homicide squad arrested him three hours later. A Memphis Grand Jury indicted the star of the Little Black Book, and 20-year-old Tommy Tucker was convicted of second-degree murder... thus ending a star-crossed career. Under conviction of involuntary manslaughter, Tucker served 11 months, 29 days at the Shelby County Penal Farm.

God help the man who gets lost in Miller's Cave
Like the bats and the bears in Miller's Cave
They're never gonna find me
cause I'm lost... In Miller's Cave

The auditorium of White Station High School was jam packed with more than 1,200 people on the night of March 26, 1965. They were attending the semifinal competition of the Miss Memphis Pageant, one of the city's most prominent social events and consequential in that the winner would go the state competitions in Nashville for the Miss Tennessee contest. The winner from there would go on to the Miss America Pageant. Among the juried panel was Memphian Linda Mead Shea who held the title of Miss America 1960. The chairman of the pageant was Joe Smith, credit manager at General Electric Credit Corporation and a leading member of the Memphis Junior Chamber of Commerce, or the Jaycees, who were the organizers and sponsors of the event. During the intermission, Joe's gorgeous 29-year-old wife, Barbara Jean, left the auditorium to drive home their three young children who'd grown restless during the break in the excitement.

She dropped the children into the arms of her cousin waiting to baby-sit them, and drove from home back to the pageant. She made it as far as the Eudora Baptist Church parking lot across from the school auditorium. After the pageant ended, Joe stayed around drinking coffee with friends, but Barbara Jean had not returned. Joe figured she'd become tired and decided to stay home. He drove home in a Buick convertible that the Pageant had furnished for the event. Barbara Jean was not there. He thought that she'd probably returned to the pageant, gone out with friends afterward, and they'd somehow missed each other. Joe fell asleep on the couch, and awoke at 4:00 a.m. in a panic. His wife was missing. Joe called all of his friends. Barbara Jean was not with them. Then he called his fellow Jaycees, who went with him to the school and began searching the grounds. They called the custodian, had the building opened, but found nothing. Meanwhile, the police had been notified and officers were already searching the area. Across the street, as Joe and his companions entered the parking lot of the church they saw the Smith's yellow Ford abandoned near the side entrance with the driver's door swung open. They combed the parking lot and as they rounded the corner of the building, about 50 yards ahead they spotted a body lying face down on the pavement. They pulled Joe away from the scene, and back to their cars where they told him that Barbara Jean was gone. She was found shot three times in the back, and then shot point-blank in the face through her right nostril.

The police theorized that Barbara Jean had been accosted by someone she knew, and had driven in the parking lot and gotten out of her car whereupon her assailant beat her so brutally about the face that a part of the wooden handle of the pistol had broken off. From the looks of the fresh footprints, it was apparent that this was a woman struggling desperately for her life. She broke away and ran to the double entrance door, but they were locked. Blood was smeared on the door glass in testimony to her vain struggle to get inside. Then she broke away again – oddly running in the opposite direction of the safety of the school auditorium where hundreds of people were still in attendance at the pageant. She ran around three sides of the church building before her assailant fired the three .38 caliber bullets out of a .357 Magnum, then finished her off with the bullet in the face. Her nose had telltale gunpowder burns around the nostril.

There was no robbery; there was no sexual molestation. With the exception of the shard of pistol handle and footprints, there was no evidence other than ballistics reports on the bullets that entered her body. Charming, with a bubbling personality, Barbara Jean, was a Berclair School PTA president, a Cub Scout den mother, and was well liked within the community. The police were baffled – there seemed to be no motive, other than what they termed a random act of violence. The murder touched off one of the most massive manhunts in the history of the Bluff

Barbara Jean & Joe Smith

City. All days off were cancelled for the homicide officers. A hundred officers and detectives scoured the crime scene and the areas around it. Divers were sent down in a nearby pond to search for the murder weapon. During the endless investigations and interrogations, Joe recalled Barbara Jean receiving numerous phone calls at home from someone asking for a date, someone who had given her a ride home once. She said the annoying calls were from a Memphis police officer, and asked Joe to report the incidents, which he did. Joe went in person to police headquarters and filed a formal complaint, although neither Barbara nor he knew the name of the officer. Evidently the police shrugged off the complaint. In time, the pestering phone calls ended and faded from immediate memory. No one knows if the homicide investigators followed through on this seemingly pertinent information. Eventually police commissioner Claude Armour announced to the press that they had gathered enough circumstantial evidence to identify the killer... but in order to strengthen their case, he again appealed to the public to those, whom they were sure had relevant knowledge of the murder, to come forward as witness for the prosecution. No one did. Two years slipped by with no indictments. Then came a bolt from the blue when a special crime committee formed by Mayor William B. Ingram announced to the press they had uncovered substantial evidence implicating a Memphis police officer of a rank higher than patrolman. The police commissioner reacted with hostility and demanded that the mayor's office name names. Ultimately no further information was divulged by the police department or by the mayor's special crime committee, and Attorney General Phil Canale let the matter lapse. To this day the case endures as an unresolved mystery, although in Tennessee for the crime of murder there is no statute of limitations, and a box of evidential artifacts remains in the back office of the Memphis Homicide Cold Case Squad.

Riding motorbikes around Memphis with Fred Queen became more of a thrill when Fred got his old lady to buy him a brand new 750cc Triumph Trident. It was a low slung, shiny black confection that was the fastest thing on the drag strip at Lakeland, a track just east of Memphis. It made an exemplary companion to my black 750 Featherbed Norton. Fred ordered the bike from Jimmy Arnold, the Triumph dealer. Arnold knew everything there was to know about a Triumph inside and out, and he knew how to ride them better than anybody. His dealership off Summer Avenue was as much a clubhouse as it was an official sales agency. Jimmy looked like a sloppy Harvard graduate, wearing Levis, a white t-shirt, and sneakers around the shop. Over the sales counter hung the framed rendering of a female torso with a hand covering one of its oversized tits. Underneath, a cryptic logo read, *be sure to grab the right one.* The clientele, of whom there were many, hanging around unshaven, chewing Bull O the Woods tobacco, wearing hunting caps and grinning lasciviously over their communion of slimy inside jokes, exuded an aura far more insidious than their leather-jacketed Harley riding brethren. The muted arrogance of Arnold was matched only by his artful sarcasm. It always seemed a pain in the neck for him to step around behind the counter to sell you spare parts. If you bought too many, he'd wisecrack, "If you're gonna buy all that, why not replace the whole damn bike?" Jimmy Arnold was man of refined good taste, however. Last time I saw him, he was restoring an Ariel Square Four to an immaculate standard. Fred Queen and Jimmy Arnold shared something of a resemblance: thin, small head and wiry constitution, except Jimmy was clean-shaven while Fred wore steel-rimmed glasses, long sideburns, and a pointed beard. They knew how to ride fast... and just how to tuck themselves in on the machine whilst tearing through a high-speed curve.

When I first met Fred Queen he was paling around with Connie Edwards, a midtown go-go dancer and stage vixen in Big Dixie Brick Co. Fred would drop by my place to shoot the breeze: usually about late night biker bars he frequented. He'd relate incidents like when some member of the Outlaws MC gang pounced on a rival, wrestled him down to the barroom floor, then whipped out a pair of pliers and yanked out the front teeth of his foul-mouthed victim. Upon depicting such altercations in graphic detail, he would then lay back on the couch with grim satisfaction and daydream about riding a BSA 650 Clubman. Acquisition of the new Trident greatly exceeded these pipe dreams, but Fred had lived through considerable Karma to attain this three-cylinder/triple-megaphone Bardo Plane.

Once he kidnapped Connie, blindfolded her, and took her someplace that she had no idea where she was. He tied her to a chair for three days while spiders nibbled her feet and had his way with her. She claimed Fred was *real* abusive – stoned on barbs *or* straight. After the tortuous end of his entanglement with Connie, Fred became engaged to young woman named Dana Bender, but ended up with her dowdy, silver-blue haired mother, Carol. After all, Mom had the savings account. One crisp autumn afternoon, I stopped by the tidy bungalow of Carol Bender in the svelte North Parkway area next to Rhodes College where Fred was staying to see if he wanted to go riding. Through the shrubbery I caught a glimpse of his black Triumph Triple resting tilted on its side stand behind the glass slot windows of the garage. Carol came to the door in a muumuu with eyes swollen shut; her face and flabby bare arms were black and blue all over. She spoke in a groggy intonation, "Freyad just stomped me... he *stomped* me..." and closed the door ruefully.

On the sultry evening of September 1st, 1968, when Fred and Connie were still living together, Timothy Murray stopped by their duplex in Midtown to swap his Volkswagen for the evening to take a joy ride on Fred's previous Triumph motorbike, a 650 Bonneville. Murray was a 19-year-old freshman enrolled in the sculpture department of the Memphis Academy of Art, and he was Fred's best friend. Connie handed Timothy the keys to Fred's cycle, and the fledging artist powered off into the darkness gripping the high-rise ape hanger handlebars of the roarty Bonneville. On Poplar Avenue a big car pulled up behind the cyclist and crowded in on him aggressively. Murray turned off into Overton Park, but the car chased him onto a side road in the park and pushed him off the pavement at terrific speed. The Triumph flew off the tarmac crashing into two trees, fracturing Murray's skull and killing him instantly. The impact was so great that it knocked the boots off his feet. The two front tires of the car blew out upon impact with the cycle, and the car was left abandoned behind a nearby by gasoline station. At first the authorities thought the crash was an accident, but testimony from a newspapers boy who was out "throwing papers" on an early morning route happened to witness the accident. Within a month the drivers of the marauding automobile were tracked down by the police and charged with first-degree murder.

Actually the pursuit and harassment of Murray was a case of mistaken identity. Fred Queen and Timothy Murray looked much alike – more so than Jimmy Arnold and Fred. Murray was driven off the road because his assailants thought that they were chasing *Fred*. They'd swerved their car at the motorcycle in the mistaken belief that Queen was the rider. Dixon Allen Robinson III, was a passenger in the car driven by Stanley Graham Burleigh, 21. Queen had met Robinson, a tall, blond, broad-shouldered, 20-year-old apprentice carpenter, at a beer party of motorcycle riders around Cordova about two months before the accident. Before Murray's death, Queen had gone to Robinson's home on Peabody Avenue, looking for prospects for the Outlaws Motorcycle Club. He appeared proud of his motorcycle outfit. Fred wore a Nazi-type crash helmet, and had megaphones on his bike to amplify the sound coming from the exhaust pipes. A quarrel ensued over a jacket marked with Hell's Angels insignia that Robinson was wearing. Queen told Robinson he had no right to wear a jacket with the insignia of a motorcycling club of which he was not a member. The quarrel escalated into an altercation, and Robinson threatened Fred with the admonition, *I definitely intend to kill you.*

"Connie drew a gun on Robinson one night when he came prowling over to my house," Fred told me later. "As any girl will do to protect the man she loves."

Once I'd asked Connie about the incident. "Oh jeez, I felt bad because Tim came by and wanted to – for the night – borrow Fred's bike and lend Fred his car. So I said okay, 'cause I had the keys to both. They looked alike on the bike with the glasses on and everything. They chased poor Tim; some little boys saw him being chased by these thugs. They ran Tim into a tree in Overton Park, right there off Poplar by Parkway."

"Why were they after Fred?"

"Fred named this motorcycle club, The Family. You may have heard of them. There was a spy among them, and they were jealous. Fred was an okay guy until he turned into a junkie. Then I began to get beat up, and tortured, and you name it. It took away my free will."

"Is that when he got on drugs?"

"He was on them lightly before that, but after he came back from New York there was no stopping him with drugs. He was a heroin addict."

"Then he started the motorcycle gang?"

"Yes. He knew some Hell's Angels in New York. He was in the Navy before that. When he joined the Navy and because they told him *not* to, Fred exposed himself to Agent Orange that was poison. It was left in some of those big canister dump trucks. He got in there and crawled all around in it. So he ended up dying from Agent Orange. He swelled up like a balloon."

The state offered both offenders 11/29 in the penal farm to plead guilty. Burleigh accepted the deal, but Robinson pleaded not guilty maintaining, "I never even saw the motorcycle until it suddenly cut in front of us and turned into the park." When the case came to trial, the prosecuting attorney demanded a 99-year prison sentence for Dixon Allen Robinson III charging him with first-degree murder. A jury of six blacks and six whites was chosen and

Fred Queen Photo: E. Baffle 1977

founf him guilty of murder in the second degree. The judge sentenced Robinson to 10 years in the state penitentiary – the payoff to "get even with Queen," while Burleigh was sentenced to six months on the county penal farm as a consequence of playing ball with the prosecution. Fred Queen continued riding Triumphs and with his treatments for drug addiction.

"I ran into Fred again," I told Connie, "late at night just before he died. He was staying at the Ambassador Hotel down on a scary part of South Main. He was hanging out with his son in the afternoons. He told me he was going to die. He had gotten remorseful about his life and he was trying to be gentle and spend time with his son."

"Well the girl took the son 'cause she didn't want Fred's influence on it, 'cause he wouldn't give up heroin. She moved to California. Her name was Rosemary. Like everyone was making the joke, *Rosemary's Baby*. The funniest things in life are true," Connie mused.

The grisly antics of Midtown maniac Howard Putt, however, made Fred Queen look like the switchblade wielding, nun chuck whirling mama's boy that he was. While awaiting trial in the county jail on charges of first-degree murder for the multiple slayings of five Memphians, George Howard "Buster" Putt passed the time by making hard-edged pencil drawings in stark firm lines of the murder tableaux. The renderings were as ritualistic as the killings. In each instance the lean 24-year-old assassin with wavy blonde hair and sunglasses towered over his victims slashing away with a butcher knife. Of the women depicted each was middle-aged or elderly with the exception of one 20 years of age, yet all were idealized as slim and youthful. The victims were portrayed with hands tied behind their backs and with a choker cinched around their necks fashioned from silk stockings that Putt had ripped off their legs. Upon request of the defense, a psychotherapist put Putt under hypnosis for a 75-minute examination to determine sanity. While in his trance, Putt projected himself into the role of both the killer and the victim for whom he substituted his mother as a young woman. The therapist contended that Putt felt rage at his mother for his abused upbringing. He viewed the pencil renderings as an example of a "compulsive, too controlled, obsessively meticulous mind that holds so tautly to a bizarre concept of reality that, like a tight band, it snaps." The psychologist went on to comment that Putt suffered from paranoid schizophrenia, characterized by grandiose delusions. One such delusion that Putt harbored was that it was God's plan to kill him. By killing someone else, he set up his own self-destruction.

Clifford, his older brother, is quoted as saying that "our father mistreated us something bad." Their father was a drifter, part time truck driver and hospital orderly; he'd done prison time for writing hot checks. "Our mother, she did what he (the father) told her or she knew she'd get a beating. I've seen him hit her in the face and break her glasses. She was scared to death of him – we all were." In reform school in Richmond, Virginia, the teachers continued to administer beatings to Buster and Clifford. "This is where the trouble really started with Buster," his brother claimed. "The school had a football team which played a much larger varsity team and George, who played quarterback, was just flattened and got cleated in the forehead. After that he started having these black out spells. He'd do things during that spell, or trance, or whatever, and he wouldn't remember it later… he took to sleepwalking with his eyes open. He'd go to a graveyard behind the high school to just sit there and think."

The summer after his injury, Richmond police arrested Buster for molesting two young girls, one of whom was stripped naked and forced to suck his dick. Psychological testing revealed Putt's morbid preoccupation with blood and gore. He managed to flee from custody one night, clad only in his undershorts, and teamed up with his brother Clifford for several days before he was recaptured. He escaped from custody again and then he abducted a 30-year-old Richmond woman at knifepoint, robbed her of $35, raped her, and fled Virginia a fugitive on felony charges. In Laredo, Texas, Putt climbed through the window of an apartment and abducted the female tenant. As he was driving the woman out of town in her own car, he spotted a police van and crashed, fleeing on foot. He was captured and sentenced to thirteen months in the Webb County jail, from where he was shipped to the maximum-security juvenile lockup at Gatesville. Then he was transferred to the Terrace School, in Laredo, but Putt escaped, then was recaptured and sent to the more secure Hilltop School reformatory. A 1965 report termed him psychotic. Buster was just turning 19. In 1967 he was perfunctorily discharged from custody on his twenty-first birthday, as he could no longer be held as a juvenile. He drifted to Tupelo, Mississippi, where his grandparents were living and found work as a hospital orderly. In a few days, Buster was fired for stealing $100 from a nurse's handbag. From there he became entangled in one petty theft after the other.

In the fall of 1967, Buster migrated to Memphis where he quickly married his brother's pregnant ex-girlfriend, Mary Bulimore. The new Mrs. Putt worked at Baptist Memorial Hospital. Buster insisted on six to eight bouts of intercourse every night, although he rarely climaxed. Mary had the baby and the couple named him George Jr. In early 1969 the couple moved on to Jackson, Mississippi, his wife and with brother Clifford. There Buster tried to rape his mother-in-law on three separate occasions. Shortly after the third rape attempt, the police suspected that he committed his first murder in Jackson, when a socially prominent bachelor was slain on April 27, 1969. Rumored to engage in homosexual affairs, the victim was stabbed fifteen times at his home, a short distance from the gas station where Buster was employed. Putt was never charged in the crime, but authorities remain convinced he was the perpetrator. In May he was arrested for burglary and sentenced to six months at the county penal farm. From there he soon escaped by simply driving off in a truck, and the couple headed for Memphis to evade the Mississippi justice system. They floundered around Memphis trying to find jobs and selling blood. They made no friends. Their last residence was on Bethel in North Memphis. Even in the Bluff City, Buster seemed "odd" to most folks he met.

Before he was fired from his last job at another gas station for stealing from the register, Buster bought a $50 Bible from a peripatetic preacher. It was just five days after Buster committed his first Memphis slaying, when an evangelist, the Reverend A. A. Ragsdale, drove into the Hudson Oil Co. at 1505 Bellevue, where Putt was working as an attendant. The Reverend claimed that day young Buster was the only one who seemed interested in his Bibles, and is quoted as saying, "He told me he was married and had one child and they were expecting another. He said, 'I sure would like to have that for my wife, but I won't get paid til the 29th. So I told him to go ahead and take the Bible and I'd come back and get my $5 down payment then. On August 30th I went back by Hudson Oil Co. and that young man paid me $5 just like he promised and was as nice and gentlemanly as you please. He seemed in good spirits and perfectly normal." This was the same day that Buster's last victim, a shapely 21-year-old office worker was viciously slain on her way home from work. Meanwhile a $10,000 reward was posted for the capture of the "cunning sex slayer" with funds collected from the City Council and from private sources.

The first victims of Putt's rage were a quiet, middle-aged couple found strangulated and savagely defiled in their garden apartment at a fashionable address in Midtown at 1133 South Cooper. On August 16, 1969, their bodies were discovered a day after the slayings by their son, a student at Memphis State University. Police director, Frank Holloman, described the murder of Roy and Bernalyn Dumas as ritualistic and the most atrocious and revolting he had seen in years. Dumas was a navy veteran of World War II, and police said he appeared to be very frail, less than 100 pounds. His wife, described by a friend as "witty and humorous", was a slender brunette, and was employed as a registered nurse at Baptist Memorial Hospital. It's possible that Buster had murdered Roy Dumas first and was waiting when Bernalyn Dumas came home from work that afternoon. Both had been bludgeoned and then strangled with ladies hosiery. It was reported, "The woman lay spread-eagle on her bed, gagged, wrists and ankles bound to the bedposts. She had also been raped, her anus and vagina afterward mutilated with a pair of surgical scissors.

Within eleven days brave Buster struck again breaking into a clapboard house in the locus of Midtown and strangulating a rather feeble spinster 82 years of age. Leila Picard Jackson was found in her bedroom by her 18-year-old grandson in much the same position as Bernalyn Dumas, with a stocking tied around her neck and her genitals mutilated with a butcher knife. Her apartment in the triplex with its aged yellowed curtains had been just short of ransacked. In the aftermath of the butchery, Putt was evidentially poking around for some chump change. Real fear now began to grip the denizens of Midtown. All vacations and days off were canceled for officers assigned to the homicide squad.

Seventeen days later Glenda Sue Harden, a ravishingly pretty typist with long auburn hair, had left work in the Falls Building downtown on Front Street and headed to a nearby bank to cash her bi-monthly paycheck of $140. Her matte gold semi-mini dress sparkled in the late afternoon sun and her lithe figure cast a long shadow as she walked west through Confederate Park past the statue of Jefferson Davis. She felt relieved to be done with the gray IBM machine in the underwriters department for another weekend. She'd told a co-worker that she was going to Sears Midtown to shop and grab a quiet bite to eat, then drive home to get ready for a date with her fiancé. They were to announce their engagement on September 7th. From the park she walked down the 39-steps of the bluff and across the railroad tracks to where her powder blue Mustang was parked in a lot by the river. At 5:00 a.m. the next morning her Mustang was found five blocks away on the cobblestones at the foot of Monroe and Riverside Drive. Her purse and shoes were inside. A dragnet was ordered and at 4:10 p.m. her body was found by two patrolmen in a secluded brushy area of Riverside Park. With her hands bound behind her back, she had been manically stabbed fourteen times as she lay helpless. Discovery of her ravaged body touched off widespread panic in Memphis.

About 30 minutes after the discovery of Glenda Sue Harden's corpse, Buster himself actually went down to police headquarters, mingled with others there, and asked homicide detectives general questions about the crime! He was quoted as describing the scene there as like "a circus with everybody running around" and the phones ringing like crazy. During the ensuing afternoons Putt would work with his brother on repairing their Buick station wagon. "I had a bad feeling every time I would see him," Clifford admitted. "He would say, 'There was another murder, another murder,' and I hadn't heard it on the news or anything. It seemed that he wanted to tell me what he had done. I knew something was wrong. He'd show me the exact houses where those deaths occurred. He pointed them out." On September 9th, an anonymous caller fingered George Putt as the fiend responsible for the slayings, but the police were too befuddled with tips and leads to act on the information.

Capture of George "Buster" Putt Sept. 11, 1969

September 11, 1969, started as a happy day for dental receptionist, Mary Pickins, who was celebrating her 59th birthday in her apartment. She had just had three new locks installed on her doors in the red brick and concrete LaBlanche Apartments at 41 N. Bellevue in Midtown. Mary Pickins was about 5 feet 10 with dark brown hair. Since her husband had been killed in World War II, she'd become active in the Bellevue Baptist Church across the street. "She was all excited and jumping around because it was her birthday", said a neighbor. "She had such a friendly smile. The last time I talked to her, we were talking about the murders. She said she wouldn't let anyone in her apartment that she didn't know." She had left work downtown in the Sterick Building early, and by 1:00 p.m. neighbors heard screams and Mary Pickins terrified voice, "Don't kill me. Please don't kill me." At that moment the lady with the friendly smile was being savagely ripped and stabbed 19 times. A German immigrant nurse, Emma Gross, heard the screams and called another neighbor, Wayne Armstrong, who had been sleeping. Armstrong, a clerk at King's Liquor Store, arose and dashed into the hallway, and saw that Mary Pickin's door had been broken. Emma Gross then approached the door to the dying woman's apartment and suddenly came face to face with Buster wearing dark sunglasses, his white shirt soaked in blood. Putt showed her the butcher knife still dripping blood and calmly walked past her. As he did so, drops of blood fell on Emma Gross' skirt. Stunned, she followed after him down the stairs. Meanwhile Armstrong had rushed back to his apartment, grabbed his .38 caliber revolver, and in his underwear gave chase to the fleeing Putt who'd broke out into a dead run once he stepped onto the parking lot. As Buster fled from the spread of bullets shot from the smoking revolver of the stocky liquor salesman, a filling station attendant saw the slight figure of Buster sail by silently. "He was one of the fastest runners I've ever seen," he said, but the area was now swarming with squad cars. Buster ripped off his shirt and climbed on top of a delivery truck, then jumped a high industrial fence, but he lost the wild and winding footrace when two uniformed officers chased him down on the Madison Avenue overpass. They handcuffed his bloody hands behind his back, and escorted the blond assassin, naked to the waist, to the county jail.

Just like everyone else Mary Putt learned the identity of Memphis' sex killer... on the evening news. Before the day was out, Buster had confessed to all five homicides. Indicted by the grand jury and convicted on October 27, 1970, of several counts of first-degree murder, George Howard Putt was sentenced to die in the electric chair. Unable to contain his mirth, Buster giggled as the judge pronounced his sentence. Yet when the Supreme Court struck down the death penalty in 1972, his punishment was altered to a term of 497 consecutive years in the state penitentiary where his custody status is listed as minimum restricted. Officially, Buster's sentence expires March 1, 2437.

Called the "Human Timekeeper", Al Jackson, Jr. grew up in Memphis, the son of a successful bandleader. He was known for the 'fatback' style of drumming that was a down-home rhythm infused with cadenced syncopation. Jackson did doubly duty in the chair of Willie Mitchell's band concurrently with the band of Ben Branch, and he enjoyed great success as the original drummer with Booker T. and the M.G.s. He also co-wrote hits for Al Green and placed his signature beat behind Rufus Thomas, Carla Thomas, Eddie Floyd, Sam & Dave, and Otis Redding. More than once I saw Al Jackson whipping the skins behind the militant bluesman Albert "Crosscut Saw" King. He was all over the drum set playing with Albert; I never saw anyone pounding the drums that rendered such romping fatback. Domestically, Al and his wife Barbara Griffin, a local R&B chanteuse, had developed a rather stormy liaison. During the course of a sulphurous argument in July of 1975, one thing led to another, and Barbara shot her husband in the chest with a pistol. The courts ruled self-defense. Al recovered, and the couple soldiered on, each with romantic attachments outside the conjugal covenant.

On the night of September 30, 1975, after attending a live broadcast of the Muhammad Ali/Joe Frazier fight at the Mid-South Coliseum, Al Jackson was scheduled to go directly to the airport to catch a plane to Atlanta. The artist changed his mind at the last minute and returned unexpectedly to his lavish home at 3885 Central Avenue. Shortly thereafter an off-duty police officer was driving past the Jackson home, and saw Barbara Jackson running around the front lawn with her hands tied behind her back, screaming. Inside lay Al Jackson on the floor, where Barbara claims an intruder had forced him at gunpoint to lie face down then fired five shots with an automatic pistol execution style into the back of his head. His wife claimed the assailant was black and that he had entered through a front window, although there was a

Pat's Pizza Photo: E. Baffle c. 1989

table under the window that remained undisturbed. She also claimed there was a white man waiting outside the entrance to the house. The *Tri-State Defender* headlines declared it an underworld slaying, but nothing in the article supported the claim. A motive was never established. There was no evidence of burglary, yet the chief of police was quoted as having a clear case. To prove it in court he said witnesses and others in the know would be needed to come forward and testify. No one did. Then the *Defender* and the *Commercial Appeal* reported that indictments were going to be issued against Barbara Jackson and the blues shouter, Denise LaSalle, and her boyfriend, Nate Johnson/Nathaniel Doyle, Jr., but the indictments never came. LaSalle was already under federal litigation for harboring Johnson/Doyle in her home, who was then a known fugitive wanted on armed robbery charges. The newspapers never again wrote about the murder. All attempts from investigators to draw information from the MPD have been futile. One police officer in the know told my colleague and researcher, Rob Bowman, that *some things… are just too horrible to remember*.

A few months after the slaying of Al Jackson, his son Tyrone – 19 years of age – was convicted sentenced to life imprisonment for snuffing his pot dealer. The murder was carried out with three 16-year-old accomplices. They dressed themselves in black hoods, and entered the home of Randy Givens about a block and a half from Tyrone's address. Givens was forced to kneel down execution style, while Tyrone Jackson shot him once through the head with a .44 caliber pistol in front of Given's wife. The fearsome four absconded with $40 and some marijuana.

Out on Summer Avenue beyond Memphis Motorcycle Co. and on the left just past the 1930s cottages at Leahy's Tourist Court, was Pat's Pizza – a rustic roach den pizzeria open from

6:00 p.m. until 6:00 a.m. It was a low brick building sandwiched in between a garage and a warehouse. Customers had to be 'buzzed' in the front door. No beer or liquor was served, just Cokes and iced tea. The menu was sparse: hamburger/cheeseburger, French fries, and the specialty of the house: either meat or plain pizza consisting of tomato paste sauce served over a saltine cracker type crust with some questionable shredded cheese sprinkled on top. Pat stood behind the counter and served customers when he wasn't in the kitchen preparing the delicacies of the house from items spread out on a rickety table. Pat invariably wore a yellowed brown wig in a Dick Van Dyke style. He was short, trim, and affable, probably due to not eating his own cooking. His waitress was called Miss Pat, although that was not her name and she was no relation to boss Pat. She was a stringy gray-haired, creaking old lady with a humped back possessing a gracious charm that redeemed her lethargic table service. Pat himself was a bit of a raconteur, and harked back to the days when his pizza parlor was considered to be outside of Memphis proper. A time when Jerry Lee and Elvis and their buddies would ride their motorcycles out to his place and hang out around the Hammond organ that now stood dusty and neglected at one end of the shadowy L-shaped room. Still lots of musicians used to go out to Pat's Pizza after gigs to nosh the cardboard-like burgers and indulge in late night jamming. Pat remembers he never once paid a musician to play. On the contrary, they couldn't resist playing for fun. What ruined Memphis was closing down the trolley cars, he reasoned: the trolleys took you everywhere, were economical and pleasant to ride, and reduced the traffic problem.

Late one still night toward the end of August I'd ridden the Norton out to Pat's and was sitting at the counter over a tumbler of iced tea pondering whether or not to challenge a cockroach that was meandering over the countertop lazily waving his antennae at me. It was about 2:00 in the morning when Pat buzzed open the door, and Billy Naylor walked in. He was a burly, bull-necked, tattooed individual who seemed to know Pat from way back. He sat at the counter and ordered a hamburger pizza. After he'd choked down about half of the pie, we struck up a conversation. "Yeah, well," Billy said, "I've been around here since about 1967. I think that's when I moved permanently to Memphis and I've been here ever since. I had a record shop up in Brownsville. Tommy Cogbill is from Brownsville originally. My mother used to baby-sit him when he was just a little baby. He was Chips Moman's sound engineer over at American Studios. I hung out over there with him and Dan Penn. I got hooked up with Stax with Estelle Axton, Packy Axton, and all those guys – Wayne Jackson.... I knew Otis Redding; I knew Isaac Hayes when he was a janitor at Stax. He was the live-in guy over at Stax Records and I used to drop by there and he'd give me demo copies of records when they'd come, the DJ copies."

"What was it like over at American? What was going on behind the scenes?"

"Well, at American it was a pretty laid back attitude. A friend of mine named George Parks kind of worked on and off with the Box Tops and he got me in over there pretty tight. I met Neil Diamond over there and Mary Lee Rush and quite a few people on and off. It was entertaining. Anybody could just walk in and out. They had the songwriters' offices next-door upstairs. They had upright pianos in all the rooms upstairs where they would write. That's where Mark James wrote 'Eyes of a New York Woman' and 'Hooked on a Feeling', and he wrote 'Suspicious Minds'. He wrote all three of those for B. J. Thomas. Elvis heard the 'Suspicious Minds' deal and he wanted to do that song. Mark James had talked to B. J. about it and he said, 'Hell, man, go ahead. You could make a lot more money off Elvis than me.' That's how Elvis got to do "Suspicious Minds". I was in the studio when Elvis cut it, sittin' down on the couch in front of the soundboard. He came in with the Memphis Mafia bunch: Red West, Gene Shaver, Richard Davis and Joe Esposito, you know, all the bunch. Elvis was pretty much running the show. He'd sing and all and he'd stop and say, 'Let's do that again.' They kind of got a little irritated with him, but it ended up the song that's out there today."

"I heard Chips Moman said Elvis was surrounded by this whole entourage and that he couldn't really talk to him in front of those people and say hey, you know, you're just a little off pitch here, or try to pick it up on this bar or work on this phrase. He had to do it kind of in private, but he said Elvis was very responsive to that."

"Yeah, he didn't like to be called down in public, that's for sure."
"How did that bunch get along?"

"Well, they were pretty good at getting along. They kind of reminded you of a whole room full of 'yes men'. I think Red West was the closest one to Elvis as far as getting in there and telling him *you ain't doing this right*, or *you need to do this*. Because Red, he was in there from the get go. I know Red very well."

"Do you talk to him very much these days?"

"I haven't in a while. Everybody used to get together. George Klein would have a party every Christmas; he did it for charity. He'd always have all kinds of people there. That's probably the last time I hooked up with anybody. He had Jerry Lee there. I was a faithful regular at that for 25 years."

"Were there a lot of girls hanging out at American, or was it mainly a men kind of crowd…?"

"Yeah, well, it's kind of hard to describe. You had the main guys that hung out and stuff like that, and then you had the girlies that were there, too, hanging out. They were kind of like groupies out beside the stage door. They were there as party favors more than anything else. That's where I met Art Baldwin. Art was one of the first guys in Memphis with the topless clubs. He was Mary Lee Rush's manager. She came in and she cut an album there. Right after that song she had out in the '60s, that single hit, 'Angel of the Morning', she did an album, and she cut that at American. Art Baldwin, he was the titty bar kingpin in Memphis that actually started topless clubs, as we know 'em today in Memphis."

"How long was he on the scene operating the titty bars?"

"Oh, I'd say Art came to Memphis probably in '72, maybe. Somewhere like that, and he was a very active element up until probably '82 or '3 when he went to prison for about six years. He got out, and got back in it again."

"What were the charges that sent him to prison?"

"Well, there were some drug charges and some other conspiracy charges. He rolled over on the governor, Ray Blanton. He was the mysterious Mr. B. at the trial of Ray Blanton. He's the one that got Ray Blanton removed. That song they wrote, 'Pardon me Ray'…when he was fixin' to be impeached as governor, and he'd just given pardons to about three or four hundred criminals. Blanton was sellin' pardons".

"Did Blanton get on the carpet because of some banking and finance irregularities? There was some kind of fraud with banks too, wasn't there?"

"Yeah, that was Jake Butcher; he was involved in that, too…. He had his hands in a lot of dirt. But Art Baldwin was the key witness for the state, and by doing that he got his time reduced by quite a bit, the jail time that he did."

"Then he came back and went back in the business again in Memphis?"

"Yeah he did, but he never got the foothold or the strength that he originally had, and eventually he just unraveled and OD'd.

"What were the names of some of those joints that he ran?"

"Well, Art, he named most of his clubs the Lucky Lady. He had like six Lucky Ladies in town and he had one called Shirley's. I worked with him at Shirley's quite a bit."

"What did you do there, Billy?"

"I was his – I don't know what you'd call it exactly, just one of the managers. I rode with him a lot, drove for him, picked the money up at the clubs, made the night drops, everything."

"Were the clubs mainly out around the airport?"

"Well, he had GG's Angels which was on Winchester right close to the airport, and then he had Shirley's which was on Winchester right just before you go under that train bridge

Danny Owens

coming up on Lamar Avenue there. When Art went to prison, Danny Owens basically forced control of all of Art's clubs and took 'em over."

"How did he do that?"

"Ah, just lack of the presence of Art and the strength of Danny. They were just a notch above organized crime here in Memphis. See, Art Baldwin came here from Seattle, Washington, and there was a strip-club Mob boss out there named Frank Colacurcio, and Art also had to get permission from Carlos Marcello in New Orleans to be able to come to Memphis to open up an operation of that caliber in the South. He also worked with the guy down in Miami. Traficante, I believe his name was. In that aspect they were connected, but it was a much more independent operation. It wasn't like the *Sopranos* or the stuff you see on TV, *Goodfellas*, and all that. They just did it the right way I guess you'd say. They tried not to step on anybody's toes. Carlos Marcello pretty much ruled the South. Especially along the Gulf coast areas there in Alabama and Mississippi and, of course, New Orleans, and all the way up into Mississippi had been his. Where Memphis touches Mississippi there, he pretty much made laid claim to it. When Frank Colacurcio set up the thing with Carlos Marcello to arrange for Art to come in and do that, apparently he gave them their blessings. I never knew of any exchange of money or anything like that for it, but of course I wouldn't probably ever have known that. Art pretty much ran it independent of anybody else."

"Did Tiffany's come along later?"

"Yeah. Tiffany's opened up in '81 or '82, and that was owned by Steve Cooper. He had two silent partners in this thing. The building that they put it in used to be Beaver Lumber Company, which I thought that was appropriate. Beaver Lumber Company was owned by Billy Hyman, who was a city councilman and a big, powerful figure back in the '70s and '80s in Memphis. It was a three-way partnership – Steve Cooper had a paint company, so he knew Billy Hyman through the painting and carpentry industry. They all got together, and he says, 'I've got this lumber building here that's not doing too well. For 1/3 partnership I will furnish that building, if you will furnish the work crew to convert it and run it for me. Our third partner will be Wyeth Chandler and he can get everything else done.' That's how the thing got started.

"You knew Mayor Chandler personally?"

"I met him a few times. The first time I ever met him was up on Overton Square when I had to pick him up in TGI Friday's and help him out to his car..."

"I was just wondering if you had ever seen him in party action... but I'm sure he went to Tiffany's quite a bit, didn't he?

"Well, he was real discreet when he did and they didn't talk very much about it. He didn't come down there that much. I didn't really see him that much in Tiffany's, but I know he was there. I helped Steve get Tiffany's going. The first time I ever met Steve Cooper, him and his general manager – a guy named James Moore, we called him Skinny – I walked in there. Art sent me down there. He said, 'Go down there and see what they're doing. I think they're fixin' to open up a club on us.' So I go down there and I go in the place, and Steve and his stepbrother are plumbin' the bar in and Skinny is unracking chairs in the back. I look around and they got three little satellite stations and then they got this gigantic stage right in the middle of the floor. There were chandeliers all in the place, and I said, 'Yep, this is a titty bar. No doubt about that.' Art Baldwin had a club right down the street. Tiffany's was at Getwell and Winchester and Shirley's was just a few blocks down the street there. The important thing is I carried a couple of girls down there with me and just wanted to see if they could get a job. I talked to Steve and everything. He told me to bring 'em on back down there in about three weeks; they should have the place going by then. I told Art about it and he processed the information, I guess. They were never what you would call bitter enemies, but they didn't like each other very much. Skinny though was a bitter enemy with Art Baldwin. Steve Cooper kinda did things a little different. He didn't seem to want to get out there and make a lot of trouble. He just wanted everything to work smooth, where Danny Owens and different ones like Art's brother Jimmy, was just notorious. He'd kill somebody at the drop of a hat.

"Baldwin and his brother came from where?"

"Actually, the whole Baldwin family, they're from Parkin, Arkansas. They went to Seattle, and they had a bunch of clubs up in Seattle. I think Jimmy killed somebody up there and they needed to leave. Parkin is about 25 miles from Memphis. Yeah, that's where they buried Art."

"There was another titty bar out in this area that one of the cycle gangs operated. Was it the Outlaws or the Family, or were they just hanging out at one of those bars? I know a couple girls, Marcia and Connie who used to dance out there somewhere."

"Danny Owens owned a strip mall right there around Airways and Winchester. He had his main club Danny's was there, and he owned the whole strip mall. At one end was the Pink Garter. The Pink Garter, it wasn't owned and operated by Danny's, but the Iron Horsemen had a very strong foothold in that club. What they did was – Danny Owens, Art, all of 'em – they used motorcycle clubs to get the girls to dance in the clubs. Most of the girls that danced and worked in those clubs were biker old ladies. Art, when he first came to Memphis, he had some Banditos with him there, a lot of them, as a matter of fact – from Texas. They supplied most of the girls when he first was getting started up in the clubs, and some of the club managers. But Danny, he worked with the Iron Horsemen and they eventually beat him almost to death, back in the early '80s. But as far as the bikers actually owning any clubs per se, I don't know of any."

Hell Angels in Memphis c. 1972

"Now the Outlaws had a chapter here, too, right?"

"Right. They were a fairly strong presence here for many, many years back in the early '70s. A matter of fact, they're still here."

"The Outlaws, from what I understand started before the Hell's Angels, have always avoided any kind of publicity. While the Angels and Sonny Barger used publicity and public opinion to their own particular advantage, the Outlaws seemed to be super underground, but well organized and more secretive."

"They kept their affairs pretty private, whereas the Hell's Angels were headline boys. They seemed to jump on publicity and made movies and stuff like that in the '60s.

"They never had a presence in Memphis, though, did they?"

"Ah, just a slight presence. The Family tried it and it just never worked. I think it was '72 when they tried to put a Hells Angels chapter here and the police just slaughtered 'em. There was a bar called the Glass Frog down on Lamar and Rozelle in that area. The Family owned that bar and they had a bunch of Hell's Angels come down for a big party and the police raided the place. There was maybe, I'd say, a hundred bikers in there and they had about 500 police officers. The headlines in the *Commercial Appeal* – back then to have a color picture on the front of the *Commercial Appeal* was just a real rarity – but the headlines on the paper the next day had a big, oh, it looked like a good 8x10 colored picture of all the Hell's Angels sitting in court with their patches and belt buckles and knives and guns laid out on this big table. They were all bandaged up… looked like that Buford Pusser movie when they were all in court. It said: *Memphis Police Department Defeats Hell's Angels*. They never came back to Memphis after that.

"When I came to Memphis, the Family was here and that was just about it. Back then the Family was kind of a combination motorcycle club, car club, party club. A lot of the guys in there then weren't bad asses or nothing like that. They were just people that liked to ride motorcycles, drink, party, and just raise hell in general. But in '68 or '69, things started kind of changin'. The Sindicate Motorcycle club was started in 1969 and they're still here. At one time the Sindicate had about 200 members in it. It's spelled different – it's 'Sin' instead of 'Syn'. They said that would differentiate them from the Mafia by changing one letter. The Outlaws came in into Memphis in 1970, maybe '69. Originally they were a club called, der Führer. They rolled over Outlaw and basically been here ever since. They get down real low every now and then, but seems like the last few times I've seen them they were on another recruitment drive. I think there's some Boozefighters here, which are not a very big club, and then there's some Vietnam Vets. The Road Barons are here; they're a pretty strong club. They were a spin-off out of the Banditos over in Arkansas. Some of them broke away and started a club called the Road Barons, and they're pretty stout. They've got chapters in Louisiana and Arkansas and Tennessee – around. They've got a few hundred members, for sure, maybe more.

"Do you go to their church meetings, any of these clubs?"

"Not per se their church meetings, but I have been to a few of their parties, and I've been over to their clubhouse; made the rounds pretty much."

"What's the distinction between these clubs in terms of the character?"

"Well, the Outlaws, they're considered to be one-percenters. In the biker world if you're a one-percenter, you're the baddest of the bad. Like the Hell's Angels are one-percenters, the Outlaws are one-percenters, and to be able to be a one-percenter club, you got to be sanctioned by an existing one-percenter club. That's kind of a touchy thing, because you got a local group that decides they want to put on the one-percenter patch, then the Outlaws or whoever is gonna come down on 'em and they're gonna want to know who sanctioned you to wear this patch. If they can't give the right answers, they'd put 'em out of business pretty quick."

"What was it like – a day in the life working with Art Baldwin?"

"It was never a dull moment. He wanted to be a success; he wanted to make money. He dressed very expensively, and he liked having the presence of women around him. He just liked being a mobster. When he first came to Memphis he had a '71 Cadillac limousine that had bright orange velvet mohair-looking upholstery in it, and it was painted purple and white. It looked like something Isaac Hayes would drive straight out of *Shaft*. He dressed, oh, like Shaft. He dressed like the blacks, with the real flamboyant sharkskin suits, but then he could dress conservatively, too. Sometimes he'd get a little crazy. He had a big gray sealskin long coat that he used to wear a lot. He never was into the big hats and the stacked shoes, but, he dressed

Art Baldwin

well, always wearing tailor-made suits. He did buy some at Lansky's. I went there with him on various occasions. A matter of fact, he bought me three suits in there."

"And he wanted you to dress a certain way? He wanted you to dress up, too, right?"

"Oh yeah, he expected all his people to, you know, dress nice. That's the way Steve Cooper is, too. He's a sharp dresser, but he's a lot more conservative. Steve's house looks like an antique museum. It's just impeccable. Steve's still doing very well for himself. He owns a couple of clubs here in Memphis still, and he's relocated to Phoenix, Arizona, now.

"What are the clubs he has in Memphis now?"

"He's got one called Christie's, which is where Night Moves used to be."

"Oh yeah, that's what Bud Chittom had something to do with – Night Moves, right?"

"Right, yeah, Bud and Steve were partners with Ralph Lunati back then. His brother Joe Lunati owns a cam company, makes cams for cars, racecars."

"Yeah, a famous camshaft company – a Memphis company. They made hot camshafts for cars and motorcycles. In fact, they'd put a cam in anything that would take a cam."

"I know Ralph real well and he's one of the nicest guys you'll ever meet in your life. He's a little guy, and he owned Platinum Plus – one of the biggest titty bars in Memphis. Platinum Plus was at Mount Moriah and the Interstate. It was originally built as a seafood restaurant called the Loft. They bought it in probably '90, and it went up as a titty bar. It was the most successful one in Memphis as far as I know, as far as just making money. The Feds busted it, and they just decided they were gonna put it out of business. So they made up everything they could figure out to make up, and the Feds finally shut it down and confiscated all the property.

"Yeah, it seems like when the Feds get on you there's just nothing you can do. You just gotta hang it up. They'll hound you to death."

"But you know Ralph and his brother Joe weren't that close. I don't think Joe agreed with Ralph's choice of occupation that much. Ralph was a self-made millionaire. It's funny because a lot of the girls that worked for him, until they got to know him a little bit, they thought he was the maintenance man at the clubs. I had one girl telling me that she lost the combination to her lock and that nice little maintenance man came in there and cut the lock off of my locker so I could get in there. I said, *maintenance man*, who you talking about? She said, 'I don't know, he's kind of bald-headed, had on a great big gold necklace with a ruby,' and I said, 'That was the guy that owns the place.' You'd catch him out there sweeping the parking lot or up on the roof fixing an air conditioner or something like that. He's just that kind of guy."

"A real hands-on kind of fella," I said.

"He'd dress okay, but to Ralph to dress up would be a nice, good pair of jeans and a nice shirt. He always had that gold chain. He got that chain from Jerry Lee Lewis. He just bought it from him. It was a nugget, a flat nugget, with a great big ruby in the middle of it and a rope chain. That was his favorite piece of jewelry."

"Did you hang much with Jerry Lee?"

"I have, on and off in the past quite a bit. I know J. W. Whitten. I've known him ever since he moved to Memphis. J. W. is Jerry Lee's right hand man. I imagine that J. W. Whitten is the only reason Jerry Lee Lewis is still alive today. Kerrie Lou, his sixth wife, almost killed Jerry Lee; she just dogged him to death. Once they got rid of her, they got Jerry Lee kind of back up on his feet a little bit. But Jerry's up in his seventies now. Last time I saw him was maybe about a year ago. They had a premiere thing, a little record signing deal at Spin Street at Poplar and Highland. Jerry Lee was down there; he had all of his band. Ol' B. J. Cunningham was there playing bass. Kenny Lovelace, he was there on guitar. All of Jerry's old people were there, ones that are still alive. But when he comes out on stage he looks like he's just a little frail, like a China doll almost, but once he sits down on that piano bench, he becomes Jerry Lee Lewis. It takes him a second – he'll sit down, he'll look around like he doesn't know where he's at, and then he'll run up and down that keyboard a few times. Then he'll start loosening up and he starts talking, but he doesn't kick the piano bench across the room anymore and he's slow in moving, but he's still rock 'n' roll."

"What did *you* do for recreation when you were working with Art Baldwin?"

"Everything – I messed with hotrods, I rode motorcycles, I hung with some of the bigger clubs for quite a few years. It seems like that biking and hotrods and nightclubs and titty bars, they all just mashed together. And so when you need money, you go work in a bar, so you can get up enough money to build another hotrod or a motorcycle or something like that. It just always seemed to work for me. When I came to Memphis and started working at the Manhattan Club, the house band over there was Willie Mitchell."

"What did you do over there, Billy?"

"I was the doorman. I worked the front door – checked IDs and collected the cover charge. I lived upstairs. They paid me $60 a week, that was my paycheck, but I was allowed to bootleg all I could. I'm talking about $200 a week doing that."

"That was before liquor by the drink, right? That's when you could only bring in a bottle."

"Yeah, you had to bring your own bottle. We had beer and set ups. After 11:00 p.m. you couldn't buy liquor. What I would do, when I'd get ready to go to work – the liquor store was right next door to the Manhattan Club – so I'd just go to the liquor store and I'd buy me a case of half pints. I think they cost me about – there was 48 half pints – it cost me $48 for a case, which took my whole paycheck. Then I would sell 'em for $3. So I was making a pretty good profit off just doing that. I'd buy about three or four cases a week and that sustained my income. But back then, you know, if you made $100 a week you were doing pretty good for yourself."

"Manhattan Club stayed open until, what, about dawn?"

"I don't know if they had a key to the front door, to be honest with you. I came on at usually about 9:00 p.m. and I never got out of there before noon. The day shift would take over when I would leave. They would come in at noon and we'd still have people left over from the night before in there. Some of them stayed four or five days and they'd never leave."

"Well, did they have girls dancing or was it just bands playing?"

"It was just a band. Quite a few of the famous musicians in Memphis played there. Willie Mitchell was the house band, and Willie would come on at 10:00 every night and he'd play until 4:00 a.m. Then after he would stop, that's when all the other musicians would come in and just sit in and have jam sessions. Phillip Dale Durham was a drummer that had a little three-piece band that played there. Later he played with Moloch. They've had some incredible jam sessions. I went down there one night and Wayne Jackson was there and Packy Axton, and they were jamming with Willie Mitchell. They stayed there until 9, 10:00 in the morning playing."

"Who owned that joint?"

"When I worked there, a guy named Asa Lewis. He looked like a penguin. Little bitty guy, bald-headed, and he was probably in his late forties, early fifties then"

"White guy?"

"He's a white guy. I think he was Jewish. He bought it from a guy named Billy Hill. Billy Hill founded the place in 1954 and it was the Manhattan Club. It was probably one of the premiere clubs in this city. He had the Manhattan Club and Lil' Abners, which was right down the street. They were kinda in competition with each other. Asa Lewis bought the Manhattan in the mid-60s. The décor in it... if you've ever been to Anderton's restaurant on Madison, it had those same cloud-like things floating in the ceiling, but somebody had painted every bit of it flat black."

"What a pity."

"One of my jobs, while I was working there, was to help Asa paint the place and clean it up. We hit that place with some bright lights and I could see all that scroll and pattern work, and those cloud-like ceiling lights in there. We went back in and got those lights working and kinda made the place look a little different."

"Yeah, Anderton's Seafood Restaurant was built with a kind of famous architecture – it had that crumbling-ruins brick façade that was an exclusive style of the 1950s. I used to go there a lot. It had this undersea motif in the dining room, with an aquamarine and silver color scheme and sparkling paint that twinkled. There were indirect lighting and cloud-type fixtures in the ceiling. The bar was constructed from an actual mahogany sailing yacht with a long mast jutting out from the bow. Fishnet and seashells were hanging everywhere. It was like going into another world, far out at sea."

"It looked that way right up 'til the day they closed the door. I went over there and ate one last time 'bout two days before they shut down, and it looked just like it did in the '50s."

"Did you ever know a guy that used to hang out at Jimmy Arnold's? He rode Triumphs; his name was Fred Queen."

"Last time I saw him was at a gun show. Came through there and I recognized him and I said, 'Do you look like a guy I used to know named Fred Queen? Is this what's left of you?' He said, 'Yep, this is what's left of it.'"

"Did you ever ride with some of the musicians? Like, Jerry Lee was riding for a long time, and Elvis rode…"

"You know, Jerry Lee – he never did ride that much, but he liked to play with motorcycles. When he was younger and he had enough strength to hold one up, he had a lot of Harleys; still does, as a matter of fact. Harley Davidson gave him a '56 Panhead, a full dresser, a white one. He's still got that one. He'd get that out on his farm down there and ride 'em around a little bit. Now Elvis, he got out and rode. He'd get out at night. See, back then helmets weren't required, but Elvis always used to wear a helmet. Well, he didn't always used to wear it, but a lot of times he would – to keep people from recognizing him."

"And who all rode with him?

"All the Memphis Mafia; they'd all get together and they'd go. They came out to the Sindicate clubhouse out on 61 Highway. It was New Year's Eve when it was. I was there; a bunch of people were there partying. Sonny West's brother, Bill West, was president of the Sindicate motorcycle club. Sonny called out there and talked to Billy and said, 'We want to come out and party. Is it safe?' And he says, 'You know you're safe here.' So they all came out, rode up, and the whole time Elvis was there he never took his helmet off. I don't know if he was scared or just didn't want to take it off. They stayed there maybe an hour or so and then they got all together and took off again. But Elvis, you know, if he had bike and he wants somebody he wanted to ride with, he'd just go buy them another motorcycle, and you just kept it."

"When you'd go riding with the Sindicate how far did you all go… where did you all ride?"

"You'd go to wherever they were having a party. A lot of times they would have hill climbs and motocross races and we'd go to that and everybody'd just sit around and get tore up. You'd go out there on a Friday and you'd get drunk as a rat and messed up, and you'd sober up Sunday and ride back home. Sometimes you never did sober up. I went to Daytona with the Sindicate in '73. That was a pretty good ride; it was four days to get there."

"You'd go out to Shake Rag?"

"Oh yeah, I went to Shake Rag. It's still there. The original old store burned down a few years ago. But as far as Shake Rag as a biker presence, it's still there. It's a weekend thing. People go out there to just – it's somewhere to go. It's about 25 miles north of Memphis. It may be in Tipton County; it may still be in Shelby County. I don't think anybody ever pays much attention to where it was, it's just if you could stay sober enough to get there. It's a good ride and you get up kind of early Sunday morning and ride out to Shake Rags, stay out there three or four hours, and then come home."

During this time Erik Morse, a buddy from Texas, was buzzed in the front door, and had picked on our conversation. "You were talking about Art Baldwin earlier. I heard that Frank Liberto was some sort of Mafia connection here in Memphis and was connected maybe with Art Baldwin. Certainly he was close to Carlos Marcello. His name comes up when they start talking about the Martin Luther King assassination. Liberto operated a little café close to Knipes on Main St. and was Marcello's logistics liaison for James Earl Ray at the time of the shooting."

"I was here in the National Guard when they assassinated him and we got activated. We were in the streets when the riots started out. It was like a day after Dr. King got assassinated. We all met at the Coliseum, the whole Tennessee National Guard. We had the commanding general of the Tennessee National Guard, we had mayor Henry Loeb, and police commissioner Claude Armour making a speech and they told everybody how brave we were and what good a thing we were doing and all this. The last thing that they told us was there's a curfew on. If you're out after six p.m. and you're white, send 'em home with a stern warning. If you're black, do what you gotta do. And out after nine p.m., lock the white people up and fire at will on the blacks. When we came into town, they made us fix bayonets and brandish ammunition for all our guns, so they would know that we didn't have blanks. Because the word had gotten out that we had blanks and we weren't gonna shoot anybody. We didn't have blanks; we had live ammunition. One high school student, one young black student was shot and killed as a result. Oh, there were quite a few of them shot and killed. I doubt if the majority of them ever made any kind of notability. But I witnessed half a dozen shootings. They'd put us on guard duty with fire engines, mostly. They were burning everything in the city, and whenever we would answer a fire call we would be under sniper fire and they were throwing Molotov cocktails at the fire engines. We had direct orders: if you see somebody that is what they called a belligerent coming at you, shoot to kill. It was basically a war zone and that's what happened."

"There was sniper fire on you?"

"Oh yeah – quite a bit. We answered a call to a fire down on Hollywood and when we pulled up they shot the windshield out of the fire engine. The bullet came through the windshield and through the back glass into the area where we were sitting behind on the hook and ladder truck. It missed me by maybe two or three inches. They shot out the whole windshield and we jumped out and hit the ground. They shot that fire engine all to pieces, shot the tires out on it and everything. Then we saw a guy who was trying to throw a Molotov cocktail and one of the guys on the back end of the truck shot him and he rolled him off the building. I mean, nothing was ever mentioned about it, but that's one account I know happened. Then we had a sniper hit us. We were standing out in front of the fire station, went outside to smoke a cigarette, and I kept hearing – sounded like a bee flying by me. I asked the guy standing next to me, I said, 'What is that noise?' Just about that time the whole window in the fire station hit the ground, and I said, 'Somebody's shooting at us.' We caught him in a drainage ditch, a culvert that went under the street at Chelsea and Watkins. He was hiding up in there. We captured him and turned him over to the police. He had a .22 rifle."

"That's a pretty light firearm, a .22, but it can really do some damage."

"They had anything they could find. They had pistols, shotguns, and little .22 rifles. They were making lots of Molotov cocktails."

"Do you remember this pretty much being all over the city of Memphis, or was it mostly coming from particular neighborhoods?"

"Well, for some odd reason, they always seemed to burn their own neighborhood. You know, they destroyed Beale Street, which was an all-black area at that time, and the area around Airways and Lamar."

"Orange Mound...?"

"Yeah, right, they burned out a lot of that. They would burn their own businesses out. But they didn't really get into the white part of Memphis that was totally controlled by white people. They didn't seem to do much damage there. I don't know if it was just more heavily guarded or whether they were just actually scared to go that far."

"Well, Billy. Let's all ride out to Shake Rag's one of these days."

"Will do, goodbuddy. Just give me a ring." Billy ordered another pizza, and we stepped out into the summer night air heavy with heat and humid drift. The Norton was waiting in the stillness under Pat's Pizza's winking red neon signage. With one crank the beast barked, shuddered to life, and breathed in hungrily through its velocity air stacks. I cast off into the eerie depths of Summer Avenue. In my rear view mirror I saw Erik retreating down the street to his cottage at Leahy's Tourist Court... to dream the dreams of a thousand tourist park ghosts.

Mack Rice, the Stax songwriter, came into town one weekend from Detroit to do a show at an obscure little joint downtown. Jud Phillips, Jr. was his manager and he invited me to join them at the club. Mack delivered a high-energy spread of his compositions including "Mustang Sally" and "Tina, the Go-Go Queen". For the encore he had three towels around his neck to protect his beige sequined jumpsuit. Mack typically received three standing ovations. In the dressing room Jud introduced me to an amicable, wholesome, round-faced gentleman named Herbie O'Mell – someone Jim Dickinson claimed as his manager. Herbie and I removed to the bar for last call cocktails. In high school and as a student at Memphis State, he started promoting sock hops and dances. "You went Central High School...," I iterated.

"I did, in fact. You know Elvis, George Klein, and I are the same age – same age and in the same grade at different schools. George Klein and I have been lifelong friends. Even in high school I used to go over to his house and visit with him. That's where I actually met Elvis. George lived directly across the street from Humes High School. If you walked out of the door of Humes High School and walked across the street, that's where George lived... but George was the big man on campus at Humes and Elvis used to come after school and visit with him. That was before he recorded or did anything. But yeah, Central is located at Bellevue and Linden and back then that was Midtown."

"Did you go to Jungle Gardens near there?"

"Yeah, that was near Central, but the Belvedere was at Belvedere and Union, and the Pig & Whistle near there, was where a lot of people went. It was a drive-in. You could stay in your car and carhops would wait on you...come to the car."

"You were organizing sock hops?"

"In the early '50s, '52-53-54, when I was putting on my dances. At that same time some of these bands were getting booked at these dances and they weren't getting their money. Some of the guys would say, 'Herbie, we'll give you 10% of what we make if you'll handle it for us and make sure we get our money.' So a lot of them were not *my* promotions, they were just being booked someplace or in a club and they were always getting cheated on their money. So when they got booked they'd call me and I'd handle it or help them get booked, or sometimes they'd just already be booked and I'd be there and I'd be the one to go collect the money. I'd get the money from the club owner or whatever. They just seemed to trust me and that's how things led into managing and promoting. When I was doing my sock hops, I'd hire Elvis. I went over there to the guys at the Chisca Hotel downtown, because George Klein and Dewey Phillips were upstairs on the radio – George was nighttime guy or he was part-time guy doing something over there, 'cause he was still in school. I went over there and I met the manager of the Chisca and made a deal with him. I paid him $50 to use the room downstairs in the basement, and made a deal with him where I didn't have to pay him until after the dance, 'cause I didn't have a fifty to give him. So, I hired Elvis and two other guys, and it wasn't Bill Black or any of those guys, just two guys for a hundred bucks. And I put on dances, and paid him a hundred and paid the Chisca guy the fifty, and I ended up with anywhere from a hundred to two hundred dollars, and I thought I'd made all the money in the world. The funny story was that we did that two or three times and Elvis came to me and told me that somebody had offered him a $150 to go play at the Eagles Nest. I thought he was lying to me and I said, 'You better go take it', so I let him go for the extra fifty.

"There was an Italian family that owned the Eagle's Nest and the skating rink out there…"

"Yeah, I think that's the Pericini family."

"How did that segue into the Penthouse…?"

"The people that were putting the Penthouse together came to me and asked me if I would get involved with it. They had just opened it and they had a band playing there in white tux coats and music stands. They were busted, and they asked me if I'd come up there. So they got out and I got in running the place. Now the Penthouse was on Cleveland Avenue at the corner of Peach Street. It was above in a building and downstairs was Cerritos Restaurant, an Italian restaurant, on one side and on the other side was Halpern's Delicatessen. You took an elevator to go up one story to the Penthouse. I got a band that was playing out on Thomas Street in a place called Club Currie. It was Ben Branch and a singing group called the Largos, and they were about the hottest group in Memphis. I hired them and then I went out and hired Duck Dunn and Charlie Freeman, some white boys, and that was the first integrated band in Memphis. Ben Branch happened to be the fellow that Dr. King was talking to when he was shot because Ben Branch was part of Operation Breadbasket. There was Ben on tenor sax, Big Bell the drummer, Mickey Collins was the piano player, Floyd Newman was on the baritone sax. In addition to the Largos, I had a singer that came up and tried out a few times in front of Ben's band. He was up there for about six months. And that was Isaac Hayes. It wasn't that he didn't like him, but Ben just didn't want to pay him. If he sang, he was going to get paid just like any of the other guys. I paid Ben and then Ben paid everybody else. I think Isaac got paid like five dollars a night when he sang. He finally took off and went somewhere else. I think everybody liked Isaac. But everybody was dancing; there weren't any slow songs. It wouldn't matter if it were you or I up there singing. They would dance to anything that sounded good. Now when I went in and opened up and did TJ's, the Manhattan Club was going and the Thunderbird was there and Caesar's was there. Ernie Barrasso had Caesar's, and he and Freddie Alfonso owned the Thunderbird together, and then he left the Thunderbird and opened up Caesar's."

"Right, toga party. I heard he was always having theme events at Caesar's, and had the girls dressed up in go-go toga outfits and that he had the hottest looking girls in town hanging out or working there."

"When I had Penthouse and I was doing, I guess you'd call it R&B music, there wasn't a white club around doing R&B music at that time. The black clubs were out on Thomas Street and down on Beale – the Hippodrome down on Beale and Club Handy – but the Penthouse was the place where the white people could come and hear that music."

"So white people could go to Club Handy and they could go to the Hippodrome?"

"Well, no. No, they really couldn't, or to the Flamingo Hotel, which was the black hotel there. The Hippodrome was a big thing. I just loved that music back then, and they were all black and you couldn't get in. I went down and a lady by the name of Miss Johnson, she lived on Beale Street, but she owned the Hippodrome building property. I asked her and she got me in where I could stand behind the bar and I got to listen to Sister Rosetta Tharpe, Thelonious Monk, and Faye Adams, and Joe Henderson. I was the only white person there. So I went by and saw Sunbeam Mitchell and got to talking to him and told him that I had been over to the Hippodrome. So he started letting me into Club Handy. I'd go up there and listen to Little Willie John and the band and Evelyn Young playing sax. The hottest sound on Beale Street was a guy people called, Bill Harvey. Bill Harvey's band…B. B. King played in it; they all played in Bill Harvey's band. I just loved it, and I was a fan. Those clubs were always packed but I only went when there was a big act playing. I mean, I wasn't in it for business; I was just a fan. Really, I got interested in the music business through that… and that is why I say the white people would come to the Penthouse."

"So, was the audience at all mixed at the Penthouse?"

"No, back then it was strictly white – young crowd. When I came in and changed it around, all of a sudden it just went boom. It was just a great atmosphere. In fact, *Route 66*, when they came through town filming that TV show, they came up there and filmed."

"Well, how long did it last, Herbie?"

"Oh, maybe a year. The Memphis police department closed it because there was an integrated band, and they just gave us a lot of trouble back then in '59. That just wasn't allowed back then."

"Couldn't they pay the police off? Weren't those people used to being paid off in those days?"

Herbie just laughed, "I don't know, I didn't know about all that...or I didn't try that. I just don't operate that way. What the police would do, because of the band being integrated and had so much talk going on about it, is that when the people would leave and get in their cars, they would stop them and check them for drunk driving. It got to be where they ran the business off. They never raided the place. But I wasn't thinking about integrating or not integrating, I was just thinking about putting a band together that people loved, that people would come out to hear and pay to hear. I was aware of what the police were doing. In fact, I had a partner; Chick Schaeffer was his name. Without me knowing about it, and I wish he hadn't done it, he went out in front of the club with a prison uniform on and a ball and chain and had the newspaper take his picture. So people stopped coming. That place got closed down pretty soon after that.

"What did you do after the Penthouse closed?"

"Well, after that I did promotions... and I used to go to the Manhattan Club almost every night. Willie Mitchell and I are lifelong friends. When he got off we'd go eat."

"What did you all eat?"

"We went to a place called Tony's. It was a little joint on a side street down off of Bellevue there. Have you seen these platters that are kind of oval shaped that they serve in some of these small restaurants? Well anyway, we'd go in there and every night we'd order a plate of chorus girls. What they'd do is, they'd open up a can of sardines and line 'em up there on the plate with onions, and they'd call 'em a line of chorus girls."

"The Manhattan was just a hole in the wall, wasn't it? But a lot of people went there."

"Yeah. It was at Bellevue and Kerr, and it was just nothing but dancing."

"It was all black, right?"

hite people were there... Willie Mitchell's band and all white people dancing, no blacks, but it was in a black neighborhood."

"You were managing too...?"

"Yeah, I managed Ronnie Millsaps, and I managed Jerry Lee Lewis, and I managed Jim Dickinson. I took care of some of Carl Perkins' business affairs; I wasn't his manager, though, but I helped Carl on a bunch of his stuff. I managed Dan Penn and Spooner Oldham for a while. Then Dan had Beautiful Sounds; he and I were in the recording business together. And Chips Moman and I were in the recording business together. In fact music lawyers would call me, and I would tell everybody I'm not a lawyer, but I would go over the contracts and make the corrections, and tell the people what they should do or shouldn't do in 'em. At the time I was an executive producer; I didn't turn the knobs. I was putting deals together, got the musicians or put the band together, found the songs. I just put people together more than anything else. Put them together with the right songs. Then about eight years after the Penthouse, I went into TJs."

"Well, when you got into TJs, wasn't Campbell Kensinger the bouncer? If there was trouble, didn't Campbell quash anything that might happen?"

"Sure, he did. I mean, the Peabody Hotel, Memphis Country Club – all of them will have a fight sooner or later. Campbell was my doorman. Something started every once in a while; we'd go over there and ask them to leave. You know, where there's whisky being served, there's always gonna be somebody break up and a fight starts, and some woman starts yelling or something. I told him I didn't want him hitting anybody, but if somebody jumps up and swung at him, he needed to protect himself. But we just tried to escort 'em out and to ask them to leave and say come back another night.

"I wonder if Campbell ever knew the Tiller brothers."

"Well sure, they came in – Albert and George came in and I said, 'Y'all can't come in here, I'm sorry – just too much trouble with you all around.' Campbell would say, 'Would you all leave?' and they left. They didn't give me any trouble at all at TJs. Of course, I knew George and Albert and Michael, and I played baseball with Dago Tiller when he was a little guy. When we were young we played baseball in the Optimist League and would go over to the fairgrounds together on the same team. So he left town and the next time I saw him, five or six years later, he was as big as a house and mean as hell. I guess I was lucky that I met him in his younger days when he was sane."

"I was just curious about the inception of TJs. I heard that somehow it wasn't going and you came in and kind of picked up the pieces."

"Some people started that club and was going along with it, and it just fell apart on 'em and they didn't do any good at all. I got a call one day from Mr. Belz. He owned the shopping center the club was in and Belz Investments and the Peabody Hotel and all that other stuff. He said, 'I understand that you can operate a club, and I have this club and would you like to take it over?' I said, 'Well yeah, I might be interested in it.' Make a long story short; he had somebody take me over there. When those people had gone out of business, they'd owed him so much money, 'cause I mean, they left the glasses, the tables, the chairs – everything. All I had to do was say OK, I'll take it, and he gave me the key and unlocked the door and I was in business. I didn't have to do anything. So, I got Ronnie Milsaps and put Ronnie in there, 'cause I had been handling Ronnie and I had just brought him to Memphis to record with Chips. I needed a place to base him out of, kinda. So it all worked out. I put Ronnie in there and the whole place just turned around overnight."

"What was the exact location of TJs?"

"TJs – do you know between Madison and Poplar where Piggly Wiggly is now? It was on Avalon right behind what was Montesi's Supermarket, but the door faces Avalon."

"Yeah, that's a hot location right in there. There used to be a little drive-in there beside it."

"The Psycho Lounge was up on the corner. It was an alternative club. They used to go in there and they'd have those wristbands with the spikes on it and get out there and dance and slap each other. It was a popular place."

"The Psycho Lounge – For People Who Need Help. That's what it was called."

"Then there was a place around on Poplar Avenue at Evergreen across from the Guild Art Theatre called the Psych Out – Psych Out Lounge. There was the Silver Slipper, too?"
"The Silver Slipper was way out on the edge of town, but it was a very nice place with dinner and an orchestra playing."

"What was the room like at TJs?"

"I had TJs downstairs and then I also had the upstairs for four years, where I had my acts. I put in Roy Hamilton, and I'd bring in acts every week upstairs like Brother Dave Gardner. He played for me a couple times and did a great job – packed the place and everybody loved him."

"He was a sharp guy though, sharp dresser and everything?"

"Oh yeah, he was quick. He was based out of Biloxi. I'll tell you who I was really impressed with, and we didn't do a whole album…but we did an album on Ringo Starr. When we were doing it, one night there was a knock at the door; they called me to the door and Bob Dylan was there. He said, 'Is Ringo in?' I said, 'Yeah.' So he came in, sat down, and so Chips was there and Chips said, 'Well, why don't you sing a song with Ringo?' Ringo said, 'Yeah!' So, Bob said, 'Okay'. He just sat on a couch. He said, 'Play it for me.' It was a new song they had been working on, and they had gotten the tracks down, and he said, 'Play it.' They played it and he said, 'Play it again.' They played it again. 'Play it again.' They played it again. He got up – did his part in one take. That impressed me. And Willie Nelson. We worked with Willie Nelson, and Willie can do the same thing… and Dionne Warwick, working with her. We finished up her track and said we got to put some voices on there, and we'll call background singers in and get that done. She said, 'You don't have to do that,' and she got over there and sang all three parts of the backup voices. Those are the kind of things that impress me. As far as a gentleman and one of the nicest people, is Carl Perkins. It's hard to beat a man like that as far as talent, producing, playing, and singing; he's as good as they come. And Jim Dickinson – he can sing, he can play that piano, and he can produce. He's just a gifted person, and he's disciplined and just so creative. I mean, Jim's a genius."

"On the business end, do you think there's a cartel of businessmen and politicians who have actually controlled a lot of the action in Memphis?"

"Yes, but it's not a cartel. It's this old, old money and bankers that have suppressed everybody – black and white people. They kept the deals and kept the money only for their friends. Even 25 years ago I knew some people that wanted to do business deals and they had to go out of town and borrow money to come do their deals in Memphis. The banks just wouldn't loan it to them. They weren't one of their good ol' boys, you know what I mean… but that's changed now."

"Back then they didn't want Memphis to really expand, in a sense," I surmised.

"They were happy where they were and they wanted to keep it there."

"At TJs, did you have any private parties?"

"I had Elvis' New Year's Eve party. We had it at TJs, and had Ronnie Millsaps and the Bar-Kays playing, and it was great. Elvis and everybody came. All the Memphis Mafia guys came with him, and they invited some of the fan club presidents. That's how they showed their appreciation to the fan club presidents, and they got to come and other invited guests."

"So Red West was there and that whole Memphis Mafia group?

"Oh yeah, George Klein, Rico, Lamar Fike, Marty Lacker, Jerry Schilling, Joe Esposito, Richard Davis, and Alan Fortas – his uncle was Supreme Court Justice, Abe Fortas. Kang Ree, Elvis' karate instructor, was at the party – just that whole crew that was with him."

"Did these people take anything larger than a Salvo tablet at that party?"

"I did see Elvis take a drink. He took one drink and it was the only time I've ever seen him take an alcoholic drink. It was a Sloe Gin Fizz. I guess I was privileged enough that Elvis, if he came in someplace, he'd say, 'Hi, Herb. It wasn't like, 'Hi, chum.' He'd call a lot of people chum – 'Hey, chum, how're you doing?' But I mean, I was invited over there and I sat at their dinner table at Graceland and ate with him and Priscilla. As a matter of fact, I always felt a little funny, 'cause all the guys that were friends, like Joe Esposito and Alan Fortas and Richard Davis and all of them, they were sitting in the kitchen eating. They didn't get to sit at the table. I felt a little funny about that. Once Elvis got to his popularity and as big a star as he was – you get people like that and they sit around and Elvis would say, 'Let's go to the movies.' Well, everybody would stand up and say, 'Let's go.' He'd say, 'Well, let's go play football,' and everybody would stand up and, 'Let's go.' It wasn't that he was so domineering, that's just what he'd say. Nobody would say, 'Oh, no, let's sit down and watch TV.'"

"What's the craziest thing that Campbell Kensinger ever did?"

"Well, one thing: he got mad over at TJs when he was working and he took a chair and threw it through my plate glass front door. I got him and said, 'Come here!' He came and he was mad and everything and I said, "Come here! You gonna stay right here,' We went upstairs, and I said, 'You're sitting here until Monday morning until I can call somebody and get that door put in,' and I made him sit there. I had Campbell sitting at the back of the main room. Upstairs was a long room and I had an office at the very back. Late Saturday night or early Sunday morning, a police car drove by and saw the broken door. So they called the Dog Squad. They got one of those police dogs, and they opened that door and let that dog loose in there. Campbell was sitting in the back there, luckily he was awake, and he looked up and that dog had run upstairs and was coming at him like a race hound. He didn't know what to do, so he took about 10 steps back and got into the office and shut the door and locked it. That dog was barking, barking, barking and he was staying in there until he heard the police yelling. He told him he was in there because he worked there and he was a watchman since somebody had broken that door. The police finally called the dog off and opened the door. Campbell and them called me and I said yeah, he's working there and he was guarding the place 'cause of the broken door. I had it fixed on Monday morning and took a little bit out of his paycheck each week."

"Did he ride cycles?"

"Yeah. He had a club. They had a club and they had a motorcycle clubhouse over there at Park and Airways in Orange Mound. He had a couple of Hell's Angels that were in town then. At least that's who he said they were."

"What the craziest thing you ever saw the Tiller brothers do?"

"Well, when I ran the Penthouse; you got on an elevator and rode up to the second floor to get in. Downstairs I kept a guy with a moneybox and you paid your cover charge to get in. I got a call once to come downstairs, so I went down and there was Dago and Mike Tiller and Albert – not George, but Albert. They were all in there raising hell and I walked up and I said, 'What's going on?' My guy down at the door said they've taken the cash box. It was like one of those little ol' fishing tackle boxes. He said they've taken the cash box, and they were standing in this little hallway and they got it in their hands. They were saying, 'We're gonna go have a good time,' and blah, blah. So, when you walk out and got to the street, there was a door there, and you'd locked the place up at night from that hallway. So they said, 'What are you doing?' I said, 'I'm reaching in my pocket for a dime,' and they said, 'What do you mean?' I said, 'Because, when you walk through that door, I'm shutting that door and locking it and calling the police and telling them you robbed me.' They said, 'What!?' One of the Tillers took that damn tackle box and threw it, and the money and change went everywhere in that hallway, and said, 'Aw, screw you,' and walked out and left. So, when they left I still locked the door. They never caused me any more trouble. A couple of times they would, one at a time, come to TJs and Campbell was at the door and he just said, 'You can't come in.' They'd say, 'Why not?' He said, 'No, you can't come in. I'm sorry. If you all want to do something, I'll meet you all afterwards, if you want to have a beer,' 'cause he knew 'em. He just come out and said, 'I'm working here, I can't have any trouble and I don't want to take a chance.' They never came in TJs, not one time."

It was 4:00 a.m. and Teenie Hodges was packing away his Steinberger guitar and Mack Rice had called for a taxi to carry him over to La Quinta Inn. The air in the industrial dressing room was dead, foul, and booze soaked. Cigarette butts were all that gave traction on the slime-soaked floor. I bid adieu to the music makers and to their promoters. In the parking lot I started up my old Thunderbird and, as if on a barge launched on dark, murky waters, cruised off toward Midtown and Cox Street with the twin glass pack mufflers humming low and my head swimming with thoughts of the turbulent 60s.

CABIN NOTES:
When I got back to my pad, I riffled through a stack of Memphis Flyers *and pulled out an interview with Ernie Barrasso, dancer Bunny Lee, and John Knott who used to write the "Nitelife" column in the* Press-Scimitar. *I lay down with the Chris Davis penned article under the celestial star-painted ceiling of my room. It read:*

"One time, John invited me to the top of the Top of the 100 Club at 100 North Main," says Barrasso. "And we had a wonderful meal. The check comes and John says, 'What's this? Don't you know me? I'm John Knott.' And the waiter says, 'So what. I'm Joe Blow.' Knott told the waiter to call the owner, who confirmed that Knott had to pay just like anybody else. The subsequent review was scathing. 'I said the peas were canned', Knott brags. The next week the Top of the 100 was packed. All it took was a mention from Knott – even a negative one."

"If the Psycho Lounge changed the color of its lights from red to blue, John would write about it," Barrasso says. "And if John Knott mentioned you or your nightclub in his column, you would be full for at least three weeks."

Knott experienced it all – the dueling pianos at the Sharecropper, the fine company at the Crown Lounge, and Charlie Feron's Vapors on Brooks Road, where Jerry Lee Lewis would play. Knott loved catching Wayne Jackson at the Junket Club, and while he thought the $3 cover charge at Billy Hill's Starlight Supper Club on Highway 51 was a bit much, you got a free chicken, so who could complain?

Knott also saw the darker side of nightclubs. He had a window seat at the Driftwood on the night when George "Dago" Tiller, one of Memphis' most notorious roughnecks, threw a barstool through the glass.

"There was a time when they didn't allow dancing on Sunday in Memphis," Knott says. "John Coll, who ran the Psycho Lounge helped fix that. He'd have dancing on Sunday at the Psycho, and the cops would get him and get him and get him until finally they said, 'The hell with all this. Let it go.' John Coll did it. He liked to fight for his rights, and that's how we finally got dancing on Sunday."

Barrasso began his career as a salesman, selling Fords for Hull-Dobbs. Then, one October day in 1961, Elvis Presley walked in and everything began to change. Presley wanted to buy a brand-new Thunderbird, loaded, and Barrasso was just the man to sell it to him. Just before Elvis drove off, a fan asked to snap a photo. That picture of Elvis, the new Thunderbird, and Barrasso ran in newspapers and magazines all around the world. The young salesman's face had become associated with an icon. His 15 minutes of fame were ticking away, so Barrasso decided it was time to parlay the exposure into a more glamorous career. He decided to open a nightclub.

"I wanted to meet a lot of girls," Barrasso says, and owning a nightclub in the Swinging Sixties seemed like just the ticket. Knott was already praising his habiliments, calling him a 'dashing young boulevardier'. He partnered with his friend Freddy Alphonso, who had been a liquor distributor.

"Freddy was selling wine. I was selling Fords. We'd both sold a lot of Thunderbird, if you know what I mean. So the Thunderbird Lounge just seemed to be the right name for the place," Barrasso says.

The Thunderbird opened in 1965 and was located at 750 Adams Avenue in the basement of the Shelborne Towers apartments. It was a New York-style walk-down with a blue room, a red room, a dance floor, and a bar. Fortunately, the club, a live music venue featuring artists such as Ronnie Millsaps, Sam & Dave, Charlie Rich, Boots Randolph, and Flash and the Board of Directors, was a big hit catering to a suits-only crowd. Even Elvis rented the club out for his New Year's Eve parties, which were slow fizzles by all accounts.

Shortly after the Thunderbird opened, Barrasso was taking regular vacations in Acapulco, and Knott was writing that "Some successful [club] operators are making movie star salaries." But it wasn't until Club Caesar opened in November 1967 that Barrasso would really hit his stride. Club Caesar was Memphis' first authentic discothèque. It featured Roman decor blended with psychedelic Aquarian iconography.

"I always traveled a lot, and I brought back a lot of ideas from Las Vegas," Barrasso says. "I figured if something would fly in Vegas, it would fly in Memphis. I got the idea for Club Caesar after attending the opening of Caesar's Palace." It was a modest club on Cleveland just south of Poplar. Club Caesar held only about 100 people.

The tables at Club Caesar were all numbered so that customers could request a song for special someone at another table, even if they didn't know that special someone's name. At one point, Barrasso planned on installing telephones at tables so patrons could request songs or dates without leaving their seats. That plan fell through. One contest at Caesar's earned the lucky winner a discount on a quality hairpiece. Sometimes winners would take home a wig, while runners-up were stuck with wiglets. There were always lots of pretty go-go dancers shaking their togas for the crowd. Sometimes Barrasso would hitch a trailer that had been converted into a stage on wheels to the back of his modified hearse and drive his go-go dancers around town. He would stop from time to time and let the shake-dancing commence.

"The whole reason for having the go-go girls was to excite the crowd," Barrasso says. "It wasn't dirty in any way. It was supposed to get everybody up and dancing. A guy can't meet a girl unless they dance, and the go-go girls could really get 'em going. All you needed to be a dancer were two things: a pretty face and great legs. And you had to be able to dance a little. And you had to be young."

But even Barrasso, who would go on to distinguish himself in the casino industry (at one point booking travel junkets for Donald Trump), was never able to hire Bunny Lee - the hottest go-go dancer in Memphis with a rocket-fueled money-maker. Her services were just too expensive.

"I was a celebrity," Lee crows. Lee caught her break accidentally. The vice squad worked the clubs constantly, making sure no bootleg liquor was served and that the bands and crowds didn't get too integrated. Lee was out partying with some friends and her dirty dancing got the full attention of the Memphis police.

"The Nite Liter's looking to hire a full-time dancer," a vice officer told Lee. Startled by the statement, Lee asked, "Who in the world would ever want to watch me dance?"

"Who wouldn't," the vice officer answered.

So Lee went down to the Nite Liter, climbed into a gilded cage, and aced her audition. "They said I had the job, and I was shocked," Lee squeals. "All I had to do was to dance one song an hour. It was never more than a little tease, baby," Lee says playfully. "It was a blast." Her go-go performances in front of the Marty Willis Combo set eyeballs to rocking. She did the swim, hitchhiked north and south, and did the Zombie.

"There wasn't a law that said blacks couldn't go to white clubs and whites couldn't go to black clubs, but that just didn't happen," Barrasso explains. "We had to stop serving beer at the Thunderbird and Caesars at quarter to one, and everybody had to be out of the club by 1:30. But a lot of the black clubs would be open till 5 or 6 in the morning. We'd call first and ask if it was okay to come by, and they would always say yes. We'd go to places like M'lundas and see Isaac Hayes, but my favorite was the Manhattan Club. It was a hole, a real dump, but it was open all night. Willie Mitchell played there, and nobody has ever had a better band than Willie Mitchell. Rufus Thomas would play there, and Wayne Jackson and Andrew Love. You would go to the Manhattan Club and stay up drinking and dancing until 5 in the morning, then walk across the street to Chenault's for breakfast."

"I'll tell you what night life was like in Memphis in the '60s," says Kathy Knott, John Knott's wife. "We all went out every single night. We slept three or four hours a night. We all had day jobs. Speed was legal. We'd get up, brush our teeth, and go into work with the same makeup on."

171

CHAPTER THE NINTH
POETS, TILLERS, OUTLAWS AND THE IRON HORSEMEN

The afternoon sun slicing through the Venetian blinds stirred me from my slumbers. On the other side of the wall I heard what sounded like heavy body blows... not sure if the thunderous commotion was coming from rough sex play between Lillian and Bob, or from an antagonistic altercation or both. After a lull I heard the abrasive voice of Lil', "Bawb, go down to the store and bring us in a six-pack of Millers." OK, I thought relieved, all's well; they're just lit up on early afternoon boilermakers. To clear the cobwebs from my still dozing brain, I decided to catch some wind and putt over to Bud Chittom's chicken shack on Beale St. and wake up with a bowl of vegan chili chased with a strawberry Daiquiri. The proprietor himself happened to behind the counter running quality control and making taste tests. I took a table on the patio, and pretty soon Bud ambled over with two Daiquiris to join me on the kind of drowsy afternoon Memphis is known for.

"Say, didn't you operate High Roller or High Cotton at one time?" I conjectured.

"I operated both of them. After that I had a place called Poets. I remember it was the early 80s."

"Poets, is that at the old Front Street Theatre location?"

"That's right. The Evans, the father and son, both were musicians. They owned that and they owned the movie theatre at Park and Airways in Orange Mound. It was called the Park Theatre. Evans is still working as a piano player at society things. He gave me the best line when I started out in the business. When he came by to meet me and introduce himself as the landlord, he said 'Son, this is a one night town. If you want more than that you're going to have to trick 'em.' And that's true. Memphis has always been a Saturday night town. If you wanted more than that, you had to trick them. The place had gone broke and I convinced Evans to let me try it. And he said as long as you can pay the rent and get me out of this lease, I'll give you the equipment at the end of it. I did and he honored his word and gave me his equipment, and I moved on from there. I sold my car to get the beer money. Yeah, verbal agreement. Before that it was an art movie house called the Capri at 1819 Madison? No. It was the Guild Theatre."

"Oh that's not on Madison. That was on Poplar. It was the Capri was on Madison."

"You're right. The Guild was at Poplar right next to Transmaximus, the recording studio that Steve Cropper operated."

"Bill Kendall ran the Guild Art Theatre. He screened foreign films and soft porn at midnight. He had a long run with the Guild in the 60s and 70s. Then Bill retired from battling city censorship, and the Guild changed to the Evergreen Theatre that just screened trash."

"You remember where everybody went late-night at Toast of the Town? The Toast was right across from the Guild."

"Then when the Capri moved and became the Guild, is that when Poets started?"

"No. Jimmy Robinson and Jerry Swift... Jimmy had had some success buying the first Friday's franchise. That was the second place on Overton Square. The first place was the Looking Glass. The second place was Friday's. And Jimmy Robinson and Jerry Swift went up the street and opened a place called the Ritz. Billy Joel opened it up. Billy Joel played the weekend. And I ran it about a year and half or so, and I moved when the lease was up because I wanted a bigger venue. It was too small. During that time, Robert Gordon was a nice show, George Thorogood was still driving himself around in an old checkered cab, Ry Cooder was a good show. The Pretenders were there first. Remember Chrissie Hynde got in a big fight down at Friday's… kicked the window out of a squad car. People went to jail. That was a good show there. From there we went on to different places."

"That was the Ritz she played that night and then got into a fight over at Friday's?"

"By that time I had it and it was called Poets then. The Ritz was still there, but they went out of business. Robinson got into drugs. It just went bad. Then some people came down from Atlanta and started Poets, and that failed after a short period of time. Then I made a deal with them to do some shows with Bob Kelly who promoted the big acts and I did the baby bands, the small acts and was able to put a few gimmick things together. Everything from a Christian or a secular Sunday night show once a month to mud wrestling.

"I saw that Robert Gordon show, by the way".

"Wasn't that a great show? You remember who was in the band? Chris Spedding from the Sharks. Spedding was playing…. It was a rockin' ass show. You remember Robert wouldn't use front monitors, he'd had these great big side fills. It looked like 1956."

"I also saw at your venue, The Ramones."

"They had just done 'Gabba Gabba Hey'!" They were touring behind what was supposed to be their popular, mainstream album, but nobody cared for that. If you remember Joey had a guy on both sides of the stage to keep him from wandering or falling off the stage. He took cigarettes from in his nose and his ears. That's how he started the show. The whole band was a mess but he in particular was low riding man. Everybody in the audience heard or subliminally knew what to do. So from the moment they started, there was a pit, people dressed the part. It was the first scene like that I had seen in Memphis or others had seen. Nobody had seen a mosh pit in Memphis until they played."

"Just curious how you got started in this?"

"I figured out that I was within a few months of getting a degree in philosophy and all I had ever done was play in bands and I had always like the promotion and marketing end. What happened was that my father had burned up in a fire when my mother and father's home burned down. And I needed to go back to work to get my mother back in order. I worked during the day at Strings 'n' Things, and at night I started doing a few shows in some secondary markets where I used my band very effectively. I knew how to work door deals. I knew how to promote. In doing so I tried to get the people who went broke at Poets to hire me to do what I ended up doing for myself. They didn't think they had the money to do it and they went broke anyway. Like I said, I called the guy in Atlanta who had put the money up and was responsible for the lease. I encouraged a partner to come in with some seed money for the band deposits and I sold my car for $500 and bought beer. A man who don't take a chance don't have one. I was a one-trick pony; all I knew how to do was to fix guitars and play in bands."

"What was the name of your band?"

"It was the latest rendition of Interstate 55. You remember 55 came to town, then they were Interstate 55, then they were Mudbone, and then they were Gambler. We stayed busy."

"Started a little later than Jim Dickinson?"

"Dickinson played in the Dixie Flyers and they already become the house band at Atlantic Records Criteria Recording Studio in Miami. Dixie Flyers and a band called the Road Apples out of Atlanta were two of the best undiscovered bands I ever saw. They were playing in '69 and '70.

"But there were some pretty good local rock bands that kept us floating at Poets. Then we did some pretty big regional and national shows, and we did a few plays. By and large our mainstay was original music. A lot of them burned out too quick. Jimmy Scott from the Pretenders died shortly after the Memphis show. Benny Mardones had a big hit called 'Into the Night'. He did the sound check without a microphone, that's how big his voice was. Then he'd collapse on the stage and cry like a baby. He was the damnedest basket of hormones I've ever seen in my life. He was taking cocaine. He was a tremendous talent. Some of those acts are better than others, and some of them go through the poses and get their money and leave. I always liked Billy Joe Shaver. I remember the first show George Thorogood worked. I mean he didn't even have a spare guitar. He talked to the crowd while he changed strings and nobody cared. And just to show me he could control the crowd, he had me turn the house lights on and off as he wanted. And it didn't matter because he just owned the house. You know what it's like when you get them in there close and everybody's of a like mind. There's a certain synergy that transcends time and place for sure. That's what happens when those great ones play. Sometimes they worked better in clubs. Robert Gordon probably couldn't work a big stage. Ry Cooder wouldn't be good on a big stage, but in a club.... Delbert McClinton is another example. He was marvelous. Roy Orbison was always a good act. That same band now plays behind Vince Gill. All of them old Memphis boys are who it is.

You look at Robert Johnson and who copied Robert Johnson and did something else with it. Green Day is nothing but Robert Johnson. I don't mean the black Robert Johnson, I mean Butch Johnson, the Frayser Flash, the boy that was from Frayser that was a very good guitar player and he had a mindset to play a certain style that was indicative of no other at that time. And those original types kinda make things work in a way that Memphis will always be able to do, and Nashville won't. Everybody still uses our studios. They still use our musicians, but they just don't do business with us. Memphis just doesn't do the business of music well.

"I started an unsigned talent showcase called Crossroads for a number of years that was a lot like South by Southwest, and I tried to get the business to connect. We've always had great rhythm sections. And when you get a great rhythm section together, you can get a Sun or Stax, Hi or American Studios. All of those had great rhythm sections. Sam the Sham came to Memphis with a big band from Louisiana. And if you remember he stopped the Beatles' 19 months at number one with 'Wooly Bully'. But when he first came to Memphis, they couldn't keep regular work and they had to go back home... because the musicians who all became great studio musicians were all playing the clubs.

"Willie Mitchell – who has the best set of ears I've ever heard in my life – when Quincy Jones got in trouble doing the first Michael Jackson record, which was 'Billie Jean', he sent for Willie Mitchell. And Willie went out there and stayed for three weeks. When he got back, I went by the studio and his comment about Michael Jackson was that he thought he was a bitch and he slept in a bag. I'll say it the best I can. 'Little freaking motherfucker thinks he's a bitch and sleeps in a bag.' That's what Willie Mitchell had to say about Michael Jackson. But when Quincy Jones got in trouble, he called Willie. When Todd Rundgren was completing an album... I saw Willie listening to Foghat. And I said, 'What are you doing?' And he said 'Rundgren sent this to me. He wants me to pick the single.' And the single turned out to be 'Three Times Lucky' which turned out to be a big hit for them. Best set of ears I've ever seen in my life. And if you listen to an Al Green record, there's no music on it. There's a count on a closed hi-hat, there's some funk fills on the guitar, there's a little counterpoint stuff going on with the organ and they're playing a little music on the choruses. Willie cut him through tubes in order to fatten his voice up. And when you listen to Al Green, you're listening to Willie Mitchell. And when he got away from Willie he didn't have a hit. When he got away from Willie, nobody else understood how to cut him cause his voice was so thin. He never had another hit. Think about it. And that rhythm section was all boys from the neighborhood that Willie taught how to play. There wasn't a guy playing on those Al Green records that was born more than five miles from here. Herbie O'Mell was around American Studios, and he could tell you. Note for note. The American studio rhythm section played on everything; they played on Elvis, they played on Streisand. Look at Booker T. and the M.G.s – same scenario."

"What've you been doing lately, Bud?"

"I do some promotion for Beale Street as far as events, festival type stuff. It's a craft you know. It's not art anymore. It's just a craft. When Stax went broke, there was such a backlash to anything musical in Memphis. Union Planters Bank got stuck for a few million dollars and we could never live it down. Anything musical, money didn't follow it. In the past, businessmen put up money to do Pop Tunes, which was Papa Joe Coughi. Coughi was the focal point of a few Italian investors that put up money. Some guys put up money for Willie Mitchell to go out on his own. Some guys put up money for Stax, and it kinda broke down and there wasn't anybody to put up very much. If you didn't already have something or weren't with something, there wasn't anything new coming up. It was all 'paint it black, charge five dollars'. At that time Beale Street was blues and soul; it was a place that people went on the weekends. Earlier on WDIA was a catalyst for rhythm and blues. That wasn't blues – that was rhythm and blues. Overton Square was a region of new entertainment that came together, but Midtown was just a cheap place to live. That's where all the young people were. That's where all the dope was. It's like where everything assembled. It was like Soho, the Village in the 60s, the Haight Ashbury.

"Dickinson and John Fry started Ardent Studios in a garage. In Nashville they all take their calculators out and figure out how much of the song they wrote at the end of the appointment. They actually count the words. Whereas in Memphis, they start a session at 10 o'clock, everybody shows up at about 11 and goes to eat, then gets high until 1 and do it by 2. It's over by 2, and it's because they got the vibe and they figured out how to lay out. First take they did they kind of run into each other a little bit. The second time they did, they figured out how to respect the holes in it. Then they laid it out where they were supposed to be, and they made a good record. Memphis never made great records; they made good sounding records. Everybody just shows up and when you get the right people, you get a nucleus, and it works. It's the randomness of it. It's the drunkard's walk. The randomness of selection, and sometimes it works damn well. When it does, you get something that's meaningful. *Northern Exposure* came in here and interviewed Dickinson and me about the difference in Memphis music. I was explaining that the drummers play a little slow behind the beat and we respect the holes and the lay-out. Nothing suited these guys. Then I took them to meet Dickinson at the Peabody. The guy asked him, *what's the difference in Memphis music?* Dickinson took his old cap off and started pulling his hair like he does, and he said, 'I don't know, but every time I leave town for eight or ten days I get to playing funny.' And that's what they wanted to hear.

"We had a pressing plant when the rest of the South didn't have one. A guy over on Chelsea at Plastic Products figured out how to press a record, how to make an acetate. It was the Kraft brothers. James Kraft. It was some Arkansas boys learned how to master. And that was a big deal because there wasn't any of that down here...I asked Willie Mitchell once, 'I figured out what "30-60-90" was.' That was one of his hits. He had four hits: 'Robin's Nest', 'Woodchopper's Ball', '30 60 90', and his biggest hit was called '2075'. 'But what's "2075"?' And he said 'I don't know. That's just what was printed on the acetate when we got it back.' And it turned out to be a really important record for Memphis. Because it was disciplined rhythm and blues, an instrumental, and Memphis had some really great instrumental guys from Lonnie Mack to Willie Mitchell to Travis Womack, to Booker T. and the M.G.s.

"When Stax closed, everybody spread out. What happened was Atlantic brought a guy in who could engineer and this guy figured out how to put a bottom on Atlantic Records. Then Wilson Pickett left Stax and went over there, and a bunch of others left and Stax got bad, and there wasn't no easy money and everybody spread out man. Then Rick Hall at Fame in Muscle Shoals picked it up."

"You're doing something at Club 152 on Beale St., right?"

"We have a couple of live rooms that I can honestly say I'm proud of the music. The Masqueraders was an old Stax/Motown doo-wop act. They work for us early evenings and the weekends. Jerry Hardy is doing a roots rock thing and their rockabilly thing that's very valid. Then there's Freeworld with Herman Green, the horn player Herman Green's band of young men. They've been around for 12 to 14 years. Captain Pete who had that great WEVL blues show on Main St. – his grandson killed him over needing money for dope. But as far as Beale Street, we don't have to raise money for benefits anymore like we did for Fred Ford. We have a healthcare plan if you make less than $30,000 and more than 50% of your income comes from music then you can get free health insurance which is an honorable thing.

"The studios aren't as necessary as they were and major labels aren't mandatory anymore. You can sell by way of downloads. You make your money playing. It's kind of got back to a 50s thing. It's kind of 'eat what you shoot' now which I think Memphis does well. Memphis never had big labels. Transmaximus, which Steve Cropper and Jerry Williams did, was the only studio paid for from big label money. Everybody else just sold sides.

"That's a shame about Captain Pete."

"That was a class guy. That whole bunch, including Polly Walker who has always been so nice to me. She was doing the business for B.B. King. Polly did the arrangements, marketing, stage work for B.B. King for forty years until Sid Seidenberg convinced him that a Jewish guy in New York could do more for him than a black woman in Memphis. I met her in '69 when I went to work at this little club, the Nite Nite Club. Her son Cato was the bandleader down there and later the bandleader for B.B.'s band. We had a little house band that played down there Thursday, Friday and Saturday nights. We played behind those old Chittlin Circuit rhythm and blues acts like Totsy Davis out of Little Rock, and Jack McDuff played B3 Hammond... almost demonic; he played it just possessed. Once in a while B.B. would play. Calvin Levy played at the Nite Nite, too. He was just like Leadbelly. Remember Leadbelly sung his way out of jail. At Cummins Prison over in Arkansas, out of your neck of the woods over there, they had a prison band. And Calvin sung his way out of jail. He wrote a hit song called 'Cummins Prison Farm'. Calvin killed somebody else and wound up back in jail just like Leadbelly. Leadbelly wrote 'Goodnight Irene', 'Midnight Special' – all great songs while he was incarcerated. And if Calvin's living he's still in jail because you can't sing your way out twice.

"Where was the Nite Nite Club?"

"South Main down by Ernestine and Hazel's by Central train station. Sunbeam Mitchell had the Club Paradise and that was the crown jewel of the Chittlin Circuit. That was the biggest room of the Chittlin Circuit, the Club Paradise. I knew Sunbeam well. When he died I went and bought his desk from the widow. Sunbeam was very nice to me. He had an illegitimate son his wife didn't know about named Vincent Taylor. His mother worked at the Paradise and her name was Ernestine Taylor. Vincent looked just like Sunbeam. Sunbeam looked like what they used to call sleepy. His eyelids came real low over his eyes. And he always had to look up to see you because his eyelids were too long. Sunbeam had a big smile, a million dollar smile. You come in to Club Paradise and if he didn't know you but you had the look of a musician, he'd treat you just like you were Albert King. He was nice to you. And he was a good, smart gambler and everybody liked him. I had a sound system that I would book out with him, and then he would send me down to Holly Springs on Sunday and we would split the door. We would do a door deal on Sundays because there wasn't no Sundays in Memphis if you were an R&B act. Now I'm sitting behind his desk, but the most blood-curdling oath I've ever heard come out of Sunbeam Mitchell's mouth – and this was so unlike Sunbeam Mitchell because he was so genteel, so nice to everybody – but a guy came into his office one night and said 'Mr. Sunbeam, So-and-So is so upset that he's going to get you and he's going to do this and do that.' And Sunbeam Mitchell said, 'You go tell Mr. So-and-So if he does, I will wade in blood to my neck to get to him,' and he meant it with every ounce of venom. There was no mistaken that he'd do what he said. "

"Who were some of the promoters?"

"Bobby Kizer, Herbie O'Mell. Kizer did rock 'n' roll; he did Southern Creed. That was the first time I ever heard 'paint it black, charge $5'. He had Club Kizer, and he had a joint out in Tipton County called the Tippin Inn. He put up the money for the deposit for Poets."

"What about Miller's Cave?"

Believed to be Johnny Aubrey Nix 1951

"Miller's Cave was just a little ol' beer joint out in Frayser run by the Miller Brothers. They were cool guys but the only thing coming out there with any speed was coming out of Millington, and that was Bobby Whitlock, and Bobby Whitlock was part of Derek and the Dominos and all of that.

"Jud Phillips?"

"Jud Phillips meant more to me than Sam. He was such a talker he could mesmerize you. He could put you in a brain lock. I mean when he got to talking, you'd get slack-jawed and have to sit down somewhere... to absorb it all because it was good."

"Campbell Kensinger...?

"I knew Campbell. Campbell had a peephole in the bathroom at Trader Dick's on Madison, and he went in there on a couple of occasions and raped women. Herbie O'Mell had Kensinger as a doorman early on when he was adorable. Later on he was a totally different animal later. Campbell finally got killed trying to collect some money from some bikers, and the boy who shot him was defending himself. He didn't get killed as much as when the cops figured out it was Campbell they let him bleed to death. They let him bleed out because they were through with him. I still don't know anybody who said they did the wrong thing, you know what I'm saying? Campbell was going to hurt someone because he liked it. All the club guys hated him. All the cops hated him. Campbell could have been good when he started, but he ended up bad. I've seen him whouped twice. He wasn't no terrible animal. With a normal man, when he got the jump, he was ferocious. And he was very, very sadistic. But an old red headed, double-jointed, big-boned old boy out in front of Trader Dick's give him all he wanted one night, and I had the good pleasure to watch that. Campbell was going to kind of nose him around and this guy took umbrage to it, and just got on him and never let up. But the best one I knew about was this boy out of Tipton County named Johnny Nix. Those Nixs are all tough boys. When Bobby Kizer opened up High Cotton on Cooper in Midtown, Campbell was one of those guys that was going to come in, tear up your joint, beat up your bartender, and do whatever he wanted to do. Bobby knew he was going to have a problem, so he got Johnny Nix sitting there. He was the doorman too. He'd been sitting there for some time. So when Campbell came in, Bobby introduced Johnny Nix to Campbell. And Johnny Nix had a claw hammer that was real close. His words were, "You're that big old bear I've been hearing about'. Nix took that claw hammer, and Campbell took off running. The only way he got away from him was that he crawled up in a dumpster. Bobby Kizer brought Johnny Nix to town especially for that."

"What about the Tiller Brothers?"

"George Tiller had all the class in the world. They just gave him 10 calendar years in last year down in Mississippi for selling 10 or 12 pain pills. The judge said, 'You really don't deserve this for just this one instance, but,' his words were, 'look upon this as a life time achievement award.' George was sixty something when he got that sentence, so that was the end of it. I sent a little money to him as did George Klein and Herbie and everybody else. But he's going to stay down there in Parchman Farm until he dies. George wasn't a mean person. Dago Tiller was a mean person, and all the rest of them were. George was just an athlete that liked to drink, but he was all kinds of tough now. Now Dago, I got away from him when I saw him. That was a very dangerous man. George was just one of those guys whose arms were too long and his hands looked like brickbats, they're real flat. He's got an iron jaw and he's very nimble, very agile on his feet. He was just a natural athlete and as such, he was a hell of a boxer. Anybody that tried him on wasn't going to like it. Whoever tells you that they saw somebody beat George Tiller, is lying."

"Did you operate Trader Dicks?"

"No, but I wound up buying it. You know, the Antenna Club down the street from there was the best joint I ever remember in Memphis and it was just a piss pit. It was the best joint by far, but it was never what you'd call clean nor well kept."

"Downtown vs. Midtown, Madison Avenue vs. Beale Street. Things have changed in Midtown, haven't they?"

"There's a new scene in Midtown. There's still a real reason to be in Midtown if you're young. Beale Street is 'fleece 'em and release 'em'. I can honestly say I've preserved a few boys that would have been wiped out of business. I'm showing people what it's like, what it sounds like. I can honestly say it's worth it because we revitalized downtown. I've got this little chicken joint that serves chicken and waffles and every table depicts something to do with the Chittlin' Circuit. You can come in there and have a good meal and read the story of the boy that did 'Pledging My Love', the guy who died playing Russian roulette – Johnny Ace, the late great Johnny Ace. I've got a lease for another 27 years. We're well funded and the same bunch has been together forever. We're going to go out together. The sum total of things is a life well lived. That's the only watermark there is."

Of the once student philosopher, now matured Euterpean savant and venerable Boniface of *Beaux Stratagem*, I took leave. Mounting my trusty British steed, I took advantage of my position on the river bluff to steer the black beast over the old Harahan Bridge into West Memphis. Cruising over the apex of the antiquated arched roadway, the wind shook the iron girders of the bridgeworks, but the Norton held fast and true to its line. In the haze, the fields and alluvial plain of Arkansas came into view. I wanted to see more. I took the first right turn off the highway and within minutes I was riding into the totemic *fin-de-siècle* town square of Marion. Still bearing right and heading back toward the mighty river, I rode out through grassy fields to a makeshift airstrip used mainly for biplane crop dusters. I paid $15 to the pilot of a creaky Piper Cub to haul me up in a glider that looked like an overgrown goose. At 3000 feet he cut me loose, and I floated in imperceptible descent over Old Man River and the dusty skyline of the Bluff City. The glider and I drifted in silence save for a slight whoosh of wind turbulence passing the cockpit. My thoughts were suspended and seemed somehow washed and filtered in the rarified air until I became thoughtless and somehow extricated, even absolved from the earthly Gomorrah that now appeared trifling and insignificant below. Thusly I drifted and drifted in a wide timeless spiral until the thermal column of air upon which I sailed let me down with a gentle thump on the terra firma of the dirt runway.

On my way back into to town I turned off of Riverside Drive onto to Beale St. As I rode over Third Street, actually Highway 61, where the old Pantaze Drug Store used to stand on the corner to my right… and there I noticed Silky O'Sullivan feeding some corn to his goats out in their pen beside his tavern. At that moment Silky looked up, saw me on the bike and waved. I hadn't talked to Silky in a coon's age, so I circled around on Fourth St. and parked the Norton in his back lot behind the goat pen. Somebody had given his goats a bath because they didn't smell quite as badly as they used to. He invited me to the bar for a shot of rye.

"Hey, Howlin' Wolf's son lives here now. His name is Little Howlin' Wolf. You're gonna love him," Silky exhorted jovially. "He just got off tour with Tina Turner. He done slept at the White House about three or four times. This guy is funnier than anything you got on HBO. He's played with Muddy Waters and Lightnin' Hopkins and all of 'em. He said he was plowin' down in Mississippi – said that every time he'd plow, that mule would jerk its tale; said he could count the oats and the corn in his ass and tell you what that mule had for lunch. He said the plantation owner down there gave him 50¢ a week raise. He said the plantation owner gave him $2.00 a week and he'd put his arm around Little Howlin' Wolf; 'Look, Little Howlin' Wolf,' he said, 'if you don't get no bigger, you gonna be my nigger.' Said he tied that mule to a tree and headed to Chicago."

"Say Silky, didn't you grow up in a castle out near Graceland?" I queried.

"Yeah, I lived on Highway 61. If you take Graceland and cut it, sliced right across going from Highway 51 over to Highway 61, that's where I lived. My father built a big castle out there about 1938. I wasn't born until '42. He was a chemical engineer from Canada, and he decided that he wanted to do something different. So he got this tough-like block out of Birmingham, Alabama, and built a house completely out of concrete. There's concrete roof, concrete ceilings, concrete beams. It could take a direct hit from a damn bomb and it wouldn't even shake it. I mean, this is about 24 inches of concrete foundation. This is just a fortress he built out there. It's a beautiful Spanish-looking house. I guess I'm a product of the '50s.

"I used to catch a bus to go downtown Memphis and I used to go to the Loew's State Theatre. I'd be sitting in there and all of a sudden in the bathroom I'd see this guy keep combing his hair, and I thought he was a greaser. He kept combing his hair all the time, looking in the mirror, combing his hair. He had ducktails. We called them ducktails back then. He had a little acne on his face and I thought, *man, who does this guy think he is, Mario Lanza?* 'Cause, I mean, they had a lot of Mario Lanza movies playing back in those days. People were listening to the McGuire Sisters and Perry Como-type music. I kept hearing these guys who were running around with this guy and yelling like he was something really important. As he was an usher there, he had on one of those uniforms that they wear…I kept hearing them call him Elvis. I didn't pay any attention to it, 'cuz you know, if you live in the same hometown, such as Roy Orbison and Jerry Lee Lewis, people don't really appreciate 'em 'til they're dead, and they don't pay any attention when they're alive, really. But, I was just getting into liking rockabilly music, and I was about in the eighth grade, and I turned on the show that was popular at the time called Dewey Phillips – *Red, Hot & Blue*. He would get Elvis' songs and play 'em about eight or ten times nonstop. Like, he'd get 'That's All Right Mama' and play it ten times in a row. All them little kids just started going crazy over wanting to hear more Elvis, more Elvis, and more

Elvis. Next thing I knew it spread like a fire – it was down in Shreveport, down in Louisiana, then it just took off nationally.

"I used to have a Cadillac – my mother had a Cadillac – and I was skinny back then, had long black hair, and I put a guitar hanging out the window one time and tried to crash through the gates at Graceland. I got about half way up in there and they caught me. They said, 'Get your ass out of here', and they kicked me out of there. You know, Elvis used to rent out the fairgrounds here and rent out the theaters. It got where he was a prisoner in his own world. He couldn't get out. He'd sneak out at night on his motorcycle and run around White Haven; had his own girls. I think he ran pretty hard with a lot of women before he got hooked up with Priscilla. He was dating all them White Haven beauties. I just think that he was a phenomenon, like a meteor that comes once every so many thousand years. He was exactly what Sam Phillips with Sun label said: he was a white man that could sing black music, and that's exactly what he found and that's exactly what he got. He was a very religious man deep down inside. He did probably as much gospel as he did popular music. He had an image that he didn't want to face and the fact that the world was gonna find out what he was really about.

"If you lived in Memphis back in those days, we had these clubs like Clearpool out there at Winchester and Lamar. It was a big place where every weekend they'd have Hank Ballard and the Midnighters or the Drifters, and they'd have these high school sorority dances. We had the Rainbow Terrace Room, which also had big shows coming in all the time. At West Memphis across the river, we had the Plantation Inn. It was a party town. You could bring your own bottle and do what you wanted to. Memphis had a drive-in network. Like they had Leonard's, they had Gilley's, they had the Pig & Whistle, Willie King's, Jungle Gardens. That was Memphis' social life. Like, in that part of town, that was your drive-in. If you went in there and you weren't from that territory you could get in trouble real easily, if you were from the rival part of town, and if you didn't know anybody like the Tillers to protect you. I happened to know the Tillers. I ran into 'em and got to know 'em. They were a good, shall I say, ally to have on your team.

"The Tillers happened to live in the part of Memphis that was kind of a white-collar area. They could beat up anybody and do anything they wanted to. They actually had kind of a respect. People were scared of 'em, but yet they liked 'em. I'd go to private parties in Memphis and the Tillers would be there, and you'd hear people over in the corner, you know, whispering and things. But wasn't nobody gonna say anything to them, 'cause they knew that they'd be in big trouble and that if you beat one of the Tillers, you'd have to go down the line. There's about five of them. If you beat one, you'd have to work your way up, and by the time you got to the third one I don't believe you could mount any kind of offense whatsoever.

The first time I met Mike Tiller it was at the Armory, out by the fairgrounds and he said, 'Let's go get in a fight.' I said, 'Yeah, let's go.' He walked down the flight of steps and he turned around at bottom and there was a big guy dancing. I guess he was about 6'7", about 290 pounds, had a pair of glasses on. Tiller tapped him on the shoulder and knocked him to the ground right in the middle of the dance. I mean, you talk about embarrassment. I thought he was kidding. I'd be in a dance and somebody would look at me crooked and I'd say, 'Hey, that guy called you a rat.' He'd go over there and hit him right at the table. They didn't play around. They came from Germantown – nice area, affluent. In fact, Dago was the valedictorian of his class. He was studying to be a doctor. He was valedictorian over at Christian Brothers High School – great baseball player. George was a great football player. He got a scholarship to University of Tennessee. He had long arms – I guess he could tie his shoes standing up, and he had a fist about twice as big as an average man. He was kind of the Muhammad Ali type; he could stand back and just drop you. He had that Jack Palance look. He'd put that look on you. He's down in prison down on Parchman Farm in Mississippi right now. The nicest guy you ever met."

"You had to have a car then…?"

"For drive-in movies, yeah. Integration shut down all the drive-ins. They just started shutting down. They started having troubles. Things had changed a lot after that. They cracked down on the liquor and drinking. You know where a drive-in is today, besides Sonic?"

"You had a place on Overton Square for a long time."

"I had a place at Overton Square. Yeah, I've been in business 36 years. I had a place called Silky's right in front of Pappy & Jimmy's Lobster Shack on Poplar. I moved everything back down to Beale Street in '92, and I'm glad I did. Beale Street's a great area. I've done very well down here. Then I opened a place in New Orleans in the French Quarter. I got tired of going down there. It's like you owning a muffler shop up in Wichita Falls. I got tired of going there, and I sold it two months before Katrina. I escaped. I got out, but I've done a lot in New Orleans. I've been king of Mardi Gras there three times. I'm king this year. So I've done a lot of wild stuff down in New Orleans.

"Well, Memphis was a great city in its day, but it's still controlled by a bunch of old families. The reason Memphis never took off like Atlanta or Houston and them places, is because a lot of old money here that's held the city down like with plantation mentality, unless they got a piece of the pie of what's going to happen. Old real estate families... they just controlled everything downtown in Memphis. Then they wanted to move everything out to shopping centers, but everything's coming back to downtown Memphis now. You know, the expressway, they wanted to come right down through the center of Memphis and you had these people that wanted to save the trees out in Overton Park here. If that expressway would have went through, Memphis would have been really booming. Then the city didn't want to give a half acre of land to the Ford plant, which was here in Memphis, and the Ford plant got mad and moved out of town. So thank goodness for people like Fred Smith at FedEx and International Paper, and AutoZone. If it wasn't for those, it would be just a little country town."

"The Belz family did well with the Peabody Hotel... and Elkington?"

"Elkington's a good part of Memphis. He's done good things with city planning. He stuck his neck out."

"That's dangerous in Memphis."

"Well, there's an old saying in Memphis: *You can always tell the leaders, they got the most arrows in their back.*"

"You knew Campbell Kensinger, right?"

"Yeah, I knew Campbell in high school. He was more of an ivy leaguer back when I knew him. Then he started running with motorcycle gang type people. You gotta be careful who you run with. You move with dogs, you get fleas on you."

"You went to Christian Brothers High School, too?"

"Yeah, Christian Brothers. That was a great school. I just got put in the Hall of Fame over there."

"So that's a Catholic school, right?"

"Yeah, the de la Salle brothers."

"How'd you get this goat farm going outside?"

"Well, I wanted to have a little mascot, so I put a couple goats out there. When I first put 'em out there, the health department came down, said, 'Silky, you know your neighbors don't want these goats – they smell and there's a livestock law in the city.' I said, 'Well let me handle that.' So I called a friend of mine at city hall. I told him to pass me a waiver where I could have my goats. The ones that knew me on city council, when they voted they said, 'Baaaah, yes, he can have the goats.' They had the headlines the next day in the paper: 'City Busts Out Barkeep's Goats.' So I kept my goats.

"About 10 weeks later, my managers called me and I said, 'What's the problem?' They said, 'You've got five guys sitting down here – looks like Blues Brothers, got big briefcases with them – waiting on you.' So I drove down there and walked in and I said, 'Gentlemen what seems to be the problem?' They said, 'Mr. Sullivan, we're from Nashville and we represent the state health department, and we got a message for you from the state health commissioner,' and I said, 'What could that be?' They said, 'Well, if those goats aren't out of here by 5:00 today, we're gonna padlock you and shut you down.' I said, 'Is that the reason you made me drive all the way down here?' They said, 'Yeah.' I said, 'Well gentlemen, not to waste my time or your time any longer, I'm gonna tell you, before you even open those briefcases: did you talk to my lawyer?' They said, 'Yeah.' I said, 'Well, what did he tell you?' They said, 'Well, he told us that you were crazy enough to take this to the Supreme Court.' I said, 'Gentlemen, he was correct,' and I said, 'You know what the first question's gonna be when I go to the Supreme Court?' And those guys kinda lean back in their chairs and gave me this very inquisitive look, and I looked at them straight in the eye and said, 'Gentlemen the first question I'm gonna ask when I go to Supreme Court is: What craps the most, 10 ducks or 2 goats?' So I said, 'Do you want to open up that can of worms with the Peabody?' They said, 'No, we don't want to do that.' I said, 'Well gentlemen, end of conversation.' So my goats are still frolicking down here very happily. I have a lot of rhythm & blues bands out there on the patio in the summertime. I have dueling pianos. I have the best barbecue in Memphis, best ribs; got all kinds of good food in there: oysters Bienville, Rockefeller….'

"You make those right, don't you – like down in New Orleans?"

"Better. There are a lot of differences, but a lot of closeness, too, between Memphis and New Orleans. I went to LSU there for a while. I went to about eight universities. Memphis had E. H. Crump and Louisiana had Huey P. Long. New Orleans is a lot wider open and a greater international type area. Of course they dealt a lot with Cuba back in the old days. It was a Latin American port in the Caribbean; they had United Fruit Company down there. They got a lot of tradition… a mixture of Texas, Mississippi, and Alabama, and a lot of the Creole, and them people – *laissez les bon temps rouler*. They like to have fun. I ran for lieutenant Governor down there four years ago; came in second. My motto was, 'Silky Sullivan, voice of the bayou.' I got broadcast in Lafayette, and I told them to put their hands on the radio, I'm getting ready to give them a message. I said the message is – I had on a white suit and suspenders – and said the message is, 'If you don't suck a head or pinch a tail [crawfish], I don't want your damn vote.' I got 80,000 damn votes out of Lafayette. Out of eight people I came in second, that ain't bad."

"That's pretty good. I think you ought to run again."

"Well, there's too many skeletons in my closet…"

"That's not going to harm you in Louisiana."

Rotund and white as Silky's Louisiana campaign suit, the sun was sinking over the muddy Mississippi, when I swung my leg over the Norton and headed toward Midtown. The Unapproachable Norton seemed to know its way back to Cox Street… certainly better than I, after that line of highballs downed with his Silkyness. I left the bike in the alley between the duplex and the adjacent manor house, climbed the front porch steps and flung myself onto the porch swing where the last rays of reddened August light lay upon me like the hands of Lucifer. I seemed to float imperceptibly in the swing as if it were the huge goose gliding high and wide over the encampment of Memphis far below… and wondered if Silky ever barbecued a goat.

The Arcade Restaurant facing Central Train Station and across from its sister Arcade Hotel is, by virtue of its proximity to main line trains that are passing through the terminal from Chicago to New Orleans, an oasis of transient urbanity in the Bluff City. Among the first class trains that once passed daily through the terminal were The Creole, The City of New Orleans, The Sunnyland Special, the Florida bound Dixie Flyer, and the Panama Limited that Bukker White immortalized in song. The 1920s edifice of the Arcade is as much a landmark as Central Station itself. The Arcade is patronized not only by the weary traveler, but also by a democratized stratum of Memphis society where railroad workers and passenger trainmen run elbows with local artists and musicians. I was seated at the counter on an aquamarine and tangerine leatherette upholstered stool waiting on my order of a vegetable plate and iced tea, when Harold Boone happened to sit down beside me and order a pork plate with all the trimmings. A feisty waitress arrived in a crisp sky blue uniform and with a toss of her platinum blonde bouffant laid out my dish of steaming peas, corn, and sweet potatoes and my frosty glass of tea. I gobbled a mouthful while exchanging pleasantries with the bearded and hairy gentlemen to my right, looking in appearance not unlike his eponymous namesake, the stalwart Tennessee frontiersman, Daniel.

"Harold," I ventured, "do you remember which Nix it was that was that the FBI contracted on that Martin Luther King detail? Red Nix...?"

"Right... he got killed in a motel."

"Did you happen to know Campbell Kensinger...?"

"Yeah, Campbell wanted to be bad so bad, it got him killed. Campbell was all right, but nobody we ever knew that was around him considered Campbell tough. To the stranger or somebody that didn't know him, he had a reputation that he was tough, but I always took Campbell for a good guy. I don't say nothing bad about him, 'cause I knew him so long. He just got into something to do with some reds, or some kind of barbiturate, and just got tore up so bad and got sideways with everybody that he dealt with. There's a guy named Hawk he did a club with. Supposed to be the guy that set him up and got him killed by Mac McCullom, but I don't know. His daddy was Chick Kensinger. You know Poplar Plaza shopping plaza at Highland? He built Poplar Plaza shopping center. They were millionaires. Chick Kensinger, he bought Campbell's little brother, Jimmy Kensinger, a Chevrolet dealership up in Dyersburg, Tennessee, after he got grown. Campbell was just a bad apple in that family – the black sheep. He couldn't get a better upbringing. I mean, he just got kind of sideways. Maybe it's because he ran around with Mike and Albert Tiller. They were an influence on a lot of people."

"What kind of influence did they have? People looked up to them?"

"Well, no, not necessarily looked up to them, the sons-a-bitches would just do anything. If you were in a jail cell with 20 people, the Tillers put 19 of them in there. George wasn't like that; Charles wasn't like that; but Mike snitched on Charles, and to tell the truth, it wasn't Mike it was Albert that snitched on him. Charles killed Mike for it, but Albert was the one that did it. He was gonna kill Albert when he found out. Said he was gonna kill George, too, because he had to kill Mike and Albert."

"He killed his two brothers?"

"They're his cousins. Charles, he was a short guy, and he got beat out of playing for the St. Louis Cardinals. He went up there and tried out for them. He was a good athlete, but he was just too small."

"Which one was called Dago?"

"That's Charles. Yeah, I got a picture of him and James Earl Ray, sitting in a cell together... at Brushy Mountain, or Riverbend Penitentiary. For a while Dago was like James Earl Ray's bodyguard. The nigs up there tricked Dago out on the recreation yard chasing, running him out there amongst 'em. Some of 'em got on him with baseball bats. That was the end of Dago. I mean, he was gonna get it one day. We used to be pretty good friends, but we had a falling out and I didn't care any more about him. I had a chance to kill the son of a bitch, didn't do it because of his mother and his brothers. I liked them... if I'd a killed him, it'd save seven lives.

"Jerry, Ronnie, Mike, Albert, and George were brothers and grew up in Germantown. Dago, Thomas, and Joe were from Memphis. They were cousins. The ones that caused all the problems were George, Dago, Mike, and Albert. It was four different personalities. Mike was pretty smart, but you couldn't trust him. Albert was pretty dumb; you sure in hell couldn't trust him. George was a good athlete, graduated from high school and got a scholarship to go to the University of Tennessee. Got kicked out of there, beat up a couple of assistant coaches, went in the Marine Corps, and boxed while he was in there. The heavyweight champion of the Marine Corps was named Johnson; George knocked him out twice. He went over the wall and was put in the stockade, and he ran off from there every night. Charles graduated from Christian Brothers and went on to Memphis State; was studying to be a dentist. He was pretty intelligent,

Dago Tiller & James Earl Ray, Brushy Mountain Prison

real smart, but there was that fine line and Charles wanted to be the toughest son of a bitch in the world. He whouped a lot of people – a lot of them.

"The toughest one out of the whole bunch was George. George was built about like Cassius Clay. He'd kick the shit out of Dago. He had those big hands and long arms, and knew how to fight, could fight, and would fight. He didn't get excited or nothing like that; he'd hit hard, real hard. George was a good boxer. There was another tough guy in Memphis, by the name of Johnny Shepherd. They called him 'Cast Iron'. When they boxed for the Mid-South Championship, everybody thought that John was gonna beat George. I said *nah, there ain't no way*. When George beat Johnny that kinda tamed Sheppard down; he got out of the limelight. Of course, George has done about 12 to 16 calendar years in the state penitentiary. Whouped a couple of policemen, whouped an FBI agent and knocked his eye out. Just whouped everybody he come across, tell you the truth about it. A likeable guy. Most everybody in Memphis has run around these bars and streets, did a little knockin', stealin', killin', shootin' or whatever the hell they had to do, knew George and respected him 'cause he was tough. I mean, he was legitimate tough, internationally tough. If you was from Russia or Cuba or China or Honduras, he wouldn't mind kicking your ass. He just didn't dog it on nobody. I mean, nobody. Not a dog in him. He was tough. He's standing ten years down in Rankin County, Mississippi. If it'd been me or you caught for the same crime, we'd get half a year at the most."

"Yeah, we heard that the judge told him this was a lifetime achievement award."

"Yep, you've worked all your life to get this. This is your lifetime achievement award. You know, people like to say things like that to people when they're sitting behind some kind of protective veil. They say that to George on the street, probably George would've slapped some of his teeth out. He's old, he's old just like I'm old. Everybody gets old. When age catches up with you, if you want to keep it up, you get your gun and go 'til it kills you or you kill them. Some of 'em ain't worth shooting. Some of them, you're glad you shot them."

"Why do you think George got into trouble like he did, other than fighting? Why do you think he ran around doing all these little petty things?"

"You got to enjoy a little of it to do it, but Mike and Albert used to pull him into that petty stuff. That's all they did. Many a time Mike would send kids into places, kids that just got to Memphis from Brownsville, or Guntown, or Tunica or somewhere like that, come to the big town, Memphis. First thing they do is start running around at night. Mike will tell them where there's a house that's got jewelry in it, or a drugstore that's got a lot of drugs in it, or a house that's got a lot of money in it. The kids would be so dumb, they'd go in there and get it. They'd get caught getting it. If they got it, they'd split it up with Mike. If Mike got in any trouble later on, he'd tell 'em about the kids did it and beat the charge. Son of a bitch."

"Well, Campbell toward the end had a motorcycle club, but he was..."

"He tried to get the Hell's Angels in here. He tried to buy up a little group called The Family, and he was going to do a number on somebody for somebody – it was for Elvis Presley. He knew some of those guys worked for Elvis. He was supposed to pop a cap on this guy that was coming in teaching Elvis Presley karate. A guy name Mike..."

"Kang Ree"

"Well, nobody worries about Kang Ree; he was a joke. It was a joke: somebody starts and gets a black belt in a week. That's some money there, that's Elvis. No, what I'm talking about is a guy used to teach Elvis private karate lessons, started screwing Priscilla."

"Stone was his name?"

"Mike Stone. He was a legitimate bad son of a bitch. So they hired Campbell – was talking about killing him just before he died. And he was trying to get the Hell's Angels in it, but they wouldn't back his play up here in Memphis.

"The Outlaws have been around awhile..."

"Yeah, the Outlaws have been around. They're just a bunch of local guys; there wasn't much to them, I didn't think. They're not supposed to be west of the Mississippi, and the Hells Angels are not supposed to be east of the Mississippi. You got some Pagans and the Banditos, and the Gooses, and all that bullshit. *Iron* Horsemen."

"The Iron Horsemen were connected with Danny Owens, weren't they?"

"Oh, all them little ol' girls, all them topless dancers they had, their little girlfriends worked there for him. You know how that goes. That's white slavery is all that is. Picked up little ol' girls, and they danced for 'em. Call 'em their old men, you know. You get a little ol' girl strung out on Quaaludes, heroin or whatever. All of them tell you they're dancing to work their way through college. Just pimpin' and whorin' – it all goes together, just like the good book says. I've never seen one of them yet that was worth a shit."

"Those one-percenters, they really couldn't stand up to people like the Tillers or the Nixes, could they?"

"You get 1500 people against the five toughest son of a bitches that walked the face of the earth, the five toughest people on the face of the earth are gone. Those bikers are strong in numbers. You got 1200 guys riding on you, or a 100 guys that stick together and made a pledge to stick together like brothers, then you got a problem... but their business of getting into trouble is generally with other bikers. As far as two or three of them running around with George Tiller, that ain't gonna happen, that ain't never gonna happen, never did happen. He just slapped the shit out of one of 'em. He didn't care nothing about 'em, about who they were, about how bad they were. I mean, Campbell was a joke to George and to Dago Tiller and them, and to Dante Raggiante and people like that. ...Dante Raggiante got killed in Atlanta in a car wreck. A little Italian boy, real small. He was nuttier than a fruitcake. It took all day to whoup him, he'd fight you all day. Raggiante, Sivangio, Springnoli, Sinciola, Gigianti, Cartosi...and all them Italian boys around here."

"Did you know any of the Liberto family?"

"Yeah, I knew the Libertos. Wasn't none of them guys tough. The people that are clannish are Italians. They stick together. The Chinese stick together. Gypsies stick together. They're clannish people, full-blooded people. All full-blooded people stick together. And it's kinda little groups going, they got the Mafia going, they got the Gypsies are thieves, and so on."

"Liberto had real strong connections with Carlos Marcello in New Orleans."

"Probably, but so have 10,000 other Italians down there, too. I just got through telling you they're clannish. You know, the people that work for a railroad, all their kids end up working for the railroad. The people that are cops; their kids become cops. The people that are pipe fitters; their kids become pipe fitters. It just goes that way. Not all of them, but I mean it's just the input is the strongest and that's the way it goes. As far as being tough in Memphis, the guys that were tough that you didn't hear nothing about that were just as tough as Dago and George were people like Sonny Bray, Dale Dean, Pretty Boy Moore, Harold Reeves, Clark Bell, Larry Bell, Joe Bell, Sonny Reeves, Johnny Shepherd, Edgar Buffalo, Herman Stephens, J. D. Rutherford, Lloyd Bobbin, Simbo Ban, Junior Jackson – I can name all them just as tough. I can name you all them people nobody's ever heard of that would go to work 40 hours, come home lay on the couch, take care of their kids and you mess with them, they get off the couch and kick the shit out of you. But they don't care about their reputation. They don't like to get out and run wild. George Tiller is probably gonna die down there in Rankin. What the hell did he prove? I admire George. He's got my admiration being so tough, but who wants to die in the penitentiary no matter what you're doing?"

"Were all these white people?"

"No, you got black people that are tough – Frank Rogers or Bone Crusher or Ernie Buford, the guy they call Railhead, Cast Iron, they were tough. But blacks and whites are completely different on being tough. A lot of people don't understand that, completely different. Your blacks are tough in Harlem. Just like the other day, I bumped into about seven or eight of them and had a little fender bender. They smacked into the back of my van. They all got out, *hey man, what you're doing*? I didn't even start my car up yet and – but *you* backed into my van. I said, *well get the fuck out of the way. I'm too old to fuck with you... or two or three of you sons a bitches are gonna get shot. Well, you said nigger awhile ago.* I said, *I didn't say nigger, but I will say nigger. Fuckin' niggers get out of the way.* I like some of 'em, but I don't like some of 'em: some are black, some are niggers. That's just the way it goes, the way it always goes, will go and has gone. Just like white people, there's white people are white niggers. They call them wiggers, same old thing. Ain't no difference."

"You think there's an underworld in Memphis?"

"No, ain't nobody gonna say nothin' about that. There's never been any Mafia here – Liberto or Gattises, or Broadnax. Probably Broadnax would be the closest to organized crime in this town. You never heard of nobody trying to rob Broadnax jewelry store, have you?"

"No, uh-uh."

"They ain't going to, neither."

"Why is that?"

"Well, I'm just telling you there's certain things you talk about and certain things you don't talk about. The real people just don't talk about them."

"How about Art Baldwin?"

"Art come here from Seattle and opened up these titty clubs. He wasn't tough, he was just dangerous. Ray Blanton – when the governor of the state of Tennessee was selling the pardons to everybody, and they kicked him out of office – he had an informant that he was getting his information from. But the Feds had busted this guy who was trying to beat a charge, and this guy had heard because of the position he was in and the people he knew, that you could buy a pardon from Ray Blanton… and through this guy, the Feds would send the money to Ray Blanton to get people pardoned. I knew a guy who used to drive the money up there to Ray Blanton, and he did it for a guy named Mr. B. You know who Mr. B was? Mr. Art Baldwin. He had that big ol' drug charge on him, but he didn't do but a year up at Maxwell Air Force Base. When he got out, Danny Owens had taken his place.

"Danny got beat up pretty bad down where they tried to kill him. Put him in the hospital. He got in a fight with a guy named No Legs, one of the Iron Horsemen. He slapped him upside the head and slapped him around and run the gang all out of his clubs, didn't want them hanging around there. They came around there to his joint, cut the phone wires, and come in there with baseball bats. They were lucky that they come in there when they did. If they came in there and there'd been some guns, one of them would've got their ass killed. They were just shit ass lucky. Then Danny was so greedy and money crazy, he got the whores to come back and work in there. But Danny's doing, what, 28 years now. He's in Lompoc federal prison. While he was in the joint he loaned some guy some money on a radio, and the guy came back to get the radio back and didn't have all the money to pay, and Danny wouldn't give the radio back. So the guy waited until Danny went to sleep, went in there and cooked up about two pints of Johnson's baby oil, got it boiling hot, and dumped it in Danny's face. It never stops when you're in that league. They put Danny in another prison, and he lack to have lost his eyes. So before that Romeo shot Danny's thumb off and his fingers off down at Ann's place in Mississippi, and they never did catch him. Another dude shot Danny two times up on Madison Ave. at J-Wags with a .357 Magnum. When they took him up to city hospital and Danny was laying there in a bed in the operating room, had bullet holes in him, and that little ol' machine that measures his heart, goes doot…doot…doot, you know makes that little sound? Danny asked the doctor how's it look, and the doctor said it don't look good. Danny said the thing then started going dootdootdootdootdoot."

"Who is this Romeo guy?"

"Just some dude. I don't know. Somebody had paid him to kill Danny. Him and his buddy, Chubby, were sitting down there at Ann's Place, when the dude come with a shotgun. Danny seen him coming, then Danny flipped the table up to get down behind the table and the guy fired the gun. It blew Danny's right finger and thumb off his hand. He laid there on the floor and the guy ran out the door. Danny's laying there with his eyes shut and Chubby got onto Danny, and Danny whispered is he gone?

"Danny got in a fight with a boy, a kid around here named Billy James that was trying to be tough, pretty good kid. He got killed. Danny threw him through a plate glass window, and he bled out before they got him to the hospital. The story got out that Danny took a knife and tried to cut his throat, but he just fell through the window. They come down there looking for Danny because a guy named Whirlwind, an old wrestler agitated that fight on. Them agitators get everybody killed. We had a guy out here named Sonny Bray, was pretty tough. Sonny ODd in '73, but he wasn't scared of nothing. Clarence Lester Elwood was crazy… Johnny Young, Claude Bedman, Scrappy Moore, they were crazy. They killed people, you know. They were dangerous just like Buford Pusser, man. Buford would kill the shit out of you. That's the reason there's not too many people breaking too many speed limits to get to McNary County."

"Pusser, he ended up on the side of the law, right?"

"Supposedly. He was just as crooked as he could be. He was dangerous, though – real dangerous."

"I heard somewhere that Mike Tiller was engaged to the daughter of a Montesi…Vicky Montesi, who was the daughter of Fred and Evelyn Montesi who had the big supermarkets"

"No, Fred was the father of Louie Montesi, and Louie was Verna Montesi's husband. Vicky Montesi, Judy Montesi, and Bobby Montesi were their kids, and Mike Tiller married Judy Montesi. He used to beat the shit out of her every month, just beat the dog shit out of her. That's the kind of guy Mike was."

"Who was the daughter of Evelyn Montesi, who was shot dead – the Montesi wife that was murdered?"

"That was Verna Montesi. That was Judy's mother. Her father was Louie. They moved from Galloway out on Perkins. When Louie shot Verna Montesi, he had to go to the penal farm for it… but the only thing about it is Louie didn't shoot his wife. A woman who was there with 'em shot her. It was Louie's mamma. They hated each other. See, Louis's momma was 85 years old. He didn't want his momma catching no charge. The story I got, he did a deal with the head of homicide, named E. C. Swan. Swan wasn't head of homicide after it happened; I know that. He went for the bucks. Yeah, Huey P. Long, his son got in trouble; he paid. Frank Sinatra paid his son out. When you got money, you pay your way out of it."

"So Mike Tiller was married to Judy Montesi… up until he was killed?"

"That's right, until Dago killed him."

"Sounds like their relationship wasn't so good."

"Well, she must have liked him; she kept coming back for more. She was a big ol' fat girl, just out about 340. She was likeable. I liked Judy, she was just married to somebody who was a woman beater."

"So why did Dago kill Mike? They were cousins, right?"

"That's right, first cousins. Dago thought that Mike snitched on him, but it wasn't Mike, it was Albert. And he tortured his ass to death. He took a screwdriver, tearing snips, or whatever you got to do. It took two days, three days to kill him. I wasn't there… but Red Nix was there, Leon was there, Thomas was there.

"But they never found the body…?"

"A finger here, a toe there, an ear here…you know."

"What happened to Albert?"

"Albert got the hell out of here. You remember Jimmy Hoffa? He was head of the teamsters and disappeared after he got through doing his time. Well, when he got out and disappeared, the guy that became head of the Teamsters, his name was Jackie Presser. Albert married his daughter, Cindy Presser, and immediately started stealing their jewelry and stuff, doing drugs. They lived down in Miami, and later on, as time passed, Albert was in the joint down there, in the county jail doin' some time. When he was sick from doing so many drugs, they let him out to die. You know, when you do all that stuff, man, trouble and misery follows you… when you dish out so much of it. Like George Tiller's son – 25, 26 years old – he committed suicide. I had a friend I ran around with, wanted to be bad, Jimmy Nelson. He got killed. I could sit here and name a hundred guys that got in these bullshit fights, that didn't have enough sense to know when to pull up, got killed. It wasn't no big surprise to me. I always knew that if a son of a bitch was mad at me I needed to get my back to the wall and get me something in my hand and make sure I got some guy on my back, and get the hell out of there. If you whoup a guy, why stay around? Why kill him and go to the joint for it? There's a bunch of people I'd like to just choke the shit out of, but you know."

"What are some of the clubs you liked to hang out in?"

"Danny's Club, Cotton Club, Plantation Inn, Gilley's, Porky's, Earl's, Kay's, Wild Gables, Little Memphis, Delmar, Sam's, Cotton Bowl, Cottage Inn, The M&M, Thunderbird, Ti-

Ki Club, Manhattan Club, and oh, the Gypsy Village – I believe everybody went in there were thieves, was the reason they called it Gypsy Village. There was one place called the Freeway Inn. After every other club closed, it opened up. You sure could get your ears cropped in there; at Lamar and Bellevue. If you didn't know anybody in there, you didn't go in that place. Here's the way it goes: bad guys don't walk up to other bad guys and slap 'em. They walk up to guys they know; they slap some people around they know they can slap around. It all boils down to this, everything breaks about even for everybody. Like the old saying goes, *we all get the same amount of ice – the rich get it in the summer and the poor get it in the winter*. That's what Bat Masterson said the day he died.

"To make a guy look bad you slap him in front of a bunch of people, but people know who to slap, who not to slap. I remember one night George slapped an old boy in a bet. We're sitting there talking about it four years later and George said, 'Man, that scared the shit out of me, when I tried to slap old John, 'cause later another guy jumped on him, slapped him, and John went back there and shot him.' I said, 'That's right. The night you slapped him, he was looking for a pistol. You be glad you got out of there.' You just can't tell, you know. Some people tell me it's better to kill someone big. I don't know whether it was or not; I know this guy had a hell of a reputation about them shoot guns. Usually what scares people off is a reputation. George and Dago really had a reputation, but they could back it up. Dago was a grappler, if he got his hands on you, you was in trouble. George would stand and knock your ass off before you could get your hands on him, and could hit hard.

"Campbell worked there at Trader Dick's. I considered that really funny if people would get scared of Campbell. He would just sucker punch the shit out of somebody, get 'em in there, get him drunk and just knock the shit out of him. He was a pretty good-sized boy, if he hit you. He worked for Herbie O'Mell down there at TJs. All that physique, growling and stuff… he liked to have messed with wrong guy one time. There was a guy named Nick Caracas, come here from Houston, Texas. He was a mobster, good for about 12 people getting killed. They run a club called the Loser's Club down on Cleveland and Union. It was on top of NBC Bank building; it spun around real slow. It was a circular club cafe. They had high-end entertainment in there like Fats Domino, Chuck Berry, the Platters, and the Drifters and all that stuff back then in the early '70s. They were selling a bunch of diamonds out of there.

"Nick Caracas went up to TJs one night and Campbell and two or three of the punks up there was going to jump on him. Well they were lucky they didn't, 'cause they would've gotten their ass killed. Later on, close to the Loser's Club, Nick Caracas was getting gas up there at Bellevue and Lamar and got into some argument with just some kids – just some kids that were getting gas – and when the kid pulled off, a guy pulled him by the jacket and pulled him out in the middle of the street and let him go, when he did, a tractor-trailer truck come through there and popped him like a melon. Just busted him right in two. That was the end of the Loser's Club. Shit happens."

A good meal at the Arcade deserves a good tip, so I tossed the platinum waitress a silver dollar, swung open the double doors of the Arcade, and stepped out onto Calhoun Street. Although they weighed down my jeans, I liked carrying silver dollars in my pocket… makes you feel flush with the world in a way that paper or plastic doesn't. On the corner I dropped a 50 cent piece into the newspaper-vending box and eased out a late edition *Commercial Appeal*. Same old crud. *Why do I buy these papers*, I reproached myself. Still flogging that "West Memphis Three" case on the front page again: three little boys were found killed in a drainage ditch, hog-tied, mutilated, one of them castrated. What a sub-standard travesty of criminal justice. While black t-shirts, death metal, jett hair dye, Marilyn Manson cartoons, and an Esbat frolic inflamed the local evangelicals, it's apparent that the adoptive father of one of the eight-year-old victims should with good reason be arraigned as the prime suspect. He has one of longest police records in Crittenden County, had undergone psychiatric treatment for abusing and terrorizing his own natural born son and his wife, and he survived as an unemployed police informant. Then his wife turns up mysteriously killed a few years after the trial of three teenagers indicted for the murder of the children. One of those indicted was retarded with an IQ of 72, and even then he had no clear idea of whom even 'Satan' might be. Another of the convicted teenagers, a high school dropout who identified with black metal and wore his hair long and black, took the fall. It's apparent that he's set to be spending the rest of his life on death row in the Varner Unit of the Arkansas corrections system.

The expert Violent Crimes Division of the Arkansas State Police had offered to join in the investigation of the three murders, but the offer was refused. The State Police expressed little surprise in being thusly rebuffed, due to the fact that the West Memphis Police Department was *already* under investigation for theft of the Crittenden County drug and narcotics enforcement bureau larder. One can harddl wonder that investigation was so badly botched. There was also something fishy about the Circuit Court judge over there who refused to entertain motions for admittance of new evidence and testing, although he accepted damning testimony in the trial from an "occult specialist" whose credentials consisted of a mail-order PhD. The judge also appears to have had explicit ties to the certified mentally deranged West Memphis PD informant, and adoptive father of the child victim who was castrated. The judge strangely *expunged* the psychopath's criminal record after the murders, and he blocked a homicide investigation upon the unexplained death of the informant's wife. What an incestuous imbroglio… kind of makes you want to puke up a good vegetable plate.

CHAPTER THE TENTH
BEHIND THE MAGNOLIA CURTAIN

Sometime during my first week in the duplex on Cox St., a high-pitched, yet gravely sound of an effeminate voice coming from the alley beside my bedroom window awoke me from a night of abysmal slumbers. It was the penetrating vociferation of George Wheeler, a no longer young native son grown into late manhood, who possessed the mind and personality of a gregarious nine-year-old boy. George lived in the voluminous, decrepit clapboard house across the alley. He was the ward of a diminutive, cross-eyed octogenarian, Maude Wheeler – the Empress of Roaches.

Maude was also a *gattara,* or a keeper of cats. She maintained revolving herd of stray cats that she fed every afternoon with dubious table scraps. Maude summoned the felines along with whichever birds and fowl of the air happened to be flying about or roosting in the many trees that surrounded us, by standing on the rotted back steps of the house and vigorously beating a warped aluminum sauce pan with an oversized tablespoon. She cooed to them in little girl articulations, "Heeeere kitty, kitty, kitty. KEEeeeetty, kitty, kitty; kitty, kitty."

Maude Wheeler was the scion of landed gentry from White Station, now the easternmost annex of Memphis. During the War of Rebellion, her family did not stand with the South. When her grandfather was a young civil engineer, the Yankees tried to hang him as a spy, but he wangled out of it by directing the scalawags where to dig up all the gold that was stashed around the home place. Later he married his own daughter, and was pardoned by the governors in three states. Within the complex lineage, the bride was actually no blood relation at all, but Maude was fond of telling the story. In fact, Maude was a raconteur of grand proportions as well as up-to-the-minute on current events. Rhetorically probing her guests in aristocratic tones what the Russians were up to, she would sit at the dining table swatting and raking off the roaches that swarmed on every surface in the house, and whose populations were legion living under the peeling wallpaper of the rooms. According to the oracular prediction of John McIntire the phylum of humble roaches would anyway one day reclaim their master of the earth as their own. One had little reason to doubt such visions of the sagacious sculptor as the day Randall died in Arkansas, John was driving his VW van along a highway in Alabama and in the instant Randall was released from his death throes John saw in his mind's eye the poet cross over the Stygian waters into the netherworld beyond.

Maude often reiterated how impoverished the family was for generations after the Civil War, and how her mother went off her rocker when Maude was a little girl. Her mother struggled as a seamstress, when they were living on the ground floor of an antediluvian house on Linden Avenue near the Midtown library. When her mother took one of her spells, she would stomp out onto the front veranda of the house, and in the most strident language curse the Pope to high heaven.

In the darkened, unpainted hallway of the old house hung a large, framed photographic portrait of George painted in delicately with Marshall's photo oil colors. It was the image of George as a young boy smiling serenely and attired in a dapper plaid suit with knickers. He kept a bicycle in the hallway that was from the 1930s, yet he rode it only a few times during the year. Instead, he was an inveterate walker. Generally unshaven, he walked everywhere in a sleeveless undershirt in summer, and with an timeworn wool overcoat and fur billed cap in winter. One hand was usually held high, more fluttering than shaking, near his throat in an unctuous, self-effacing manner. His favorite jaunt was brisk walk over to the Fairgrounds about three blocks

George Wheeler Photo: E. Baffle c.1977

east, especially when the Royal American Shows carnival was encamped in town and the midway was running full tilt. George absolutely lived for the carnival to come every September. Maude bought him a season ticket, and he would spend the entire day there, every day the carnival was open. He rode all the rides, but not the terrifying ones. He'd climb aboard the Ferris Wheel, Tilt-a-Whirl, the Merry-Go-Round, the Lilliputian steam train, and he was thrilled with the Pippin roller coaster that was constructed on a small scale of wooden planks and ran jolly red and white cars on a narrow gauge track. Between rides he would eat foot-long corn dogs with plenty of mustard, swig Pepsi-Cola from paper cups, and finish off those snacks with a big pink fluff of cotton candy spun out on a paper cone. During the carnival season, he'd be seen walking home invariably carrying high a little whirly-gig on a stick. Its red and blue propeller would spin merrily as it caught the draft initiated by his swift gait.

George adored having his picture taken, and whenever he saw me with a camera hanging from my neck, he would stop and pose and say; *now you can take my picture*. Although in mind and spirit, he was youthful and blithesome, there was something ineffably tragic and darkly Shakespearian about the aura that emanated like a halo around his being. After I had left Cox Street and returned to Memphis after a particularly lengthy absence, I passed by my old address at 704, and was astonished to see that the Wheeler home had vanished. Nothing left but an empty grassy lot and a few trees standing at the back. Upon inquiry, I learned that Maude had joined her mother in the hereafter, and that before her passage young George Wheeler had stepped off the curb into the busy parkway facing the Fairgrounds and had been struck by oncoming car and killed. I hope instantly.

The sun shone brightly and the wind was calm on this fair day in April, when I mounted my second line motorbike – a 650 Triumph Tiger that I'd bought off a deputy sheriff in Bryant, Arkansas. The deputy had routinely used the bike to run through cow pastures feeding hay bales to his cattle. After I'd rebuilt the Triumph from the ground up, I lost enthusiasm for it one night on a ride over the Mississippi River Bridge, when high winds caught the leeward side of the bike and blew it around the bridge pavement like a Dixie Cup. That kind of behavior was never an issue on the Norton, which – with its "Featherbed" double-looped, Rex McCandless designed frame – was a staunch road-holder under even the most adverse conditions. During the rebuild process which took an entire summer, I thought it wise to ride to Jimmy Arnold's on Jackson Avenue out in the Nutbush area to pick up a couple of replacement air filters for the Triumph. As I was cruising down the high overpass over the railroad tracks by the National Cemetery, I saw a dense blue-gray cloud moving across the road. It was a noxious effluvia pouring from the hazardous-waste incinerator of the Velsicol plant. Looking like a huge refinery, the chemical plant stretched off to the left seemingly to the horizon. It was a grim vertical tableau of gray stacks, chutes, massive conduits, holding tanks, fuming reaction vaults, and parched, dead earth. Organochlorine and polybrominated biphenyl pesticides, such as DDT, dieldrin, endrin, aldrin, chlordane, heptachlor, and heptachlor-epoxide were manufactured at the facility. The Memphis Fire Department lived in continual mortal fear of having to respond to an emergency call at the Velsicol plant.

Although company propaganda insisted that the presence of these substances does "not indicate any imminent risk" for human beings, exposure to these Pan Bad Actor Carcinogens induce immediate convulsions, seizures, respiratory depression, coma, and death. It's still a hot area. One really ought to wear a Hazmat suit just to drive past the plant. Velsicol dumped enough endrin into the Mississippi River to kill millions of fish down stream. There were massive spray campaigns that dowsed whole regions of the South with hydrocarbons that killed off not only the fish, but killed off the birds, the rabbits, the snakes, and every insect and rodent. Chlorinated hydrocarbon doesn't break down – it's always *there*; it's always potent. These colorless, odorless poisons were dumped all over to control fire ants, and sprayed to destroy mosquito vectors, while wildlife was being totally decimated. Following that, organo-phosphate – which is basically nerve gas – was used. A lot of farm workers died because if they would get this on their bodies in pure form, they died if they didn't take the antidote and wash off. And still a lot of people would be sprayed. They'd walk through the fields and get the residue on their bodies and they would die. Thus the outrage of *Silent Spring* has gone on and on and on. I spun the Triumph around in the middle of the road and high-tailed it back to Midtown. Better, I thought, to mail order those air filters from J. C. Whitney.

Meanwhile, I jammed over to Whiteway Pharmacy on Cleveland Avenue. Leonard was the cheery and bearded pharmacist always on duty and was well know for helping out the musicians in town. I sat at the lunch counter and ordered my Whiteway favorite: grilled pimento cheese sandwich on whole wheat with a vanilla malt. Sublime. From there I turned my bike onto Watkins and rode down the street to John McIntire's house near Madison. John had moved after Beatnik Manor began to draw too much heat. WEVL, totally independent guerilla radio, was just starting up in a private house in the neighborhood. I had dropped in to make another installment payment on the 1941 Bolex 16mm movie camera that I had bought from John for $50. Living with John then were a longhaired, goateed filmmaker with Ostrogothic appearance from Ponotoc, Mississippi, named Carl Orr, along with his filmmaker bride, Jo Lynn. In an adjacent room to Carl's was ensconced Randall Lyon. Carl seemed to have the whole Red Army dancing in his head, and was ever propounding theory from Sergei Eisenstein and Dziga Vertov. He and Jo Lynn had just completed a short film entitled, *Don't Be Cruel*. The most attention the film received was the *Commercial Appeal* article reporting its mysterious loss by the roadside somewhere in Mississippi. Carl was usually typing on a script of some kind or other, often for days at a time without sleeping. He was typically operating on a short fuse, which could, and did, ignite at the slightest provocation. Hanging at their Watkins house as much as I did, I was soon cast in a Carl Orr black and white 8mm film production set in *fin-de-siécle* Memphis. They greased my head for the part wherein I played the central role of an unfortunate, yet cooperative victim of ritual sacrifice. My scenes filmed on an Expressionistic staircase – in a fragile, yet

Carl Orr & John McIntire c.1968

shattering manner – were the most memorable. Of course, that film was ultimately lost, too. Carl eventually split with Jo Lynn to Hollywood – a film capitol, which he thought, was unfairly underrated.

Just as I had made my irregular $10 camera payment to John, an apparition named Horace Hull walked in with his consort. She was as petite and ripe as he was tall and gaunt. Horace was well dressed in a three-piece suit and with shoulder length hair falling straight as a window curtain. He exuded a Burroughsian charm that was not unjustified in that the once golden-throated banjo player was considered to be most notorious addict in Midtown. His cocktail of choice was straight up pharmaceutical Dilaudid, although H would do in a pinch. Horace and his belligerent, woman-beater, younger brother, Charlie, were in direct line of descent from Cordell Hull of Tennessee, who was appointed Secretary of State under Franklin D. Roosevelt, and was awarded the Nobel Peace Prize in 1945.

In Memphis jobs can be hard to come by, yet as a recently entrenched émigré from Arkansas, I figured I needed one. I had heard Randall Lyon often speak of Bill Eggleston – the handsome, aristocratic photographer from Sumner, Mississippi. He lived in a manor house on Central Avenue in the arboretum of the Annesdale garden district with his wife, Rosa, an exceedingly attractive and cultured belle of the true South. The house was set on expansive grounds and had a Mediterranean flair with large Romanesque windows and a fluted, red-tiled roof. The home and been previously occupied by the family of local supermarket magnet, Fred Montesi. The planters from whom Rosa descends owned the town of Lula, Mississippi, and more farm lands around it than most anyone. The couple had been childhood sweethearts. Bill had attended a number of schools at various times studying painting. After he dropped out of the last one, Sewanee University of the South, Rosa bought Bill a Ferrari as a gift and later a special handcrafted Bentley sports convertible that he still drives upon occasion. Bill had his suits tailored on Saville Row, smoked Winstons constantly, and favored straight bourbon whiskey over ice. William J. Eggleston was indeed a photographer, but not of the commercial variety. He was what you might call an artist of the camera, and began his efforts as a devotee of Henri-Cartier Bresson, although later he would claim to be "at war" with Magnum photographers and their style and concept of picture making. Randall claimed Bill had a 16mm Arriflex movie camera sitting in a basket on the floor of his personal photo laboratory. The thought of such a camera was enticing. I had learned photographic film processing and printing in a makeshift darkroom set up in a toilet at the University of Arkansas. A sculpture professor came in for one session and showed me how to develop a roll of film; that was the last I saw of him for the duration of the course.

Armed with this basic training, I decided to approach Bill Eggleston for a job in his lab. I rode the Norton up to the manor house on Central and dismounted in the drive way. Bill must have heard the exhausts of the motorbike signaling my arrival, as he came out the side door of the house and greeted me amiably by the hedges. In the afternoons, he was typically dressed like a plantation overseer in a white shirt, kakis, and high lace-up boots of the kind worn in the fields as protection against stepping on snakes. Bill put me to work immediately. The Arri he had not used in quite a long time; his current preoccupation was printing hundreds of 8 x 10s for a forthcoming exhibition at the Museum of Modern Art in New York. This would be his last airing in black and white before the monumental color solo exhibition that John Szarkowski would mount for him at MOMA in 1976. Rosa and Bill invited me to dine with them that night. They were serving lamb, so I politely demurred... besides there was lots of work to be done. We used Leitz enlarging equipment, which complimented his allegiance to Leica cameras. Late at night Bill would come in the lab that was connected by a breezeway to the main house. He came with his glass of bourbon and ice and worked with me. Eventually the maestro taught everything he knew about black and white processing and printing. Under his counsel, I took over the lab and worked with him steadily for the next two years. In Eggleston's home I met houseguests such as photographer Lee Friedlander, and was introduced to Gary Winogrand.

Every afternoon Bill would go out – oftentimes in his Bentley – and shoot five to six rolls of film under what we called the "Egglestonian light": essentially the hours of crepuscule when the slanting rays of the sun spread a golden mantle over all Memphis. While I was processing the film, Bill would sit at his Steinway grand piano in the parlor and play Chopin and Bach melodies with an extraordinary fervor. I hurried to get the film processed and into the water-rinsing bath, so I could go in to sit on the Persian rug and lean my head against the leg of the piano. One day Bill pulled into the driveway in a 1961 Pontiac Bonneville that he had just gotten painted solid black. In the back seat he had a huge Tectronix video monitor in a cardboard box. This marked the beginning of Bill's foray into portable, hand-held video making. He went to Cambridge to teach a semester for Ricky Leacock at MIT. While he was there, he built an acutely low-light sensitive, black and white video camera to which he attached a Switar wide-angle Swiss lens. The resulting effect was stunning. Randall and I assisted Bill on a number of missions with that outfit around Memphis and New Orleans, which in turn inspired us to form our own video art-action group called, TeleVista. Concurrently, Bill was moving more and more into color photography. Many evenings he would call me in from the dark room, to view color diapositives that he would project onto the white bedroom wall. We sat for hours

Bill Eggleston with Tectronix monitor in Pontiac Bonneville Photo: E. Baffle 1975

evaluating the images, many of which were later printed as large format, color photographs utilizing the expensive dye-transfer process. It was fascinating to observe how *every* frame that came out of his camera was a keeper and was in context. He never cropped an image, but was adamant about presenting everything full frame, and he never shot for a single picture, editing out those that did not conform to this purpose. He photographed in series. Every frame was intrinsic and essential in a literary way, yet stood alone as a non-verbal abstraction of deconstructed composition and tones. His pictures are mainly untitled. Hardcore examples would be the photograph of a stark green tiled shower stall, or the dark interior of a kitchen stove oven, or the flash photo of a nest of old shoes and socks under his bed.

Rosa named Bill's Bonneville, the "Pimp Mobile". In the serendipitous moment that he got hold of an exquisite Linhof 5 x 7 sheet film camera, Bill took up with dancer, Marcia Hare. Together they fused as two insouciant and fearsome running party dogs whose astonishing stamina and public conniptions became near legendary in Memphis, New York, and Washington, DC. Randall and Marcia and I also assisted Bill on his missions with the cumbersome Linhof camera and strobe outfit when he was photographing in various bars and clubs. Unlike the main body of Eggleston's oeuvre, these efforts produced ultra large-scale portraits. Many of the images Bill was producing were now being published in editions of collector type books funded by his boon companion, the enormously successful Memphis cotton merchant, Julien Hohenberg. This was before Julien's company went bust in the wake of his extravagant speculation in the cotton futures market. If his family and advisors had allowed Julien's positions play out, they would have reaped fortunes, but they were a little too nervous and had lost confidence in the bodacious Memphis entrepreneur. As a decorated naval war hero, Julien had nerves of steel. Although he treated his employees and staff like royalty and heaped lavish incentive rewards upon them, one also had to have nerves of steel to keep up with the dashing luminary of global cotton commodity trading. About Julien's cavalier attitude, Eggleston remarked, "He told me right before the cataclysmic thing happened, that he expected it and he had almost asked for it and didn't care one way or the other. He still feels that way. Like anyone like him, he was resented a lot and they ganged up on him, and frankly he didn't care."

Attractive and enviable as Julien appeared to his guests during the endless rooftop parties at his penthouse overlooking Overton Park, he proved not entirely victorious in his amorous affair with Fred Queen's former girlfriend, Marcia's pal, and our colleague in Big Dixie. With the flirtatious and seductive Connie Gidwani Edwards, it seemed that Julien had undaunted competition. The rival of Julien was the gifted mulatto painter, Dewitt Jordan. He came to Memphis from Helena, Arkansas, where his father farmed and his mother operated the black funeral home, which was located next to a juke joint called the Dreamland Café. As a child, Dewitt drew sketches of corpses and studied art books from the library. In the entrance to the funeral home hung a small Rembrandtish painting that Dewitt did when he was 15 depicting death as a winged angel coming to get a man. His parents became wealthy and they encouraged his formal study at the Chouinard Art Institute and at the California School of Arts and Crafts in Oakland. After completing his studies, he joined the illustrating department of Warner Brothers Studios in Hollywood in the late '50s, and worked as a sketch artist producing posters and show cards to promote movies.

Like that of Phineas Newborn, the flourishing career of Dewitt Jordan went into eclipse for a lost decade purportedly due to problems of instability. Determined to make a fresh start, Dewitt returned to the South. His career got a boost in 1964 when Memphis developer Harry Bloomfield purchased *Birth of the Blues* to hang in the lobby of the old Rivermont Hotel. Dewitt was a pipe smoker with a gregarious personality, but when he drank an annoying side of his personality could surface. Beverly Sousoulas, another of Dewitt's patrons once confided, "Dewitt had this drinking problem and whenever he was down and out and had no money, he'd go to Bloomfield who'd pay him to do another painting. So Bloomfield got a lot of paintings at very good prices. Some of those paintings he had from Dewitt are probably worth $20,000… but it made Dewitt be more prolific than he probably would have been. Dewitt had a story about every painting he ever did. You know, it depends on who he was talking to what the story was at the time, but he had a version."

By the early 70s, he had gained national recognition for his thematic and historical works in *Newsweek* and *Time* magazine, which rated him as one of the Top 10 American Artists. He was painting portraits of leading Memphians and of Sammy Davis Jr., Danny Thomas, Charley Pride, and Tennessee Ernie Ford. The themes of Dewitt's paintings, which emphasized the traditional lives of African Americans, drew criticism for their treatment and subject matter and were thought to be exploitive portrayals of Uncle Tom slow shuffling down in Dixie. He refuted his critics by telling them, "That's my heritage. Hell, man that's the South. I paint all God's children."

To review his oeuvre, I made a date with Beverley for lunch at the Peabody Café. From there we walked over to First Tennessee Bank to scrutinize Dewitt's murals. "Unbelievable," I exclaimed, "the guitar, the banjo, the saxophone, the horns, the hands, and the expressions… it's absolutely vibrant. It's pictorial, but it's not bourgeois realism; it's something far beyond that. It's a vision!"

"It's called genius," Beverley declared. "Now how does he know where to put all that stuff? Well, he just had an instinct for it. I would ask him, *how do you know how to do that*? He said, 'God tells me.' I said, 'Would you take pictures of musical instruments that you want to put in?' He said no. He said it's just in his mind. He just knows."

"The way he treats the water and the clouds and the tableau, the dramatic expressions, and the little dogs and the cotton on the wharf here, the cotton balls of fluff. The gesture, the expression… I mean, he's like Gauguin. Absolutely vibrant, *in vivo veritas*."

"This is his daughter in the painting. This is my son, Earl, and Cynthia his daughter, and they were best friends. The kids loved her because her answer to everything was, 'Yes, Lawdy'. She grew up in Helena and in Memphis, and then in Chicago. After Dollnetta and Dewitt were divorced, she moved with the kids to Chicago where they all still live."

"And there's Danny Thomas, Elvis, and the tractor driver…"

"This is Hugo Dixon, who donated the Dixon Gallery, and the King and Queen of

Dewitt Jordan, Dollnetta, & little Cynthia Photo: courtesy Eddie Jones

Cotton Carnival, Martin Luther King, and *Crump*, E.H. Crump, looked exactly like that.

"The airport – look at the planes flying over the city."

"This is Nathan Bedford Forrest, Confederate commander. This is the statue that's in Forest Park; he and his wife are buried under it. There's a ship burning and going down. Look at his face – that's Jefferson Davis, and there's Davy Crockett.

"When I'd first seen some of Dewitt's work I was just, *awww! I can't believe this!* I was determined to have a piece of his work. I was still married at the time to Frank, and it was close to Valentine's Day and we got in touch with Dewitt in Helena and had him come to our house and bring several paintings that he had done, and I just liked them all. So as a Valentine's present to me, Frank bought one that was called, *My Mother's Eyes*. It's an elderly white woman, and Dewitt said he was commissioned by her family to do a much larger portrait of her. He said she was so wonderful and so sweet, he just couldn't get her out of his mind, so then he had done this one little portrait of her to keep for himself. But he brought it along, and naturally that was the one I wanted.

"Then my children and I had driven down to Helena to talk to Dewitt because I wanted him to come and do these paintings for me for the Opera Ball. So we had coffee in his house and the children had a soft drink, and we just had a wonderful conversation and convinced him to come back to Memphis with us. The set designer at the opera company had stretched the canvasses to fit in where the mirrors are in the Peabody Skyway, and I wanted him to see those and see exactly what I wanted him to do. So he said that sounds great. He got in the car with us, came back to Memphis, and when we got to my house the phone was ringing. I answered it and it was Dewitt's father. They had burned Dewitt's house to the ground. The reason they knew it was arson is whoever burned the house had gone in, and Dewitt had a lot of work all over his house as well as at his studio that was downtown at the funeral home, and they had slashed all the paintings and burned the house to the ground. It was heartbreaking, but as far as Dewitt was concerned, *well, I can do that again,* and of course he could."

"When I met him he was living in your home in Annesdale on Carr in Central Gardens."

"After he was burned out in Helena, we had Dewitt stay in our house where I had a studio set up. It had heat, air conditioning, everything, and then for the opera thing, because the canvasses were so big, he painted those upstairs in the den. My northern wall had an all-glass back, so the light was really nice for painting. He would paint and I'd peek in to see what he was doing, and I'd go to bed. He was sleeping on the third floor of our house and was just going to paint; he'd paint until four or five o'clock in the morning. Then he wanted to have a baloney sandwich and go to bed. So when I'd go to bed, there'd be on this canvas an elderly black man with a hat. In the morning I'd go down and it was a young black man with a scarf around his neck and a bald head, and I'd say, 'Well, where's the other painting?' And he'd say, 'Well, I just painted over that.' I'd say, '*Why?* Because Dewitt, you could've had two paintings.' I was thinking about his money and what he needed to live. I'd say, 'The other one was beautiful. Why didn't you just take another canvas and paint a new painting?' He'd say, 'Because it wasn't the way I wanted it to be.' He might paint four or five different subjects on the same canvas before he finally settled for one.

"Dewitt was a marvelous dancer and he was a smash at the Opera Ball. He looked like he was Hawaiian, and was so handsome in his tuxedo. He had that islands look, like Trinidad. He had two brothers and they were both light skinned. His mother was a very light skinned person and her husband was a medium African American, as far as his color was concerned. She told me that when they were younger and first married, they had a Cadillac car, and when they traveled, because she looked so white, she would sit in the back of the car and her husband would drive it like he was her chauffeur, so they wouldn't get in any trouble going through all these southern towns – you know, they lived out in Arkansas. If they were going to Florida, they were going through Mississippi and Georgia and places, and so they always did that to protect themselves.

"Well, he stayed at my house for a period of time and then he rented a house out in Eads, and he loved it out there. He painted, but he drank half the time and painted the other half of the time. He was a genius, not just a serious artist. He was just a genius that had a God given talent. But he drank, and that is the only reason that during his own lifetime he didn't have huge success with his artwork. He told me this story that one time he had this show in Nashville and he had promised the woman that ran the gallery that he'd be present for the opening, but he went out drinking and didn't make it in time. He said he got in just about at the end of the thing when people were ready to leave. He said he walked through the door and this lady was just steaming mad and she said, 'Well here comes the drunk now.' People would see his work and they wanted him in their gallery and they wanted him to be successful, but he was his own worst enemy.

"Dewitt would do strange things. One night I had a babysitter at my house, and I came home late and the babysitter was so distraught. Dewitt had come over there, knocked on the door, and of course the babysitter wasn't going to open the door and let in someone that he didn't know when I wasn't there. Dewitt goes around to the side of the house, knocks in the side door, and he steals three paintings from my house and takes them away. So the babysitter is just hysterical not knowing what to do. These were paintings I owned that had been done by him, and one of them was *My Mother's Eyes*. Another one was a painting of a young white woman with her hands in cuffs and she's being led away by the sheriff, and Dewitt's story was that they had discovered that she had one drop of black blood in her, even though she's got this long, blond hair. So they're taking her off to sell her in the slave market. He had all these wild stories about his paintings. The next day he came back and brought *My Mother's Eyes* and told me that one of the other paintings of a young man – he had gone down to Harold Ford, Sr.'s office and sold him that painting for fifty dollars, and he said to go down and get it. He wanted *me* to go down and cause controversy with our congressman! I said, '*No*, you go get my painting.' I said, 'I didn't sell it to him. *You* sold my painting.' He never did go get my painting. The other one he said was at his house, and he said, 'I'll get it for you'. But I never saw that painting again, either."

Despite the fame and provisional success he was enjoying among the new patrons he'd found, Dewitt's personal life was once again in chaos. When Lillian finally moved out of the duplex on Cox St., Connie moved in. One of her admiring visitors was the crazy drummer in Jerry Lee Lewis' band. Though Connie had already moved out of the house she'd been living in that belonged to Julien Hohenberg, the cotton magnate also visited from time to time on Cox St. Dewitt, however, was the most frequent and favored suitor. She introduced me to her brother, Jimmy, on the front porch just before he went off to the penal farm on felony charges for aggravated assault. Eventually Dewitt and Connie decamped to his farmhouse in Eads just outside of Memphis, where Dewitt had set up a painting studio and over a stretch of domestic bliss, Connie became his model for numerous sittings.

At Eads Connie had displaced the third wife of Dewitt, a nurse named Janet Martindale to whom Beverley had introduced him and whom he married two weeks later. Beverley claimed that, "Dewitt was not a drug user, he was an alcohol user and he was very frightened by the fact that people took pills and smoked marijuana. That just freaked him out. He said, 'I like Connie, but it scares me. It *scares* me that they do all these drugs.' He just didn't want any part of it, but when he'd be drunk and nobody else would let him in the door, she always would. Dewitt was a hard person, I'm sure, to live with." Eventually, Connie would find it expedient to spend more time at her brother's house upon his release from prison.

"The night he was murdered," Beverley recalls, "he was back with Janet and they'd had a fight. This was told to me by Dewitt through the door at my house, 'cause I could tell he was drunk. He came over beating on the door, 'I need to talk to you, I need to talk to you.' I said, 'No, you need to go home. What's the matter with you?' He said, 'Well, Janet and I got into a fight and she's mad at me,' and so she left to go visit her family. I said, 'Well, you need to go home and go to bed and get sober.' 'No, no, I need to talk to you, I need to talk to you now.' I said, 'No, Dewitt, you need to go home and go to bed.' He said, 'Well, I got a show in Nashville and I need somebody to go to Nashville with me.' I said, 'You don't need to go to Nashville, nobody needs to go to Nashville, you need to go home and go to bed.' And I said, 'I'm not opening this door, so don't expect me to.' Apparently he left and went to Connie's house, and that's when her brother shot him."

On the night of October 9, 1977, Dewitt was shot once in the forehead by Connie's brother, Jimmy Richards Edwards. The self-proclaimed "Delta Fox" was shot dead at the age of 44. Feeling compelled to talk about Dewitt, and to somehow fathom the absurdity of his death, to decipher the enigma of his talent and his will to somehow destroy what he had created while violating his own self image, I decided to stop by Connie's apartment where she was living in a high rise at Central Avenue and Highland adjacent to Memphis State University. "Did you know I ended up having twelve electroshock therapy treatments after seeing that," spoke Connie beatifically. "I wouldn't say it was murder... I was the only one in the room that wasn't drunk. My brother, Jimmy, was there, I was there, Dewitt was there, my father was there. And there was some guy that came with my brother from a bar, that was there. I don't remember his name; he lived in New York. See, Dewitt was sitting on the sofa, and I had my legs over his lap, because I had that Stein-Leventhal Syndrome – the cancer that killed Gilda Radner – and I had a heating pad on my stomach. My brother was there, but I don't think that's fair just to tell one side of the story. Dewitt's family has never been anything but nice to me. By that I mean his mother, his father, his children. Now Calvin and Frank, his two brothers, are full of it. And...if they could, they'd like to put a hit on my brother.

"What happened?"

"Our apartment had been broken into when I wasn't at home, and my brother had brought his gun over and was showin' me how to use it. I told him no, I don't want guns out – put 'em away. Dewitt picked up a hammer and banged it against the table, and after he picked up the hammer he said, 'I'm the biggest, baddest, blackest motherfucker in the world. If anyone tries to break in on Connie, I'll take care of it.' And my brother said – uh, I don't remember what. And the next thing I know Dewitt fell over on the floor furnace with a hole in his head. I jumped up and called 911."

"When Dewitt made that declaration, he was still seated on the sofa?"

"He jumped up that very second...that stray bullet could've hit anyone in the room. He

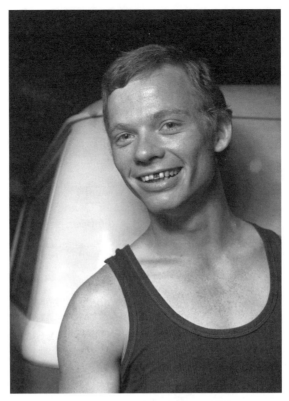

Jimmy Edwards Photo: William Eggleston c. 1976

coulda hit me, he coulda hit our dad, he coulda hit that guy in the room, or it could of hit no one."

"So your brother didn't take aim at Dewitt."

"No! Everyone in the room was drunk but me, and I'm the one that should've been. I'm there with a heating pad on my stomach, 'cause it's hurting, and I had my legs across Dewitt's lap and we were sitting on the sofa. Jim is in the chair next to him, my father is in the chair by the door, and that guy, I don't remember his name, was sitting somewhere in the room in a chair. There was no argument. You got a bunch of drunks too drunk all talking too much.

"There was no anger? In the newspapers you were quoted as saying, 'It was a freak accident'."

"Exactly. The police came and, and they tied my hands behind me all night. Then the cops got me and pushed me down the stairs with my hands behind me, and kept putting the bright lights in my face and saying, 'Okay Connie, we know you're lying, 'cause your story doesn't match your brother's story. Tell the truth.' And I said, 'I'm not lying; I'm telling the truth. If anyone's lying, it's not me.' That went on all night long. I asked my brother later did they do that with him and he said *no*. My brother and I got put in jail that night on the excuse of questioning.

"I'd called 911. I'm not wasting my time with the cops or nobody else, I'm calling 911. I still didn't know he was dead... but that close of an angle would've killed him instantly. He would've felt nothing. But when I was asked to move out – for which I was glad because I didn't want to live there anymore, anyways – under the floor furnace on the ground, there was a bunch of blood. I put newspaper down there, by taking the top off of the floor furnace. Someone's made some kind of conspiracy theory about that, but there wasn't one."

"Had Jimmy and Dewitt got along before? Did they ever have a conflict?"

"They didn't care for one another. My brother never cared for anyone I'm interested in… 'cause he's my brother. I could care less who he's involved with."

"Where's Jimmy now?"

"Hopefully he's across the hall. You want me to go get him?"

"Well, I don't know."

"I would feel better. You know, 'cause that's not fair, if someone tells lies and stuff. Luckily my brother's picked me up off the floor here more times than I can count." She yelled over for Jimmy. "See, he won't talk.

"Mrs. Jordan told me, don't come to the funeral. She was afraid for *me*… that his brothers Calvin or Frank may pull something. And she told me to not try to get her to take this chest back that was Dewitt's grandmother's and give it to his little girl. She said, 'No, honey, anything that Dewitt gave to you, D and I – D is what she called his dad, Dewitt, Sr. – D and I want you to have it.' And she said, 'You take care of Connie, and we love you.' And Dewitt told me people were always telling him he's gonna die in some white woman's house. I didn't have a hang-up about color, Dewitt did."

"The way I look at it, Dewitt, you, I – all of us involved – we're responsible for each other in some way."

"I went into shock from having that experience and being there. I had twelve shock treatments after that. You know, that's where they use electricity and they burn out the frontal lobe of your brain and it makes you forget stuff. And strange thing was – another time before that when I was in the hospital – my psychiatrist would allow Dewitt to come in and see me, but he wouldn't let Julien in to see me."

"Well, Julien *was* a friend of yours, wasn't he?"

"He was my boyfriend."

"Around the same time that Dewitt was your boyfriend, too, right?"

"*At the same time*. Dewitt came over to my duplex one day, and my father was over there 'cause I didn't know what to do with him – he was homeless. Dewitt pretended that his wife Janet had given him some drugs and even got so far as, like James Brown, pretending he's choking, and then laying in the floor in the kitchen and rolling around. Then my dad looked at me funny. I just got up, called up Dewitt's mom on the phone and said, 'Dewitt, your mother wants to talk to you.' Boy he came to real quick.

"Dewitt choked his twin brother in the womb, like that Elvis thing. That happened to Dewitt, too. They said that Dewitt strangled him with the umbilical cord. Dewitt always in his mind felt guilty that he had murdered his brother. He'd ask me did I think he was guilty. And I said you can't be guilty. It can't make sense if you hadn't even been born yet. Dewitt believed that he had that much force, because he had his dead twin's strength. Also when his mother was nursing him, Dewitt bit off one of her nipples. That's not being denied anything, just a hungry baby. She had to go to the hospital and everything about it.

"Now, I did get locked up in, I guess the guardhouse in Mississippi. We were leaving Helena on our way back to Memphis, and again, Dewitt was drunk. They stopped him and they put him in the jail, and they put me in the house out back. I was terrified. The sheriff came out there and pulled the phone out of the wall so I couldn't call. I thought the next picture wasn't gonna be very good. But with Dewitt's one call he called Aidan Barlow, and it took him a couple hours but Aidan Barlow came and picked us up and we went to Aidan's house.

"But I left Dewitt, and Julien made up the note for what to say, and it worked. It worked real good. Then later I saw Dewitt, and he was pretending to cry and tell me that, 'Did you know that whole time you were gone, I was sitting there trying to paint wearing your panties?' And I thought, *what?!*"

"That's exciting."

"That's just funny."

"Aidan Barlow, who is he, an attorney in Memphis?"

"He's dead now. He was a doctor, and he got busted selling prescriptions in the name of dead people. He was one of Beverly Sousoulas' best friends. He got Dewitt involved with Beverly. Her grandpa invented the Bush Hog. A bush hog is an African bush hog; it's a wild boar."

"I thought you meant that farm tractor thing."

"Yeah, he invented them."

"That's where she got all the money. Well, I thought Beverly had a real straight background."

"No, no, no. If you had Michael Jones living with you, what do you think?"

"She had Michael Jones living with her? He was a hustler. Michael stole a Gibson electric guitar out of my duplex that belonged to a friend from Arkansas. I ran into him later in New York. Called himself 'Busta Jones' there."

"He was an all right bass player, but I don't know; she saw something in him. She was giving him money, totally supporting him, got him the gig with Albert King."

"I saw him playing with Albert King one night out at Roseland on Lamar."

"When I knew her during that period she was into witchcraft. She would save up bowls of menstrual blood. That gave me the first clue something's wrong here.

"Beverly had been in on the opera and the ballet. She told Dewitt, it's gonna make him famous to paint all the opera stars, 'cause she was running for president of the opera for that year. Dewitt did the portraits, but somehow Beverly got a hold of the check from Nancy and Wiley Tatum – they're opera singers – and she wouldn't give Dewitt his check. Dewitt asked Wiley why he couldn't just write another one, and he said, 'No, Dewitt, that's your check, she has to give it to you. Get that check back.' So Dewitt had to get Randall Lyon to go over with him to Beverly's, but before that they stopped by the Tatum's to tell them what's going on. Then, out of embarrassment, she gave Dewitt his check for work he had already finished.

"While I was modeling at the Art Academy, which is the way I supported myself at that time, when I got off from work and got home, she had dropped him off and all of his stuff on my front porch, there on the corner of McNeil and Poplar. He had nowhere to go, nothing to eat, nowhere to put his stuff. I'm very tenderhearted, so I told Dewitt, well I guess he could stay there until he could make other arrangements. But that's how we first got together is she threw him out and took him and all his stuff and dumped it on me. She wanted him to marry her but he wouldn't do it.

"Dewitt came when I was going through analysis to see how many scrambled eggs I had left in my brain. He came to the hospital and we'd take the day off, to go play with him, go get in the car and go riding somewhere. At that time he had gotten his car from Helena. I told him, 'Look, don't let them kick me out. The only way I'll do it is if you come with me and talk to the boss man and get him to say I got the day off.' And he said, 'Well, make some more coffee.' So I did, and we went over there to this Jewish mental hospital. My psychiatrist had sent me there for testing, and believe it or not, the director was thrilled to meet Dewitt and all of the rest of them were too. They told me go ahead and take the day off and I'm not in trouble.

"Here's where another character stepped in, Charles Enzer. He's an artist. He was tortured under the Nazis. He had a place over there between Garland and McNeil on Poplar, and he also owned the properties, the brick one we were in and a wooden one across the street, the two-story one. He came over and Dewitt was at home painting, and I'm in the kitchen fixing something to eat, but most of the time I was his model… in fact, all of the time, for free. Dewitt would put the painting out and I would model for it until we finished the thing and could sell it. Blow that money – although he would always give his children some money and his ex-mother-in-law. Make sure that they had money and some clothes, and he paid room and board for them. He'd call them and they could come over on the weekends anytime. They knew they were welcome. He was a stroker – a master, one of the 10 top painters of the United States. There's a picture of Dewitt in *Time* magazine, but I don't know what year. But Enzer got mad and said that he has the studio separate, 'cause his studio was around the corner from there, and that Dewitt wasn't allowed to be over there painting. The real reason was that Dewitt's paintings looked better than his, and these were the grounds he was going to kick us out on. So from there we ended up out in Eads, and I said, 'Well, let's just get the hell away from everybody, and you'll get more work done.'

"It must've been nice, Connie, being with Dewitt out in the country in Eads."

"You wouldn't believe his talent. And the thing is, he could push his own time limit to it. He started to getting me to put pot in his pipe. He didn't stop drinking, but he started smoking pot in his pipe and it chilled him out, and his work showed it. The one time he did take LSD was with me. He said he saw colors like he'd never seen before in his life, and that he thought as the artist, he could create any color that existed, and that he saw stars, all colors."

"Dewitt told me once that he had studied mural painting for a time with Diego Rivera."

"Yes, with Diego Rivera in Mexico. He got with some Mexican girl, got drunk, married her, went home with her; woke up the next day, and her brother had worn his shoes off; another brother had taken his pants. He ended up naked down there in Mexico, married to some little *chiquita*. It's funny you know, to be such a genius in one way and in another so silly.

"We would go to Helena to visit his parents and Dewitt would take the biggest house in town and go up there. If they knew him, he'd get us invited in, get himself a drink and sell them a portrait before he left. They would pay him a third upfront, and he'd do it. But with just he and I there in Eads, and I'm the only model, and he's gotta work. That's what a lot of people didn't understand, is that's how we're gonna pay the rent and buy the food."

"About some of his paintings I kept feeling, even of black women, I kept feeling like I was seeing you in the painting."

"How did you know that? Well, I was… especially in *Scarlet Ribbons*, the little girl with the red ribbons in her hair, and *Monica Blue*. I even modeled for *Lt. George Lee* – that's hanging over in the state capitol building in Nashville. He kept getting the chest messed up and he couldn't figure it out and then he said, 'Oh! He doesn't have any breasts!' So he got that straight. I modeled everybody… except the mules; Dewitt modeled those himself."

"When you left Dewitt for Julien Hohenberg… this was after the death you were with Julien?"

"No, no – I saw him before, during, and after. What scared me about Julien, he was serious. This is after I'd got out of the hospital from getting twelve electric shock treatments."

"Did it help, Connie?"

"No. I don't think you can erase something like that. When they go in there, they don't know what they're erasing. After the death of Dewitt, Julien was giving me a ride. We'd been out that night and he was giving me a ride home the next day. He kept begging me to marry him. I didn't want to do it and I said no, and he'd say why, and I'd say, 'Because all you want to do is make money.' And he said, 'But what if I lost all my money?' I said, 'Julien, I know you. You'd just be busy trying to think of some way to get some more.' Then I told him, 'Look, I'm too crazy to marry anybody.' And then Julien said, 'If you think you're crazy, you ought to marry me!' And it just sent chills through me. It's like somebody saying, *marry me if you want to see how crazy I am.*

"Our first date was, he was gonna meet me in Boston, which he did do, then we went on to Washington. The reason he had to go to Washington was to go to court because he was facing charges on manipulating the cotton markets."

"Those were the charges, but I think the underlying problem was that Julien figured out how to make more money out of cotton than anybody else. He knew how to make money with cotton in a new way, and I think that the cotton industry tried to control him and they lobbied to press charges against him. Whether for right or wrong, they wanted to stop him; they wanted to pull him back."

"Oh, you know when the Rolling Stones played in Memphis last time, Furry Lewis and

I were in the back of the Stones' limousine, and they pushed me and Furry in the back of it and it was hurting our legs even though we were the shortest. Furry was afraid they were gonna pop off his artificial leg, while the promoter, Irving Salky and the fat cats have the big seats up front. Then Furry kept pushing the seat and telling them, 'Man, get up. You're hurting my leg. You're gonna pop it off.' And then he turned to me and whispered in my ear, 'Good God, man, does Barnum and Bailey know about you people?' I started laughing. The more I'd laugh the more Furry would tell me, 'Don't you tell 'em now, don't you tell 'em.' And the more he'd tell me don't tell 'em, the funnier it became. Irving and his cronies were turning around, 'What's he saying to you?' I said, 'I'm not telling.' Even though Furry was going to open the show that night at the stadium, he didn't want them to get no pleasure out of his company right then, 'cause they were about to pop off his leg."

"Bunch of whitebread gringos, thinking they could put Furry Lewis in the backseat. They got him in the back of the bus again."

"You know those little Poor Clares at the monastery, at 1310 Dellwood in Frayser? They're a cloistered order; they don't leave the convent. Order of Saint Clare, and you can visit them. You can call them on the phone. You can ask for requests."

"Are they praying for you?"

"Yes, they are. They're a praying order, and they pray for the whole city."

"It needs some prayers."

"Whenever you need a favor or a prayer, call them up and tell them. If they have their recording on, they're at prayer, leave a message. They know me. They know Connie."

Among the artists, photographers, journalists, socialites, and scenesters that I encountered in the drawing room of Eggleston's villa, was Stanley Booth, author of *Rhythm Oil*, and sundry texts. He got wind of photos I'd taken of Furry Lewis at a joint called Procope on Cleveland St. (in the original Café Procope of the 17th century at Place Odeon, I would dine some thirty years later), and he ordered some prints from me. In dealing with Booth and his hissy fits, I was to learn how righteously he and those of his ilk had sucked the cock of arrogance. Neither William, nor his agent Cotty Chubb, heir to the Chubb Insurance fortune, ever – to their credit – condescended to such behavior as this gentleman author from Rome, Georgia.

Stanley Booth, Jim Dickinson Photo: E. Baffle c.1976

Working with Eggleston was invariably a rewarding, if not ticklish venture. After the invasions of Midtown bars armed with the majestic Linhof camera, tripod, and umbrella, we began a series photographing freshly decorated graves in Memphis cemeteries late in the night with a high-powered strobe unit. Then Bill flew me into New Orleans to bring a particular video lens for shooting scenes in Matassa's Bar on Dauphine Street. Bill met me at the airport wearing a white linen suit and a panama hat. On the way to the French Quarter, Bill drove the Bonneville down St. Charles Avenue with his chic and enchanting first cousin, Maude Skyler, next to him in the front seat. Maude was a dead-ringer for a young Coco Chanel or closer perhaps to a Gustav Klimt rendering of Emilie Flöge. We stopped off at the Pontchartrain Hotel and entered the decadent downstairs bar where Bill ordered a round of Old Fashioneds that he claimed were the best in the city – a claim I had little cause to dispute, especially in the town that had invented cocktails. We listened to the piano player listlessly tinkling over a slew of standards in improvised syncopation. Gleaming rays from the sinking sun coruscated through the beveled glass windows of the palm bar while Maude, with a glint in her dark eyes, spoke ardently of our mission, and how she intended to become a photographer herself.

When we arrived at Mastassa's Bar, Bill changed his linen suit for khakis and a fresh white shirt. The oppressive heat of the day was mitigating, and I felt obliged to go barefoot on the cool mosaic floor of the barroom. Bill swung the special low-light video camera onto his shoulder, flipped on the power switch, and began focusing on a bear-like, former Caterpillar driver from Fort Smith, Arkansas. His name was Russell, and he lived in the quarter and handcrafted Italianate Mardi Gras masks that he sold in the shops of the Vieux Carre. The hefty artisan was drinking steadily at the bar and he spoke in rhymes that he punctuated with elaborate gestures from the Elizabethan period.

To complement Russell's histrionics, Bill had already hired a geek by proxy to come to the bar to bite off the head of a chicken, so he could video tape what he envisioned would be a kind of off-carnival Happening. The geek was late… and so was the chicken. As the street lamps and dingy neon illuminated the darkness that fell upon the old quarter, an otherwise dreary Dauphine Street became transformed into what seemed like a shadowy Elizabethan stage. In about an hour a taxi driver and compatriot of Bill's from Greenwood, Mississippi, named Vernon drove up in his taxicab with the geek and with a chicken in a gunnysack in the trunk. The geek was perfect. He was paper-thin, greasy-haired, half toothless, and his jeans were about to fall off. His face was contorted in a permanent smirk of carnie disdain. Only problem we soon found out that the geek was not so inclined to bite off the head of a chicken. Bill paid him $50. The geek was happier, but still not so convinced. Bill mounted his camera, handed the geek another $25 and told him he'd damn well better bite off the head of that chicken. Through this prologue the tape was rolling.

We're on the pavement in front of Matassa's under the canopy, and the geek pulled the chicken out of the gunny sack by its neck and held it at arm's length. The bird's wings were flapping like mad, white feathers flying everywhere, and the chicken squawking for all it's worth. Then like a pro, the geek brought the head of the bird to his lips and in one swift twisting motion, opened the hole of his mouth and bit the head clean off. He dropped the headless creature to the pavement while blood was squirting from it like the fountain of Jean Lafitte. Eggleston demanded, *Now swallow it!* But the geek spit the head out into the street, and sauntered into the bar for toddy. End of tape, and the beginning of Eggleston's most celebrated collection of moving pictures, *Stranded in Canton*.

Our travail having consummated for the evening, we withdrew to Chez Helene's off of St. Bernard, for plates of oysters Bienville and various remolades. If something were not prepared to the perfection for which the Creole eatery was famous, Egg would have it sent back for chef Austin Leslie to do over. Then the patriarch of Creole-Soul chefs would come out to personally serve the resurrected dish with the genteel appreciation of satisfying the good taste of a customer he'd fed on many occasions. After nightcaps Bill and Maude retired to the room

Biloxi Photo: E. Baffle 1975

they'd shared for some days at the Downtown Burgundy Hotel in the quarter, and I took the floor of a room with Brett, a lanky attorney friend of Bill's over from Biloxi. Next day we drove the Bonneville to the marina in Biloxi for lunch. In the ocean breeze, palm trees waved sullenly over our sun-drenched repast. Afterward, Bill, Maude, and I drove out into the bayous to take photographs.

In the evening there was a soirée at Brett's house on the beach that was bourbon soaked as a mint julep and as loaded with Southern belles as an Ole Miss sorority rush party. The morning after Brett took Maude back to New Orleans and she flew out to somewhere, while Bill and I drove the sleek black Pontiac straight up the middle of the state toward Memphis.

The next nine hours burning up Mississippi highways and byways gave us time to bat around a few ideas. As the Bonneville was cruising through the swampy bayous and cemeteries of Bogue Chitto, elaborate tombs bleaching in the sun whizzed by on either side of the road. I suddenly felt urged to interrogate Bill about how he justified his métier.

"Sometimes people appear in your photographs, and you've even done a series of portraits, but the majority of your photographs are devoid of people. Rather, we see the footprint of humanity in almost everything you do."

"That's right," Bill agreed.

"... and the trace of something moral, yet amoral at the same time, or totally devoid of moral sense."

"I thought what people *did* was more interesting than the people themselves."

"Isn't this idea of what people did rather than what they're doing in a picture, lend itself perfectly to the nature of a literal medium like photography in that the unmanipulated

Maude & Bill Photo: E. Baffle 1975

photographic image is not so much a cynical view, as it is without conscience; the dumb view of an articulate machine?"

"Yes, I would agree with you."

"The viewpoint or social or political conscience is evoked after the photograph, through selection and context. So, we have pictures of record and then we have pictures of reportage infused with viewpoint," I posited.

"I think that is well put."

"… and beyond those we have pictures, whether by intent or not, that possess poetic content, atmosphere, and that ineffable quality we call art. That draws us emotionally as well as intellectually into the picture."

"I shall agree with you," affirmed Bill.

"Because when one picks up a brush or a pencil or some tool to render an image by hand, immediately the resulting image seems to fall into what we consider a subjective form of art."

"What do you mean by subjective?"

"I mean a very personal, non-objective way of looking."

"OK, that's better put."

"One the other hand, when you aimed a lens at the sky and captured perhaps your most abstract series of pictures, you seemed to claim little of what is thought of as art. Yet, that ineffable quality is there in spite of itself. Almost in a cynical way, in spite of itself, it's there."

"You know what's funny? I don't call those abstract. They're quite realistic," Bill retorted with subtle laughter.

"Yes, OK. They're quite literal. Now, you also achieve that result when you aimed your lens at a puddle of water or at a dark corner under a bed."

"The same thing, yes."

"Where nothing of art seems to exist, yet these pictures which are almost diametrically opposed are infused with the same heightened abstraction or literal realism. Abstract to the extreme and literal to the extreme, yet seeming to verge on each other. It's the same as in the cloud pictures. Under the bed, there's the footprint of humanity; in the sky there is no evidence of man, yet the poetic effect is the same. How do you account for this?"

"Well, because man was pointing the camera up," Bill laughed. "Meaning, of course, that man is still involved period."

The Pontiac was plowing up into the yellow pine country. The trees were going by so fast they looked like a solid wall of tree bark. We shot past Crystal Springs and upward on 51 Highway. I laid back under the angled wing vent window of the convertible hardtop and changed the topic.

"What about the so-called Memphis cartel? The people who were actually in political control behind political figures like Henry Turley; Robert Snowden; Julien Hohenberg; Burch, Porter and Johnson, and the people who were in the satellite – the power satellite around the Egyptian secret societies in Memphis? How do you see Lucius Burch, for instance, in relation to the Edward Crump regime?"

"Well Lucius was brought here from Nashville to break the Crump machine, and accordingly, as you know, I had a close relationship to the whole family. Burch, the Burches, they all intensely believed this happened. Whether it did or not, I don't know. 'I knew everyone, I knew it was around, but kept out of it. Because I had other things to do, let's put it that way."

"You know something of the Hull family – you knew Horace Hull."

"Of course, everyone there. Horace and I were completely different kinds of friends, friends of the times – in the 60s when we were all doing a lot of pills, and for me that was about it. Horace was into other things and a lot of very hard drugs."

"Randall Lyon was a friend of Horace. You once said, when Randall got into trouble somewhere, *Oh, Randall – well, he's one of our freest people!* As if he should be rescued from whatever trouble he was in."

"Well, our relationship probably is most reflected in the video tapes we've created. His speech is a brilliant and wonderful improvisation."

"Indeed Randall was eloquent and he was poetic and certainly a contrarian, yet he also embraced old-line as well alternative society. He was paradoxical in that."

North of Jackson we crossed the Yazoo River and had strayed off onto Highway 49. Somewhere beyond Greenwood, Bill swerved the Pontiac off the highway toward Carrollton, onto a back road and drove until the road became two ruts of dirt. Within the distance of a half-mile, a long derelict antebellum house of two stories loomed up in an abandoned field. A white haired, seemingly disaffected couple was living there in what appeared to be complete isolation. Good friends of Bill, they invited us in for tea, which they served on a rickety table in the foyer. The front entrance divided the house and had no door, but was of a girth that must have at one time permitted the passage of carriages. The floor of the foyer was of the same dirt as that of the road leading into the place. We parted with jovial goodbyes and Bill, quite at home on Mississippi back roads, threaded our way back to the highway, and pointed the black Bonneville north to magic Memphis.

We veered back onto 51 leaving the broad, all-embracing alluvial plain of the Mississippi delta far behind. We ran past Duck Hill, scene of infamous blowtorch lynchings in 1937, rolled over the Yalobusha River and sped onward with Bill at the helm thrashing the Pontiac like Ahab flogging the Pequod.

"How do you envision the landscape of Memphis versus Drew, Mississippi, versus Biloxi versus Tokyo?" I wondered. "Is there a different palate? Does this palate change for you as you move from the city out to the surrounding country...?"

"I don't think so. I think I regard them all equally."

"You carry this palate with you wherever you go."

"I think so, yes."

"How did your perception of space change, Bill, when you left black and white, not behind, but when you began to concentrate on color?"

"I didn't notice it to be any different, as a challenge to make work."

"Space, framing...is this an intuitive view that you have, or an intellectual view, or a combination?"

"Well, I don't think that I ever – still don't – regard working in color as any different from working without color," Bill contended, "it's something that was there. One more thing, which I always knew in the back of my mind, but without thinking about it, was that I was already thinking in color."

"Even when you were doing strictly black and white? Because color is what you see through the lens."

"Black and white is what the lens was seeing on film; that's not what I was seeing. But when color started working in, I didn't notice any change of attitude in myself and in the concerns of constructing images a bit. I still feel that way and I probably always will."

"Well, in terms of exterior spaces and interior spaces, do they exist for you as separate worlds or are they..."

"Not a bit. Every space has its own things, components to solve. I don't think it makes any difference whether they're inside or outside. They are different, but making these things, let's say, work – I don't see any difference there of making images within the frame and beyond the frame in terms of imagination and looking at what turned out.

Somewhere around Panola, Bill pulled the Bonneville off to the left toward the Tallahatchie River and stopped in front of Billie's Circle Inn. While the attendant pumped in a full tank of ethyl, Bill and I noshed grilled sandwiches and drank root beers standing at the counter. Getting back in the Pimp Mobile, I asked Bill, "Well when you go out and photograph in Memphis and Mississippi and the areas that you've lived in and grew up in, do you see this terrain in terms of neighborhoods, histories, landmarks, or one large organic flow of space? What are the important places and how did they affect the way you envision the city and the

Highway 51 Photo: E. Baffle 1975

country? Do you see the city purely spatially, or is there a strong temporal component to the way you try to capture what is ever changing – buildings being replaced, studios disappearing?"

"I've never tried to, or wanted to, structure my works to have anything to do with various chronologies which lead to political, social changes. It's there, but not a part of my conscious mind. For instance, civil rights came and went, and it was to me as if it never existed. I never noticed it. Not intentionally – I was just thinking about other things. I use civil rights because that's on the calendar somewhere."

"Well, that's what Cartier Bresson was all about and Eugene Atget and you. But there again, you have someone like Robert Capa who achieved poetic results aiming his camera at political and historical phenomena."

"In that way we're not a bit the same."

"But somehow the results merge."

"Well, they have to because what's out there at such a date, whether it's 1945 or 2045... something's going be out there. You can take pictures of it, and that's going to come out – the times and what's going on. Even if that's not what you're up for capturing."

"Of course, Capa didn't manipulate his images; you really don't manipulate yours. There is a verisimilitude right out of the camera that is uncompromised and it's the view of a machine, but with yours being held in the hands of a man... yet it's a chemical or electronic process."

"Well, I'll quote John Szarkowski. We had many debates, and I remember one where it got down to the bitter end and he said, *William, godammit, it's about photography!*" Bill laughed. "And I couldn't disagree. John would always insist, *what you're doing is about photography. You are not doing what Robert Capa did. You're using the same medium, but not doing the same thing a bit.* We could also say that it's up to the one holding the camera to want to try to make sure that the distortion of their works doesn't happen – and I think that subconsciously goes through our minds always – which photojournalism is full of."

"That's what we're talking about: subjectivity. Whereas I think what you and John Szarkowski are talking about is really objectivity. In Germany they once called it the *Neue Sachlichkeit*, the New Objectivity and they were trying to reach a new level of objective perception. I think if there's one medium that will bring you there, it's unmanipulated photography."

"I think you're absolutely right."

"Only the chosen moment and the redundancy of images can form a personal, yet objective view. I know that you are always thinking of your pictures in terms of series, in terms of numbers of images seen together. Not just the single image, not just the one portrait or the one view or the one plate, but 500 together – that was what you wanted to present, was the totality."

"I think I should say right now that I do have a personal discipline and that's only to take one picture of one thing. Which translates into if there's a 36-exposure roll in the camera, then 36 different pictures. That eliminates the problem of editing," Bill mused. "And they print them all. So, in editing, I never do it. I leave it up to people I trust, the first one having been John Szarkowski at the Modern. And during the process of working, the last thing on one's mind – in my mind in this case – is what anyone else is thinking either about these pictures or images or anything else I'm doing. That's necessary."

The Bonneville was doing 110 mph when we rode out of the flat country, past Walls, Mississippi, and crossing the state line on the other side of Horn Lake Road. Then Bill pulled the flaps down on the black bird and made a smooth landing into South Memphis. As he nosed the limo into his driveway on Central Avenue, Bill admitted, "It's been delightful trip." Of the same mind, I withdrew to the Norton parked by the hedges and putted home to Cox St.

Eugene Baffle with Norton Photo: Eggleston 1974

CABIN NOTES:
Some decades later I spoke with Bill after a screening of his video work at the Brooks Museum in Overton Park. "Other than the obvious pragmatic aspects, do you feel we have lost or gained aesthetic value with the ascendancy of digital technology versus film?" I queried.

"I don't know yet. I'm still trying to figure out digital," Bill replied.

"For me, Stranded in Canton has a cathode ray tube television image very much unlike a digital flat-screen image. I think that the lower definition, softer video image taken with the Swiss lens on the camera, evokes more empathy from the viewer than the cold, super crisp high-resolution, digital image that we have today."

"I think you probably are absolutely right."

"The high-resolution image digital image that we have today often appears so cold and so electronic that it borders on ennui."

"True," quoth the maestro.

Bill and Marcia Hare ran together for about five years. In the aftermath of the affair with Marcia, he began spending more and more time in the company of Lucia, daughter of the influential liberal attorney, Lucius Burch. Essentially, Bill was living at the three-story mansion of the Burch family on the easternmost perimeter of Midtown and had more or less become a member of the household. William and Lucia were social and at times even spectacular when the stimulants they consumed brought out the more fractious aspects of their personalities. Whenever I visited the home, Lucia was genial, lucid, and warmly entertaining. Memphis police were keeping an eye on the Burch estate, which was set on a tree-dotted, landscaped plot of green meadow. Lounging around the lawn tables on Burch private property, Bill was arrested more than once on charges of public drunkeness. These ludicrous charges were invariably dropped, but his DWIs were not. Of course William preserved the main household where he and Rosa and their children had moved from the chateau on Central Avenue into an elaborate villa in east Memphis. Their new residence was built in 1925 according to Florentine proportions by a Memphis architect upon his return from an inspiring junket to Tuscany. The structure was gorgeous and featured a two story massive stained glass Romanesque window, balconies overlooking Italianate shrubbery and flower gardens, and a portico leading to the garages where the Bentley roadster was kept. The manor was placed on a full city block of manicured tree-lined grounds surrounded by tall hedges. To the side of the villa was situated an expansive rectangular sunken pool punctuated with decadent floral urns. Lilly pads and lotus blossoms floated on its surface; still I was always tempted to swim in the brackish water.

After Lucia died, Bill returned to the Florentine villa and could often be found there in the kitchen puffing Winstons, sipping bourbon, and receiving late night visitors. Bill was fascinated with electronics and state of the art technologies, and he was crazy for hi-fi equipment. He had electrostatic hi-fi speakers placed discreetly in the parlor that looked like living room curtains yet produced the power and fidelity of a live orchestra as if it were playing in the next room. He would invite nocturnal guests into the parlor for booming playback sessions of Bach and Hayden.

Some considered Lucia's premature death a slow OD and blamed it on the substance abusive lifestyle that she and Bill had cultivated. Bill eventually took up with a young woman named Lee Hazelip, who had in fact once accompanied Randall Lyon and I to Magnolia, Arkansas, on a TeleVista videotaping mission for the Archaeology Dept. of Southern State College. A patriarch of her family had been one of the signers and witnesses of the original charter of the city of Memphis in 1825. Lee was a stunning beauty when she joined TeleVista on the sortie across the river and was elated to be pursing her interests in video production. Although I tried to kiss her a couple of times on that excursion, I did not see her again until she and William hooked up considerably later. By then Lee had developed into an appealing and loquaciously convivial woman. She and Bill hung out at a little bungalow Lee had rented near Midtown, and when I'd go out of town they'd let the keep my Thunderbird on the lawn behind the house so nobody would steal the hubcaps off of it parked on the street. Considerably into their relationship, I met Lee and Bill for tea at a coffeehouse on Cooper Avenue called, Otherlands. I must admit my shock to behold how sulphurous their personal liaison had become. They spit vitriol at each other with such fury that I could hardly swallow my croissant. Many moons later when I returned to Memphis after another protracted absence, I learned that Lee had died... much in the same way as Lucia.

CABIN NOTES:

The original Peabody was built by Colonel Robert C. Brinkley in 1869. Just prior to its opening, Brinkley received news of the death in London of his good friend, philanthropist George Peabody, who was the principal benefactor in building Brinkley's proposed railroad line from Little Rock to Memphis. As a sign of respect for Peabody, who also endowed George Peabody College in Nashville and contributed much to the disadvantaged children of the South, the new hotel was named The Peabody.

From its beginning the Peabody Hotel was considered one of the finest in the South. It had 75 rooms with private baths, a ballroom, saloon, and lobby. It cost $3 to $4 a day for a room and meals, extra for a fire or gaslight. In 1869 Colonel Brinkley gave The Peabody to his daughter,

HOTEL PEABODY -- MEMPHIS, TENN.

Anne Overton Brinkley, as a wedding gift when she married Robert Bogardus Snowden. For the next 96 years, the Snowden heirs would be connected with the affairs of the hotel. The Peabody was host to Presidents Andrew Johnson and William McKinley and Confederate Generals Robert E. Lee, Nathan Bedford Forrest and Jubal Early. Plantation owners, professional gamblers and movie stars frequented the grand hotel. In 1925, a $5 million Peabody designed by architect Walter Ahlschlager, opened at its present downtown Memphis location on Union Avenue. Ownership remained in the hands of R. Brinkley Snowden, great-grandson of the original builder. His son, the namesake of Robert Bogardus Snowden, once bought and sold the Peabody within hours.

Vis-à-vis the University Club on Central Avenue in Annesdale is a stone fortress called Ashlar Hall. Across from Ashlar Hall on the south side of Lamar Avenue is Snowden Circle – a heavily enforestated circular plot of land surrounding a voluminous turn-of-the-last-century manor house. To the passerby the Snowden mansion looks darkly forlorn. It is festooned with ancient ivy and knarled vines reaching down from the overhanging trees that with clinging melancholy hang onto the roof and walls. A tall wrought iron double gate protects the entrance to the winding drive that disappears from view before it reaches the main house. Through the gloom of dense thickets and wildly growing shrubbery, one seems never to get a clear view of the dreary mansion itself.

"Back in the alley when the games gets fast,
ain't no piece of paper gonna save your ass."
–Lee Baker

Sally Snowden McKay was reared in Ashlar Hall. Her grandfather, R. Brinkley Snowden, made a fortune in real estate and banking and built Snowden Circle mansion. She was one of three daughters of his son, Robert Bogardus and Grace Snowden who also owned a plantation home in Hughes, Arkansas, and owned extensive land holdings in Crittenden County around Horseshoe Lake. As a child she attended Lausanne School in Memphis and graduated from Vassar in the 1940s. Though McKay lived the life of a blueblood Memphian growing up in the Gothic-style Ashlar Hall mansion, Sally McKay preferred jeans and sandals and smoked Camel cigarettes. Once as a young woman she met an English lord on a ship during one of her many travels abroad. He had fallen madly in love with her, but his mother was not charmed. Asked why she did not marry him, Sally replied that she simply didn't want to get dressed up all the time. She was also a theater lover and sat on the board of directors of Playhouse on the Square.

Sally's nephew was a hot Memphis guitarist named Lee Baker, and they shared a house Snowden owned on Horseshoe Lake about 35 miles outside of Memphis. When Lee wasn't gigging, he rode a tractor brush hogging the neighbor's property and he generally took care of keeping the oxbow lake porpereties tidy. Oftentimes during the hot Delta summers, Baker worked the fields with black farmers, and hung out in Wheeler Taylor's juke joint at night. Growing up, the chubby, sensitive youth became captivated by the emerging SUN records sounds and the records of Elvis. In 1954 he got his first guitar, quiffed his hair into ducktails, and learned the King's repertoire. Lee attended East High School, trimmed his physique and formed his first band, the Aztecs, in 1960. He started the band with a 14-year-old kid named Jimmy Segerson, a lifelong friend who followed Baker in many bands, notably Moloch and the Agitators. His next school band was the Blazers. They played in a Booker T and the M.G.s groove, primarily for sororities and fraternities at proms and sock hops at the Peabody Skyway. When the psychedelic 60s hit Memphis, Lee was among the first to undergo a radical transformation. He turned on, tuned in, and adopted a full beard and shoulder length hair quiffed into a weedy flyaway bush.

Part of the warp in Lee Baker's social orientation, his embracing of alternative music, culture, and radical stance may be not indirectly related to the dominating hegemony of the patriarch of the family, Robert Bogardus Snowden. The millionaire landowner had spearheaded an ultra rightist alliance called The Campaign for the 48 States, and he proselytized all with whom he came in contact to bring them into the fold by persuasion or by more stringent measures. He had plenty of money and resources of his own, plus thousands upon thousands of dollars at his disposal from other wealthy Americans, and he had the active backing of many congressmen and influential people. His organization was flourishing and had become a resounding success. At one point he flew up to Washington from Memphis to attend a meeting put together by George Lincoln Rockwell, the *fuehrer* of the American Nazi Party. Snowden basically took the meeting over and eclipsed Rockwell's pitch with his own. Next day he called the chagrined *fuehrer* to his suit at the Congressional Hotel and hired *him* to work for his campaign. Rockwell reported in his memoirs:

I hung up the phone and scurried over to his suite in the hotel, which was right next to the halls of Congress. He was in his BVD'S, drinking whiskey from a tumbler. He offered me some in his hearty, bluff manner and I accepted. I liked him. He was big, florid of fact, outspoken, even blunt, and he obviously 'knew the score', as it is termed among the looseness of people called 'the movement'.
"I liked your pitch," he growled. "You've got the stuff we need. I want to put you on the payroll. How about it?"
"Doing what?" I asked. "And for how much?"
"Helping me organize the Campaign, raising funds and writing scripts for TV films."
"What's the payroll?"
"Eight thousand."

Lee Baker found gigs accompanying SUN luminary Charlie Rich, and with Rufus Thomas, and the Mar-Keys. He played the Bitter Lemon acoustically with Don Nix in a formation called Sewer Pipe & the White Trash. Baker was busted only once and convicted in 1968 on charges of dispensing marijuana. Rather than the penal farm, he opted for six months in a federal rehabilitation unit at Lexington, Kentucky. When he came back to Memphis I bumped into him in front of Katz drugstore beside TJs and saw that Lee had newly adopted a lean and hungry look. His next group reflected his *just-released-from-the-joint* temperament. It was the fire-breathing psychedelic blues-rock band called Moloch, named after the terrifying deity to whom

217

Serigraph: Tim McSweeny 1972

children were burned alive in sacrifice. Moloch made one record for the Stax subsidiary Enterprise in 1970 produced by Don Nix. The heavy-duty outfit, with band members including Eugene Wilkins on vocals, Busta Jones on bass, and Phillip Dale Durham on drums, went through several turbulent years of near-fame. "People were telling us we were stars, but we were starving," rhythm guitarist Segerson told CA reporter Bill Ellis. "It was the beast that wouldn't die and wouldn't get well."

After Moloch disbanded Lee became lead guitarist in the unpredictable and explosive, cult-roots aggregation, Mudboy and the Neutrons with leader Jim Dickinson and core members Jimmy Crosthwait and Sid Selvidge. Dickinson described Lee's playing style as angular, jump blues, while I would hear added eccentric atonal gradients and transported cosmic fugues that were inimitable. Sid Selvidge termed Baker as the linchpin of Mudboy. Their first show was on Halloween 1972 under the banner of Behold the Children of the Night! For the occasion Lee Baker had become what he called "Negative Man" and came out onstage in black face. Big Dixie was also featured on the bill. Randall premiered his character, Guru Biloxi and delivered a

Lee Baker & Furry Lewis at Procopé Photo: E. Baffle c. 1974

incendiary rant that brought the festival goers to their feet, while I probed my character as Tube Man. Tim McSweeny designed and screened printed Children of the Night posters: an image of a death's skull wearing a straw hat with boar tusks coming out both sides of its mouth and flanked with the theatrical masks of tragedy on one side of the head and comedy on the other.

Throughout his career Lee Baker continued to play acoustic as well as electric guitar. He often appeared as accompanist for Bukka White, Gus Cannon, Sleepy John Estes and Fred McDowell. With Furry Lewis, he formed his deepest relationship. For over 15-years Lee accompanied Furry Lewis backing him up on guitar, helping him on and off stage, and becoming the protector on whom Furry depended. For this Lee was rewarded with an uncommon bond of friendship, with Furry's National Steel guitar, and with the tutelage of the blues master.

Every musician in Memphis knew Lee Baker and was awed by his quintessential playing and his provocative stance. Dickinson said that Baker used to affect a kind of bopster walk and talked bebop when nobody else did. At the legendary first Memphis Blues Festival in Overton Park Shell, Baker came out fronting an outrageous rock group he called, Funky Down Home and the Electric Blue Watermelon. At the second festival in 1967 the Watermelon proved overripe for some. Baker emerged from an outhouse riding a Harley Davidson, picking electric guitar and wearing a lady's dress. Mudboy washboard player, Jimmy Crosthwait, told *Commercial Appeal* reporter, Bill Ellis, "One day over at Horseshoe Lake I was smelling a little fishy and the consensus was it would be a good idea to toss me in the lake. A bar of soap was thrown in and I washed and climbed out. Lee turned to me and said, 'Jimmy, you left a ring around the whole lake!'"

Baker loved to go to Molly's La Casita for Mexican food. The café was a cramped, ramshackle affair situated right on the side of the street at 1910 Lamar in what had been built years before as the very first Toddle House by Fred Smith, the father of the founder of FedEx.

The food at Molly's was prepared in huge blackened iron skillets in which the contents seemed to be added to each day, rather than cooked anew, still the results were fabulous. We were having a rambunctious dinner there one night with Lee and Randall and a contingent of turned-on females, before moving over a few blocks to the W.C. Handy Theatre on Orange Mound. The Howlin' Wolf was playing, and the experience totally turned my bread around. The Wolf loomed out onto the stage – all six foot six, 300 pounds of him – crooning, booming, and mugging his way through a rollicking set list long as his right arm. His was the most dramatic, fearsome, yet warmly human stage show I've every witnessed – a *real* simian showstopper. His four-piece band belted out blazing blues numbers like machine gun fire. The virtuosos were dressed in iridescent sharkskin suits of gold or of maroon that looked like they'd been slept in for three weeks. Behind Wolf's reverberating roar and his raucous harmonica fugues, Hubert Summlin played lyrical electric guitar colorations that heightened the drama to the sublime. Holding the microphone on a cord, Wolf would leap from the stage into the audience and crawl on his knees up to tables of buxom black women who had come for serious partying. On their tables were white paper plates, upon which laid an assiétte of sour pickles and cheese strips, fenced in by bottles and flasks of sundry liquors. From his knees Wolf would croon, moan, and howl up into the faces of each one. Before the evening was done, more than a few table dances cut loose by women transported by Wolf's euphonious exhortations.

Of the first time he saw Howling Wolf on stage, Johnny Shines declared, "I thought he was magic, man. They had an old saying about people who sold their soul to the Devil to be able to play better than anyone else. I thought Wolf was one of these." Actually Wolf didn't get off the plantation until he was 39. He had learned guitar from the popular delta blues icon of the 1920s and 1930s, Charlie Patton. To that, Wolf had attempted to master the blue yodeling style of Jimmie Rodgers, but his signature howl erupted instead. To that he added his exuberant stage antics.

The show of Howling Wolf was so galvanizing and inspiring that we all decided to go see Albert King the next night at the Rosewood Club way out on Lamar Avenue. Every pimp in Memphis who had a three-piece suit and a Cadillac was already there escorting fashionable protégés, when we entered the capacious night club. Not to be out done, Lee Baker came in naked to the waist except for a huge *white* fluffy, sleeveless vest of thick, wild fur. As the case in the W.C. Handy Theater the night before, our coterie represented the only white people in the joint. The mirage of Lee provided a striking contrast against the swell of dusky celebrants, as Albert King and his high-energy band ripped and razored through three-dozen wicked country blues and vamped seamlessly the entire show. No dead air.

> *I'm a crosscut saw,*
> *baby, drag me across your log,*
> *I can cut your wood for you,*
> *you can't help but say, hot dog*
>   – Albert King, 1969

Albert King had learned personal discipline plowing behind two blue-nosed mules in the cotton fields of the Arkansas delta. He had fists twice the size of those of a normal man, and he wore a ring on his finger that was an inch wide emblazoned with the initials "AK" in rough-cut diamonds. Albert had adopted a militant posture toward the white establishment and stood only slightly to the right of the Black Panthers. He was a clean-living individual and enforced a no drinking and no drugs policy in his band. When traveling on the road, his band members lived in fear of seeing Albert coming out of a truck stop or roadside service station carrying a banana and a comic book, because whenever he fired someone, he always sent him home on a Greyhound with something to eat and something to read. If a musician were fired for drinking or drug taking, Albert whipped him first before putting him on the bus home.

Eugene Baffle, Howling Wolf, Unknown, Randall Lyon 1968

In Lee Baker's electric guitar playing, no one influenced him more than Albert. Yet his devotion and life long commitment to the music of Memphis and its hinterlands and to the people who played it were no protection against an undercurrent of darker forces that are ever lurking and liable to strike without warning. Almost 15-years to the day after Furry died, and a month after Lee's own house on Horseshoe Lake had been burned to the ground, he and his aunt Sally Snowden McKay were found by the state police, shot to death in her still burning lakeside home on September 10th, 1996. The house had been burglarized then set afire. Sally's idling Toyota Camry was found on a side road about a mile from her home. It is speculated that Lee had walked in on the burglary and tried to save his aunt. Baker was not the sort to take any grief off punks, and probably had walked in on his aunt looking down the wrong end of a pistol. Baker was 51 and his aunt had not so long before celebrated her 70th birthday in style with three other women on a 43-foot sailboat they'd rented in the Virgin Islands.

At the memorial service in Calvary Episcopal Church on North Second Street, the silver tones of a mournful trumpet and tolling bells were heard as a thousand people filled the tabernacle to remember Lee Baker and his favorite aunt, Sally McKay. A month after the killings police detectives charged a 16-year-old Hughes High School sophomore, Travis Santay Lewis, with two counts of capital murder and one count of burglarizing for the double slaying immolation. As the trial was about to begin in the Marion, Arkansas courthouse, Lewis pleaded guilty to all indictments. Circuit Court Judge David Burnett sentenced Lewis to twenty-eight years in the state penitentiary. He would be eligible for parole in 20 years. The niece of Sally McKay was quoted in the papers as saying, "Based on what we knew and the evidence that we were aware of, the family felt like this was the best resolution."

CHAPTER THE ELEVENTH
MUD BOY AND THE DECONSTRUCTION
OF PANTHER BURNS

It was around Christmas time that Sid Selvidge harelipped Randall Lyon with a stick of firewood during a social visit to Sid's commodious Victorian home on Autumn St. by Overton Park. That Christmas season was when I first heard people talking of Panther Burn. Sid came from planter society in Greenville in the middle of the Mississippi delta. He became a teenage DJ on WDDT radio (an acronym for cotton poison?) owned by Hodding Carter of the progressive *Delta Democrat Times* in Jackson. He attended McCallie military academy in Chattanooga, Tennessee at 16, entered Rhodes College in Memphis at age 18, and went on to teach anthropology there. Sid arrived in the Bluff City singing Elizabethan ballads under the influence of American composer and folklorist, John Jacob Niles, and had already developed a concert style folk/blues vocal gamut ranging from basso profundo to high falsetto. He complimented his vocals with masterful delta fingerpicking styles on his Gibson J45 acoustic guitar. A handsome and powerful performer, Sid became a popular solo artist in the Bluff City. About these – to my ears – strange sounding words, *Panther Burn,* which I'd heard spoken in conversation between Selvidge his delta compatriots, I asked Sid. I learned that it was the name of a thriving plantation just north of Greenville, Mississippi off Highway 61, and that it was once owned in part and developed in 1919 by Leroy Percy, Jr. of the Percy family of writers and poets. During this early period Percy was investigated on allegations of holding Italian tenant farmers in peonage on the Sunnyside plantation he had leased in Arkansas, but the powerful influence he held with Congress and with his bear-hunting crony, President Theodore Roosevelt, resulted in the reports being buried in the federal bureaucracy and no action ever taken against Percy.

Rumor had got around the usual unreliable places that Mudboy was going to do a show on the grand stage of the renowned vaudeville house of the South, the Orpheum Theatre at Main & Beale. This was going to be more than a Halloween spectacle, it was to be the *Last Waltz* performance of Mudboy and the Neutrons, a fashionable trend at the time... but, of course, Mudboy did not terminate with this show, and the group soldiered on for decades. I had been appearing as a dancer with Mudboy for some time and as a performer within the context of our art-action troupe, Big Dixie Brick Co., which had formed parallel to Mudboy and as an appendage. On this occasion, Randall Lyon boycotted the show as he'd decided to distance himself from RnR musicians for a spell. So Marcia and Connie and I showed up at the theatre for sound check. In keeping with the tone of the event, I felt I should deliver a gesture symbolic of the splitting asunder of a rock 'n' roll band, and I asked Jim Dickinson if I might deliver a statement *entre l'acte* of Mudboy. Jim perfunctorily gave permission, *sure, why not.*

Quickly, I prepared the stage behind the curtain with two straight-backed chairs center stage, and an electric skill saw placed on a stool to the right and an electric chain saw placed on a stool to the left. On a stand further right forward, I placed a humongous black & white television monitor facing the audience, and hooked it in-line to a portable video camera operated by Little Bill, the nine-year-old son of photographer William Eggleston, who would be circling me onstage hand-holding the camera. The curtain raised, and I stepped out alone on the big stage as Eugene Baffle, unmasked, dressed in evening clothes – a black frock coat and tails and white gloves with the finger tips cut away so I could pick and chord the $5 electric Silvertone guitar I had purchased from a neighbor. Immediately I plugged the warped instrument into a 1956 Stromberg-Carlson monophonic tube amplifier scavenged from a phonograph apparatus that Lee Baker had junked. The amp was output to a Bell & Howell motion picture projector cabinet housing a 12-inch speaker, which in turn was captured by a microphone, connected to the massive sound re-enforcement PA system of the theatre.

As I stepped up to the vocal microphone placed on a gooseneck straight stand center stage, I noticed three formidable broadcast TV cameras from the network affiliates moving in close. I then launched into a rudimentary rendition of the "Bourgeois Blues" by Leadbelly picking the strings of the Silvertone in the country blues style of Mississippi honky-tonk artist, Rural Burnside.

> *Home of the brave, land of the free –*
> *I don't want to be mistreated by no bourgeoisie.*

Being a lone voice and a lone instrument amplified by this powerful, ultra high-fidelity sound system, my every word, every breath, every cacophonic guitar note was faithfully reproduced with crystal-clear accuracy down to the finest microtones.

> *Now you people, listen to me*
> *Don't try to find a home in Memphis, Tennessee*
> *'Cause it's a bourgeoisie town*
> *It's the Bourgeoisie Blues,*
> *Spread the news all around*

At the height of this protestive anthem, and with the audience becoming increasingly restive under the avalanche of verbal innuendo and de-tuned dissonant guitar drone, I produced a police whistle from my coat pocket and began to blow it in the shrillest fashion possible. Then I unstrapped the Silvertone and laid it across the two chairs. I picked up the electric Skillsaw with the whirling circular steel blade, and with its whirling circular steel blade I sawed halfway through the back of the guitar in a straight, yet jagged line. With the police whistle screeching and with the instrument still plugged into the theatre sound system, the resulting eruption of cacophony and industrial tearing, ripping, metallic slicing and clanging sounded like the Titanic breaching an iceberg the size of Texas. Instantly I threw down the whizzing circle saw, and reached for the electric chain saw. Wielding it overhead, I brought the blade down in a decisive gesture laying its grinding chain deep into the wood of the guitar and finishing it off until wire, knobs, tuning keys, and wooden splinters were flying everywhere like shrapnel. The ensuing exploding, popping, grating, and frying sounds seemed to be gaining algorithmically in an uncontrollable frenetic intensity toward the brink of a terrifying threshold, and THEN!... *poof.* It was over. The room was aghast. Stone silence, and I passed out.

Moments later after being dragged off stage, I awoke with hysterical screams ringing in my ears and the cries and shrieks of a shocked, bewildered, and half riotous audience jumping out of their seats. Since I was a boy on my daddy's farm in Arkansas and I blew off the head of a coiled King Snake with a shotgun for no good reason, I have to this day abhorred violence in any form – musical or otherwise. This shredding of the Silvertone guitar on the occasion of the Mudboy farewell performance was not intended as an act of vehemence, rather it was a gesture celebrating the temporal and divisive nature of music and the transient aspects of musicians who instigate it.

Some weeks after the Last Waltz of Mudboy at the Orpheum Theater and the art-action gesticulation I delivered as Eugene Baffle, which is how I continue to style myself, I was having a soirée one evening in my hovel on Cox St. where the bass player of an all girl group called the

KLITZ, happened to be hanging out. She called Alex Chilton on my telephone, and during their conversation he heard in the background my playing a raw electric blues fugue on another $5 Silvertone guitar replacement I'd found that had a little loud speaker built into the body. He remembered my dubious feat at the Orpheum as he was among those howling in the audience when the ruckus had reached insalubrious proportions. Within the hour Alex had found his way over to our party. When he arrived, I remembered him from a TeleVista video taping of a recording session he and Lesa Aldridge had done at Phillips studio a year before.

Alex was amusing because he played guitar effortlessly and had fun singing songs like put-on charades. In his hands golden tones poured from my Silvertone, and before the night was out I realized he could play a lot more than a little guitar. He had long sturdy fingers like Chuck Berry's and he could nail down power chords the same as Chuck when I saw him play up close once in Arkansas. Right in the face Alex looked like a cross between the actors Robert Morse and Marlon Brando, only more impish and gleefully maniacal in expression. Yet there was little to reveal he was the *enfant terrible* that I would learn he was reputed to be. Playing my Silvertone guitar, he sang a ludicrously interminable version of "96 Tears" by Question Mark and the Mysterians, while we made impromptu videos with the TeleVista camera that first night, and the party raved on until the wee hours.

Soon Alex began dropping by my place unannounced. I played the most callow country blues – a form he didn't know. And he played RnR – something I never thought I could do. We started to exchange notes: while Alex was listening to songs like "Death Cab for Cutie" and artists like Van Dyke Parks, I was tuned into the solid blues sender Dick "Kane" Cole show on WLOK. (When Prince came to Memphis he tried to get on the Dick "Kane" Cole show, but was rebuffed when "Kane" proclaimed on the air that wasn't going to happen because he played only genuine variety, non-imitation, stone blues on his program. Pity in a way, because such clichés can be explosive – especially on a radio show.) While I was mainly into country blues, on the one hand, and experimentalists like La Monte Young, on the other, Alex was enthused by the Sex Pistols whom he'd just seen play at the Taliesin Ballroom.

The Taliesin was on the mezzanine of the 19th Century Club mansion at 1433 Union Avenue in Midtown. The Club was formed in 1890 as an intellectual center for ranking women of elite society to pursue socially conscious civic activities, something unheard of in Memphis at the time. The club remained quite active, and I had seen Jim Dickinson and Johnny Woods, the sharecropper, harmonica player from Senatobia, play the Taliesin just before the Pistols came to town on their tour which had consisted of only southern cities. Randall, Marcia, and Connie had gone to the Pistols' gig, but I'd missed it.

One night in summer very late after the bars closed, I woke up to sounds of the side window opening in my bedroom on Cox St. Someone raised the window in the darkness and lifted himself into the room. It was Alex. He slipped silently into bed beside me. I figured he had nowhere to go other than his parents' home on Harbert Avenue. Usually after the bars closed, he would go with some fellow Midtown imbiber, like with Huggie Foote or his sister, Maggie Foote, to their pad listen to records and drink up all the liquor in the house before calling it a night. There must've been no pals around at last call tonight, or no liquor left in Huggie's… I dozed in the darkness. At dawn Alex was gone, as silently as he came.

After his nocturnal visit, whenever Alex dropped by, he would talk about making music together and encouraged me, in fact, to think about starting a band. He offered to play guitar in the group for a while… all we needed, he said, was a drummer, a name, and an identity. He brought the drummer, Ross Johnson, a renegade librarian, and I brought the name, from the extant and anomalous plantation in Mississippi that I'd been hearing about. I baptized the band, *Panther Burns.* There were Muddy Waters, the Rolling Stones, and now… the Unapproachable PANTHER BURNS.

When in the late 19th century land was being cleared in the delta for further cultivation of cotton, legend had it that a cunning panther stalked and terrorized the local population around the plantation that became known as Panther Burn. It howled all night, raided the chicken coops of the farmers, and became an irascible nuisance. The planters formed a posse to track the creature down. They set traps, but the animal eluded their traps. They tried to shoot it, but it evaded their rifle fire, and the shooters missed. Finally, they corralled the critter into a cane break and set it aflame. According to witnesses, the shrieks and screams coming from the panther were an unholy amalgam of animal lust and divine transubstantiation, which continue to curse the plantation. Thus *Panther Burns* would become the name most fitting a rock 'n' roll band.

Around this time a singular individual was spotted around Midtown. He was gaunt, combed his dark hair slicked back on the sides, and he often wore a pink gabardine shirt with a black placket down the front and with black cuffs turned back and the black underside of the collar turned up. Under that he adopted black trousers with a thin, translucent chartreuse belt around his waist. On his feet he put white socks and pointed, woven black Aristocrat shoes of the type favored by pimps, and he wore vintage "Chad" model Ray Ban sunglasses, even at night. We happened to meet at Zinnie's Bar at the corner of Madison and Belvedere on the night that some thugs had jumped on Phineas Newborn, Jr. by the side entrance and proceeded to break all the fingers of the illustrious jazz pianist. His mother rushed to the scene and arrived just as the ambulance did. Mama Newborn looked at his fingers and said, "You'll play again." Phineas would play again, but none of us, who'd come out of the notorious late-night swill pit and saw him lying there on the sidewalk, were so sure of it. It had happen so fast. We re-entered the tavern and drank grimly.

The boy behind the sunglasses and I sat at the bar next to each other. He removed his shades and we spoke in low tones about the beating and how the bartender happened to look over his shoulder through the big plate glass window and caught sight of the culprits stomping Phineas' hands. By the time he got to the side door with a billy club, the punks had scattered. We talked about the last time we'd seen Phineas play. We'd both seen him at the Whirlaway club on Lamar. I found out that the boy was actually a grown man of the age Howling Wolf was, when he finally moved off Dockery Plantation. We had a lot in common it turned out – in music: Stockhausen; in art: Giacometti; in theatre: Artaud; in film: Murnau; in cars: Thunderbird; in bikes: Norton. On the strength of this common ground, I invited him over to my hovel on Cox St. to listen to my collection of Jimmie Rodgers records. He had an odd name. He called himself, *Tav*... Tav Falco.

We sipped straight bourbon through a straw and listened to Jimmie Rodgers yodeling until dawn. Then he split on the first bus downtown to the "Y" where he had a room. Next day he came over to my place, and the day after that. We started messing around with the TeleVista video camera, talking about films, and playing guitar and beating an old snare drum head I had laying around the front room. I showed him everything I knew about the guitar – most of it he already knew, and he was acquainted with most of the musicians and artists that I knew in town. These sessions went on for days, and pretty soon Falco was practically living at my duplex on Cox St. In fact, it gradually became apparent he *was* living at the duplex, sleeping on the couch, driving the T-Bird, riding the Norton, and talking on the telephone. When Alex came over I introduced him to Falco, and they got along famously. Pretty soon I got the notion that Falco might be a good choice for the singer of the band – of the Panther Burns. I talked it over with Alex, and he said why not audition him. We brought Ross over, and Tav and he and Alex jammed on the Sonny Burgess tune, "Red Headed Woman". Ross sounded like a pack of hound dogs let loose on the drum set, and Falco came off pretty rough, but we saw a spark of potential in him. His vocal had a peculiar tone: not a wail, and not a whimper; it was more like a detuned, modal yowl with a touch of angst. Later his voice would be described, not unfairly, as sounding like Marlene Dietrich under torture.

Still, having Tav Falco around the house was not so much of a problem. He was tidy enough and generally stayed out of people's way. Not only did we think alike, but also we looked something alike which would prove useful later. So it was decided, with the approval of Alex who was a bone-fide musician that Falco would get a shot at lead singer of Panther Burns, and I would kind of orchestrate the movements and the concept of the band. We had a couple of rehearsals, not more, and decided we were ready to test the band before an audience. Alex thought of a swanky little bar downtown eponymously named, Court Square, where Sid Selvidge had a steady solo gig. Ross was out of pocket, so Falco and Alex went as a duo. Sid allowed the interlopers a few minutes on the tiny bandstand between his sets. He stood a safe distance at the back of the bar and seemed rather amused with what followed. Who wouldn't? Alex was in his typically gray over blue/gray jeans attire, but this guy Falco was dressed in what appeared to be a metallic foil garbage bag turned inside out with his over-long chartreuse belt wrapped around it in such a way as to keep the whole thing from flying away. The duo abruptly burst into the chorus of the rave, "Red Headed Woman", as Falco had already forgotten the intro verse. He did remember the verses and chorus properly in the second and last song of the little spectacle. That was a kind of fractured tango called, "Drop Your Mask". The tune was intact, but still something not fully gelled about it: something rhythmically strange, or tonally weird. It was hard to say which. The audience was a bit bewildered and seemed not to really want to look at them, yet they could not avert their eyes either, which I thought was a good sign. They came off the bandstand, and there was no applause, which I thought was an even better sign. Falco and Alex met me at the bar thirsty for wine spritzers. We downed those and split to Midtown in the T-Bird.

Alex would invite us over to listen to records in the big three-story stone house on Harbert where he lived with his parents in Annesdale central gardens. First time I saw it, I was impressed with the gold 7-inch disc that was hanging in a frame above the stairwell. The title printed under the center hole was, "The Letter". There was another one father up the staircase wall: "Cry Like A Baby". His folks, Mary and Sidney Chilton, were a focal point for modern art and culture in Memphis in the 1950s. They had conducted what could be considered a salon for artists, writers, and musicians. From her home Mary operated an informal art gallery and she represented William Eggleston – equally informally – securing commissions for him when he started out photographing the children of her clients. Sidney Chilton owned a theatrical lighting company in Midtown, and he was a talented tenor saxophonist, pianist, and jazz theorist. He and his jazz band played a Sunday afternoon gig at Trader Dick's on Madison Avenue in Midtown well into the 80s. Those who were enthused about contemporary art and music were drawn to the Chiltons and to the intimate soirées they hosted for Memphian intelligentsia. Alex's older brother, Howard, was a card-carrying member of the Spartacist League of young Trotskyites, and was jocose conversationalist. The youngest of the brothers had drowned in the bathtub as a child, which left an indelible mark of melancholy on Alexander, as his mother would often refer to him.

The next foray of the Panther Burns would be considered their first show. For the occasion I rented a cotton-grading loft at 96 S. South Front St. for fifty bucks, and I designed the Burning Panther Head logo for the flyer: a growling black panther head with red flames shooting out the top, outlined in white and set on a black field.

The band still uses this emblem. We had two stage risers that I'd borrowed from David Rice at the Cotton Carnival warehouse. He was a theatre department comrade from the U. of A., and he had them delivered gratis to Front St. All we had to do was drag these abominably heavy wooden risers up two flights of narrow stairs, which proved to be a Herculean task. I bought two kegs of beer, and got a few cases of obscure 7-inch RnR records from my neighbor. He had the discs left over from some abortive promotion, but his main deal was publisher of the John Lead *how to play electric guitar* series of study guides. We wrote on the flyer, "free records", and "free beer" and RnR. So on February 11, 1979, the loft on Front St. was packed with every strata of Memphis society, hardly knowing what to expect other than free booze and free 45s. Mostly, however, the audience was underage kids. Since the band knew only eight

songs and I figured they could only repeat that twice during the show, I asked Jim Dickinson and Lee Baker to do a set on electric guitars. They brought Jimmy Crosthwait to play percussion, and Amy Gamine from the KLITZ to play bass. Erstwhile we had brought Erik Hill into Panther Burns to play synthesizer. Erik was a fashionable gay blade who was a total non-musician. He played the mini-Korg with his knuckles and had that intuitive *je ne sais quoi* touch to bring Panther Burns over the top. Two flailing guitars, explosive drums, and squalling synthesizer was the recipe for the most sublime of cacophonies. On that chill February night the cotton loft was turned into a flying saucer.

Erik Hill Photo: E. Baffle 1979

Amy Gamine Photo: E. Baffle c. 1982

Panther Burns produced a number of self-promoted shows at the cotton loft over the next few months. When Amy's parents were off on a junket to the white silver sands of Destin, Falco began to spend time at the house in Central Gardens that her father had designed in a Zen, postmodern style. There were parties of course. Black motorcycle jacketed punks came and Midtown girls in fur coats –graduates of Lausanne or Hutchinson schools for girls came to hang with the bike boys who'd actually never ridden a motorbike. Falco was the only one among them who was a rider. Amy liked to entertain in a 3/4-length fur coat with a plain white slip underneath: an outfit that seemed to compliment the charm of her addictive personality. She was pale as a lotus blossom, and like the flower her allure seemed to bloom only at night. Her pallor was accentuated by rouge and a generous outline of glossy lipstick, while her diction of sly emasculations was punctuated with exhalations of the ever present cigarette, often smoked through a slim onyx holder. The total effect of her foggy presence seemed a perfect simulacrum of the high-strung Viennese from whom she descended. The parties were beer and wine-soaked affairs of Dionysian exuberance. Wine glasses were thrown against the walls and shards ground into the floor with motorcycle boots, yet these soirées hardly compared to the orgies in Oxford that Amy claimed to have had attended as a teenager after Ole Miss football games.

Following the first Panther Burns event, Van Zula Hunt and Mose Vinson appeared as guests on the next loft show. They played nothing but cathouse blues, and it was a stone groove for the essentially puerile audience. The voice of Van Zula was so highly modulated she didn't a microphone. She just belted over the heads of everyone, and the room started breathing like a catfish. On the third show we had Charlie Feathers and his son Bubba. He brought the whole family and a rocking chair to sit in. Charlie thrilled and titillated the crowd like they'd never thought possible. By the end of the night the loft room was vibrating and reverberating like a huge guitar sounding-box. Other than full size posters that I designed and printed for the events, the shows were unannounced, but the crowds grew until music lovers were lined up before the Front St. doorway to get upstairs. The shows went on until the MPD finally shut us down, due to violations of city codes and a litany of other infractions.

By the end of this string of lofty shows, Panther Burns had honed the edges of a brutal, yet lyrical assault on blues, rockabilly, tango, and pop standards that seemed to affront all known criteria of accepted taste. Our motto was: "You compose 'em; we decompose 'em," and the battle cry onstage was, "every man for himself." Our proclaimed identity, "the last steam engine train left on the track that don't do nothing but run and blow." Looking for a venue to replace the cotton loft was easier than we had imagined. A nutty little S&M bar at 1588 Madison Avenue at Avalon called the Mouse Trap had closed and the joint re-opened as The Well with a country jukebox and fresh coat of black paint. It had a square stage with a full mirror wall behind it for reflecting the tits and derrière of the terpsichorean beauties who once lifted a leg on the august platform. The joint was operated by Frank Durrell and his partner Jackie – a tall, hatchet-faced woman with a heart of gold. Frank and Jackie gave Panther Burns a Wednesday night to audition the group. A nice little crowd of rowdies and their girlfriends came to see the band, and from there on it was no sweat to book Wednesdays at The Well. As the audience grew, Panther Burns were booked on weekends along with a 60s style power pop group called the Randy Band. The Well had flowered into a venue for wimps, losers, fops, college dropouts, errant sorority girls, punk rockers, hillbilly ravers, warped musical aficionados with ears for the atonal and the unexpected, and general Midtown flotsam.

Down from The Well on Willet St., between Madison and Union, a spacious one-room church had been recently converted to a club backed by the Godfather of the Sax, Ace Canon, who'd released "TUFF" among other smash instrumentals during the golden era. The joint opened as the House of Canon and had a relief of a canon shooting canon balls sunk into the refurbished façade. It was operated by a hillbilly promoter, himself from before the golden era, attired in a three-piece suit and a Beatle wig. We booked Panther Burns in there for a Saturday night, and designed posters for the event that we wheatpasted around town and put in all the

Syd Fenwick, Rick Ivy, Kathy Johnson of the Burnettes Photo: E. Baffle c. 1980

record shops, cafes, rag and head shops, art supply stores, and branch libraries. Come Saturday, the church house was packed, and the band delivered a ruthlessly abandoned show with kids storming the stage, and Alex booting them off like soccer balls without missing a note.

Sid Selvidge had lent Alex an incredible, jazz-type Gibson 335 electric guitar that had been super-hopped up for RnR. It was of a non-descript dull brown color, and seemed to be bigger, wider, and with a deeper hollow body, than most 335s. The guitar had two open *"f"* holes that caught the amplified sound waves from his Fender Super Reverb amp, and fed back layers of noise and sheared tonalities that Alex masterfully layered upon layer until he'd built a crescendo of rapacious sound waves – a proverbial wall of rippling sound – that carried the melodies of Panther Burns to sonic heights never dreamed of by mere mortals. That Gibson, which one-day regrettably had to go back to its rightful owner, combined with the Super Reverb pumping four x ten-inch speakers, provided a musical platform of unbridled, overdriven sonic intensity that Alex would never again quite attain.

The hillbilly promoter – he called Tav, "Tavo", because that's what I had printed on the poster, but it sounded funny when he said it – was elated, and wanted to record the band with the newly formed Burnettes. This was indeed the debut of the Burnettes, a rotating coterie of junior high girls from Lausanne girl's school in east Memphis, who'd become the background singers and dancers for Panther Burns. Namely, the Burnettes were Syd Fenwick, daughter of a Spanish literature instructor at Memphis State – the darkly tantalizing 15-year-old of whom Alex was enamored – and her bubbly pal Kathy Johnson. Around this time we added another non-musician to the line-up to round out the sound on trumpet. He was a painting student at the Art Academy named Rick Ivy, and he enjoyed a brief tenure with the group squawking on horn. Regarding the hillbilly promoter's recording offer, however, I advised the band to pass on it and to wait a spell. I sensed bigger, though perhaps not better things were in the making.

Concurrently, the KLITZ were on the scene – an all girl group fronted by the Mia Farrow-looking, Lesa Aldrich, another cousin of Bill Eggleston, daughter of a minister, and Alex' ex. The KLITZ also began to play at The Well, and on some hairy occasions on a double bill with Panther Burns. The Well wasn't the only action in Midtown. We'd heard there was going to be a benefit for Don Ezell, the chauffeur for SUN records in the golden era. He was laid up in the hospital in pretty bad shape, partly a complicated consequence of wife beating. Memphis musicians were good about throwing benefits for ailing colleagues; rest of the time, the scene was, as Charlie Feathers had warned me, fairly cutthroat. Alex, Tav Falco, Ross, and I showed up at the Western Sizzlin' Steakhouse & Lounge on Madison situated somewhat farther down the avenue from The Well. Inside it seemed like every musician in town had squeezed in the tavern. A chubby MC in a farmer's straw hat was introducing singers and guitar players and flogging the audience for donations with the constantly repetitive exhortation, *We really appreciate the dog shit out of it. Now, we really appreciate….* over and over and over, until the phrase was forever burned into our neural synapses. When the MC would take off his straw hat and wave up his insufferable exhortations, as if wafting up clouds of sacrificial smoke of which there was more than plenty in the room, he looked a lot like Mike Ladd, the guitarist. At one point, the MC placed a simple straight back chair center of the small stage, and the *real*, quasi-legendary Mike Ladd jumped from the audience and up on the chair playing electric guitar like a fiend from Hell. Memphis seemed full of such star-crossed identities.

Cordell Jackson was in the audience at Western Sizzlin' and was somehow impressed when Tav, Alex, and Ross took the stage as a three-piece for the occasion. She came up to us after the abbreviated set, introduced herself, and said that the band reminded her of a group called Alan Page and the Big Four that she had produced and released on her own record label back in the '50s called Moon Records. She claimed to be the first lady recording engineer. Next afternoon Cordell showed up at our place on Cox St. toting a stack of Moon Records 45s, that she played for us on our turntable through the Stromberg-Carlson amp. Cordell was a tall, distinguished Southern lady with fine features, a bouffant hairdo, and an effervescent

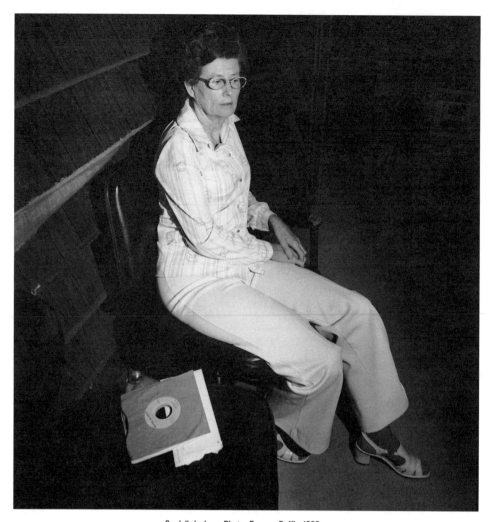

Cordell Jackson Photo: Eugene Baffle 1980

personality. Her records sounded equally as lilting and engaging as her Dixie-fried personality. She urged us to play two of her songs in the band: "Dateless Night" and "She's the One That's Got It". When Alex heard the songs, he too was delighted, and the group worked up the tunes. To this day, the two songs remain in the repertoire of the Panther Burns and are played on most every live show.

TeleVista got booked on the *Marge Thrasher Show*, a morning talk show on WHBQ-TV, an ABC affiliate. It was going to be an art-action Happening, live video hook-up between four art-action groups in North America: Center For New Art Activities in New York; Relay in San Francisco; Open Space in Victoria, British Columbia; and TeleVista in Memphis. The live hook-up was achieved utilizing a slow-scan encoder device that encoded the video signal from our hand-held video camera into audio frequencies, which permitted the four telecommunication-art groups to send/receive a video image scanned out every few seconds over such conventional audio transmission equipment as an ordinary telephone. We had engaged the Panther Burns to go on the show and serve as the TeleVista orchestra.

When we arrived at the TV station at 8:00 a.m., we ran into Marge Thrasher – the frumpy host of the show – with her hair in pin curlers, as we were connecting our slow-scan unit to the pay phone in the corridor. Marge did not take kindly to be seen in such untidy fashion, and *harrumphed,* past us to her dressing room. Once connected, the multi-million dollar technological encumbrance of TV equipment, segment producers, and line directors could not interfere with our video picture displayed on the same huge B&W video monitor that was used by Eugene Baffle at the Orpheum. The crew had a massive TV studio camera focused on our monitor, and the director had only the option to transit our image or to cut away; he could not control the content. The floor crew seemed amused with our array of guerrilla TV equipment, but the rest of the staff was not so charmed.

Panther Burns arrived six strong that morning with added personnel of trumpeter Rick Ivy who appeared in a loud solid plaid three-piece suit and Tyrolean hat with a grouse feather sticking out. As we could no longer borrow the Mini-Korg from Phillips studio, we were offered a cumbersome synthesizer that was so big it required two people to play it. So we were obliged to allow its owner, a Visigoth from the Art Academy, to appear alongside our core member, Erik Hill. Vincent Wrenn, author of solid black oil painted canvases, proved hardly more of a musician than Erik, but was endowed with like powers of the imagination.

Randall Lyon, as president of TeleVista, chatted with Marge for about 15-minutes, while the send/receive video images began flickering on our monitor, and the switcher in the control room was cutting between the interview and our live image feed. As Randall was explaining how TeleVista was sending video images from our camera that I was pointing around the studio, by means of the encoder device hooked to the pay phone in the hallway, and was also receiving images through the same telephone hookup from three other alternative art groups scattered around the continent, and talking about what a grand telecommunications experiment it all was, the inevitable female live nude popped up on our monitor. The encoder was in the receive mode and the modernist dancing nude had been piped in from Relay on the west coast. Before the director could react, the nude images had been broadcast into a million households in the Bible-belt tri-state area, as the viewers were finishing morning coffee.

Marge was visibly shaken by this unexpected breach of television broadcasting codes, but she and Randall did their best to smooth it over, while the director cut to a commercial. It was the month of May, and the King and Queen of Cotton Carnival went on next to promote the upcoming celebrations. Meanwhile, Panther Burns had set up on the studio floor to present the musical wing of the TeleVista telecommunications experiment. After the Carnival royalty segment and a cut to another commercial, the show came back. Three enormous TV studio cameras lit up and the Panther Burns were on the air. What followed is not easy to describe. Although Falco looked greasier than usual – due I think to the high heat of the studio lights – he still appeared suave in his pink and black shirt and the pointed Aristocrat shoes. As a nod to *les printemps,* he had draped a white naval officer's jacket over one shoulder, that I lent to Falco for the occasion, and which he later alleged was the naval officer's jacket that his own father had bequeathed him after drowning in the South Seas. The others in the group were reasonably well groomed in collegiate pastels, or Gothic pure black, or in the case of Ivy, Scottish tartan. The real problem was what we shall term the caliber of *music* that seemed to *exude* in an oily, low-fi fashion from their instruments, combined with the dismal whining and low squeal of the refrigerator-sized synthesizer. The voice of Falco was questionable as well, sounding like a flat disharmonic croak... due in part to the dead acoustics of the room. When the "Train Kept a Rollin" number ended to the relief of most everyone present including the band, there was a brief silence. Marge knitted her eyebrows, looked directly at Falco and asked, "Gustavo (he used his complete name for billing on this show), that's really just about the worst sounding thing I've ever heard. Do you really expect to make money with *that*?"

"Marge," Falco replied humbly, "we're not in it for the money".

"Tell me, Gustavo, just what are you *on*?"

"I'm not on anything!" Falco proclaimed, "I'm just on WHBQ at *nine o'clock in the morning.*"

There was more chatter where Falco was forced to justify the existence of the band and

Tav Falco, Alex Chilton, Rick Ivy, Erik Hill, Ross Johnson Photo: 704 S. Cox St. porch

its salvage operations and live excavations of Memphis music.

"Well, we have another song that we'd like to…"

"Just hold on, Gustavo. We're not so sure there's going to be another song from your group – what's it called?"

"Panther Burns, ma'am."

Cut to commercial. That Falco was always doing something unexpected. *Now*, he was hob-nobbing off camera with the King and Queen of Cotton Carnival. He had taken the tambourine from the drum set and was coaching the Queen how to beat it. Cut back to the show, and the camera crew in a kind of mutinous maneuver turned their cameras onto the band, rather than the dais upon which Marge sat. Falco saw the red lights on the TV cameras pop on and he launched into a deconstructed tango "Drop Your Mask" in homage to the Queen, who now was out on the studio floor dancing with the band and slapping the tambourine in rhythm, while the King was at her side merrily keeping time with his royal scepter. The somewhat structureless tango wound to an end in a more jocular fashion than the previous tune. Marge however, was not so entertained, and even seemed a bit violated. She uttered an aside, "I think I feel dirty." Then she looked straight into the camera and declared, "I really feel like I need a bath after that." And… that was it – the first golden Memphis moment for Panther Burns.

In the same month, the first Panther Burns record was released on their titular band label, and the side was called, *Frenzi 2000*. It was a four song 7-inch EP of live tracks recorded at The Well and at the Evergreen Theatre on Poplar, which was the former Guild Art Cinema. We had 500 copies pressed in Nashville, and we screen-printed the record labels and covers ourselves on the side porch of our hovel. In Midtown Panther Burns were becoming hot as a firecracker. In the fall the Cramps arrived in town from New York to record their album *Songs the Lord Taught Us,* and Alex was set to produce it at Sam Phillips Recording Studio on lower Madison Avenue.

The Cramps Photo: E. Baffle 1980

Poison Ivy on Cox St. Photo: E. Baffle 1980

Meeting the Cramps, already icons among the cognoscenti in Memphis, was like meeting invaders from Mars. They had the sound with Ivy Rorschach's surfabilly guitar; they had the beat, with Nick Knox savage boom; they had the fuzz with Brian Gregory's flying "V" electric guitar; and they had the bite with the vocal attack of Lux Interior. In Phillips studio The Cramps wanted to achieve a live show effect. Without exception they dressed like tribal batmen and batwomen at all times. Lux and Ivy were true music lovers; Nick was addicted to pounding the skins, while Brian was in a Gothic universe of his own. He knew a few chords, but essentially played guitar by intuitive feel alone in the manner of Eric Hill – who happened to be one of Gregory's most ardent admirers. The Cramps were friendly enough, considering some of them were as hopped up as they were. They placed the drum set in the middle of the floor in Studio A, and would come in late at night and practically wreck the place – within limits – and in the end had destroyed only some standing ashtrays and twisted up a few microphone stands. During takes, however, there was a lot of leaping around on amplifier cabinets and organ and piano tops. Alex was seen from time to time mainlining a solution of some chunky cocaine granules of dubious quality while sitting at the control board orchestrating the recording of tracks and coaching individual group members through the intercom. Richard Roseborough was the engineer, and I was the gopher.

After the album was completed, Ivy invited Falco to appear on a Cramps gig at Irving Plaza around 15th St. in New York. Before the Cramps came onstage, the Arkansan thrashed and screeched through a blistering 15-minute set with the Cramps' roadie standing in on guitar, and someone like Will Rigby on drums. Soon as the first note was struck, Falco later reported, the guitar player froze stiff as a zombie, and the Beale St. Blues Bopper – as Falco called himself – had to carry the spectacle with his own meager talents. Ivy was nice to him, he said. She even paid him $50 for the lackluster gig. With that Falco thought he was really in show business in New York. In the dressing room after the gig, Falco told us that a couple of junior high rockers from Long Island had tried to get backstage where the band was lounging, and Miles Copeland, the Cramps manager at the time and that of a boorish group called the Police, jumped on these two kids and beat the holy tar out of them. Big bad Miles: obviously hopped up to the point where his underlying sadistic nature took precedence. Falco himself would occasionally become engaged in fisticuffs, especially with unmannerly British stage bouncers. Invariably he was *un*victorious and usually stomped to the floor, resulting in a proverbial black eye that generally seemed to linger on and on. Falco was not, however, ever inclined to or accused of pouncing on junior high school kids.

Smitten by the big city vibe, before long Falco returned to New York by invitation of Jim Fouratt, the blonde house booker at Danceteria. Alex agreed to go along, and Will Rigby from the DBs took the drum chair. By that time, synthesizers had become impossible for the group to get hold of, and they had been playing as a three piece, until a stranger named Ron Miller at last convinced the band to give him a shot at playing contrabass. Ron had come from New York to fill in a season with the Memphis symphony, but he was a jazzer, having played and studied with Kenny Burrell in Ann Arbor, and he had traveled Europe making music for the Living Theatre ensemble of Julian Beck and Judith Malina. He was an erudite cat with a dour Yankee personality that emerged prominently in his oblique style of playing. Yet Ron was totally mad for the Panther music, threw everything he had to offer at the band, and became a devoted and faithful member of the group until some months later when he kicked Falco out of the townhouse in Greenwich Village that he shared with his heiress wife, Louise Lynx. The removal of Falco from the townhouse was predicated upon accusation of conspiring with other bass players. Ron then joined up with James Chance, or James White and the Blacks as he was later called. But on this initial foray as a four piece, Panther Burns played around New York for a week, including the anchor date at Danceteria, which proved fortuitous in that Geoff Travis from Rough Trade in London signed up the band that night to record their first album, *Behind the Magnolia Curtain*.

After those first bookings in New York with Panther Burns, Falco lingered for a while on the downtown scene. He ventured into a little joint also on 15th St, called Tramps, operated by an agreeable Irishman, Terry Dunn, who gave the Beale St. Blues Bopper as solo shot on a Wednesday night. It was opening for jump blues legend, Big Joe Turner. Actually Big Joe *was* big, over six feet and big all around except for his shiny pomaded head. He came into the club on crutches, sat down, and ate two whole chickens before he went on the bandstand.

Tramps was a little more tidy than most joints downtown. Journalists would hang out there, and record producers like Marty Thau who operated below 23rd St. David Johansen had just re-incarnated himself as Buster Poindexter, and he had a regular weekend headliner spot at Tramps fronting his sharp trio of fashionable young men. The group wore tuxedos and Buster's patent leather shoe shone glibly as he belted out such standards as "Mohair Sam". A comrade, Jeffrey Lee Pierce, from Gun Club showed up to witness Falco's first solo gig. The Arky sat on the bandstand in a straight-backed chair, tuned his ratty steel-stringed acoustic guitar up and down for a spell, and then launched to an obscure, turpentine camp blues that he'd patched together.

Well, two little puppies and one old shaggy hound
Well, two little puppies and one old shaggy hound
Goin' up on the mountain, track my baby down,

Gonna build me a mansion way out on dago hill
Gonna build me a mansion way out on dago hill
Gonna drink my whiskey, baby right from the still.

At the cotton loft on Front St. back in Memphis, Falco had astonishing success flogging the audience with such abstruse, bucolic lyrics, but the audience in Manhattan was an oil painting. They sat there with dumb looks, and here they *did* avert their eyes. I heard Pierce try to console Falco saying, *solo shows are not so easy*, but it was the same scenario on the next Wednesday.

After the Cramps album was mixed back in the Bluff City, a triple-header was booked at the Orpheum Theatre downtown at Main and Beale, and WEVL Radio promoted the show heavily. The KLITZ opened the show, and when the Panther Burns took the stage Falco pulled another of his stunts. Mid-set he tore off his latest Silvertone guitar and barehanded smashed it on the floor of the stage into a hundred pieces. He then announced to the crowd, *we don't need guitars to play this music*!

Hardly upstaged, when it became Cramps time, Lux Interior entered the theatre from the back of the auditorium wearing a black cape. Over the tops of the backs of the theatre seats, he ran straight up the middle of the auditorium to the orchestra pit, which he leaped in a single bound and landed on the apron of the stage. From there Lux delivered another larger than humanly possible performance. For Memphian high school and college kids hungry for the music of the Cramps, it was a sensation of sheer outer space.

A few days before the Cramps split town, the Panther Burns played a New Year's Eve show at the newly transformed Well. A local hairdresser named Jimmy Barker bought out the interests of Jackie and Frank – no longer would Falco be chased around the club threatened by Frank with his billy club because the club didn't sell enough beer on his last song. Barker threw up glittery black and red paint on the interior, installed some TV monitors, and dubbed the joint *Antenna Club*. On that first Antenna Club New Year's party, Falco drank Champaign on stage from the high heel slippers of the Burnettes and Alex played the gig barefoot in his pajamas. Falco was telling his dumb Lone Ranger jokes while Ross would accent the punch line with a drum roll and bass drum crash:

Panther Burns Palace Theater, Los Angeles Photo: Richard Pleuger 2006

Meanwhile back at the ranch:
the Lone Ranger, not knowing Tonto was disguised as a pool table,
racked his balls!

and

Meanwhile back at the ranch:
the Lone Ranger, not knowing Tonto was disguised as a tripod,
kicked off his third leg!

That night Lux knighted the Burns as liege lords of the Antenna.

The new album was completed in a jiffy at Ardent studios, and Rough Trade issued it in Europe and through their San Francisco office for North America. The album received attention in rags like *NY Rocker*, *East Village Eye*, from Glenn O'Brien in *Andy Warhol's Interview*, and in the *New York Times* from Robert Palmer who wrote up the group in some half page spreads. The band started flying in to New York from Memphis for gigs at Peppermint Lounge, the Mudd Club, and CBGBs. A Yale law student from Humboldt, Tennessee, Bibi Ford, and her sister Sarah were avid fans and regulars at Panther Burns gigs at the Antenna. Bibi booked Panther Burns into a mammoth dining hall at Yale University and the *Yale Daily News*, the nation's oldest college daily, published an advance article. There must have been 800 Yalies at the gig, the largest audience for the band thus far. On the strength of this flurry of interest, Ron Miller got the band a New York booking agent and drove his station wagon down to

Antenna Club Photo: E. Baffle 1992

Memphis to carry the band on the first of countless cross-country tours. The first gig on the tour was opening for the Cramps in New Orleans. The music of the band was jangly and still not quite solidified, but that didn't slow them down. Although far from perfect – as few things are in this world – the show established Panther Burns in New Orleans for a long time to come.

From there the band played its way out to Los Angeles where it opened for the Cramps again on their annual Halloween Show. Vampira was on the bill, and made a scene onstage rising out of her coffin. Again the band was far from perfect, but as in the Crescent City, they endeared themselves to hordes of young music lovers in tinsel town. Same scenario in San Francisco, and on across the country, the band played every RnR toilet and hardcore pit from the west coast to the east. For this roadwork, drummer Jim Sclavunos joined the band from New York, and played on the follow up record for Rough Trade that was recorded in the orchestral studio at Radio City Music Hall on 6th Avenue. Some of the Rockettes sang back up.

The next phase involved offers to tour Australia as the result of a promoter's daughter from Sidney beholding the Panther Burns at the Cat Club in New York. Panther Burns racked up gigs from Melbourne and up the Gold Coast to the rain forests in Mullumbimby. The promoters rented an antique wooden ferryboat, and the band played a sodden all-day cruise in Sidney harbor. This gave Falco the idea to do a similar cruise on the Memphis Belle riverboat back home, and the band sold out two consecutive nights on the faux paddle-wheeler. The group took most any offer just to keep gas in the T-bird. Once they took on a three-nighter: Nashville, Athens, and Atlanta. The Thunderbird puffed the 200 miles to Nashville, and Ross left a couple hours later on his own, but turned back about 45-minutes out of Memphis, because he got "the fear". Jim Dickinson was with us and he pulled his cap down over his eyes and filled in on the drums... and the drums were all that he did play; he never once touched a cymbal. What a fabulous drummer! Jim drove to Memphis after the gig in a tiff because he'd had to shout down the Nashville promoter – a college kid who ran Praxis Records – who reneged on paying the band enough even for gas.

On the following day we drove to the house trailer where the guitar player in the opening band from the night before was sleeping. We woke him from an intoxicated slumber, and shanghaied him to play drums on the next two dates. We stuffed the bear-like hillbilly into the back seat of the T-Bird and struck out to Athens. About forty miles away from the venue, we heard a loud *ka-pow*, immediately followed by another *ka-pow* as both retreaded, back tires blew out. I held onto the steering wheel for dear life, while the big T-bird swerved, careened wildly, and skidded to a halt. We got help from some farmers passing by, and managed to get some used tires on the Ford. By this time Alex had become morose and withdrawn.

When the T-bird finally pulled up in front of the 40 Watt Club, the bearded promoter came to the door, and advised us we were 15-minutes late for show time. He told Falco, *I know you all are good, but you're cancelled*. I thought sure that Falco was going to sock the hippy promoter in the nose, but he didn't… too winded from changing flat fires, I suppose, and I guess he wanted to protect his fingers for the next show. When the group arrived in Atlanta the venue was large scale and professional. The hillbilly guitar-player-turned-drummer we'd brought from Nashville sounded half sober and passable at sound check, but once into the show that night, he was foul with liquor, and all over the drums in not a good way. Falco started staring down at his feet, and muttering lyrics, while Alex literally sneaked behind his amplifier to hide. There'd been good press on the show, but the reality was a complete fizzle. If the promoters had a rail, they would have ridden us out of town on it.

As a result of intercession by the Cramps, one day Falco received a hand-written letter from New Rose Records in Paris. Shortly thereafter Panther Burns went into Phillips studio and recorded the first of several albums they would record over time for the Parisian label. Although Geoff Travis thought there was not enough interest to warrant Panther Burns touring in Europe, Patrick Mathé at New Rose thought differently. He hired Prestige Talent in London to put the group out on tour in British Isles and across the continent. Again Panther Burns played every toilet, mosh pit, and RnR venue large and small from Amsterdam to Budapest. That was before the "wall" came down and artificial cities like Berlin were chimerical and exotic.

Back in the Bluff City, Panther Burns went into a studio on Deadrick Avenue in the Orange Mound area around Lamar and Airways Boulevard. Among three tunes I penned for the album was "Vampire From Havana" for which I tuned down the guitar strings in open D-chord so Falco could attain a deeply resonating and haunting guitar drive. The hit-popping producer Chips Moman, with funds derived from the success of a 7-inch Sapphic paean recorded by the Jaynettes in 1963 on the Tuff label entitled, "Sally Go Round the Roses", had putatively built the structure from the ground up as a two story recording facility, then he turned around and lost the new facility in a gambling ruse. Whether half-truth or the kind of rumor that appeals to musicians of a certain ilk, Panther Burns were attracted to the mystique of the studio and marched in with high expectations and with LX, as we called him, once again at the controls. Ours was the first album project upon the reopening of the studio after many years of disuse by Easley/McCain partnership. The vibe of the space was ultra vintage. Upstairs there was a voluminous echo chamber wired to the control room on the first floor. Underneath my exuberant feeling was more than a tinge of remorse in having pulled out at the last minute on recording the album with Roland Janes at Phillips Studio. LX, in collusion with Easley's older brother who was on the session as a guitarist, had mandated switching the production to the refurbished Easley studio, citing the first failed attempt to record Panther Burns at Phillips with Stan Kessler and the entombed sound that had resulted. It was said that there were so many "ghosts in the control board" at Phillips, and one could never be sure what you were getting on tape. Maybe that was part of the attraction/avoidance syndrome of recording at Phillips. Roland had telephoned me numerous times to remind me to bring the band in the studio and get started. Finally, I had to ride the Norton down there and explain what was happening. Roland's displeasure, especially with LX's involvement in the decision, was clearly apparent and certainly not unwarranted. One day… I will find a way to record the group with Roland.

At the Deadrick studio, LX permitted Falco only four or five vocal takes, and of those he seemed disinterested, speaking over intercom, "I've got what I need, but you can do another one if you *really* want to." I knew Falco could do a better take; guess Alex didn't think it mattered. Like most producers using multi-track recording systems, LX's credo was, *forget it, we'll fix it in the mix*. Still, there is a lot that cannot be fixed in the mix. When they got to the most challenging song on the album, the obscure Crudup classic "I'm Gonna Dig Myself a Hole", the session turned into a nightmare. Falco's rhythm was so snaky that the vocal had to be recorded live with Ross on drums and with Jim Dickinson playing acoustic guitar. Jim carried the tune and Falco tried to lay himself in the groove somewhere. After about 15-takes, LX got on the intercom and ruthlessly denounced Falco's efforts. On the subsequent takes, his voice became thinner and thinner until the point when he did manage to fall acceptably into the groove, his voice had denigrated into nothing more than a whisper.

Jud Phillips, Jr., the business manager of the group, dropped by the sessions with a representative from Gibson. They were giving away guitars on endorsement. They offered a new model to Alex, but he refused to endorse their product – not because of quality issues, but he simply did not want to act as an advertisement. LX could, at times, display a surprising degree of integrity. Jud, Jr. had brought me into contact with another of his clients, Teenie Mabon Hodges, who with his brothers, Leroy and Charles, formed the core of the Hi Records rhythm section. I invited Teenie to play on the sessions along with his cousin, Roland Robinson, who had been the bass player and band manager for Eddie Floyd since he was fourteen. Teenie and Roland were 'cool' personified without even trying. Guess it was born right in them. They were elegant and cordial young men as well... although Teenie did carry a loaded pistol. Still, lots of singers in Memphis were armed with guns: Eddie Floyd, Issac Hayes, Jerry Lee.

Roland told me about traveling with Eddie Floyd. When they'd arrive in some southern town for a concert and drive up to the venue, if there were any women holding papers around the entrance, Eddie would tell the chauffeur to just keep on driving right out of town. Not only was apprehension by Treasury agents due tax evasion a constant threat, but the consequences of unresolved paternity suits made life on the road in the US particularly turbulent for the singer of "Knock on Wood".

Another marvelous aspect of making music with Teenie and Roland was that they invited the group over to rehearse at their place in Midtown. Members of Panther Burns had always disdained rehearsals, and when the group hit the stage it was every man for himself. On the other hand, maybe they sensed that Falco in particular could benefit from a rehearsal, but Teenie and Roland didn't seem to care if you could play or not... evidentially they just assumed you could play. They never talked about it, maybe because we were honkys and so it didn't matter anyway, but rehearsals with them were fun and relaxed, and a party with all the trimmings. Teenie contributed one of his original songs for the album, "What's Wrong?" and he played guitar as brilliantly as did Roland on Fender bass. Behind the scenes, LX castigated their playing on the record, claiming that we did not need them. At least in attempting to subvert our miscegenation, he did not sabotage getting Teenie and Roland on tape.

During a weekend break the sessions Teenie and Roland were going to play a live date with Panther Burns over in Little Rock at a joint called Juanita's. Teenie rode to Arkansas in the Thunderbird with Falco and I.

"Well what did you do, Teenie, when you were growing up in Arkansas around Blackfish Lake...?"

"Fished... and hunt. The first band I saw live was the James Cotton band at nine years old. Then, a couple of weeks later I saw B.B. King's band. It was a place called the Top Hat."

"What about your father – a musician, too?"

"He played keyboards, and I didn't know he played until I was 12 years old. I knew we always had a piano in our house from the time I can remember, growing up. Well, we had 12 children: seven boys and five girls. His name was Leroy Hodges. I wanted to be a baseball player and he thought I was too little to play. I was his favorite kid out of the 12 and he always thought I'd get hurt playing baseball, because I never weighed over 132 pounds. But I was a catcher, so he was trying to find something else for me to do. My first recording session was actually through BowLegs Miller. The first time I recorded for him I was 14. When I was growing up BowLegs Miller's band and Willie Mitchell's band were the two biggest bands in this area. He was a trumpet player, comedian-type person."

"How did you start song-writing, was that at Stax Records?"

"Yes… 16 years old – David Porter and Isaac Hayes, I have to thank them for that. I never knew I could write; I always wanted to, but I never had an idea. They called me to do a session on Sam and Dave. They were finishing an album on him. I got to the studio, they asked me to help them write their song and I said I don't know anything about writing it, and they said, 'Yeah you do, you can play, you have great ideas, let's go upstairs and write this song. We'll show you.' We went up and in about 20 minutes we wrote the song, came back down and recorded it. The title of the song is 'I Take What I Want'. That particular song went gold on Aretha Franklin years later. The biggest record I have I think would be 'Love and Happiness' and then, maybe, 'Here I Am, Come and Take Me' – a group called UB40, they had the biggest record on it, actually. UB40 and Al Green; they're the only two that I can think of. I always tried to get artists to record it, like the album *Toots in Memphis* on Toots Hilbert. I told him somebody would record it and it was going to be a hit, and maybe two years later they did, and it was. I was listening to a group called Redbone, and then thinking about the way I'd heard music, perceived music, that would be *Indian*. I just tried to come up with something, two notes against each other, the way I did, "da, da, *da*, da, da, dahn, da", and just from there, but with Al Green in mind that I did it. It's the same thing; it only took about 15 minutes."

"How did you get started with Willie Mitchell?"

"I asked Willie for a job, to put a window in his home. This was a year after I was out of high school, and he had told me when I was about 15 or 16 that I never would be a good guitar player. And when I asked him to put this window in at his home, he said, 'No,' he said, 'I won't hire you to do that but I will hire you to play in my band.' I didn't believe it, you know. I said, 'You're kidding.' He said, 'No I'm not kidding, I'm hiring you to play in my band.' So we worked something out with my father. He adopted me, Willie did, when I was 18, and I started living with him

"Maybe six months afterwards, my brother Leroy, the bass player who had done this *Sunrise Serenade* album with Willie Mitchell while he was in high school, came into the group. Then six months later my brother Charles came into the group, who I didn't even know played keyboards; I didn't know he could play! When Willie asked me about him I was saying he can't play. 'What're you talking' about?' he said. 'Well I hear he's the best keyboard player in town.' I said, 'Well I don't know nothing about him playing.' So he joined the band after Al Jackson left the Willie Mitchell group to be exclusively at Stax with Booker T. & the M.G.s. Jeff Grill played drums with us but Jeff was a jazz drummer and Jeff kept telling Willie he had to find another drummer because he didn't like playing rock 'n' roll. So I found this drummer, Howard Grimes, with Flash & the Board of Directors and talked to him about joining the group, and he did. Then in 1966 we stopped doing live performances and went into the recording studio exclusively… and I had met different artists already, like O. V. Wright and Bobby Bland – I knew Bobby Bland from years back; he's in my family actually on my mother's side some kind of way.

Then Al Green happened. We met him in Midland, Texas, and talked him into coming to Memphis. It was just something about Al Green that was special. I knew from watching him the first time we played – backed him in Midland, Texas – he was something special… around the third song that he *was* special. Then actually Al had decided not to write anymore. He thought it was wrong and I told him his lyrics were right, but he just didn't know music and that if he and I wrote together, that it would come out much better. So that's when I did 'Love and Happiness'… *we* wrote 'Love and Happiness'. Got together, actually wrote the song watching wrestling on TV Saturday morning, channel 5, watching Jerry Lawler and all of them. Took about 15 minutes, you know, the whole idea, but when I got with Al the lyrics changed somewhat, but it was the same title and the same idea and everything."

"What distinguished the identity of Memphis, in your mind, from other music centers?"

"Well, the three-state area, for one thing: Arkansas, Mississippi, and Tennessee; the musicians come from there. The music, the whole industry, for years has been the three states, and being so close together with Memphis right at the border of it. I guess everybody just congregated here. Listen, everybody played different anyway; everybody played the same note differently, even. I know myself, but I don't know what it is that makes me know that it's a Memphis musician or it was recorded in Memphis."

"You were all together last night, playing in a little place on Beale Street...."

"Leroy and Howard Grimes and I've just done another album, which I hope to be released by early spring. I'm interested in doing movies, also, or scores for movies – as a matter of fact, the group just did the Tom Cruise movie "The Firm". Doing movie scores and playing in places like coliseums and things like that. Definitely touring for at least 90 days a year, but probably no more than that."

"We saw you in Paris last summer with Albert Collins, the "Ice Man" in a large stadium on the *peripherique*. Around 60,000 people there, and a spectacular performance, I must admit – with you on electric guitar and Charles, your brother, on keyboards and Albert Collins on guitar. It was a damned stunning. But back to Stax Records and Hi..."

"Well, Hi was bigger than Stax at first because Willie Mitchell was there. He won the instrumentalist of the year for five, six, seven years. Then after Booker T. & the M.G.s started recording, it would be between the two of them, from year to year. But Bill Black was also on Hi Records, and he had the song "Smokie", which was a million seller. I think that was before Stax had a million seller.

"With the Bill Black Combo."

"Right. You know, Bill played bass with Elvis Presley."

"What was it like to do a session at Hi Records...?"

"Choose a song or bring a song, you know, we had writers – one immediately comes to mind is Errol Randall. We would hear the song for the first time and sit down, the whole band, and go through the song, maybe 15 minutes; then we would record it, and it usually took us no more than three takes to record any song. We never rehearsed on a song to record it, you know, like days before or something, weeks before; never pre-produced a song, we just went in the studio and did it from the floor."

Surprisingly the Panther Burns were invited to open a heritage festival at the Midsouth Coliseum where Alex and I had both seen the Beatles play in 1966. Theirs was an abortive 30-minute set due to scare of fireworks going off and their being pelted with a hail of girl's shoes and jellybeans. On this occasion of ours, Ronnie Hawkins was headlining. Hawkins was a monster talent who had made a transition from Arkansas to Canada where he became a star. He was gifted with incredible pipes – a voice that was a powerful as it was tunefully incomparable. The man breathed RnR like fire, and as always, he had a hot band. What distinguished Ronnie Hawkins, and Roy Orbison, and the best of the best, was that they weren't shouters; they were singers, and highly melodic ones.

Shortly before going on stage, Falco pulled yet another of his pranks. From the dressing room pay phone, he telephoned all three broadcast TV stations in town and told them in a disguised voice that Tav Falco and Panther Burns were going to commit some guerilla type provocation at the festival at the Fairgrounds, and they'd better get a TV news crew over there pronto. The caveat worked, and three network camera crews were at the stage when Panther Burns stepped out. On the six o'clock news that evening television viewers in three states had the dubious pleasure of watching Tav Falco hanging upside down off the apron of the festival stage bellowing the blues as only he could do, with his paragons of RnR thrashing behind him.

Tav Falco & Ron Miller, Memphis in May Festival Photo: BuZ Blurr c.1983

What most impressed me at the festival was the uncanny performance of Clarence Gatemouth Brown. He was a tall, lanky Texan who fused blues with a variety of styles and genres such as jazz, R&B, swing, country, and Cajun. He played a big Fender Jaguar electric guitar with a capo, but what was totally strange was that at times, he actually fretted the strings *behind* the capo! Then he would lay a white cloth over his guitar as he stood there playing, and his fingers would be picking the strings *underneath* the cloth. The music he played was enthralling, vibrant, and unique. Gatemouth was an original. But the astonishing thing about him was that halfway through his concert, he began to pin people in the crowd – from the stage,

Alex Chilton with modified Gidson, Memphis in May Festival Photo: BuZ Blurr c.1982

and started *reading their minds!* Gatemouth would read an individual's mind and then tell the audience over the microphone what that person was thinking!!! Those persons whose thoughts were revealed, reacted slack-jawed like, *how does he know that?* It was the most eerie and bizarrely preternatural phenomena I have ever seen anywhere. Gatemouth's set was in the afternoon, and I was stone sober, stone straight. I can never forget, and in vivid detail, how this sorcerer of the blues exercised these remarkable telepathic powers on a festival stage in broad daylight.

CHAPTER THE TWELFTH
JIM DICKINSON – GODHEAD, GURU, & ÜBERMENSCH

When Panther Burns were recording an earlier album for New Rose called, *Sugar Ditch Revisited,* in Phillips B-studio, Roland Janes was engineering and Jim Dickinson was the producer. Jim had just produced a track with Andrew Love and Ben Cauley of the Memphis Horns; and was elated with the modulated, sensual saxophone tonalities. Because Ben Cauley had been the only survivor of the plane crash that had claimed the lives of the Bar-Kays, Jim said that every note that comes out of Ben's horn sounds like *I'm just lucky to be alive!*

We heard Roland Janes speaking from the control room over the intercom, "Alex, you're holding back, we can barely get a signal from your guitar on the tape…" The output from the rusty derelict Mosrite guitar that hadn't had the strings changed since it left the pawnshop, was just the opposite as that of the hopped-up big Gibson 335 jazzer that Alex had played in the initial phase of the Panther Burns. The kilter of his Mosrite guitar reflected the present psychic predicament of the artist in that he had abated his drinking of booze, lost considerable weight, and had withdrawn to his room at his parent's home. His personality had lost something of its penetrating edge. Jim covertly advised Roland to leave Alex to his doldrums, and that they'd bump up the volume on the board and fix it later.

Ben Cauley, Sugar Ditch Sessions Photo: E. Baffle 1985

Not long after the sessions, on the day following his father's death, Alex left Memphis and moved permanently to New Orleans, the scene of Panther Burns' many underground triumphs. Eventually he bought a decrepit 18th century cottage off of Esplanade Avenue on the edge of the French Quarter. Later on, while he was doing a mini-tour of solo dates in Europe, his charming mother perished in a fire that destroyed her deluxe apartment on Eastmoreland. It seems she had left a pot on the stove, forgotten about it, and a fire was ignited that roared through the wooden structure in a matter of minutes. Occasionally Alex would return to Memphis invited on a festival to revive a Box Tops show, or to play a club date of new solo material, but he never seemed content with such reunions, and would ever speak of the Bluff City in negative tones.

While Alex was tinkling on the Mosrite and Falco was typically struggling with his vocals, I was taking a respite from my gophering duties and thinking that I had now begun to more fully fathom the mind of studio ringmaster and guru Jim Dickinson. Some six or seven albums later, I was again in a Memphis recording studio sitting across the control board from Jim as he was paused mid-production while the engineer was rendering some Panther Burns tracks. I suddenly felt compelled to find out even more about the mentor revered by so many, yet understood by so few.

"Yeah well, my family is from Arkansas. So I was born in Little Rock. We moved to Memphis in '49. Arkansas is a funny place, and Little Rock in particular. As with many Southern people, you really can't tell when somebody from Little Rock is serious or when they're putting you on. There's a very complicated Little Rock put-on that my mother was the master of, and still there are many things that she told me that I still don't know whether she was serious or not.

"Over the years it's been hard for musicians to escape from Arkansas. Rockabilly, it was a year and a half that was really *it*. It was like from late '56 to '58 when Elvis went in the Army and then *every*thing changed, and rockabilly vanished. I think that the commercialization and the sellout of rock 'n' roll can be measured alongside the deterioration of the friendship between Dewey Phillips and Elvis. I think the first time Elvis took Dewey to Hollywood, he was embarrassed. You know, Dewey was Dewey and didn't stop being Dewey, and it embarrassed Elvis. From that point on, I think Elvis made the decision: well, I can either be commercially successful beyond anyone's wildest dream or I can stay true to the personality that I developed in Memphis, and it looks pretty obvious what he did. Taking nothing away from Elvis, 'cause one of his true geniuses was that he could sing crap and still be Elvis. And the movies are the same thing: he could perform absolute garbage and still be compelling to his audience.

When Dewey was thrown off the air in Memphis, he went to Little Rock assuming that he could do the same thing there, and he couldn't. People hated him in Little Rock. Memphis is a unique place. Certainly Dewey Phillips could have happened nowhere else, nor could Elvis have come to the public and been accepted anywhere else on Earth. I have a crazy friend in California, who still wears ducktails and says that both true bluegrass and Southern gospel were destroyed by hand-held microphones. All of a sudden everybody wanted their *own* mic and that mix, that blend, and the bleed into a single mic stopped happening and it destroyed the music.

"The territory that was Southern white gospel and black gospel was exactly the same for rockabilly. Like Charlie Feathers said, the bluegrass finger picking and cotton patch blues somehow came together with gospel music. Even with the leg shaking, as Elvis said in all those interviews, he saw nothing wrong with what he was doing. He said that he had learned it in church. Go back to the Statesmen or any of those gospel quartets or quintets and there it was. The Big Chief, he did the whole spreading leg things. Big Chief was the bass singer in the white gospel group, the Statesmen. He had a moustache, but he also had ducktails. A lot of Elvis's shtick, especially the physical stuff, came from the Big Chief. And even the gold suit came from an enormously popular Baptist evangelist named Angel Martinez; he was Mexican, and he wore a gold lamé suit – he was a big deal. Elvis was just doing what he learned in church, so how could that be wrong? The thing that Guralnick's book about Elvis, is so erroneous about is – taking nothing away from the brilliance of Elvis Presley – but they treat him like he was a space alien, who just landed with this *thing* that he was doing. Elvis represented a way of life that already existed in Memphis. There were plenty of people doing what he was doing. Not as well, not as dramatically, but hell, it wasn't even his haircut; it was Robert Mitchum's haircut. All he did was go to Lansky's and buy some shirts – I did *that*! In the rest of the world maybe it was unique, but it was not that unique in Memphis. My father said to me when I grew my ducktails out, 'What do you want with a truck driver's haircut?' And that's what it was!

"Back then the racial division was so drastic; it was like a concrete wall. The black radio stations were WDIA and WLOK and the white were WMC, WREC and WMPS. And the racial lines – except for Dewey – were set in stone. When Dewey went on the air, after he played his intro theme, he would say, 'Oh-oh good people.' 'Cause that's what he was doing, he was playing good music to good people without color line – he'd play Sister Rosetta Tharpe, and then play Hank Williams, 'cause it was all good music to Dewey. As mundane as that seems now, in 1956 that was a revolutionary concept. If you go back to those original five singles that Elvis cut on SUN, in each case there's a black jump blues on one side and there's a country ballad on the other side. And that in itself is an *idea*. You know, who the hell was makin' records with ideas behind them? *No one!* Takin' nothing away from Sam Phillips, who I love like a father – I don't think that was Sam's idea. We all know that moment, where they first recorded 'That's All Right Mama'. When you read the various rock historians, most of the point of view is Scotty Moore's. He's the one who basically tells the story over and over: how they were just fooling around and they'd put their instruments up and all of a sudden Elvis started doing this *thing* and they just started doing it, and nobody did it consciously. Sam even said himself that he heard 'em doin' it, and he turned the tape recorder on. He didn't tell 'em to do it; it was not his idea. So Sam didn't know what was going on. Well, that's as far as most people take this story.

"You've heard the famous Elvis outtakes, from later in his life when he's really screwed up; the most interesting ones to me are the ones from the American Studios – the Chips Moman session – where Reggie Young tells him, 'You can keep playing the guitar if you want to, but it really sucks.' In these studio conversations you get a truer glimpse of Elvis's personality than you get from the slicked-up final product. The rehearsal takes are very revealing: where he's rehearsing the Ronnie Tut band, I guess in Graceland, and you hear him makin' fun of the lyrics – and playin' around basically. Again, you get an insight into the man's personality, and listening to that one day it dawned on me: maybe, when he was 18-19 years old, maybe *he* knew what he was doing. Nobody ever gives him the credit that, by God, maybe this 19-year-old truck driver *knew* what he was doing when he sang 'That's All Right Mama'. If you think about that, it changes the whole picture. And where did Elvis get – where did he hear 'That's All Right Mama'? He heard it on Dewey's show, of course! And that's where he got the idea of *OK, here is this blues song and here is this country song – what about that!* And nobody ever gives him the credit that maybe he had it planned, all of it! Even the movies, 'cause that's what he wanted to be, anyway, was a movie star; that was his goal."

"He wanted to sing like Dean Martin…"

"Yes! Yes! Yes! He wanted to *croon*. The first on-camera interview Sam ever did, it was very different than his subsequent interviews – what we all got used to seeing, when he was really puttin' on a show. He did it in the office upstairs at the studio – coat, tie, straight as if he was teachin' Sunday school class. He distinctly said, of course he changed his story later, 'I know you hear people say that I've said if I could find a white man who could sing like a black man I could make him into a star', and Sam said, 'I never had that thought.' Of course he realized that isn't what people wanted to hear him say so he quit saying it, but at this time he said it. And he also said, 'I heard in Elvis's voice…,' and he called the name of one of the Ink Spots. And that did appear in Elvis's voice when Elvis started doing the ballad thing. But Sam heard it then! So, it's hard to say what they thought they were doing. Yeah, Sam was just looking for *something* – for something unique, as he said over and over and over."

"He was working with black artists, too..."

"Up to that point, and the real question is when he stopped working with black artists, he utterly stopped. There was no gray period; he shifted gears completely. That would be really interesting to know why. Other than the fact that I think he felt burned by the Chess Records situation."

"Charlie Feathers would say that Sleepy Eyed John was the one who really broke Elvis in Memphis on the radio."

"Yeah, well, that was one of Charlie's backward statements. Sleepy Eyed John was a lot more professional than Dewey and therefore a lot more cautious than Dewey. He kinda waited for Dewey to do the dirty work. He was OK; he was a morning jock, also, but his importance I think has been exaggerated. Dewey's show had the impact it had because of when it was on – afternoon, right when school was out, and then he went on at night after he became more successful. But I don't think the importance of Charlie Feathers can be exaggerated. I think Charlie was a big part of what happened in rockabilly, not just with Elvis but also with a lot of people. I think he influenced the genre as much as anybody else did, and more than most. Think about this: if you were a producer and you were producing the young Elvis Presley, and you had heard something that was like magic and you wanted to get more of it – what would you do? You couldn't sit back and play records and say, *why don't you do this, Elvis?* 'cause there weren't any records of it, yet. I think Sam played Elvis tapes of Charlie Feathers and tapes of Harmonica Frank Floyd. I think Harmonica Frank was probably as important as Charlie in terms of turning that corner. Where did the hiccup come from, for instance? I think the hiccup is unquestionably Charlie's. Like "Tongue-Tied Jill" itself... Sam wouldn't buy "Tongue-Tied Jill" because, the quote was, 'It ridiculed the afflicted'. That's as close as Charlie ever got for sure, is "Tongue-Tied Jill". He had moments of brilliance later on. I really think it goes back to 'Tongue-Tied Jill' and the fact that he must've thought, *I've got it*, when he did that, and to have Sam just turn it down flat like he did – I don't think he ever recovered from that, personally or artistically."

"In my opinion, most everything Charlie touched was equally as brilliant."

"My father was a wholesale match salesman; he worked for Diamond Match Company. He was head of a district, and he just kept demoting himself until he was just a salesman. They kept trying to move him to New York; he wouldn't go. On Saturdays I would go around with him to warehouses. We were in this tobacco warehouse in West Memphis, and he and the warehouse guy were off counting cartons of clothespins somewhere, and I heard this music. So I followed the music until I went up these stairs and there was this glass door with a lightening bolt on it and *KWAM*. There were four, maybe, five black – looked like field hands – they were dressed like they had been picking cotton – playing music, and one of them was this great big guy. I could hear it through the door but I couldn't really tell what was going on. Then my father found me and we left, but I realized it was a radio station. So in my father's car I dialed it in until I found this *sound*, and it was Howlin' Wolf. Maybe he had some records out, but it was certainly before the album, 'cause I saw the album – first the grey one with the drawing of the Wolf on it – at Ruben Cherry's Home of the Blues record store some years later. And still as a little kid, I carried it up to the checkout cashier and Ruben said, 'Oh, you're gonna get the *blues*!' Howlin' Wolf was a lot broader character than you would imagine."

"What plantation was he on?"

"I don't know which one he was on, but either Dockery or Stovall."

"It was Dockery."

"No chord progression...and John Lee Hooker, I think, has been mislabeled as a Delta blues musician. They were both playing hill country blues; nobody knew what to call it. And the mystery of Howlin' Wolf – the mystery of his music – is second only to Robert Johnson, and only that because there's so much less of Robert Johnson. The impact, the strangeness, of Howlin' Wolf can't be equated to anybody."

"Do you think that's attributable in part to his leaving the plantation, then going to Arkansas, to West Memphis?"

"It could easily be."

"If you look at Mark Twain's writing about Arkansas in *Huckleberry Finn*, for instance, when they're on the Helena side of the river, and there's a mob over there and they're about to lynch somebody, they got somebody up on a roof, and there's a mob mentality portrayed. In the whole book, this is the most sinister passage."

"Yeah, even the dirt is a different color on that side of the river. The Mississippi is the dividing line. Back then, of course, it was almost impenetrable, I mean, you were on one side or the other."

"Albert King was over there, too."

"A true darkness. Of course Memphis is still not part of Tennessee, and back then, truly it was the capital of Arkansas and Mississippi. 'Cause by population, by demographics, however you want to cut it, there were no major towns in Arkansas or Mississippi; they were states full of small towns, and the capital of both these states was Memphis. Anybody's idea of escaping his or her environment began with going to Memphis. Maybe you were going to go to Chicago later, but by God you went to Memphis first."

"It was a gateway…"

"Yeah, and Mr. Crump was God… and some people got caught. I'm caught – I can't leave. There's something here I drastically need musically. I've tried to leave twice; it was a miserable failure both times. There's something here that communicates with musicians, unquestionably."

"Well, no matter how far I go, and I'm not trying to, but I can't escape Memphis."

"No, no. What you do is Memphis. Yeah, it won't come off. There's a real difference in the way you and Tav are perceived outside Memphis. 'Cause I've played with Tav in Nashville and I've played with him in New Orleans and the audience perceives him entirely differently than a Memphis audience does. And it's both a good thing and a bad thing, but I guess it's because in Memphis they know what it is – they recognize what may appear to be strange elsewhere."

"Well in Memphis Tav was never quite something that even audiences here could totally identify with; there was something of a mutation about his existence both onstage and off, really."

"Yeah," laughed Jim, "you realize that none of these people who are now great fans and interpreters of the hill country blues, without what Panther Burns did, none of them would be doing it. You all utterly resurrected R. L. Burnside. That whole phenomenon is a result, I think, directly of what y'all did with the earliest stages of Panther Burns."

"Well, it had an influence. I must admit that what I've heard some of the other artists do who connected themselves with Burnside later, outside of his own family, was somewhat misguided."

"Yeah, I think that's safe to say. You're being kind to them. What can you expect from a bunch of Yankees?"

"What was your first band?"

"The Regents, which was the telephone exchange in West Memphis – Regency. That's where we got the name. We played anything that was on SUN Records and Chuck Berry. We were really a rockabilly band. I like to call myself a pioneer of suburban rock, 'cause we were the first East Memphis band who played nothing but rock 'n' roll, 'cause it was all we *could* play. Everybody else at that point, they had some supper club music or some jazz or something that they could fake. We couldn't do anything but what we did, and it was rock 'n' roll. I played Orbison and some of the more obscure stuff.

"We really didn't relate to anything but East Memphis. We were playing first house parties, then fraternity sorority parties, and we were just the East Memphis band. There was Jerry

McGill and the Topcoats, but they were like greasier and we were a little more fraternity-friendly than they were. Jerry McGill, one of the stars of Eggleston's *Stranded in Canton*, was in jail at the same time as George Howard Putt. In an attempt to intimidate Jerry, they put him in a cell with Putt, and of course they got along like brothers. Jerry had a Gideon Bible that was signed by George Howard Putt: 'The Shadow Over Memphis'. They captured him in an alley not far from the old Sounds of Memphis studio.

"I've gotten to know Charlie Musselwhite, 'cause he toured with my sons and we did a little work together, and we're almost exactly the same age. He knew Furry Lewis and he knew Will Shade, and yet I never saw him then. The big difference was he went to Tech High School and I went to White Station, and he was that much closer to downtown where these black musicians were. He has pictures of himself with Will Shade in 1958-59, and then he moved to Chicago right into the thick of the blues community. Very erudite – he's very sharp. He's got the pure style. How we could have been so close in space and time and never met really shows how separate the worlds were back then. In Memphis, even to this day, everything comes down – all issues come down – to either race or where you went to high school.

"There was Tech High, it was a vocational school. It was the school in Midtown that you went to if you didn't go to Central, and Central was the social upper crust at that point. East High School was on the border of East Memphis – we at White Station thought of them as foreigners. They weren't quite far enough east, and if you went too far east you were in Germantown. When I came to White Station in the second grade, it was half suburban – what would become yuppies – and half farmers. Literally, in my homeroom in high school, there were two desk rows of suburban people, a blank row, which I usually sat in, and then two rows of farmer kids. It gradually shifted to where it became all suburban. I changed classes in the first grade. My art teacher had a navel jewel in her forehead, was from India. When I came to White Station I thought a terrible mistake had been made. I thought, *well this is obviously where farmers come from; this is a school for farmers*. It took me a long time to get over my prejudice. I thought we moved to Hell."

"In Arkansas I went to a backwoods school with loggers and dirt farmers. Up until sixth grade, many of the kids went barefooted winter and summer."

"Oh yeah, they would let school out at pickin' time, and for chopping in the spring, and I thought, *what the hell is this? These people get out of school to chop cotton?* White Station was a county school. East Memphis just grew up around me. When we moved in the county, we had three acres square; it was like a city block. Big ol' Southern house and there was a cotton field in front of our house and truck gardens behind our house, and a black community right down the road, which thank God, 'cause that's where my whole character comes from, is from that environment and the yardman that my parents hired when we moved here.

"So that stayed far from the Tech High School area where Charlie Musselwhite went to school and became integrated in the community that wasn't really Midtown, but more connected to downtown, just below the Pinch area. And then Alex Chilton was purely Midtown... Alex was about twelve then. I think of Alex as an art brat, because of his mother with the art galleries. Think about how small the art community was in Memphis in the '50s, and his father was a jazz clarinetist. Alex grew up on the perimeter of this tiny art community, which was Midtown. It wasn't until the '60s that, if you were in ballet then you were in ballet, if you were in fine art then you were in fine art, and if you were in music you were highly questionable; and these things didn't come together until the '60s, when they came together with a vengeance."

"Panther Burns were a product of Midtown, although most of our first nine months took place – our performances were downtown in cotton lofts. I knew the cotton lofts because TeleVista had rented a cotton loft on Front Street to do art-actions there. When Panther Burns started happening, I was drawn back down there. I knew what those spaces could be."

"That first show was amazing. I'll never forget it."

"Eric Hill rehearsed Tav the night before, just on the stage down there; we'd brought the stage from the Cotton Carnival warehouse, then we constructed an art-action environment around it."

"I was outside at one point, and the windows – it was like a cartoon, where you see the buildings pumping; it was literally like that. The windows were like, swelling with the sound. It was a remarkable night. I played with Baker and Crosthwait and Amy, wearing the mask. That was quite a show. Tav was still reading the lyrics off notebook paper."

"Yeah, the band had eight songs: four blues, three rockabilly, and one tango."

"And Tav was hoarse from rehearsing. Oh, that was fabulous, man. And Alex wouldn't get off the stage."

"Alex actually peed off the stage."

"Yeah," Jim laughed, "he had a great arch – it was impressive."

"But there were no bathrooms to get to..."

"Right...then Vernon Richards, Bill Eggleston's chum from Greenwood, was singing at the time. Ross Johnson and I were standing by the window and – Ross was always uncomfortable in public anyway – he was just getting ready to leave then Vernon started singing 'Gonna Tie my Pecker to a Tree' and Ross says, 'Well, I can't leave now, my *favorite* vocalist is performing.' Vernon's memorable lyric was, 'Last time I seen him and I ain't seen him since, he was jacking off a nigger through a barbed wire fence'.

"And David Evans, the ethnomusicologist, was standing there with his eyes spinning around like Mr. Toad in *Wind in the Willows* saying, 'I'll never forget this. I'll never forget this'. Unfortunately, I think he did. There's never been a folklorist who wasn't trying to affect the art. It's the great fallacy of folklore."

"Well I thought their approach was to record it with a minimum of intrusion..."

"It should be. Go all the way back to Lomax and that's not what it was. They all had their agenda; folklore is very agenda driven. It's not like anthropology. Those recordings should have been made by anthropologists."

"There's a heated debate now between anthropology and folklore. Cultural anthropologists have eclipsed – theoretically – folklorists. They've developed an antithetical relationship."

"I call it the Trobriander Effect, wherein you affect and notably destroy the thing that you discover that you love, by interacting too much. For the folklorists it was like: here, chew on this straw, or wear the checkered shirt, or bring the overalls next time. This seems like an innocent thing, but it isn't."

"Well, the ethos of Big Dixie and of Randall was a factor in the conceptual impetus for the formation of Panther Burns."

"Randall Lyon's importance can't possibly be over-emphasized. He was one of the ones who crossed all the lines and had a true artistic vision, apart from just stumbling along. He had intellectualized, probably beyond anybody, what was actually taking place on a day-to-day basis."

"It's true though, Randall was like one of those novelists who talks their book away."

"Yeah, there's very little art shell left one could call art because his performance – his very being – was the art. Again a perfect example of Little Rock. You know, how do you put your finger on Randall? There ain't no way. You remember that performance where Tav performed solo and Randall performed with the Band of Ones?"

"That was downtown in some off-beat room... maybe on Second Street."

"That was remarkable. I saw Randall do a lot of cool things, but that night he didn't even take his overcoat off. He was a star. It was *incredible*, and I tried to tell him that afterwards and of course it made him mad. You couldn't compliment him; that's not what he wanted. I think he was resentful. He realized how much he had given. Eggleston performed that night, too – the keyboard thing. I remember Tav had that new black guitar. I was really impressed by that guitar!"

"Falco got that Gibson on endorsement in Hamburg, Germany. It had mother-of-pearl stars inlaid in the fretboard; they just gave him the damned guitar. He still has it."

"The Bitter Lemon was right at the border of East Memphis, literally, and Randall was involved there, too, with John McIntire. But the Lemon could have probably happened anyplace. I think that was just happenstance as to where it was geographically. 'Cause what became Overton Square was certainly more concentrated in terms of an art colony or what would become kind of an art colony, and that's because of its proximity to the Art Academy in Overton Park – pure and simple. It was the graphic artists from the art academy who reached out first, who started to accept other schools of thought and apply that to their art. People like Jerry Finberg, who was purely a graphic artist, yet he's the person who introduced me to the guitarist, Charlie Freeman, and it was because he said, *You need to know each other*.

"Around what became known as the Beatnik Manor, John McIntire was viewed as a social enigma, but he was very open to other forms of art and other expressions. In that area Burkle's Bakery was a cheap plate lunch; it was a great place to congregate, and a good plate lunch. The local community resisted the changeover – *bare feet don't eat*, that kind of thing. So it was not like anybody was making it easy for us; it all met with considerable resistance. Especially when the first hippies showed up, 'cause then it got real obvious. I remember Bill Barth and Warren Gardner, in particular, who was the first one busted for drugs. Jim Arwood – he had a Karate dojo – he and two other people opened up the sandal shop on Third Street just off Beale, which was the first hippie emporium of any nature in Memphis, and they brought the heat sure enough, which is what I thought the first time I saw him – *oh my God, we've been getting' away with it; now it's over*. However, I resisted Barth; I fought against Barth in the musical community, 'cause I didn't think the two things should mix: the old blues players and the hippie musicians. And I was wrong; I was dead wrong.

"We did the first Memphis Blues Festival on a check that I had from Sam Phillips for 'Cadillac Man', which was like, $65, and Charlie Brown claimed to have put up $100 which I still don't believe, and a lump of hashish the size of a soft ball that Barth had – that was all the resources we had to put on the first Blues Festival. And Barth, had I known what was coming later, with the Steve Leveres and the real pirates that were coming, I'd a kissed him on the mouth. 'Cause Barth – say what you will about him – he loved the music. And he saw a bigger picture than any of us were looking at. Supposedly prison really changed him and embittered him. He was in prison for a good while, and it really embittered him racially, from what I understood. He got real bitter about black people as a result of prison, and moved to Amsterdam. One of the regrets of my life is that I didn't understand who Bill was, in time."

"Lee Baker was on the Blues Festivals. He came from an established family?"

"Yeah, Baker was Arkansas as well, it can't be denied. You can't get that stubborn anywhere but, God bless him, Arkansas."

"You all came together at the Bitter Lemon?"

"Yeah, and we all played the Blue Festival, but none of us played it together. We were the white boys from the blues festival."

"You had the Jim Dickinson Blues Band and Lee had his own band at that time, right?"

"Yep, well that was the first argument we had, was about whether or not to play mixed – not age mixed but racially mixed – on that first blues festival. And I thought the point was not to, at least initially. So I played with an all-white band and Baker played mixed. Then the next year when he did the Electric Blue Watermelon, let's just say I boycotted. This was the first year there was truly what could be called the Insect Trust. Randall and Barth and Robert Palmer and Nancy Jeffries had performed on the first festival, but it wasn't quite a band yet; it was more of just an art project. By the second year it had become a band."

"There was that Harley Davidson on stage."

"Yeah, Baker had all of the Buddha and the Uncle Sam regalia and he was wearing this dress that had big flowers on it, and he rode a Harley Davidson out of this set that was an outhouse, playing 'Stormy Monday' with a black horn section and a black rhythm section, who all thought he was crazy. They had no idea – they were just there making $10 or getting their lump of hash or whatever it was. But Baker, he was utterly right; I was utterly wrong. Fortunately I got to tell him that before he died."

"So Baker was living in Eads for quite a while."

"Yeah, with Randall, in an old schoolhouse. By then Moloch was no more; we were in Mudboy by that time."

"Now, at the end, Lee was living with his aunt."

"No – they both had houses on Horseshoe Lake. Lee had become like the groundskeeper of the estate for Colonel Bob Snowden – the Snowden family. If you go back ironically… the little cartoon, the racist cartoon, *Hambone*, that used to run in the Memphis paper – one of the running things that Hambone would talk about was 'Colonel Bob', and he was talking about Colonel Snowden. The old man was quite a piece of work. He had all girls, so Baker was the sole male Snowden heir. It all fell to him, like the menial tasks and cutting the grass and that kind of stuff, for 60 pieces of property. If you can believe the theory of how he was murdered, which I'm not sure I do, it was over that – over the custodianship. The 14-year-old kid that was convicted of murdering him and his aunt was in a family that he had just evicted from one of the sharecropper cabins, which was one of Lee's jobs – to go collect the rent. And ironically Baker, who was as non-racist as anyone could possibly be, in fact I usually say, *it's not what he was, it's* who *he was that got him killed*. It was his grandfather and the legacy of that family – just the wrong place at the wrong time. I've got a lot of friends, musicians and otherwise, who have died young from a multitude of reasons, but Baker is the one I just can't deal with. I can barely listen to the music.

"He was unique – what he did as a musician was so utterly unique – that something is gone from Earth. My son plays a little bit like him; Steve Selvidge plays a little bit like him, and I don't think it ever went across Baker's mind that he was having an impact. That people, kids, literally, were absorbing what he did, but they did. I can't bring myself to listen to it. It's like he put an emphasis on *every* note. There's almost a crackling to the way he played – every note. I could do a thing with Lee…now I've played pretty well with Ry Cooder, we got to the point where we could communicate mentally, and I've played pretty well with my son – we can literally play the same thing at the same time – but I could do a thing with Baker where we pushed each other up and out. Over and over like… *oh yeah, man*, and I can't do it anymore. It's gone from Earth."

"The Snowden family had a mansion on Central Avenue at Snowden Circle."

"Yeah, must have gone back at least one or more generation of big money, big cotton money."

"They owned Ashlar Hall?"

"Oh yeah, there were tunnels and secret rooms at Ashlar Hall that Baker knew about. For sale again, Ashlar Hall. You know Prince Mongo owns it, which is kind of ironic. Mongo is so mysterious. I'd always heard Mongo was from some Virginia family up east that paid him to stay away. Now we've lived in the area of Hernando, Mississippi, for 20 years, and his mother and mentally retarded brother lived in Hernando until not long ago, and Mongo would visit periodically. It was an old antebellum house that had fallen into disrepair – you know, the crazy brother in the attic, and a very Tennessee Williams type of scenario. He's been in Memphis since the '60s or '70s, just as a local strange person who runs for mayor periodically. But, he owns Ashlar Hall."

"He'd had some stellar visitation. There was a resulting lawsuit of some kind, and he was awarded an extraordinary amount of money by the court because he began to have visions. From the lawsuit he must have earned the money to purchase something like Ashlar Hall. Mongo contends he's from the planet Zambodia, sent here as an ambassador for an alien race

Furry Lewis Photo: Eugene Baffle c. 1975

of micro-midgets that would bring peace and happiness to Earth. He claims to have been born on Zambodia and was sent to Earth as a kind of Supermann riding a meteorite. He was obsessed with the number 33. He says he's 333 years old, says he can travel to Zambodia in 33 minutes (or 33 seconds if in a hurry), and he's awaiting the arrival of 333,000 of his fellow aliens. Downtown on Front Street he had Prince Mongo's Planet – a pizza parlor/art gallery/cosmic emporium. Panther Burns even played there once and Evelyn Young walked in and started jamming with the band on saxophone."

"I remember seeing the pictures in the paper of him in court, wearing his grass skirt with the skulls around his neck. *60 Minutes* or something like came through town and did this piece on Mongo."

"Procopé was another venue that was like a folk venue but also had blues where Lee Baker and Furry Lewis played. They'd become almost inseparable."

"Again, I'd fought with him about that. I said, 'Baker, Furry is so much better without you.' He said, 'I don't care – I'm playing with him anyway.' And of course it became necessary, I mean, for Furry really needed Lee. But at the beginning it was like just Lee, you know, *here I am; I'm playing.*"

"He took Furry to that movie set in Nashville. Whose movie was that?"

"It was Burt Reynolds – *W.W. and the Dixie Dancekings. Uncle Furry* they called him!"

"Lee told me that they tried to pay Furry with a check that day after filming, and Furry pulled a knife out on them."

"He didn't take no checks. The director – whoever he was – was giving Furry heat about drinking. 'Cause Furry drank a pint of whisky every day – that's what killed him. They put him in the hospital, dried him out, and he died. But the guy was giving him heat about his drinking and finally Furry said, 'Lookie here, mister, I could *be* drunk. Point is: I'm not drunk, but I *could* be drunk.' The next day Burt Reynolds brought him a fifth of whisky, in front of the director. Oh, Furry was a force of nature, man. He took Baker with him when he played on *The Tonight Show* promoting that awful movie, which really is a terrible movie, and Lee showed up with him, and they didn't – oh no – want to see no white boy on the screen, so they made Lee sit over with the Tonight Show Band. He was miked and everything; you could hear him, but you couldn't see him. Furry did "Going to Brownsville". In the middle of the song he stopped for the solo, and by this time Lee was taking the solos. Furry was just kinda hangin' out. So Lee is getting in the solo and Furry says – you know he called him Lee Bailey – inexplicably he always called him Lee Bailey – he's in the middle of the solo and Furry says, *Po' ol' Lee Bailey.*"

"So Furry was a Midtown musician, right?"

"Downtown."

"Downtown? 'Cause the place he was burned out in, I thought was in Midtown."

"It was closer to Midtown, yeah, but when we first did the Blues Festival he was living on Fourth and Beale – same place as Will Shade."

"Oh yeah, and Van Hunt."

"Van Hunt lived there, too. It was like an old blues guys' retirement home, almost. Fourth and Beale – that had been one of the famous whorehouses."

"Like that was the very beginning of South Memphis in the old days..."

"I'm not sure South Memphis was ever anything, really, until now. When they ran the blacks out of downtown, basically that's where they went."

"Well, Stax, wasn't that...?"

"I guess you could call that South Memphis, but when Stax started out that was not a black neighborhood. It was a mixed neighborhood that had been largely white. But North Memphis is important musically because so many damn guitar players came from there: Roland Janes being the first, and Travis Womack, and all the Frayser guitar players. It was something in the water up in North Memphis that produced very aggressive guitar players. Travis Womack was totally unique. He used to play a Les Paul with a Bigsby and he played with the Bigsby in his hand, and he picked in and out like that, with every note – he was shaking with the Bigsby. Charlie Freeman once said, 'cause people used to ridicule Travis and make fun of him, 'If he'd ever turn loose with that Bigsby, people wouldn't believe it.'"

"Was Miller's Cave going at that time?"

"I never go up there. You know, you need a passport. If you're from East Memphis you're not supposed to go *there*. Bobby Whitlock came out of North Memphis, too."

"What was your first record deal?"

"I signed my first recording contract with Ruben Cherry, Home of the Blues, and Bowlegs Miller was supposed to be my producer, and my manager was supposed to be a disc jockey on WLOK, called Hunky Dory. One of the first real problems of my career was when I'd call WLOK, and I didn't know whether to ask for Hunky, or Mr. Dory. It was a dilemma.

"Ruben Cherry would take me places where we were the only two white people. One night there was this event at the Flamingo Club, which was upstairs at Beale and Pontotoc over the Pantaze drug store, and Ruben didn't show up. They were presenting Rufus and Carla with a father and daughter of the year award, some black organization. So there were three white people there – Henry Loeb, who was the mayor; Steve Cropper, who was sitting on the dais; and me. I was sitting with Bowlegs and his wife. And you got the picture, Bowlegs had a goiter the size of softball on his neck, which you couldn't help but notice. We're sitting there and Henry Loeb is just glaring like that, you know, *what the hell are you doing here?* Cropper, of course, we knew each other; he was trying not to look at me. Legs said to me, 'I'd let you dance with my wife, but I don't think the mayor would dig it.'

"We never put out a record on Home of the Blues. It got sold to Vee-Jay and I got lost in the sale somehow. But, Ruben used to call me Little Muddy, 'cause he thought I sounded black. I thought I sounded like Ricky Nelson; it never sounded black to me, but I was singing blues. He would play my tape for a room full of black people and have them try and guess who it was, and they would guess everybody but me. Ruben Cherry was a very interesting Memphis person. Home of the Blues record store on Beale figured prominently in the whole scene… that's where Elvis bought his records. Ronnie Hawkins talks about it – coming over from Arkansas to go to Home of the Blues.

The store had been there for generations. A Jewish family. Ruben was kin to the Camps, who controlled the jukeboxes. But none of it could have happened without Buster Williams. The whole Memphis sound was dependent on Buster Williams at Southern Amusement 'cause he extended credit to everybody, and he pressed the records, too. Plastic Products was where they were all pressed up, in Coldwater, Mississippi. First, up there on Chelsea, by Chips' studio, but later the big plant was in Coldwater, Mississippi. It was the largest independent pressing plant in America. John Fry and I used to go down there 'cause we never even issued a thousand records. We were making them five hundred at a time – a limited run – and they'd do the limited runs in the middle of the night. So we went down there one night and Buster was there. He was a big, fat man with a real low, gruff voice. He was talking to me – he said, 'Boy, if you want to be in the record business, you got to get your hands in the shit.' He was talking about the vinyl mix, and he said, 'Stick your hands down in there, boy.' I've always been glad I did it.

"The studios were all in ghettos because of cheap real estate. SUN was different 'cause Sam moved out of the original studio in '58 into the newly built one on Madison Avenue."

"He moved out of the radiator shop?"

"Right, to around the corner on Madison in '58, and everything drastically changed in '58, anyway. My main guitar player Stanley Neal had just been drafted and my band was kind of in flux. Ronnie Stoots and Charles Heinz were the singers – pretty-boy ducktail singers – in my band. Charles Heinz made the second record on Satellite, 'Prove Your Love' and then subsequently was in a car wreck, broke all his teeth out and quit singing. He ended up a minister of music, I mean, he went back to the church and sang in church, but he never did rock 'n' roll after 'Prove Your Love'. But Ronnie Stoots, who became Ronnie Angel – he toured with the Marquees – was my singer. At this point my band – me and Ronnie and Steady Eddie Tauber and Rick Ireland – went to Ardent, which was in John Fry's house."

"Rick Ireland was in your band? He's the little guy I used to see at Phillips studio plugging in wires."

"Yeah, he literally formed the band that became mine. Rick Ireland started me in this hideous business. We recorded something and that's the first time I ever met John Fry, and we didn't stick. I mean, it didn't continue, it was just a hit-or-miss thing. Then, a couple of years later, I was married, living in the veteran's student housing at Memphis State, and Fry's house on Grandview – I could jump in the ditch behind the veteran's housing, and go down the ditch and come up in John Fry's backyard. Bobby Fisher, who owns a music store in Memphis, called me up one day and said, 'Can you write a song like The Kinks?' And I said, 'Yeah, sure.' He said, 'Can you do it in 45 minutes?' And I said, 'Well, I can try. What's the deal?' And he said, 'Well, if you can write a song, I'll come over and pick it up.' So, OK – I had a little sound-on-sound tape recorder and I went back in the bedroom and wrote this stupid song, and 45 minutes later here comes Fisher. I said, 'Well, I've got your song now Bobby, but tell me what you're gonna do with it.' He said, 'Well, I found this band. They're 15 years old and they all play great.' Well both of those things were a lie. He said, 'I'm gonna go to John Fry's house and make a record.' And I said, 'Well, you can have the song, but you gotta take me with you.' So the song was 'Back for More', the group was Lawson & Four More, and before the end of the day, Fisher was sitting there with his thumb up his butt, and I was producing my first record. So it just grew from there.

"When the university bought the Fry's house, we found the property over on National and built what is now called the old studio. We were under construction for six months, because we were next door to a plumbing supply house that had a short-wave radio, and in the middle of a session you would hear 'KFY-99D'. I'll never forget it, it's burned into my mind, and we searched and searched and we couldn't get an effective ground – we drove spikes into the earth, we did everything conceivable, and we couldn't ground out this radio station. Six months it took us to find this place between two of the bud cabinets – the rack that had the auxiliary gear in it. A screw had fallen down between the two bud cabinets and grounded through the paint, and that is what was pulling in the RF. So we were there what seemed like six months before we actually opened. My wife was the first receptionist and she claims that the first day that she put anything on paper – a bill or whatever – was 6-6-'66, which may have been significant, I don't know.

"When the incident happened with Lawson & Four More I'd been working for Chips Moman at American Studio playing piano, and I didn't know the difference between a producer and an engineer, because all the 'producers' in Memphis were engineers. It looked to me like they were all just retired guitar players. So I didn't see anything special about what they were doing until I met John Fry, and I thought I wanted to be an engineer. John told me, 'Well, Jim, I don't think you're emotionally suited to being an engineer.' And once again, he was right; I was wrong.

"What's John Fry's background in engineering?"

"John, at that time, had only been in one studio, which was a place down in Florida where all the equipment was plugged into an extension chord and they turned it on with a light switch. For John, it all came from books; he had more applicable audio knowledge than probably anybody in the city – certainly anybody that was actively sitting at a console. That always was what Ardent had to sell, was that it was cutting edge and it was gonna work. You weren't gonna have to fix it before you recorded, which was generally the case wherever else you went. Roland had Sonic at the time, which was mono and very, very primitive, and American was mono – just mono quarter-inch tape machines – and SUN was three-track; Stax was mono. When we got the first eight-track people were furious, the rest of the community. Chips Moman told Fry, 'You've just set the recording in Memphis back ten years.' And Fry to his credit said, 'Well you get ready for the dark ages.' The consoles – he built one for Stax and one for Ardent, and that was like the Starship Enterprise around here. Nobody had ever seen anything like that. Musicians, and I mean sophisticated musicians, like Tommy Cogbill, they would come into Ardent and just stare – *What's this?* – you know?"

"He was a bass player, Cogbill?"

"Yeah, he was actually a guitarist but he became famous as a bass player, and as Chips Moman's partner. Chips' first hit out of Memphis was 'Keep on Dancing' by The Gentrys. I knew Larry Raspberry, the singer, as a kid. I had refused a couple of road jobs because I had just gotten married and I figured, well I could either stay married or I could go on the road; I can't do both. So, I turned down a Marquee tour and a couple other things and it was kind of known around town that I wouldn't tour. So again, living in vet's village and the phone rings about 9:00 at night, and it's Raspberry. He's desperate. He said, 'Man, I got a number 15 record, a 15 with a bullet, and half my band just quit 'cause they're in high school; won't go on the road, and MGM wants an album from me and Chips won't cut an album until I got a full band. Will you go on the road with The Gentrys?' I said, 'Hell no, Larry, I won't go on the road with The Gentrys.' He said, 'Well, will you come down here and tell Chips you will?' And I thought, *yeah, sure I'll do that*. I knew Chips anyway.

"My wife and I went down, we got to the studio down at Chelsea Avenue and Thomas, in the middle of the for-*real* ghetto, about 10:30 at night. Chips says, 'Hey, you're going on the road with The Gentrys?' And I said, 'Yeah, sure Chips,' and I started talking to somebody; I didn't notice what was going on – Chips got up and locked the door, and he wouldn't let us out; he didn't unlock the door until noon the next day, by which time we had made The Gentrys whole first album and half of the second album. Chips says to me, 'Boy, you're too good to go on the road with The Gentrys.' And I go, 'Well, that's what I think too, Chips.' And I had my first job. The whole rhythm section was me and Tommy Cogbill and Clarence Nelson, this black, brilliant blues guitar player, and Clarence had to sweep up.

"Chips would just plug us in to whoever came in with whatever band, and Cogbill was a fantastic jazz guitarist – and he hated playing bass, and he didn't own a bass. So Chips had this real piece of crap Hagstrom baby blue plastic bass. I mean it was an insult to play the thing – sounded awful. He would only let me play with my left hand. Cogbill would sit right there beside me and I would double Cogbill's bass part with the left hand of the piano. I would come out of those sessions with my hand like a claw, but I developed a hell of a left hand doin' it. Chips, if his pill kicked in or something and he started feeling good, he'd say, 'Hey, Jim, you can chord on the bridge if you want to.' Much as I ever got to do. But I quit Chips to go to work for John Fry, because I thought John would teach me how to run the board and I could be an engineer. Well the first thing Chips did after I quit was hire an engineer. That was one of the brilliant moves of my career.

"The first thing I know of that Chips Moman did that was successful was as a writer. He'd written "This Time" released by Troy Shondell. He was like 17 or 18 when he wrote it. Then he did time – six months for income tax evasion in Georgia, and came to Memphis. The first time I saw Chips must have been '59. 'Cause Ricky Ireland, my guitar player, was going to West Memphis to Danny's Club to audition for Brenda Lee. There was a package tour and she had lost her guitar player or whatever, and Chips got the job. Gene Vincent was on the package tour and was there that day. He had his Stratocaster case laying open on the stage, and there was a .38 snub nose and a bag of marijuana in his guitar case, and I thought: *man, this is it – we hit the big time!* Well, Chips got that job and went with Brenda Lee to the West Coast where Johnny and Dorsey Burnette were just starting to write songs for Ricky Nelson. Chips – little known fact – replaced James Burton in Ricky Nelson's band; I don't know for how long, but he was guitarist for Ricky Nelson and then came back to Memphis and the proceedings began to commence, as it were. American Studios was already there, and Seymour Rosenberg and Don Crews owned it, and Chips came in – took Seymour's place.

"I graduated high school in 1960, went to Texas and I did two years at Baylor University, because there was a fabulous theater department there: Paul Baker's Baylor Theater. We had a room designed by Frank Lloyd Wright – it was an amazing theater. Because you had to stay at school to stay out of the Vietnam draft, I thought when I went to Texas that I was through with music. I figured that was it. It was just something I did in high school, you know, to have fun and be drunk. When I went to Texas, first people I met were musicians, and they didn't know anything compared to me. I didn't realize there was anything special about Memphis until then. Like, go back to Dewey: Dewey would play a record and he'd say, 'It's a hit!' Well, hell, I thought it was. I didn't realize nobody outside of 300 miles from Memphis had ever heard "My Gal Is Red Hot". I thought everybody had heard that. Well, in Waco, Texas, I was like a musical god. All of a sudden I had these great credentials that I was unaware of. So I fell back into music gradually.

"When I busted out of Baylor the second time and came back to Memphis – 1962 – folk music was just starting to happen. It was just too damn easy; I couldn't resist it. I went up to Cambridge. I had a friend doing a master's degree at Harvard, and I saw Kweskin's Jug Band and the Holy Modal Rounders, and I thought, *damn, and these people – they're playing my music.* I mean, *this is jug band, what the hell?* It's too easy; I gotta do it. So I started playing folk music. I wasn't quite through with theater, so me and two other guys rented space in the farmer's market; this is '63. We built a small theater. Well, the fire marshal wouldn't let us open, so we found – you know, the way you do things in Memphis – somebody to pay off, and it was one of my partner's, Phil Arnell's, uncles on the building commission. He said, 'How many seats have you got?' and I said, '50'. He said, 'Tear one seat out and you're not a theater. Because you have less than 50, and none of these laws apply.' So that's what we did. Of course I'd get

200 people in there. We were doing one-act plays with folk music as an opening act. Then on the weekends we were doing, for want of a better word – hootenannies – which always offended me, and they were packin' out. I mean, I was literally turning people away."

"Where was that farmer's market?"

"It was at the corner of Poplar and Cleveland. It's a Kroger's now. When we ripped out a wall in order to put our stage up, we found crossbeams that had bark on them – it was that homemade. Place was unbelievable; no way to air condition it or heat it. But, we did five or six one-act plays over the course of three months, and at the end of the run there was a discrepancy in the books. One of my partners had paid himself a little too much, so I had to compensate for it.

"Then I was the first person to rent the municipal shell. I went before the Park Commission and somebody who knew my father – played poker with my father – said, 'Yeah sure, you can rent it, but if you wait two weeks until the end of the season, you can have it for $75.' I said, 'Book it'. So we put on what we advertised as the First and Only Memphis Folk Festival and with people no one had ever heard of: Jim Vincent, Sid Selvidge and Horace Hull. Sid with Horace Hull was one of the best acts I ever saw of any type of music; it was like magic. Horace Hull was probably the most talented musician in Memphis of my generation. He was trained on a pipe organ. He would go into one of the churches by himself and do this Bach stuff on the pipe organ. But he had a longneck mountain banjo, and he and Sid had this incredible kind of Louvin Brothers tip, where they would go in and out of harmony and shift parts. Of course, then Horace was beautiful – he looked like an angel. They dressed alike and they had this kind of proletariat thing. I mean it was an unbelievable act."

"Horace Hull was hardly proletarian, I think."

"No, hardly. And couldn't speak a coherent sentence; he stuttered, but he sang like an angel. He couldn't talk between songs, but just sang. He brought the first real marijuana to Memphis, from across the seas in his banjo case in '63; which was also revolutionary.

"Anyway, we put on this show. Bob Frank was on the show; Valerie Lord, who was like a 13-year old girl with a Joan Baez voice; Colin and Kathleen Heath – Colin Heath went to the Ozarks and started building geodesic domes. I put one ad in the Thursday newspaper, 'cause that's when the movies changed and I put it on the movie page, and I went on what became George Klein's television show. It was *Dance Party* at this point. Wink Martindale had it for years. It was a guy named Ron Maroni, who later was arrested for some sex crime, who was running the show at this time and because they would have high school couples each week that danced, they had to stop because of integration. Nobody wanted to see white folks and black folks dancing together on television in 1963. I was on the first show where there were no dancers, and they didn't know what to do. So they talked to me for 15 minutes about this damn show that I was puttin' on at the Shell. Well, I had gone to Little Rock with my parents for the earlier part of the weekend, and they came back and let me off at the Shell – there was a traffic jam. There were cops there, I mean, I had packed the show. A dollar a head for people that *nobody had ever heard of.* So there was a picture in the newspaper of me with my guitar, the guitar that Sid Selvidge still plays to this day. One of the stupidest things I ever did was selling that guitar."

"That Gibson J45?"

"Yes sir. It was red, and I saw a picture of myself playing it and I decided it was too red, so I sold it to Sid. Really dumb. It actually isn't red anymore; I mean, if I had just *waited...* But I had my Bob Dylan neck rack in the picture of me in the paper, and they referred to me as the 'Decibel King'. I guess I was a little loud for the venue; I don't know. But the story also ran in the Nashville paper. Bill Justis, who had been one of the co-producers at SUN Studio with Cowboy Jack Clement, was in Nashville working for Mercury/Smash making what they used to call 'party records', where he would do an instrumental version of hits, just a string of hits. He had a plan to do a record, which they called *Dixieland Folkstyle*, which was going to be a

Dixieland band playing all these folk songs. He had seen this publicity, and I knew Justis halfway – he knew who I was, I'll put it that way – and he had a trumpet player that I had been in a high school fraternity with, and who played in my brother-in-law's band, named George Tidwell. Justis said, 'You know how to get a hold of Dickinson?' He saw this picture in the paper, you know.

"So Tidwell calls me up and says, 'Come to Nashville and make this. Get two more folk singers and come to Nashville.' Had I been smart I would have gotten Sid and Horace, but I got Colin and Kay 'cause I thought they wanted legitimate folk singers. What they wanted though was me, was like something kind of rough. Justis, who was not a racist, had always referred to what I did as *niggerbilly*, which is pretty good, really. So I get up there, carrying my banjo case with a bag of Horace's pot in it on the airplane, innocent as the day is long, and we're in the old Columbia Quonset Hut... "

"Owen Bradley's studio?"

"Absolutely. It was the Nashville cats: it was Bill Purcell, Buddy Harman, Bob Moore, Boots Randolph, Grady Martin – it was the *cats*, man. Five guitar players, a guy playing a banjo with a flat pick, and the Jordanaires, and three of the Anita Kerr Singers, and *me*, and we made this album – my first album. Justis was seated at the board saying, 'Give me some more of that niggerbilly, Dickinson.'

"Afterwards I got a contract with Justis and we did the New Beale Street Sheiks – the thing with Crosthwait and the jug band thing, which was really my first record, recorded at Sam Phillips Studio. When we went in to make the record. Justis had, I thought, booked this date at Sam Phillips. Crosthwait and George Gillis and I showed up Saturday morning, and there's Scotty Moore and Bill Black and nobody else was there – oh and the repairman, the guy who fixed the gear. And Justis had failed to book the date. So I said, 'Oh, come on Scotty, call Justis. I promise you this is real.' Bill Black liked me; he thought I was funny, so he said, 'Oh, come on, Scotty'. So he calls Justis and they set it all up and we made the record. Tommy Rousie – the repairman – engineered, and I found out later it was the only session he had ever recorded. Into two RCA microphones we recorded "You'll Do It All The Time" and "Nobody Wants You When You're Down & Out". I wanted to take the tape and send it to Bill; Scotty wouldn't let me have it; doesn't trust me. And I said, 'Oh, come on man,' and he said, 'No, I'm going to Nashville Tuesday and I'll give the tape to Justis.' Well, I don't hear back and I don't hear back. Finally I call Justis myself. I said, 'Man, what's the deal?' and he said, 'Oh, we have the tape; the record will be out Thursday.' I said, '*What?* That...that was a *demo*!' He said, 'Oh, man, you could never do it that bad again.' And I said, 'Bill, you have no concept how bad I could do it.' What happened: I got reviews in *Cashbox*, in *Billboard;* Chet Atkins tried to buy it. People thought it was a hit, 'cause it was so weird."

"And this is with Jimmy Crosthwait on washboard?"

"Crosthwait on washboard. He had been playing a washboard three days when we did the record. But the record came out on Thursday, and that Sunday the Beatles were on Ed Sullivan for the first time."

"Folk music kind of started to..."

"Ended. The whole American record industry was over for six months. The record got played in Nashville. John R. played it twice on his radio show. The first time he said, 'There's some kind of noise going on in the parking lot and I'm going to drop the microphone out the window and see what it is.' Then he played my record. The second time he said, 'I've been in the music business for 30 years – this is without a doubt the worst record I ever heard.' Then he played it," Jim chuckled.

"But that first record you did at the Quonset Hut with Justis, that wasn't an instrumental record..."

"No, I was singing lead, and the Jordanaires and the Anita Kerr Singers were singing background."

"Was that your material?"

"It was like corny folk stuff, like 'Michael Row Your Boat Ashore' and that kind of thing. There had been a record called 'Midnight in Moscow' which was instrumental. The idea was to have like a Dixieland band, like on 'Midnight in Moscow' – kind of jacked-up Dixieland – playin' behind this folk material. There's a pretty good version of 'St. James Infirmary'. The rest of it is pretty corny."

"You had Grady Martin on guitar?"

"Yep, and Fred Carter from Arkansas."

"It's come out that on 'Train Kept a Rollin' that Owen Bradley recorded at the Quonset Hut with the Johnny Burnette and the Rock 'n' Roll Trio, it was actually Grady Martin playing guitar."

"I would believe it. Takin' nothing away from Paul Burlison, but he couldn't play the part. I mean, he didn't even know how it was done – the pitch string, fugue thing. It makes more sense than what I had heard, that it was Dorsey Burnette playing guitar; I don't think so. It makes perfect sense it was Grady Martin. And the first recordings, "You're Undecided" and "Tear it Up" – it's the same thing; it doesn't sound like Burlison. "You're Undecided"… that's a very underrated song. That's what the Rock 'n' Roll Trio did when they won the Ted Mack Amateur Hour in New York, was "Tear it Up" and "You're Undecided". They were hot band, too – *phew*. I used to sneak out of my house when they played at the Bon Air club down on Summer Avenue in the Berclair neighborhood where I grew up, and we couldn't get in but they had one of those metal speakers in the parking lot. I used to listen to them on that metal speaker.

"Everybody like Jim Stewart and Chips Moman and Homer Ray Harris, who all ran studios, I think they all saw the possibility of what Sam Phillips had done, and didn't see why they couldn't do it, too. Stax, originally Satellite, was in a barn in Brunswick, Tennessee, behind a Dairy Queen, first time I was ever in it. Jim Stewart and Estelle Axton had borrowed money on Estelle's husband's house and bought just barely enough equipment to cut a tape. "Last Night" was recorded there; "Gee Whiz", too, I guess. Chips was the engineer/producer per se at that point at Stax and when they moved to the movie theater, and he and Jim had a falling out, he bought Seymour out of American Studios, as I said.

"Lyn-Lou was initially Bill Black's studio. Willie Mitchell – he was an artist and an arranger, but he didn't emerge until after Ray Harris was gone from Hi records. Then the emphasis changed instantly from the Bill Black Combo sound, which was very rigid and tight and white. But that's where the basis of their success was, from those white records, which sold an incredible amount because they were jukebox hits. Joe Coughi at Poplar Tunes and Myra Camp with Camp Electronics had the jukebox companies. You could sell a half million records to jukeboxes alone back in those days.

"The studios that emerged in Memphis in the '60s were all really low level, very *un-*technical facilities, where basically everybody was just an old guitar player who plugged some wires together. There was nothing sophisticated until Ardent, and subsequently Stax. And Stax was an accident. When you look at Jim Stewart or Estelle Axton, it's very hard to equate them with the idea of recording black music. It was Packy's idea, Estelle's son. He brought in the band from the Plantation Inn. He brought Ben Branch and the Largos to the old studio. Neither Jim Stewart nor Estelle would've ever had the idea of, *Oh, let's go get some black musicians and cut some R&B.*

"Jim Stewart was a hillbilly fiddle player. I think the brilliance of Jim Stewart – which the longer I live the more respect I have for Jim Stewart – was that he could see what was going on and what was proceeding in front of his eyes and he could follow that. When a door opened, he was smart enough to stick his foot in the door, rather than belligerent, typical Memphis *no, I'm gonna do it my way.* So I'm not taking anything away from Jim, I'm just sayin' it wasn't his idea; it was Packy's idea. It was Packy Axton , and you won't hear this from anybody else in this building, but it was Packy who brought Stax inadvertently to Ardent. Because Packy tried to strangle Jim and they had a bad fight, and he was barred from the studio at a certain point. So he and his partner – black partner Bongo Johnny Keyes – started recording at Ardent. And the people at Stax heard it and went, *damn! Let's go there!*

"When he had the fight with Jim he went to LA and he made a record with Montague, the famous black 'Burn Baby Burn' disc jockey. The group was called The Packers; the side was called "Hole in the Wall" and it was a semi-hit. Packy got screwed on the deal so he came back home, and he started recording the same kind of phony instrumentals on a band he called The Martinis, which was Carl Cunningham, a brilliant drummer that died in the plane crash with the Bar-Kays and Otis Redding; James Alexander; Teenie Hodges; and Willie Mitchell's oldest son, Hubbie. Packy would record these instrumentals and as Fry used to say, *sell 'em by the inch*. I mean, he'd just cut off two minutes, three minutes, however much he wanted.

"The people at Stax heard this stuff, and their stuff sounded like it was coming through petroleum jelly compared to Ardent. They heard the stuff and pretty soon here comes Al Bell, and a relationship was formed. Generally they would record band tracks in their studio and then come to Ardent to bump it up, 'cause we had an eight track when they had a four track. The same thing brought Chips there, initially. Dan Penn is the one who came from American first, and then Chips came afterwards, because he heard the stuff and what it sounded like. Of course with eight tracks, they had another track for strings and horns and voices, and it was that much better. Willie Mitchell had his own 8-track, an old tube 8-track, but he didn't have a console that would mix like Fry's. And Cosmo from New Orleans – this is back when it was a four track – Cosmo Matassa, he recorded without a console. He plugged the mic straight into the back of the tape recorder. The first time he came to Ardent, Fry asked him – they were talking about gear and whatever – what kind of mixing board…and he said, 'Well, I don't have a board; that's why I'm here.'

"But Willie – I remember this vividly – he and Joe Coughi from Pop Tunes showed up together the first time. Coughi had a big ol' jar of pig's feet; he was eating pig's feet, and drinking this black Italian coffee that looked like motor oil. Coughi looked like an old man when he was a young man. I don't think John Fry knew quite what to think, why they were there. Willie had this homemade eight track, like mine, with the old tube electronics. It was really noisy, and Fry had this brand new gorgeous Scully tape recorder. John puts the tape on and punches play, and it hits the head and you hear this, 'Sssssss' like a nest of snakes. Fry says to Willie, 'Ah, well, I think you got a little noise there,' and Willie says, 'Yeah, it sound good, don't it!' But they saw Fry as a rocket scientist. It was like, *Oooh… do magic*. The R&B guys would just stand around in awe. John Fry always wore a tie, not a coat, but a white shirt and a tie, and when he started to work he would take that tie and flip it over his shoulder. He was just a kid, you know. He was 20 years old."

"How about Dan Penn …?"

"It's hard to say why Dan left Muscle Shoals. Probably conflict with Rick Hall, because they're two very strong personalities. He came to Chips as a songwriter, but like me he wanted to be an engineer, who produces. There was a group called Ronnie and the DeVilles. Ronnie Jordan, who later became a pretty famous disc jockey and recorded for a record that I produced for Hip, which was the Stax white label, as the Honey Jug. When I was working for Chips, basically his two main acts were the Gentrys and the DeVilles, and I guess their biggest record was "Cindy's Carousel". But Ronny was real smart aleck, and Chips hated him. I used to tell him, I said, 'Chips, look man, Raspberry's OK, but this Jordan kid is really hot.' 'Ay, little bastard,' he said. So it reached the point where he told that group that he wouldn't record 'em with Ronnie, so they fired Ronnie and hired Alex, and it became the Box Tops. And right at that point Chips was so pissed off at him that he said to Dan Penn, 'Hey, you wanna produce – produce this.' So they showed up for their first session thinking Chips was gonna cut it, and it was Dan Penn. They recorded "The Letter". It was the second time Alex had ever sung into a microphone. He now says he was 15; the math works out to 14. It was right before his birthday, and as they say: the rest is history.

"The first album was the group – the kids playing. Well, imagine how mad it made Chips, when it was a hit. So the second album Chips told 'em they had to record with the rhythm section – Reggie Young and the American rhythm section. "Cry Like a Baby" is the first thing with the studio musicians on it. That album, the second album – the *Cry Like a Baby* album – which was made at the same period of time as *Dusty in Memphis*, the Dusty Springfield album, those two records to me are the high water mark of pop music in Memphis. I don't think it ever got better than that. And if you listen to them, you can even hear a similarity. That second Box Tops album, which Alex won't even talk about, is brilliant. There's a song called "Weeping Analeah", another called "Deep in Kentucky" – I mean, if they were released now they would sound contemporary. Dan Penn mixed them at Ardent; that was the first time he came to Ardent. I had left Ardent at that point, but I was fascinated by Dan Penn. I would come and sit in the reception area and listen to him through the wall. 'Cause Dan Penn is real country and he has a very hardheaded belligerent approach to what he does. I learned a lot from his mistakes."

"Chips Moman played guitar…?"

"Oh Chips was spectacular, on things that he's un-credited for – he played on some of the Joe Tex records before they had enough money to hire Reggie Young. The original American rhythm section, half of it had come from Stan Kessler's group, was Reggie Young on guitar, who had been with Eddie Bond and the Stompers when he first came to Memphis; Tommy Cogbill playin' bass; Bobby Woods playing piano; Bobby Emmons playing organ; and in the case of both *Dusty in Memphis* and the Box Tops, Spooner Oldham as well, playing electric piano."

"Where is Spooner Oldham now?"

"He's playing with, of all people, the Drive-By Truckers, which is David Hood's son's band – Patterson Hood. I think they still live in Alabama, most of them. Spooner's been in and out of Nashville for years – played with Neil Young for a while, Dylan during the gospel period. Brilliant – a *brilliant* musician. Oh, I left out Gene Chrisman, the drummer – utterly unique drummer. The second best drummer I ever heard come over a microphone."

"Who's the best drummer?"

"Oh Jim Keltner in LA, without question. All the other drummers are in one category and Keltner is over here by himself – he's that good. But Chrisman is probably more unique in his own weird way. First time I saw Gene Chrisman I was working for Chips, and this weird looking guy with his hair all standing out from his head came in the back door and started taking the drums apart and leaving with them. I thought he was stealing the drums and he looked so weird I was gonna let him, but it turned out to be Chrisman. But they were Stan Kessler's band. Tommy Cogbill was Chips' partner, and he basically just hired 'em away from Stan. Then the band that became the Dixie Flyers, which was Charlie Freeman, Tommy McClure, Sammy Creason and me, same thing: Jerry Wexler at Atlantic hired them; it didn't cross my mind about them being in Stan's group, and I negotiated the deal. Stan still won't believe that. I've apologized to him. There's no doubt about it, I did Stan Kessler wrong. I freely admit it."

"Stan Kessler produced Panther Burns' first effort in the studio at Phillips. Mid-stream, the band pulled out to move to Ardent because they wanted more of a live sound, but Stan could hardly be second-guessed when he said, *I've never heard anything like this – these boys don't even play in meter.*"

"I used to describe Tav, and I hope you don't take this the wrong way, I'd say, 'Tav can play in one rhythm and sing in another rhythm, and neither one of them be right.' Always amazed me he could do it… and not stop. That was the importance of Mudboy. Somebody said about Mudboy that we would reach the point where any other band would stop and we would extend it. That's what we were trying to do."

"The club scene followed a certain evolution…?"

"In Memphis in the '50s there was no liquor by the drink. The significant musical clubs

Matchbook Courtesy of Jim Cole

were in West Memphis. There were two redneck joints, which were Danny's Club and Cotton Club, and there was the Plantation Inn, which was black music for white people. Plantation Inn is where what they claim the Memphis sound came from: Ben Branch and the Largos and before that, Phineas Newborn, Sr., Phineas' father with the family band, and that's where the concept of the light horn section, the heavy rhythm section literally came from. Everybody my age, every band that called itself a band, played "Stormy Weather", and that's where it came from, from the Largos' arrangement. The "5" Royales would come through town periodically and that's where they performed. They both affected the Memphis community and were affected by the Memphis community. If you wake Steve Cropper up in the middle of the night, tonight, and ask him who he's trying to play like, he's going to say Lowman Pauling, the guitar player for the "5" Royales. 'Cause he was like, the coolest thing anybody ever saw in 1959. "Dedicated to the One I Love", "The Slummer the Slum", "Think" – a lot of stuff. For a while they were on Ruben Cherry's Home of the Blues label.

   "Club-wise, there was nothing in Memphis to compare with the Plantation Inn. Prince Gabe and the Millionaires played at the Whirlaway on Lamar Avenue; he used to sneak me in the back door. But it was real small. The Manhattan Club was Willie Mitchell's home base, and what made Willie unique was that that band, which was largely the Hodges family, could catch a groove at a real low volume, so that it was a little more acceptable to white folks. These are strictly white clubs now, you got to understand. This was utterly, racially segregated: black musicians only – no black *and* white musicians. It was literally illegal to play with black musicians. Herbie O'Mell will tell you he had the first club with an integrated band – the Penthouse.

"Plantation Inn was like a typical roadhouse from the '20s or '30s. It was like something back in time, because it was a plantation-looking structure. It had been there for God knows how long. My parents went to it. It was owned by Morris Berger; he was white. One of the places when they were looking for Hoffa's body, one of the things they dug up, was the parking lot at Pancho's Restaurant which replaced the Plantation Inn. There was some connection to the Berger family. They just had a big nostalgic celebration of the Plantation Inn; they were talking about the black musicians and the white. It was never pointed out these black musicians had to come in the back door and sit in the kitchen. It was the *Plantation* Inn – it was a whole racist scene. Plantation Inn was right as you first got to where the old highway curves down into West Memphis – before you get to Earl's Hot Biscuits.

"Sunbeam Mitchell had Club Handy, which was on Beale St. at Hernando. Upstairs was the hotel, where most of the musicians stayed, there was a whorehouse, and Ernestine & Hazel's on Calhoun St. was the same deal. It was all the same people; it was Sunbeam Mitchell's widow. Later Sunbeam got the bowling alley and made Club Paradise, which was off Crump Blvd. between Annesdale and the Missouri Pacific train yards. Abe Plough, the cosmetics and pharmaceuticals tycoon actually owned it. I've always thought that Sunbeam was fronting it for Abe Plough because it was too big – it was too big an operation. Abe Plough had his hand in everything; he and Philip Belz. I remember reading an article in *Time* magazine, it was talking about downtown Tel Aviv, and said that this huge, multi-block area was owned by two men in Memphis, and it was Abe Plough and Philip Belz.

"Philip came to town and started a furniture store, and then a furniture manufacturing plant, and then a foam rubber plant – that sold foam rubber to the furniture plant, and he bought up unwanted real estate property, that people thought he was crazy for buying. The first of which was Poplar Plaza. He bought all the outlying areas that became shopping centers. You hear all this stuff about the reason the interstate highway didn't go through Overton Park and the center of Memphis? The real reason was, the exchange would have been right at Philip Belz's driveway, and it just wasn't gonna happen. At one point Colonel Snowden, Baker's grandfather, and my great-uncle owned the Peabody. It had been closed; it was closed and vacant, and everybody said, 'Tear it down – it's worth more as a parking lot,' and the Belz family took it over and restored it in the '70s. Then they turned it over to Gary Belz, their teenage heir. In West Memphis, Danny's Club was strictly a redneck joint. It was just before you get to the dog-racing track. They had dancing girls."

"Where did Charlie Rich play?"

"He'd play at the Sharecropper solo – that was downtown in the old city bus barn. Sometimes Reggie Young would come in and play with him. Bill Justis always loved Charlie Rich. He was a jazz player. He showed up from Arkansas as a piano player and Sam Phillips just pulled it out of him, so to speak. I've heard Sam say that it was one of his regrets that he didn't get what he wanted from Charlie Rich. Sure, he had roots in country music and rock 'n' roll, but he was a jazz musician and nobody ever let him play jazz. He wrote "Lonely Weekends" for Jerry Lee Lewis and Jerry Lee wouldn't record it, or didn't record it for whatever reason."

"What about the murder of Al Jackson? Do you think that was like a conspiracy?"

"Everybody lays it off on the wife. I tend to think it was something different… because the studios were very separate. If you worked for Chips, you didn't work for Stax and vice-versa, and Al Jackson was *the* drummer at two studios. There were several attempts by organized crime to move into the Memphis music community. If you wanted to hurt the Memphis music community, in a way that they couldn't overcome, killing a drummer was the way to do it. I think it goes deeper than the wife. Al Jackson was a real gentleman."

"Do you think it's a coincidence in that the six months previous to the assassination, she'd shot him with a pistol?"

"I really do think it's pure coincidence. I think that was just a domestic dispute. 'Cause it was so obviously a hit, and I don't think she could have put that together. There is no organized crime in Memphis to this day, and there are reasons for that. Attempts to take over or become partners, shall I say, with individuals in the Memphis music community have all failed. So, I think it was retribution. You probably won't find anybody else who says that, but that's what it looked like to me. It was too much of a big city hit; I don't think it could have been pulled off locally."

"What was the purpose, other than just a vendetta?"

"Yes, just to hurt Stax and Hi. There was no replacement; there was no way to replace Al Jackson – period. If you had tried to make a move on somebody…"

"The Mafia had tried?"

"Oh, yeah, they tried with Chips, too. You remember Campbell Kensinger? That's why Chips hired Campbell as a bodyguard really for his family. It was like, people on the roof getting shot. It got pretty nasty a couple of times. I think the reason Sam Phillips retired was because they came to him and said, *OK, either you have a partner or quit doin' it.* And he quit doin' it."

"There was the same claim made that this is why Sam Phillips sold Elvis to RCA."

"Never heard that, but it could easily be. Now the reason I think Sam sold Elvis is, if you look at those first five records – there's a jump blues on one side and a country song on the other, and that's an idea, I mean, that's a concept. I think that when Sam sold Elvis that idea was almost gone, 'cause you look at the rest of Elvis's career, and there are only little spikes where you can hear that again; and I think Sam knew it. I think Sam knew that he was at the end of the road, creatively, with Elvis Presley, and he had just discovered Jerry Lee Lewis – where the road went on forever."

"What was the pitch from the Mafia to someone like Chips Moman?"

"Meet your new partner."

"What about the Lucchesi family in this sphere…?"

"I don't think so. I think that they certainly were connected, but in an unorganized way. At one point, during the Crump era – this is documented – the *boys* came to town, airplane landed, when they got out of the airplane, there was a line of state troopers – who at the time were referred to as 'Crump's Cowboys' – and they got back on their plane and went away. There are crime figures in Memphis who can't leave. It's like a home – not home base – but home free if you're playing tag. Like, either we'll kill you, or you can go to Memphis. It's literally that, and it's because there is no organized crime here. And like, the Mafia's very ashamed of their gay membership, so they're all here. And I mean, I've dealt with them, one to one. I know this to be the fact."

"Well, how do they survive here? Do they do things here?"

"They have to keep the lid on it; it has to all be small and unconnected. Think about it – a town this size, with the history this town has, there should be organized crime here, and there's not. There's plenty of *dis*organized crime."

"When we're talking about the Mob, you were talking about the Mafia – like Italian…"

"Yes, as opposed to the Dixie Mafia which is everywhere."

"But you're talking about all outside people; these are not people that grew up here out of the roots of Germans and Italians that migrated."

"No, these are all people who have come here because if they leave here somebody will shoot 'em. I don't know where all they came from…especially during the '70s and the active drug era. Again, it became obvious to me that I had not been lied to – that this was true."

"Campbell Kensinger also acted as a body guard on a few Mudboy and the Neutrons shows…"

"Well, Herbie O'Mell was one of Campbell's closest friends and probably the only person who could control him. I'd known him since high school. Me and Kensinger snorted yellow jackets in the room that used to be Fry's office, and as we sat there with tears rolling down our face – 'cause you know, with yellow jackets you're not supposed to snort 'em – Campbell looked at me and he said, 'Man, you know the difference between you and me?' I said, 'What's that Campbell?' He said, 'You really like this.' It was unfortunately true."

"So Kensinger did this bodyguard thing as just like something he did with friends – he wasn't a professional bodyguard?"

"Oh yeah, he was. He was trained in eight martial arts; he was at the Bay of Pigs. He was very much a professional. He got busted for something after high school, wherein he was given the choice of join the Marines or go to prison. It was like, not be a Marine, but train, and he was in Hawaii training – the Alpha 66 force, which is who went into the Bay of Pigs. When asked if he was at the Bay of Pigs, Campbell's reply was, 'Shooting women and children.'"

"He was shot in his house…"

"No, it wasn't his house. I think he was assassinated by the police. The motorcycle gang that he had, that he took it over, was the Family Nomads, which was the Family and the Nomads put together. He had taken what was a rag tag motorcycle gang of methed-out hillbillies and made them into a paramilitary force. He'd take them out in the country and drill them and put them through a weekend of maneuvers, and he'd beat the shit out of them until they understood what was going on. He had friends in the police department. As Campbell used to say, in any kind of organization there's two sides to the story, and he had friends and he had enemies – and the enemies became stronger than the friends.

"One by one they separated him from his gang, they separated him from his friends, they separated him from his dog, even – because he had a killer dog to protect him. He lived in what they called the Compound. He was bartender at Huey's at the time. The day that he actually was killed, to tempt him into this situation, this tattoo artist – real famous amongst tattoo artists – guy was brought in to town by somebody, who I figure was the cops, and they lured Campbell to this situation where he was by himself, as stoned as a human being could possibly be on every type of drug, and when Campbell got high he wanted to fight because he loved to fight and it made him feel good. And he went over to this guy's house to beat him up, literally, having already done it God knows how many times to the same guy. Broke the door down and was coming after the guy; the guy emptied his gun. Shot him nine times including through the brain. The last – he was alive when the cops got there – his last act was to throw a telephone at the police. And the guy who killed him, allegedly, had been on the phone to the cops saying, 'Kensinger's at the door. I'm not going to stand this again.' And supposedly the cops reply was, 'Smoke him and be sure he's done.' Who knows?

"They used to say in the early '60s that in Memphis you could play cops and robbers and be on the same side. They also said that the reason the Freedom Riders didn't come to Memphis was because they were afraid the cops would steal the bus. Machine Gun Kelly and that whorehouse that was on Fourth Street: the story from the Beale St. raconteur, Thomas Pinkston, how Machine Gun Kelly got busted was they had raided that whorehouse, and there was a big Memphis cop, I think he was vice squad, named Rainey, and apparently the Madame at that whorehouse was his old lady, as Pinkston put it. Thomas used to say, 'He was bootleggin' down on Beale Street at the Gray Mule, and that's how they done it – done messed around and got po' ol' Machine Gun Kelly.' He was just a two-bit thug, and they made him into this high-crime figure and busted him to get the whorehouse raid out of the newspaper.

"What they used to say as I was growing up is: *Memphis – the Jews own it, the dagos run it, and the niggers enjoy it.* That was the common phrase of Memphis. If you think about it geographically, it's been leapfrog from downtown Memphis to Midtown to East Memphis. It's been between the Jews and the Italians, just in the real estate aspect of who owns what. For instance, when I rented the curb market for the theater events, we couldn't find out who the hell

Memphi Insignia

owned it! Or who to even talk to. It turns out CBC (Catholic High School) owned it – 'Cadillac High School', and they rented it to this thug, that I ended up doing business with, for a dollar a year."

"I've also been told there were a number of secret societies that existed in Memphis."

"Well that's all part of the cotton hierarchy and they still exist. In fact, John Fry and I were both honored recently by Carnival Memphis, which is what's left of the Cotton Carnival, and it's all still RaMet, Sphinx, Memphi. It's all still there. The King of the Cotton Carnival this year is Howard Stovall – Stovall Plantation. His grandfather owned Muddy Waters' mother."

Jim rattled the small change in his pocket like gris-gris bones and slid back in his swivel chair with a sigh, heaving like an ocean of woe. I thought again of Alex and his innumerable rights of passage, and of his collaborator, Chris Bell, of whom I know little. "What is so esoteric about Chris Bell and *I Am The Cosmos*?"

"He's been largely mis-portrayed in the Big Star legend, in that they make him appear to be far more serious than he was. He basically was an *I don't care* kind of guy. I just don't see all this darkness that supposedly surrounded Chris; I never saw that. Even after Alex forced him out of Big Star, or whatever happened, I didn't see any bitterness. I played on some of his stuff after that and there was probably ill feeling, but it didn't wreck his life. It didn't destroy him and force him into suicide – that's all crap. He had a drug problem, sure, and he was probably screwed up when he hit the light pole, but..."

"Alex told me Chris was taking Mandrax that night he ran his car into a light pole."

"Yeah, I would imagine it's about that simple. Remember – you probably saw this, too, Alex used to do it – they used to shoot Demerol down their throat. Not injecting it, just use a needle to shoot it down. Which would do nothing but knock you out, really. I doubt if it would even get you high. Well the first night of Big Star *Third*, Alex did that with me in the control room, just basically to show me where it was at. 'Cause again, if you think Alex Chilton cared – you're sadly mistaken, because he did *not* give a shit. Chris may have cared a little more than Alex, but not much. I just don't buy all this darkness of personality, hell-bent for suicide crap. I just don't see it that way. He would ask me to overdub on something or 'Would you play on this? Would you do that?', and I would just do it. It was no more than anybody else in the community, really, who would ask me to play. That's what I do.

"The interesting transition, that I've never seen anybody touch on, is what happened to Alex in New York. 'Cause the Alex that came back – he spent a summer, best I can figure, in New York with Keith Sykes – came back a very different person, with the new voice: the new Jim McGuinn-Lou Reed voice. Where people say that Alex won't do the old voice… that's not true. He *can't* do it. I've heard him try; it just isn't in him anymore. When he came back from New York he was strangely silent, in conversation. He would sit in a room for hours and not say anything, which says to me: psychedelic drug experience. But, that's just a guess. He slowly came out of it, and as he came out of it he took the band away from Chris, and Chris let him. There wasn't much to take, because it wasn't much of a band. I'm not saying anything derogatory, because God knows my reputation is built on that record, Big Star *Third*, but it wasn't much of a band. They didn't play that much, they weren't active as a band, they didn't mix together as a band – they were basically over-privileged white kids who had a recording studio to play in.

"Artistically I'm very interested in decomposition and decay, and by the time they came to me with *Third*, it was well into decomposition and decay. The relationships were falling apart, Stax was going out of business. It wasn't just the group – everything was decaying around the group, and that's what I recorded. Many of the stories are exaggerated, although it did get a little hairy. Lesa Aldridge was the absolute muse of the record, and is in my opinion a musical genius. You get you one of these little homemade recordings they got of the KLITZ, and it'll answer that question for you. I recorded the KLITZ later on and I thought the stuff I did was good, but you should hear the stuff that Alex did, and the stuff they did by themselves. It's just barely even stuck to the tape, but it's just flaming brilliant. They have a version of 'Land of a Thousand Dances' they cut at ballad tempo, that's just good as anything I've ever heard. Alex reached a point on both records I did with him where he started erasing Lesa's parts, the things she'd done. I stopped him, on both of them. I said, 'No, you can erase that if you want to, but you're not going to touch *this*', because it was just so good. I think the contrast between my two records – I think Big Star *Third* continues to be significant largely because of John Fry, because it is technically so good, and because it is the last set of consistent performances Alex Chilton ever delivered. You can't find a place on that record where Alex is purposely screwing it up."

"That syndrome where you create something just so you can have the pleasure of destroying it…?"

"Oh, there are always little flashes of brilliance on Alex's records, but never any more than that."

"And *Flies on Sherbert*?"

"Oh, that was his revenge. As Alex claims he was excluded from the mixing of *Third* – which he was, but it was utterly necessary – I was excluded from the mixing of *Flies on Sherbert*. So as far as I'm concerned it's a very flawed record. I mean, I know people who genuflect to it; whole careers have been based on that record. I heard about a guy who wrote a master's thesis on the introduction to one of the songs – I mean, like the first eight bars. Supposedly the group Pavement was inspired by it. But I lost the mix. So much of it was recorded at Phillips through dubious equipment that it really needed a little fixing, in the mixing, and it didn't get it. Of course Mike Ladd is all over *Flies on Sherbert*.

"Mike Ladd grew up next door to me. He had the first big amplifier I ever saw. He was a couple of years younger than me. I'd be in my room practicing; I'd hear Ladd next door. He'd crank his up and start. He'd hear me and play along with me. He was just a hack kid; then one day he took this solo, and I thought, *damn! What's happened to Mike Ladd?* Clarence Nelson was the one who taught him, at Holiday Inn Records, which was something Chips participated in. Ladd's father was vice-president of Holiday Inn, and Mike had been down there hangin' around, and Clarence Nelson showed him. He's an amazing guitarist."

"Lesa was involved in that, too."

"Very much so. She's playing guitar and piano and any number of things on *Flies*. The only thing that remains of Lesa on *Third* is the background voice on 'Femme Fatale', which I absolutely refused to let Alex destroy. That may be the only place that she remains, other than as an inspiration. Like, 'Holocaust', which is supposed to be so dark – it's about Lesa's mama; it's not particularly dark. The thing I didn't realize about *Third* until recently is that it's about Midtown. There's geography behind each one of those songs. You can go down the list and say, well that's about Lafayette's Music Room, and that's about Lesa's mama's house, and it's all geographically about Midtown.

"'Nighttime' is the thing that got me. I realized one night when I was thinking about 'Nighttime', that it's not even really an album, it is a group of recordings. It was never finished, and when they finally put it all out this last time, they asked me to sequence it and they asked Alex to sequence it, and we both refused. I went back and I still had notes   I'm so neurotic, I still have production notes – and our ideas of what the final album was to be, were very different. Now, we agreed on the first song and the last song and everything else was different. 'Nighttime', which is now my favorite song on the record, I wanted to exclude. But, as I came to understand what it was about, I could see him walking around the corner down there at Cooper, up Madison, with the scarf; I mean, there it is – undeniably 'Nighttime'. And I can tell you exactly what 'Kangaroo' is about, and I may be the only person on Earth who can: Anita Kerr's niece, and she's married to Bob Simon now. Alex encountered her at some house party, and basically rubbing up against her butt in the party, was masturbating. That's what the song is about. 'I want you like a Kangaroo' – there it is. Alex let me know one night, in a fit of weakness, what it was about.

"Even the title; *Sister Lovers* was never supposed to be the title. Sister Lovers was the name of a group, a kind of side project group, when at one point Alex and Jody were going with sisters. *Third* was never supposed to be the title; the only title we ever discussed was *Beale Street Green*, which was from 'Dream Lovers', which was never on any of the records until the last time it came out – and is in fact, I think, the point of the record. The big thing that's wrong with all the versions of the record is that everybody has lumped the rock stuff and the dark stuff, and it was not supposed to be that way. See, Alex doesn't think the record is dark. I don't either, frankly. It's supposed to begin with 'Thank You Friends' and end with 'Take Care', and 'Take Care' to Alex is a little blessing. It's about terminating his relationship with Lesa, certainly, but it's nonetheless, in Alex's view, a little love song. It's sad, but there is a difference between sad and dark. When we went to New York and tried to sell that record, I was accused of destroying his career, people thought it was perverted and sick and evil. *Evil* was a word they said, and it isn't! It may be a little scary here and there, but I think it is a very sensitive, delicate rendering for Alex, compared to some of the other things he's done, which are, for want of a better word, more cruel. I don't detect any cruelty on *Third*.

"Where I gained Alex' trust, and he did trust me up to the point where he was excluded from the mix, was with my own production technique. Understand that I don't inspire trust – it's nonetheless necessary for me to get it from the artist. On 'Kangaroo' – at that point he had keys to the studio and he would come in the middle of the night to work on stuff, which is where the solo on 'Thank You Friends' came from, and which I think is one of the best, most coherent guitar solos anybody could find. This is a long way around to explain 'Kangaroo', but the first time he played me that solo, it was something he'd done in the middle of the night with Lesa running the board. The solo was chaos; it was dog shit. I said, 'Yeah, sure, that's OK, good.' So three or four days later he played me the solo again, and he had worked on it again, and there were parts of it that were just like the first chaotic version, but it was starting to refine itself. I said, 'Yeah, Alex, that's better.' Well, maybe a week later he played me the solo and there it was. Whereas if I had said, 'No Alex, that solo is dog shit – you have to do it over,' it would have been dog shit. Point being, he would work on things by himself and then seek approval.

"Well, I came in one morning and he said 'I've got a new track for you.' And I said,

'Alright, play it for me.' And he plays me the vocal and acoustic 12-string of 'Kangaroo', both recorded on the same track, with the needle just laying on the end and quivering. I listened to it, and Alex gets that little sarcastic, satanic smile on his face and says, 'Produce that, Mr. Producer.' So I said, 'OK.' So I went out and started feeding back and laying down the tracks one at a time – I think I did the Mellotron first, actually – and it really worked well; it worked right away. And Alex just kind of perky, you know, looking around. I was feeding back my Burns of London guitar – I still play that guitar – and Alex comes out and says, 'Can I play, too?' I said, 'Yeah, sure Alex.' He gets his Stratocaster and starts playing it with a drumstick. It was then that I gained his confidence.

"What I think I did for Alex, is I removed the yoke of dictatorial production, because Dan Penn definitely did that and Fry did, too, and Terry Manning before that. I didn't. That's why he came to me, because no one else had ever told him to do anything besides, *sit down and shut up*. He would come up with a crazy idea and they'd say, *That's crazy, Alex, shut up*. When I produced him, he would come up with a crazy idea and I would figure out how to do it. Most of his ideas were sound. The one song on the record that suffered was 'Downs'. Fry made the mistake of saying, 'Oh I really like that song. I could hear it on the radio; it could be a single.' Well, again here came that smile, and I thought, *oh, OK, there goes that one*. And Alex said, 'Oh, well that's good, but I hear the snare drum sounding like a basketball.' I said, 'There's a basketball right back there in the equipment room, let's go get it,' and it ruined the song, of course. But that's what Fry gets for saying the wrong thing at the wrong time. 'Stroke it Noel' was the title that was added later because he was making fun of the violin player who was a friend of his father's, Noel Gilbert. He had a bodyguard at the time, who was a friend of mine from high school; 'stroke it' was one of his phrases. 'Stroke it Noel' is brilliant and it leads right up to *Flies on Sherbert*. It's almost the next moment; is the beginning of *Flies on Sherbert*, to me.

"We made the album in fits and starts. It wasn't like a coherent, *let's go in for 30 days and make a record*. I remember three periods of recording. I don't even think about it like it was making an album. We were just recording. Had we jammed it all together it would've definitely gotten ugly and been bad. But that didn't happen as far as I'm concerned. I know at a certain point Fry said to me, 'I know you're not done, but you have to mix what you've got; I can't stand this anymore.' My answer was – he said something about how bad Alex was treating him – I said, 'John, I figured that was the way he always treated you,' which is what I thought. To me it wasn't that bad, but it wasn't my relationship. I can't judge it by that, but we were not done.

"The thing that pushed John over the edge was Slim – the ol' street alcoholic – that Alex and the bodyguard brought in to overdub. Slim – we were working on 'Whole Lotta Shakin' and I don't know what he expected Slim to do, but Alex brought him in, put headphones on him, and gave him a microphone. About halfway through the cut, he started to weep uncontrollably, and that pushed John over the edge. John thought it was cruel and pointless. I've never quite understood exactly what that was about. One way or the other, we didn't get to finish it. But that was the point at which John said this is too much.

"There's a reason we recorded so much, is because we were waiting for Stax to go out of business. We thought if we keep going with this, Stax is going to go out of business and we can sell it. Well, Stax went out of business, but we could not sell it. Nobody wanted it. Jerry Wexler at Atlantic Records, whom I'd worked for and was friends with, once said, 'Baby, this record makes me feel very uncomfortable', and I thought that was a good sign. Lenny Waronker, who's one of the most brilliant record men I've ever known, said, 'I don't have to listen to that again, do I?' *It's up to you, man* – you know?"

"Erik Morse sees a parallel between what Chris Bell was doing with his recordings for *I am the Cosmos*, and what Alex was doing with *Third* – roughly parallel, and sonically unique."

"Oh, I think there's definitely a parallel. *Cosmos* came in pieces, too. I think there's probably several years involved in that. Certainly both albums were drawn from the same well;

they're taking water from the same well, and their influences are similar. They were both trying for kind of an orchestral concept. That's the way I looked at *Third*, anyway. I wouldn't be surprised if Chris wasn't going for the same kind of full sound spectrum. A lot of it had to do with the fact that they both had experienced John Fry, and just what you could really make a guitar sound like. As you listen to that Ardent anthology, you're gonna see the guitar sound that Fry produced goes back a long way. The guitar on the first song on that anthology, which is the 'Ole Miss Down Beats', is something that's in Fry's head, to this day."

"Alex played a little bit with Chris on some of those sessions…"

"On Chris's sessions for *Cosmos*, yeah, but Chris did not play on *Third*. Alex was more upset by Chris's presence than Chris was by Alex's. Like if Chris came around, Alex shut down. For me it goes back to what I said about Chris, is that he didn't care. He may have cared intensely; I may be wrong about that. But he definitely appeared more comfortable around Alex than Alex did around him. Of course Alex wants control and he wants to be the sharpest pencil in the box, too."

"Will Rigby who was drumming for the DBs has made references to homosexual liaisons around the studio throughout that period of recording."

"It's almost like 'Kangaroo': I chose to ignore it, and treat it as if it was just another day at the glue factory. And again, it predates anything that's on *Third*. I may have been guilty of manipulating it, not manipulating it, but getting as much out of it as I could. I may have been guilty of that, I'm not sure.

"Eggleston now denies that's him playing piano on 'Nature Boy', and it *absolutely* is him playing. I promise you on my immortal soul that is him playing. He was walking with a crutch at the time and the crutch falls over – you can hear it fall over – and that's Little Bill, his son, playing the organ. And Fry says, 'Oh, can't we make…' and I said, 'No, no John, just let him.' And Eggleston was reading it off sheet music, which I still have, and Alex was singing along. I always thought that was part of the record. Nat King Cole had the hit; it was the movie theme to *The Boy with Green Hair*.

"I quit once, at one point. Alex said something like, 'Well, quit if you want to.' I said, 'OK, I quit.' I'm a known quitter. I quit with a flourish. I quit better than I produce, actually. And Alex followed me all the way – I was living out towards Eads, and he followed me all the way home. Followed me into the house, upstairs, into the little space in the attic that I had and pled with me to come back, and I said, 'Sure, Alex – I'll be there tomorrow.' Part of the reason he let me do as much as I did, was I reminded him of his brother that drowned in the bathtub, and that's one of the early tragedies of his life. Something about me reminds him of that. Alex is deep, there's no doubt about it. Without him, I would've never done the Replacements, and then I really wouldn't have had a career. But in terms of sensitivity, Paul Westerberg makes Alex look like the man on the street. By far the most sensitive artist I ever dealt with. Everything affected him – everything. He hates for me to say that.

"Memphis is not about the bars, it's not about the venues, it's not about live music – the history of Memphis music is recorded music, and there's something like magnetic fields happening here that makes it different."

CHAPTER THE THIRTEENTH
DISCOURSE OF RAGE, CONJURATION, & EXILE

Under the spell of a Herschell Gordon Lewis movie, *She Devils on Wheels*, I watched Falco and his coterie of hangers-on, stymied students, losers, and thwarted artists merrily embark on another road to folly and disillusion. This time the idea was to form an all girls sister group to Panther Burns. The band was named after the theme song to the Lewis movie about a gang of female motorcyclists: *the Hellcats*.

> *We are the Hellcats nobody likes,*
> *Maneaters on motorbikes,*
> *When you hear the roar of our cut-out exhausts*
> *Get off the road or you'll get your rear-end tossed.*

Before the posse of felines self-destructed – as any self-respecting sorority of hellcats are apt to do – both groups made a trip to New York during a particularly intense heat wave by invitation of Central Park Conservatory Summerstage. Again I acted as gopher on the journey and had promoted Cordell Jackson's addition to the bill. Both bands delivered as righteous a performance as they were capable of, but Cordell stole the show. While the Panther Burns rode in their new replacement to the Thunderbird, a long black 1963 Chrysler LeBaron limousine, Cordell had driven her canary yellow Cadillac up from Memphis, and stayed on in Gotham for a few days promoting herself as the 'Rock n Roll Granny'. A tireless self-promoter, the efforts of the lady from Moon Records paid off in spades. She was ecstatic to be offered two Budweiser commercials, a shot at Letterman and another of those nameless late night yak shows. Cordell returned to Memphis a jubilant rocker in full glory.

1963 Chrysler LeBaron Photo: E. Baffle 1987

Not long after the Central Park Conservatory triumph, the next time these two incestuous wildcat groups appeared together was the LSU, Louisiana State University, graduation party on the USS Kidd naval destroyer docked in the Mississippi River harbor at Baton Rouge. More babies were conceived on that saturnalia and more graduates jumped overboard, were pushed, or fell into the harbor, than on any other party known in the annals of the university.

Shortly after the USS Kidd bacchanal, Midtown was stunned one Friday when the jejune husband of Amy Gamine, bass player of the KLITZ, was shot down in broad daylight as the couple were leaving Pappy and Jimmy's Lobster Shack on Poplar Avenue at Hollywood. Amy and James Starks were darlings of the art scene – she herself bearing a striking resemblance to Natalie Wood, and James a promising artist and painter employed by the prestigious Dixon Gallery and Gardens.

Amy's grandfather, Julius Gassner, served as *maître d'*of *the* Sacher Hotel in Vienna before he to moved to NYC where reigned as *maître d'* for the New York Athletic Club for over 30 years. Francis, Amy's father, had gone to school with Andy Warhol at Carnegie Tech on the GI bill. Andy had a crush on her father who also was the apartment manager of a Victorian pile called the Castle. Andy lived there for a while and that's how she came into possession of an early, quasi-cubist Andy Warhol painting of a saxophonist, which her father bequeathed to her. Twenty-five years later she sold it for a pittance during the depths of a distraught lifestyle.

Francis was eighteen when he married and Dolly, seventeen. He studied one summer under Frank Lloyd Wright and then the couple moved to Greenwich Village for several years where she worked in fashion and he practiced architecture and gigged on stand up bass in a jazz combo. In 1959 they moved to Memphis when Francis got a job with architect Al Aedilott. They immediately were drawn to the academic and to the architecture crowd: Francis Mah, and Roy Harrover (who designed the Art Academy and Memphis Airport, and who is married to Stephanie, the sister of Bill Eggleston). The couple also traveled in the sphere of Marcus Orr, the historian, novelist Shelby Foote, and faculty from the Art Academy. They worked with actor George Touliatas at Front Street Theater: Dolly on costumes, Francis on sets. Structures that Francis designed included the Library at LeMoyne Owen College – for which he commissioned artist Ben Shawn to paint a mural – the Theater and Music building at the University of Memphis, Sears Building on Poplar Ave, Temple Israel, and the obliquely *avant garde* C&I Bank downtown with the angular glassed-roofed tropical garden in the lobby.

Francis Gassner was well liked and lived on the cutting edge in his love of flying, fast cars, audio equipment, musical evasions, equal rights, and eventually younger women. On his baby grand, he played hours and hours of Chopin and Beethoven. He traveled in Europe, Africa, and South America and spoke several languages. Architectural junkets took him several times behind the Iron Curtain to Russia and Hungary.

The stress of replacing Main Street with the creation of a pedestrian mall and the tribulations inherent in dealing with city hall politicians and building authorities affected Francis' health, not to mention the cigarettes and the nightly routine of beer, manhattans, wine, and aperitifs. For the Mid-America Mall, he commissioned a monumental organic sculpture called, *The Muse*, designed and executed by John McIntire. It was cast by the artist and Randall Lyon in white concrete and marble chips. A champion of civil rights, Francis marched with rabbis and clergy to end the sanitation strike the day after King's assassination. Then worked with civic leaders to help secure and dedicate land for Martin Luther King Park in South Memphis adjacent to the Chaucalissa Indian Mounds beside the Mississippi River.

On that payday Friday afternoon in September of 1984, the Francis' daughter and her husband, James, were walking out to their car in the parking lot after a fine meal at the lobster shack, when three youths strolled by and one of them brushed against Amy's jeans. The couple kept on walking and as they turned the corner of the building they noticed that the black kids were running after them. The three imps were pursuing them pointing guns. Beside their car the boys were trying to get Amy in the car with them. She was able to calm down the boy that was pointing a gun at her; he was the youngest and she gave him her money. Unfortunately James decided to fight back and refused to cooperate. First he was pistol-whipped, then as he attempted to approach Amy's side of the car, he was shot through the back with an expensive chrome-plated pistol. Amy screamed maddeningly, and the knaves quickly ran away.

The couple managed to get back into the restaurant and call the ambulance. Their favorite waitresses were now only complaining about the blood that was falling on their carpet. By this time Amy was hysterical. The ambulance drivers saved James' life by keeping him awake on the drive to the hospital. The bullet grazed his heart as it traveled through several organs. He spent six weeks in intensive care with a 50% chance of pulling through. The night he was shot a chaplain came to tell Amy that James probably wouldn't make it, but maybe prayer works.

The adolescent offenders were summarily caught because the next day they went to school and in their art class at East High School, they bragged about shooting a white boy. The police then had a good idea who had done it and the shooter was quickly apprehended. Just a few days previous, the *Commercial Appeal* had published a lengthy interview with James that featured his paintings, so the art schoolteacher at East High was aware of him. At the trial, the assailant licked his lips horribly when he saw Amy in the courtroom. The juvenile served eight years at the penal farm, while James Starks miraculously survived and went on to bring forth many more paintings. His injuries, however, have caused him tremendous residual pain and engendered more than his share of psychological duress.

The Memphis Music Heritage Festivals in May began to leave wider and wider gaps in the cultural landscape, especially concerning the alternative art scene. To address this sense of neglect felt by an emerging weed patch of artists and musicians, Falco got the stubborn idea in his head to present the best and the worst of them in the setting of an alternative festival. He and Alex dubbed it COUNTERFEST. In 1985 the first Counterfest was held at 96 S. Front St. back in the same cotton loft of the original Panther Burns show, which had for quite some time languished in disuse. It was a two-day event with artists and musicians working together in utter anarchy and with no support other than what personal resources they might conjure up. Bizarre environments were constructed; psychedelic lighting and diffraction gradients were fabricated and installed in the wide-open rooms. Stage risers from the Cotton Carnival warehouse were again dragged up the stairs. Suddenly there was a waiting list of participants eager to join in. Again the TV news crews came to capture another Falco-instigated *art-action*. Their cameras happened to catch the precise moment when Falco wielded a wood-chopping axe over his head and brought it down full force, crashing onto and splintering an electric can opener he had placed on the makeshift stage, while spontaneously invoking an incendiary manifesto for the stodgy ears and perceptive faculties of the Midsouth viewing audience:

LOUNGERS, RAKES, LOAFERS, FOPS, EXHAUST QUEENS, MIDINETTES, PUPPET HEADS, IMPERIALIST RUNNING DOGS, & BACKSLIDING HEIFERS –
WE ARE THE NEO-RUMORIST FESTIVAL – *COUNTERFEST*!
WE ARE THE DITCH-DIGGERS IN AMERICAN ART AND MUSIC –
UNDER THE PSYCHOTROPIC RED GLARE OF THE AUGUST MOON,
TONIGHT IS THE NIGHT TO FORGE A TRAGIC ALLIANCE WITH THE UNDERGROUND!
TONIGHT IS THE NIGHT TO *CRACK* THE IMPERIALIST BLACK EGG!
TONIGHT IS THE NIGHT TO GET YOUR ASHES HAULED!
WE'RE NOT TALKING ABOUT PIE AND CAKES, CLUTCHES AND BRAKES,
OR THE HIGH SOCIETY SCHOOL OF THE ARTS –
ALL PHRANKING PRIVILEGES ARE REVOKED!
PANTHER PHOBIA, PANTHER PHOBIA, PANTHER PHOBIA!
BURN, BURN, BURN! – BURN, BURN, BURN!

Then Falco swung the axe head around again and plunged it through the picture tube of a waiting and useless TV set stationed on the other side of the stage from where the once intact electric can opener had so naïvely stood. This guy Falco was continually coming up with absurd ideas and gestures. I'm not sure anyone truly understood what the heck he was doing... I'm not sure he even did.

COUNTERFEST events were mounted for five years on an annual basis. The last one was held on an industrial barge floating at the dockside of the river harbor. I had been out on the road with Panther Burns filming their concerts, and when we returned to the Bluff City we found Jim Jarmusch winding up the production of his movie, *Mystery Train*. A friend from the East Village named Red Rockets was acting in the role of a night clerk in the film, getting gunned down in a 7/11 – Rockets fell like an avalanche when he took the bullet. Jarmusch was filming in the abandoned Arcade Hotel at Main St. and Calhoun, where I had filmed the opening sequence two years earlier for the Panther Burns short, *Memphis Beat*. Jim brought the entire cast and crew down to the barge for COUNTERFEST. Meanwhile he'd come by our place and looked at our short films, and somehow Falco got him interested in the rebuilt Triumph motorbike sitting next to the Norton in our living room. Next thing I knew, Jim Jarmusch had bought the Triumph with cash from his production office. Often I've thought Falco would have made a better salesman than a singer.

One day I was stretched out on the porch swing with the newspaper reading the help wanted ads. Some people like to read crossword puzzles, but I read the tightly spaced help-wanted columns for the same reasons. There's no danger of getting hired or of even trying to... as it's extremely unlikely a disaffected white boy has the ghost of a chance finding any sort of job in the Bluff City other than the most menial of tasks. Such perplexing youth do not look, talk, or smell good to the eyes, ears, and noses of sanctimonious Dixie-fried Baptists who drive the markets of the petty bourgeoisie in this citadel of the Bible Belt. On the page behind the help wanted there appeared a truncated column under the rubric: Houses For Rent. Usually there were not more than five or six listings in that column, but that day I saw a curious listing for a *farmhouse* in Binghampton = $150 monthly. As the quarters were becoming a little cramped, shared with Falco and his burgeoning entourage who kept all kinds of bizarre operational hours, I decided to call up about the 'farmhouse'. The price was right, although a bit more expensive than the Cox St. duplex.

The call proved a perspicuous stroke of Fate. The wife of the farmer who owned the house gave me the address, and I hopped on the Norton and rolled over to Binghampton to scope out the place. I parked the bike on the natty front lawn that fronted an otherwise dilapidated bungalow. The porch was rotten and the roof over the porch was just as rotten, as well as the bathroom floor, which I would find out later was rotted out due to a standing pool of water under the house. All in all though, it looked like a good deal. Yet the more I poked around the sagging old house I felt a strange twinge of *déja vu* ... like I had already been there once, had in the distant past already encountered the moldering old bungalow, had already seen the forlorn streets around it, and the sullen trees that overhung its peeling white walls. In a couple of days the farmer came to Cox St. driving an extra long pickup truck; we piled all my junk onto it and headed over to Princeton St. in Binghampton looking like a couple of Arkys fleeing to the Promised Land. The Cox St. duplex and the Thunderbird I left to the custody of Falco and his seething camarilla.

It was twilight when we unloaded the last two boxes of books onto the coruscated front porch. That peculiar feeling came over me again that somehow, at sometime in the foggy past I had known this spot in Binghampton. Perhaps it was the heavy fragrance of the petals from a gardenia bush set at the northern corner of the house that had fallen on the dewy earth in a perfect circle that evoked this necromantic reverie. The blooms of gardenia, yellowed from their whiteness, last only a few days before dropping from the bush, which will remain barren for the rest of the year. As the old farmer cast off into the murky light, I thought I heard the high timbre of an indefinable voice… yes it was a voice. Someone was speaking in the half-light, in the shadows. It was not an effeminate voice, yet not masculine, nor was it the utterance of a child. The intonations were emanating from the side driveway between my bungalow and a high homemade clapboard fence, much higher than the height of a grown man. The odd hodge-podge fence surrounded a colossal, decrepit farmhouse. I peered into the veneer of darkness toward the direction of the waggish voice, and discerned the outline of a wrinkled truck fender of a gray color that blended perfectly with the evening dusk and with the dirt of the alley. The door of the truck appeared open and two reclining feet and forelegs were sticking out from the truck seat. I drew closer to the apparition and saw that one of the feet was not actually a foot, but was a bandaged nub.

Suddenly the brute hulk of a man swung up on the seat. A gnome in short pants and Coke bottle eyeglasses darted around the side of the truck carrying a set of wooden crutches which she handed to the bearded, glowering creature. The leviathan lunged forward and rested his armpits on the crutches. Hooked up at me with cold white, narrow-set eyes and his narrow face split into a wide grin. He introduced himself as Sammy Lee, and the gnome as his daughter. He lived in the fenced-in compound next to my bungalow with his daughter, his dwarfish wife, and a pack of ornery hound dogs that he had trained to attack the front fence line whenever someone walked past. The rubes were from the hill country in Mississippi, I learned, and were friendly as could be for new neighbors.

Sammy Lee, like Charlie Feathers, was part Indian and he could mimic all the bird and animal calls from the forests and swamps. He was perennially attired in farmers' overalls, and usually wore a soiled red-plaid hunting cap on his pecan-shaped head. Sammy's wife kept Sammy Lee's head of hair close cut with a pair of old fashioned, Sears buzz clippers. My new friends invited me into their compound on that first chill autumnal evening on Princeton St. The daughter gnome opened the wide boarded gate and ushered us in while the hounds growled and yelped and leaped all around me higher than a man's shoulders. I was sure the dogs were going to take off an arm or at least a few fingers before I got in the door, but upon the entreaties of their masters, they obediently forebeared from tearing me to pieces.

Inside the barn like structure, there was a wood fire burning in a small iron fireplace of the kind once used in Memphis for burning coal. The glowing embers were cheery, and Sammy Lee was hoisted onto the middle of a king size iron bed by his minions of dwarf and gnome. He said, "Now walk *lightly* in here, son. I got two cases of live grenades sitting under the bed. When the lid blows off, they're not going to get us out of here without a fight, I'll guarantee you that!" Sammy Lee spent the next hour demonstrating how he manufactured his own bullets by pouring molten lead into metal moulds. There was an arsenal of antiquated rifles that he had stacked on racks against the walls of the bedroom. Of the few decorations around the room, there were a John Deere tractor calendar on one peeling wall, and over the bedstead was a red-robed Christ figure pasted on a solid paper fan with a flat balsa wood handle of the kind ladies fan themselves with on a hot summer's day at evangelical revival meetings. The hound dogs would repeatedly run through the bedroom vying for Sammy Lee's attention, but he brushed them away with a vigorous swipe of his crutch.

The philosophy of Sammy was that of a survivalist. His sole ambition in life was simply to survive on his Ponderosa with his brood and his pack of hounds: an illustrious example of the robust individualist. Although Sammy Lee looked studious when he wore his wire rimmed eyeglasses doing precise tasks like pouring bullets, he could neither read nor write. He eked out a living of sorts as a junker, meaning that he and his family collected junk and debris discarded on the streets and in the alleys of Memphis. A good part of this scavenging included Genie, his wife, and their daughter diving into industrial dumpsters scattered around the area and retrieving choice scraps of copper wire and junk metal. Then the loot would be sorted through, gloated over, and recycled and resold to junkyards on the edge of town.

To transport these raw materials Sammy Lee had a fleet of three derelict pick up trucks of which at least one was operational at any given time. The trucks had high side panels that the three of them had fabricated from cast off scraps of lumber, so the truck beds could be piled with junk to the point of the such top heaviness that the whole rig seemed ready to topple over at the slightest provocation. Yet, when Sammy drove these behemoths, he showed no mercy and no fear of driving at top speed with the accelerator mashed to the floorboard. Due to the carburetors on the truck motors being totally worn out, top speed was rather limited. When Sammy gunned the motor of his truck on the street in front of our houses just to show everyone what his truck could do, he would hang out of the driver's window with his elbow over the door sill and look back in glory at the plumes of smoke spewing from the exhaust pipes as his rig sputtered, coughed, bucked, choked, and lurched ahead. The color of the exhaust smoke, of their clothes and skin, and of the truck bodies were of the same color of the asphalt upon which they rode.

The foot of Sammy Lee was lost in a motorcycle accident. He told me that he was riding a 400 cc Honda down Poplar and when he got to Highland Avenue, the little motorbike carrying this gargantuan junker tangled with a bob truck. The encounter resulted in him getting completely run over by the bob truck. He said when the ambulance came the paramedics put him in two body bags, sure that he was dead. Sammy Lee survived, but when he woke up in the hospital he discovered they had taken off his foot. That had happened some years before I met Sammy. The problem was that after the foot was amputated, the nub that was left had never healed. The doctors had him back in the hospital a number of times to drain it, pack it with antibiotics, cauterize it, yet nothing proved effective. The gauze at the end of the nub was continually wet with redness, and Sammy Lee told me, among other repugnant stories, that once when he was out on the compound in his wheel chair supervising his wife digging a post hole, he removed the bandage from the nub for a moment and a little white worm wiggled out and fell on the ground. Even he was sickened by the sight of it.

When Sammy Lee and his wife and their gnome weren't out in the pick up truck scavenging and junking, Sammy Lee had them building the surrounding fence of the compound higher and higher and reinforcing any suspect pickets. Crowning their protective barrier were strands of intertwined barbed wire they had scavenged from here and there. Sammy Lee ruled over the toil of his two laborers like a fractious, crippled tyrant. When their handiwork did not meet the expectations of their lord and master, a cruel crutch would whip through the air and knock them to the ground. More than once I would hear the gnomish girl squeal with the pain of the oafish battering, and I would come to the window to see her weeping and running to escape another blow.

When Sammy Lee had some distance to perambulate, he rode in a wheelchair pushed by either Genie or his daughter. He was not without his own brand of good humor, and was often amusing simply because he would find *himself* so amusing. Falco even took a liking to the hillbilly. Once he came over with the band, and handed Sammy Lee a camera to take album cover photographs. Sammy's first effort behind the camera was a success, and his pictures of the group were accepted and distributed by the Parisian record label. Seems the French dote on anything authentically bizarre. Falco then cast Sammy Lee and his family in a short film called, *Shade Tree Mechanic,* which a student from the San Francisco Art Institute had come to town to make with Panther Burns. The prodigious brio of Sammy Lee shone on celluloid with exultant triumph. Falco was dabbling around a lot with films and pictures. I still think he would have made a better salesman – used cars or something.

Once after a gig in Oxford, Falco and his camarilla rode the Thunderbird into a ditch on their way back to Memphis. They hitchhiked back to town, but they couldn't remember where they had left the car. Sammy Lee drove me down to Mississippi to find the T-Bird, which we found about ten miles north of Will Faulkner's stomping ground. Sammy had a log chain that we tied to the front bumper of the T-Bird and hauled the heavy barge out of the ditch then on up the highway to the Bluff City. Even though I had advised there was no pay on this mission, once on the road Sammy Lee insisted on two cheeseburgers. We stopped at a roadside burger joint, and while he munched the burgers, he asked me if I had ever taken someone out in the woods and tied them up. I admitted that I had not. Sammy Lee proceeded to describe in lucid detail how he had tied up two hapless individuals to a tree deep in the woods, and had molested and violated them until it wasn't funny anymore. His mirthful, yet livid eyes betrayed his straight face in telling me that no matter how much they screamed and hollered, there was no one and nobody to hear them except disinterested animals and birds hiding in the silence of the forest.

After an extended sojourn out of the country, I came back to Memphis at one point and learned that in my absence, while a section of the protective fence was being reinforced, Sammy Lee had been knocked over in his wheelchair by his wife and his daughter during a fit of mutinous rebellion, and the Draconian hillbilly had died there in the dirt of a heart attack. His hounds howled all night.

BOMB magazine called up from New York one weekend and set up a lengthy phoner with Falco. Before they called back, I coached Tav the best I could, and I had to give him some ammunition from my own background to round out the interview. In the end I don't think the magazine published much of the extended, overwrought discourse.

BOMB: From where does this confluence between 'hillbilly' music indigenous to the South and extremely dark, European-style Gothicism spring? What is its origin and why do you believe it's one of the dominant and recurring motifs of roots music? It seems to run from the paradigm of Robert Johnson meeting the Devil at the crossroads to the murder ballads of Hasil Adkins to the skulls and coffins of Screamin' Jay Hawkins. What is it exactly about the music of Panther Burns that so often aligns itself with the terrifying and the exotic?

TAV: There was a notion afoot that America was an extension of Europe. As in most such aphoristic statements there is a particle of truth in it. More than other Americans, Southerners, the closer you get to New Orleans, seem more connected, consciously or unconsciously, to European legacies. The lineages are there to be traced and ruminated over... the persecutions, the migrations, the witch-hunts, the hangings, the burnings, the exaltations, the apostasies, the betrayals, the avarice, the peonage, the enslavements: themes elaborated in the writings of the Virginia bard, Edgar Poe. Paralleled in the last century, further sinister and distortive evocations from devastated lands in Europe entered our consciousness in the shadowed form of Expressionism. The South is a land of lost causes, brother against brother, burning mansions, of splendor, twilight, and exile... sharing an affinity with similar regions of central Europe. Burying ground ballads, hellhound blues, ghostly military waltzes, vigilante gavottes were played by Southerners who picked up European instruments and pressed them into the service of music and song that was reflective of analogous events, and of a spiritual nature shared with their European ancestors and brethren. The Panther Burns are only a mirror of such disenfranchisements, torments, and ecstasies.

BOMB: While Panther Burns was steeped in the tradition of the blues, the band also went well beyond mere revisionism, reinventing obscure songs of the past rather than simply performing old classics.

TAV: This is the literal part of our mission and how we approach it. While deconstructing formal harmony and pattern, we embrace a merry/sinister Gothicism in lyric and melody that harkens back to the dark mythologies not only of the blues, but also of parallel genres like mountain balladry, tango, and funeral marches.

BOMB: Your music has its own sonic palette, using heavy feedback and distortion, synthesizers, and incorporating other kinds of exotica... the experimental-meets-traditional. Traditional country, soul, and blues didn't delve much into atonality, feedback, and dissonance.

TAV: If your eyes and ears were open in the 60s, one could not help being exposed to everything at once. Histories and glyphs from the European avant-guard overlaid with strains of gypsy violins, Transylvanian harpsichords, and with gradients of noise generating devices of the Italian Futurists, were laid out on a mosaic gestalt of tapestry side by side with country blues traditions, hillbilly hollers, and motorcycle exhausts. It was an expansive, holistic, ever expanding, mind flogging 'magic carpet' for you to go stomping around on. For example, the Velvets had the experimentalist, John Cale, and a fashion model, Nico, with a German background. The group once played an unauthorized gig on the lawn of the HL Hunt mansion in Dallas, Texas, that was more of an art/noise happening than a RnR show.

BOMB: *From where did the decision to incorporate more of these dissonant and experimental textures into Panther's music come? Was it a result of Alex Chilton's and Jim Dickinson's influence? I'm automatically reminded of tracks like 'Kangaroo' from Third/Sister Lovers, which used mellotron and guitar feedback to similar dizzying effect. Did your earliest gigs meet a lot of resistance from Memphis purists for these reasons?*

TAV: The "Kangaroo" track I've heard somewhere along the line, but the recollection is foggy. "Bangkok" I recall vividly and here one can savor the jaunty dissonance and distortion that Alex was cultivating at the time. Later during his tenure in Panther Burns, he attained even more heightened transports of feedback and crafted spontaneous, atonal electric guitar fugues that were astounding. A taste of this can be heard on the Rough Trade single of "Train Kept a Rollin'". Jim Dickinson was more into a bag of extreme electro/acoustic distortion and pink noise which was oblique to the thrust of Panther Burns... the influence derived from him was focused more along the lines of dramatic content and theatrical intervention. During those early gigs in Memphis, musicians who knew better than I, warned me to turn down the volume, turn down the reverb, drop the hideous feedback, and learn to play in meter, if I were ever going to become a musician. I am afraid that was I unable to heed their council, and have yet to attain the stature of an honest or earnest musician.

BOMB: *As the 80s underground music scene expanded beyond punk, many of the stylistic and musical cues of Panther Burns were used by bands like Primal Scream, Spacemen 3, The Gun Club, The Meat Puppets, Big Black, Pussy Galore/The Blues Explosion. Some like The Gun Club and The Meat Puppets merged country-blues and punk while others assimilated a wider range of soul, psychedelia, and garage-rock. They were all essentially necrophagists, consuming and digesting the music of the past into new product. This methodology reached its apex in indie music by 1986 with Pussy Galore's bootleg cover of Exile on Main Street. The album is a track-by-track recording of the classic Rolling Stones LP but their translations are nearly unnerving blasts of noise with bits of Stones' lyrics thrown in. It is an intense listening experience. However the whole concept seems to be an extension of the Panther Burns/Cramps' method of recontextualizing old lyrics and melodies to form an entirely new composition.*

TAV: There are different kinds of noise, e.g. white noise, pink noise, brown noise. Some forms of noise have little redeeming value. Hence groups who produce useless and misguided noise are no better than the racket they make. Just because a group can manage to blithely savage an existing opus with unnerving blasts of unmitigated noise cannot be construed as elevating, revealing, extending, or even deconstructive of anything of more significance than a Coke bottle. If you are going to deconstruct something, you have to go on to reconfigure it and *add* something to what is left... or you end up with a worthless heap of meaningless fragments. *Nothing* is left in such operations except traces of anger and frustration that sooner or later fade into oblivion. It is misguided to make cases for such actions. Distortion for the sake of distortion is a dead end. Distortion is an application... as applied to something that is free of distortion, hence something unusual results. Or distortion is an inherent condition that can be made more distorted, but only in degree... then when distortion is removed or taken away, the condition changes in kind and something unseen is revealed. The dynamic of NOISE operates the same. Noise is what you find in a sack of *gris gris*, and although it can be dispensed with abandon, it

Sharecropper cabin Photo: E. Baffle c. 1976

must be used carefully. As applied, I embrace the term 'necrophagist'. Panther Burns *are* 'necrophiliac', and purveyors of pink noise specializing in 'Live Excavations'.

BOMB: These bands also did much to literally dismantle and destroy the traditional timbres of the guitar in order to record the death shrieks of guitar music, very reminiscent of your chainsaw debut. Do you think this type of music took the guitar to its limit or signaled the end of a certain kind of guitar experimentation? Could you foresee the end of the guitar as the focal pop icon?

TAV: Before the guitar became the focal pop icon, it was the tenor saxophone... esp. in jazz and jump blues which are essentially popular music forms. Out of destruction comes rebirth. Out of the death rattle comes the fresh wailings of the newborn. Out of dichotomy and annihilation comes the *Pantherbourne*. Whether the device is a guitar, or a saxophone, or a string of baling wire strung up on the side of a cabin, or a humble fife cut from a stick of cane... it is the hand that plays it, the mouth that blows it, the mind that perceives it, the soul that feels it, which matters in the end. There is no limit.

BOMB: I find it interesting that you have had the quasi-technological element of 'TONE SCIENCE' added to the Panther Burns moniker. What was your reasoning behind that decision?

TAV: Not unlike other artists, Panther Burns draw from a palette of tones and colors and gradations. Underlying an array of 'found' noises, drones, musical tonalities, and noise effects are two fundamental wellsprings of the din of Panther Music. The traditional musical aspect is drawn from the Devil's interval and chordal syncopations of African-American deep gospel instrumentation; the other aspect is drawn from unintentional, often industrial sounds, e.g. noises and syncopations of trains running up and down the rails... both tonalities overlap and both enchanted me from an early age when steam locomotives came chugging and puffing through the remote Arkansas railhead near where I grew up, and covered our town in huge clouds of coal black smoke. Later when I was working as a brakeman on the Missouri Pacific railroad, the reiterative and cadenced sounds of riding the rails were running through my head night and day. In the evenings the train might be dragging a cut of freight cars past a country church, or a sharecropper's cabin, or saw mill worker's front porch where electric guitars were being picked in the groove of Jimmy Reed, or church chords were heard coming out of distorted windows hung on unpainted clapboard walls. Until this day I am still entranced by both layers of this tonal palette and thus comes music as heard by a swarthy and dusty Panther as he rolls over in his slumbers under the palpable shade of a pine grove not so far from the R/R tracks.

BOMB: I've found that so many innovative 'noise' musicians (whether they be electronic, electro-acoustic, or electric) tend to have a fetishistic relationship with their gear that borders on the scientific; namely, they are very precise on what brands of instruments they like and what kind of 'sound' they are searching for. Are there any particular types of guitar (Fender Telecaster, Silvertone surf guitars, etc.) and playing methods (strange tunings, how you play your feedback, the ever-present twang of a tremolo pedal, etc.) that you've married to the overall Panther Burns sound? Do you believe these kinds of textural components are as essential to your music as the more traditional elements of rhythm, harmony, and melody?

TAV: The thrust of Panther Burns as a group has always been an electric two-guitars sound. Early in my development with Panther Burns, I made a transition from black Silvertone guitars to the black 1963, violin-shaped hollow body, six-string Höfner with the built-in, push-button active, factory fuzz tone unit. Since then I've played the same guitar, and I am not sure that another instrument could ever achieve the sonic thrust of the Panther Burns as well and as faithfully. I eschew all types of intermediary effects devices, and plug directly into a Fender tube amplifier equipped with a long, three-spring reverb tank and with dual or quadruple 10-inch speakers. Occasionally I have campaigned a National tube amp running 2 x 12-inch speakers – the model with the chrome icebox door handle on top – with sterling results. Using a flat pick or three National steel finger picks and a thumb pick, I often attack the instrument with a "slide" tube of chrome steel over my finger. Lush echo and a splash of reverb are essential to the vocals of Panther Burns... I cannot see committing to a Panther Burns performance without the aforementioned. As for the complimentary guitar, we prefer a hollow body Gretsch, or Gibson, or National, or Burns of London powered by likewise amplification. When we can get it, we employ an amplified stand-up contrabass or Fotdella, otherwise a hollow-body electric bass guitar is acceptable. A trap drum set is required outfitted with tambourine and a long cowbell. Added to these essentials can be any number and configuration of ancillary instruments and sounding devices, depending on the application, from Theremin to bandoneon, to singing saw, Leslie oscillator, etc. It is with these tools that we evoke the rhythms, (dis) harmonies, and melodies of Panther Burns.

BOMB: While most pop music historians look to the mid/late 60s as the earliest flirtations between rock and experimental music (the aforementioned elements of feedback, synthesis, an emphasis on the 'sound' of production) it still seems as though the 50s were chockfull of studio invention. From Les Paul to Joe Meek's earliest space opera. The 'Memphis' sound appeared to be a hotbed of experimentation, particularly in its use of echo/delay and gospel multi-instrumentation to low fidelity distortion. Looking back over the vast catalogue of rockabilly classics, from labels like Sun to King to Meteor etc., do you have any particular favorites that you believe made seminal contributions to 'noise rock'?

TAV: Worthy of mention is the innovative fuzz guitar used by Pat Hare on songs like, "I'm Gonna Murder My Baby". Certainly the sonic universe concocted by Joe Meek extends beyond the pale of invention and far ahead of his time and far into the future. *No one* has really matched the impeccably fastidious dynamic contours of sonic brilliance and atmospheric elegance that he achieved on his recordings. In Panther Burns we did the best we could with recording his anthem of teen angst, "Have I the Right?" (upon careful scrutiny, essentially a rockabilly song), yet we hardly attained the unearthly and divinely inhuman ferocity of the vocalizations recorded by the Honeycombs. If only Joe Meek could re-materialize and produce Panther Burns as we are ready to prostrate ourselves before the altar of his cosmic wizardry.

BOMB: I wonder if you'd consider the 'slap echo' the very first psychedelic studio effect, the way in which its undulatory gradations would simulate hypnotic propulsion throughout the background of the track, e.g. its eerie use in Charlie Feather's "Jungle Fever"? To me, it bears an uncanny resemblance to the 13th Floor Elevators' later use of the electric jug. It's also completely organic to the song, c.f. the 'novelty' effect of certain modulators in 60s psych songs like "Baby Your Phrasing's Bad" with its cheesy phase shifting.

TAV: Well, I adore funky 60s effects. I had no idea 13th Floor Elevators made use of an electric jug! I am mightily impressed to hear this about a group that I've already held in the highest esteem. 'Slap back' tape echo is surely a psychedelic effect, and it has existed since the advent of tape recording machines. What is significant is *who* applied it, and *how*, and to *what*... as much as when. It is thought that the radio engineer, Sam C. Phillips, and his early colleague, Charlie Feathers, were perhaps the first to apply tape echo to actual tape recordings as an aesthetic device. When Charlie Feathers finally got in a position to apply the effect to his own material, as evidenced by the hauntingly exquisite echo he produced on "Jungle Fever", an erotically thrilling new threshold was achieved in sonic reverberation. To attain the maximum, aesthetically pleasing delivery of the effect on a track, as Charlie explained it, required considerable experimentation, finesse, and delicate fine-tuning.

BOMB: I am not a musician per se, but I am fascinated by the style and image of the studio musician – the Electric Warrior as Marc Bolan put it so beautifully – as a kind of scientist or alchemist who sat in his laboratory channeling unknown forces through various alembics. Of course, in their time alchemists from Nicholas Flammel to Gilles de Rais were feared as magicians and occultists – in the same way, certain musicians who played bagpipes, the hurdy gurdy, and other drone instruments were executed for invoking evil spirits. Do you see a connection between the status of the noise musician and, say, the Outlaw or the Witch or the Alchemist? Do you think there is still a general cultural aversion to the experimental nature of noisy or distorted music as somehow verboten?

TAV: The image of the artist or musician as alchemist is utterly fascinating. Music –
an unseen force – magic, the occult, and alchemy all seem to be interconnected. One cannot deny that the spell of music is mysterious. I had friends from Dubrovnik who were in a band called the Scientists. Mercurial individuals, whose music was strictly alchemical. The first thing I do when I go onstage is to cast a spell. When people surrender to our rhythms without inhibition and dance, they go home thinking about it the next day, and the next. I have also witnessed Panther Burns polarize audiences – those reaching out in ecstatic embrace side by side with others spewing howls of contempt and derision. Casting a spell in the crucible of a recording studio, where there is no live audience, is another matter. In that case, one must rely on *conjurations*. In Venice one day I saw a strange man in the shadows of a portico playing bagpipes constructed with white flour sacks and with long pitch pipes. Part of the instrument he drove with an extended foot pedal. The Italians were captivated by the atmospheric droning he was generating, as was I. He was not entertaining with his deadpan grinding as much as he was saturating us with ancient, penetrating and ominously wheezing tonalities that could not be easily evaded or dismissed.

BOMB: How important a component is dancing to your music? After Panther Burns' initial forays into rockabilly, your albums tended to incorporate elements of tango and samba. Interesting because so much of early rock 'n roll was based on its ability to incite these massive audiences into flailing dervishes, whether it be at the juke joint or the Sunday social.

TAV: Bien sûr, Panther Burns is above all a dance band. Dancing is the response elicited by Panther Burns... other considerations are residual. Dance is an essential form of expression, and one that cannot be overlooked literally or in its profounder manifestations. Argentine tango, for instance, is reflective of passionate sensual, yet philosophic relationships between men and women, although its origins are derived from more primitive forms of human contact and cadences.

BOMB: But after the punk days of pogo-ing and gobbing, traditional rock audiences rarely danced beyond the occasional rigid shuffle which makes a song like "Tina, The Go-Go Queen" all the more anomalous. In your opinion what is it that has changed the rock audience from 'movers 'n' shakers' to merely spectators?

TAV: Popular dances and dance crazes in America ranging from *fin-de-siècle* Cakewalk and 1920s Black Bottom to the Madison and the Hully Gully of the early 60s were predicated on the blatant sensuality and syncopated structures of blues, ragtime, and jazz rhythms. When rock music, as a product of these forms, shifted toward heavy instrumentation and mind-expanding psychedelia, the body was left to re-orient itself within a tribal context, rather than to interpret musical cadences within the refined structure of paired couples and defined lines of dance. What had been a dance on Saturday night became a rock 'n' roll concert or free-form revival meeting. What had once been a house party with Fats Waller grooving at the piano while couples danced the shimmy became a sit down concert with Thelonious Monk at Birdland. Music makes its own demands. Though personally, I have no trouble dancing to the chording of Monk. The body is esoteric and holds its own mysteries and collective memories. What is evoked from it, as movement, is more like phenomena. The mind has thought; the body has movement. When they get together under the spell of music, the phenomenon of dance appears. Unless it is a complicated form of communal solo dancing like flamenco, dancing in couples is more demanding than dancing alone and brings with it a certain degree of socialization and acculturation. Dancing alone or head banging at a rock concert is free expression. When the music changes, the feet change accordingly. When hemlines on skirts come down or go up, the style of dancing changes. When music contains more intellectual import or becomes ultra cool, audiences tend to sit and ponder rather than get up and dance with each other. Audiences become introspective when listening to protest music or music with a message – when they are too occupied figuring out meaning to do anything other than tap their foot. Dancing before such thoughtful music might seem frivolous... but when the music gets hot and sexy, people are seen cutting scissor steps between each other's legs. Of course, when a performance becomes nothing more than sheer spectacle, the audience becomes nothing more than spectators at a circus. Dancing in couples is ritualistic and reflective of more stratified rites of courting and mating. Unstructured dancing alone or alone within a group is more like free jazz. Infused in the gaucheries of Panther Burns are aspects of all these forms of music and dance. Personally, I find dancing in couples most rewarding. I would be bored stiff at a rock concert unless it were the Doors or Suicide.

BOMB: *Do you think there has been an elevated sense of intellectualism infused in pop music over the last twenty years, i.e. the birth of the indie rocker, which has shifted the focus away from becoming a part of the 'ritual' of the live gig to a theatrical distance, in other words, observing it?*

TAV: The ground is always shifting underneath the artist... and Theatre takes many forms. Intellectual gradients do not necessarily preclude ritualistic sensuality and movement as in dance. Bob Dylan embodies a certain balance between these elements. On the other hand, what form of dancing are people doing to Nine Inch Nails...? Or to Marilyn Manson? No doubt these groups are eminently danceable.

BOMB: *Not sure if you are a follower of the electronica sub-culture, but do you think with the last decade's popularity of electronic dance music – rave, hardcore, drum 'n' bass, grime, 2-step – that there has been a real 'shift' in 'common' cultural/musical experience from melody/harmony back to rhythm? I say 'back' because, in a sense, rave and electronica audiences seemed to return to rock's traditional primacy of R&B and the beat, Bo Diddley, Chuck Berry, Howlin' Wolf, Link Wray, all of which have been part your focus for decades?*

TAV: Has the two-step come back around again...? If primal rhythm is withdrawn, melody and harmony are depotentiated and robbed of their throbbing pulsations. What you have left is Third Stream jazz or 12-tone structures of Arnold Schönberg... which I can groove on. I adore heavenly arrhythmic arias and atonal fugues, yet I live to throb = *andante, adagio, o larghetto.*

BOMB: *In several of your past interviews, you mentioned your influences/connections with female*

Jesse Mae Hemphill Courtesy: Highwater Records

rockabilly musicians like Jesse Mae Hemphill, Cordell Jackson and Memphis Minnie. However, the contribution of women, and, in a larger sense, the feminine mystique seems scarce in the rough 'n tumble world of rockabilly. Similarly, in interviews I'm currently conducting with noise-rock and electronic musicians, I've pointed out that the role played by women in the history of 'experimental' music seems to be overwhelmingly minute (exceptions of course, Pauline Oliveros to Delia Derbyshire to Laurie Anderson to Poison Ivy to Kim Gordon)...

TAV: Jesse Mae Hemphill and Memphis Minnie were country blues artists, while Cordell Jackson was more of a rock 'n' roll player than rockabilly, yet she was one of the most noisy, spontaneous thrashers of electric guitar (a red Hagstrom) that I have seen on stage anywhere of any gender. Extraordinary. She attacked the guitar like a field hand driving a posthole, while her femininity remained intact and uncompromised. What matters most, may be the quality of that which is contributed by the few, rather than the quantity of what may be dished up the many. Sheer numbers ultimately have little significance toward validating the role of women in these genres. Certainly no male has outstripped the stature of the women you have cited.

BOMB: Do you think there is an 'elemental' disconnect between women and noise music, whether it be feedback-drenched rockabilly or atonal electronica? Why do you think these kinds of music, with their emphasis on dissonant textures and droning harmonics, have remained by and large a boys' club while other genres like acoustic folk, country, and melodious pop have expanded to include larger numbers of female artists and female audiences?

TAV: The gender distinction between these genres is due to notions of confused femininity. The more traditional music forms have attracted female adherents whose femininity are never threatened and are often, by conventional standards, enhanced. In the area of generated tone and noise music, we find technologically and aesthetically experimental mind sets at work. Outside of computing and scientific fields and notables like Mme. Curie, we do not find so many women tinkering and toiling in sound labs. This is a pity because of the fertile contributions women are capable of making to any field. Women ought to be attracted to experimental activity with promise that is not sexually subtractive. There is so much to be derived by their inclusion. Much ink has been spilt, for instance, over the role of women in rock 'n' roll, and the nature of their playing. I love to hear women playing rock n roll instruments; it sounds so different from men playing – irresistibly different to masturbatory impulses of men.

BOMB: I'd read that you started your career as a film documentarian in a group called TeleVista, traveling around the South in search of blues and country figures of the past before deciding to pick up the guitar yourself. Would you mind telling me some of your more interesting experiences while on the road?

TAV: Before Panther Burns, there was TeleVista – an art-action group with a video-making thrust. The Arkansas poet, Randall Lyon, was its president, and I was the secretary and videographer of TeleVista. One TeleVista mission was a trip to the mountainside home in the Ozarks of former governor of Arkansas, the Honorable Orval E. Faubus. This controversial politician proved to be a suave, cordial, highly articulate, cunning, and utterly charming individual who embodied a number of unexpected complexities and inconsistencies, especially involving his origins and background. Randall made the interview and I made the camera, but before we could start we had to wait for his new girlfriend's teenage son to finish band practice. The kid had his rock 'n' roll group set up in the middle of the living room. His mother was aa approving shapely and busty Madison County brunette.

We stepped out on the terrace overlooking an expansive range of the Ozark mountains, turned on the camera, focused in the Swiss lens, and learned that the father of Orville Faubus had been a pacifist and had been arrested in the county seat of Huntsville for passing out seditious anti-war literature during the first World War. When the young Orville became of age, he was sent to Commonwealth College – a communist institution of higher learning in Mena. During this period Arkansas cultivated a tradition of acceptance and tolerance for sects, movements, institutes, churches, and temples of various and extreme religious and political persuasions.

Even though Faubus will be remembered as the populist leader who was the first governor in the South to dispute the 1954 Supreme Court decision to enforce racial integration, the story does not end there. In some very nasty and sad confrontations at Central High School between his constituency and federal integration officials, Orville stood his ground and was quickly summoned to Washington by Eisenhower. There he refused to concede any compromise and maintained his contrarian stance until Ike was forced to send in Airborne Federal troops to Little Rock to quell the situation so that nine black children could attend classes in the white school.

Still, he knew that no one could be governor of Arkansas without winning the black vote, which represented 30% of the electorate. Orville knew how to get the black vote. Black voters knew where he stood, they knew they could trust him, and he got their vote... going on to enjoy four consecutive terms as governor of the state. Yet Orville Faubus always thought of himself in the perspective of an American liberal, and during his tenure as governor did much to improve conditions in the state especially in the area of education and opportunities for blacks and whites alike.

BOMB: Who were the musicians you encountered and who eventually turned you onto making music yourself? Was it R.L. Burnside? Did you find something more primary in making the music that simply videoing it could not provide?

TAV: Once I was introduced to the charismatic, magical individual known as Rural Burnside in the backwoods of Panola county in north Mississippi, and I heard his haunting, trance-dirge guitar and filmed him through an interminable night in his honky tonk, I fell then completely under the spell of his snaking, swamp infested rhythms. I had never heard anything quite like these darkly melodious strains of erotic yearning and torment that seemed to flow effortlessly from his body and from his battered, de-tuned electric guitar. His honky tonk was like a secular church. Sharecroppers and their women came there for serious merrymaking, for the voluptuous guitar sounds, and howling vociferations as heard from the seemingly farthest reaches and corners of hell itself. The tenant farmers and tractor drivers came for the camaraderie, for the

Rural Burnside on guitar, honky tonk Como, Mississippi Photo: E. Baffle 1974

chicken frying all night in an iron skillet, for the endless cases of cold Schlitz, and they came for miles around to wager on the vagaries of the tumbling dice shaking in a leather dice horn, and for the girls working the back room. At some point during this period I began to see no separation between what was in front of the camera and what was behind it... between being behind the camera and being in front of it, no separation between the observer and the observed.

As a youth I had acquired my first Sears Silvertone guitar, but never learned how to really play it. I only made sounds on it, in part because in my isolation, I had no live models to learn from, and I learn from people's hands. Eventually I traded the guitar for a Webcor open reel field tape recorder. When I encountered Burnside and Charlie Feathers and others, I had models playing before me for the first time. And I had made films and tapes of them playing, and could now playback sound and picture of their playing *ad infinitum*. It was then, and it still is, just as natural to reach for a funky guitar, as it was to pick up a film or video camera.

BOMB: Similarly, I've always thought the most imaginative music had an inherent synaesthetic component in the way that it could blend visual 'tones' and 'colors' with aural harmonics. I've found this to be particularly true with rockabilly, where the heavy use of echoed vocals and reverbed guitar yields an ethereal, nocturnal lament and a perfect mood 'soundtrack' for late-night listening. Do you think your music was influenced by film making or particular genres of cinema, for example, the works of Fellini, Jodorowsky, Lynch, Waters, etc.? Do you write or record your music with any cinematic perspective for the way guitar timbres or textures might be mixed?

TAV: When I first started listening to electric blues records as a youth, I used to lay back and close my eyes and experience visual hallucinations orchestrated by and syncopated with the musical tones and phrases. This form of snyaesthesia is cinematic in abstract form. For me, pure cinema *is* visual music. Yet in my mind, pure cinema is mute – it is silent cinema. Still, it is quite apparent that sound and picture go together very well... and it is the strength of an art form how well it interfaces with another form or medium. As Marshall McLuhan pointed out, new art forms or technologies have the characteristic and capability of 'wrapping around' an earlier art form or technology. Like, for example, television wrapping around film. Then there is music arranged especially for film, often called soundtrack music, conversely film is also conceived for illustrating musical pieces.

Admittedly, I am captivated by Italian movie music from the 60s, which is a genre in itself. For instance, the music to the *La Decima Vittima* is irresistible and totally integrated cinematically. We have produced short films illustrating our songs. The atmosphere of B&W appears most suited to Panther Music, as exemplified by the piece entitled, "Born Too Late". Before we filmed it in Budapest at the 19th century Club Fések, I had met Alejandro Jodorowsky in Paris and was invited to his home one evening. I had the notion of asking him to direct the film. He demurred, but not before giving me a number of his ideas for realizing the song filmicly. In the end, we used none of his rather Dadaist visualizations, but I perceived how his mind worked in terms of a moving picture treatment of musical and lyrical content. When I conceptualized the Panther Burns album, *Hour of the Shadow Dancer*, I thought of it as music designed for a feature film. After recording the album, I collaborated writing a scenario, *Shadow Dancer: the Movie* with Rainer Kirberg, the scenarist in Berlin and director of "Born Too Late". In the process of creating our films, I found that syncing tones, sounds, and music to picture and to moving images produces an intriguing visualization and a very dynamic one with unlimited dramatic possibilities of montage.

BOMB: In another interview you said, "The influence of William Eggleston on my work is in being introduced to a symphony of color and sound while looking at seemingly mundane objects." Would you mind elaborating on what exactly it was about Eggleston's photography that inspired you? Was it exactly the kind of nocturnal, shadowy tone mentioned above? While your music always coaxed a stark black-and-white mood in my mind, were you more inspired by his color or non-color photos?

TAV: To elaborate on that impression of the Eggleston *oeuvre*, not only color relationships but innovative *de*compositional aspects and Expressionistic distortions drew me into the Egglestonian cosmos – a visionary realm of ambiguity and ironic, and unresolved consequences presented on a fabric woven with the most literal and prosaic of objects and icons and with the people – whether seen or unseen – who are attached to them in often alarming ways. Before Panther Burns, I assisted Eggleston on nocturnal missions filming in color with stroboscopic lighting and yielding images of unearthly spectra.... as if Edgar Poe had been dropkicked into post-modern Virginia wielding a Leica lens. As much as his color compositions, his earlier, lengthy B&W essays enthrall me. You are right to perceive our music in black & white imagery. In my own 16mm and 35mm short films, I am most drawn to those filmed in B&W, and all future filmic work I intend to be done in monochrome. On the contrary, in his personal work Eggleston long ago lost contact with the genre of B&W.

BOMB: At the time of Panther Burns' formation in 1979, what was the general vibe of Memphis music culture? With Sun and Stax Records along with numerous other soul labels like Hi, etc., gone or on the decline, I'm curious whether or not there was still a strong sense of identity to the city's music? What else was happening there at the time? Were the city's other 'forward thinking' musicians looking elsewhere at NY or LA punk for inspiration?

TAV: Even with Gospel groups, the nature of music in Memphis has over the years been ostensibly a commercial enterprise. Even before Panther Burns, my comrades were fed up with the status quo. One of the groundbreaking events that brought attention and focus on indigenous musicians and their music was the annual series of Memphis Country Blues Festivals held in Overton Park Shell. Here the great artists of the non-commercial world of country blues and gospel were presented before a new generation eager to experience and to absorb what had by then become traditional genres and forms. By the mid-70s Stax studio was a burned out, bombed out carcass of a movie house. When real money started to be made really fast, and Memphis banks and record company executives exploited and abused the still ascendant popularity of soul music, failing to properly cultivate the phenomena and its artists, the scene deteriorated and went down fast. All record companies of any significance pulled out of Memphis. Burned as badly as they were, the major labels and record companies still have not returned.

Anyway that scene was for rich bond daddies and fancy pimps driving canary yellow Cadillacs and wearing Stetson hats. *Who cares?* Those sorts of bubbles always blow themselves out. What is important is that the music survives. There will always be blues in Memphis. There will always be a Saturday night in Memphis for some nigger or dago – for white or black – to go out and shake a tail feather, or to court his good gal on the front porch with a steel stringed guitar. That is indigenous music. This is the fountainhead, the lodestone, the Mojo Hand, the High John the Conqueroo *root* of black inspired music, and that is the music of America which distinguishes our music from all others. It is a wild root that cannot be weeded out. It is the swamp root from which grows all forms of American popular music that travels upriver to commercial centers and then gets packaged and re-sold and pretty soon Madame LaZonga is doing the Conga on Broadway, and it all comes back down river again. The long silver thread of the blues is unbroken and always connected, yet to most it remains invisible. So the Cramps or the Sex Pistols can come to Memphis and consciously re-fry a fine cooked Southern meal in a way that no one down home has ever quite seen before. Point is: blues, jazz, rock 'n' roll have become universally recognizable and like any great and genuine genre, it lends itself to universal interpretation and re-invention. It is natural then that Memphis musicians connected with the rest of the world, and vice versa. Inspiration is where you find it: in traditions, in trends, in extremes, in multi-cultures.

BOMB: I read that you had not met Alex Chilton before and was not aware of his previous work. True?

TAV: Well, "The Letter" I had heard on the radio, but I had little awareness of a group called the Box Tops. The woods were full of hit records in Memphis and rock 'n' roll stars on every corner.

BOMB: With all the revisionist chatter that surrounds Big Star nowadays, it's difficult to gauge their impact in Memphis at the time. How did you view the Big Star/Ardent Studio influence in your early days? Was it a bit too poppy and jangly for your tastes or did it really open up a new 'sound' to rival Stax/Volt in the 70s?

TAV: Apologies, but I had no knowledge of the band, Big Star, at that time, and still don't know much about them. During the 60s & 70s, I was listening to cotton patch blues, to psychedelia, and to Karl Heinz Stockhausen.

BOMB: How important do you think Panther Burns was in resurrecting Alex's career and all of the critical attention surrounding his work?

TAV: If Panther Burns were responsible for anything concerning this gifted artist, surely it was nothing more than personal diversion and a few kicks.

BOMB: Similarly James Luther Dickinson was a kind of one-man institution stretching back to his inclusion on The Rolling Stones' Sticky Fingers *and his production on Sun Record's finale "Cadillac Man". What was your introduction to him musically and how did he fit into the philosophy of Panther Burns?*

TAV: Jim Dickinson in my mind is hardly a one-man institution, rather he is representative of a community of artists and their audiences, and he is a spokesperson for those artists and for the aficionados attached to them. Jim understands the axiom that for there are to be great poets, there must be great audiences. In that sense, Jim Dickinson characteristic of the 'people' in the most poetic and robustly independent and American sense. From the beginning Jim Dickinson was fully cognizant of the realm of the theatre of Utopian Anarchy from which Panther Burns sprang... and as our mentor he showed Panther Burns how to sing and dance the songs and shuffles of electric medicine show minstrels. As Piano Red before him, Jim – like Panther Burns – was and is still running on Train Time.

BOMB: Many of your records, particularly the early material like Behind the Magnolia Curtain, *were infamous for their very minimal production, where songs were performed 'live' and often in one take. You had said in an interview that, "Most of the tracks are one-take. We didn't do any real mixing, and of course, there were no overdubs. We went into Ardent, and we recorded all the tracks in two afternoons of three-hour sessions. A couple of the tunes we did two takes of, but usually there was just no stopping." Although this was the norm for most traditional blues and country records of the bygone era, it's almost unheard of in the age of big studios and multi-track players. I believe around the same time you and Alex Chilton were working on these recordings in Memphis, he was also producing The Cramps' early material, much of which had a similar production value. Do you recall how much of Panther Burns' stripped-down approach was a collaborative effort and how much of an influence Alex had in mimicking the sounds of early Sun records?*

TAV: Behind the Magnolia Curtain *was in fact recorded in one and two-takes within about 6-hours. There was the presence of the Tate County, Mississippi, marching drum band, members of which were stalwarts in Napoleon Stricklin's Cane Fife & Drum band. The Drum Corps appeared on four tracks marching around Studio B of Ardent and were recorded simultaneously with Panther Burns – all of us playing and thrashing at once. We were *bon vivants* of the swamps living it up on ample doses of fried chicken and short pints of bourbon whiskey. The ensuing threshold of noise was so far overreached that the engineer of the session gave up entirely on observing any recognized parameters of recording standards in a desperate attempt to just get the mess on tape. The battle cry raised by Alex as we waded into each new number was, "I'm *right* behind you, man." There was no real mixing... there was a modicum of EQing during the dumping of the 16-track material onto 1/2-track reels for engraving onto an acetate master disc. Nor was there any er, production... or anyone in charge of production as I remember. As always in those early days of Panther Burns, it was every man for himself.

When the mastering engineer began the task of cutting the acetate production disc from the 1/2 track material, the level of uncontrollable noise that saturated every frequency appalled him. The resulting grooves cut into the soft acetate master disc were so shallow and so close together due to the density of noise present, that fidelity was compromised and the acceptable industry standard for total program length of a vinyl album was exceeded by over three minutes per side. The Cramps' early recordings as produced by Alex and by Jim Dickinson had consciously achieved a level of sonic excellence and dynamic presence, whereas the first Panther Burns album just sort of 'happened' by a process of spontaneous generation.

BOMB: Can you remember what kind of relationship you and Alex had in the studio and what your working dynamic was like? Were you more of the 'idea' and 'music' man while he was the guy behind the controls or was it more of an equal writing/playing relationship?

TAV: Sure we had our recording idols as reference and the studio sounds of SUN Records and the inimitable Joe Meeks productions that we idolized, but we found it impossible to even begin to emulate such sonic wizardry. The equipment and techniques used in those innovative recordings had long disappeared... except for the acoustic, walk-in echo chambers, which we used extensively in our maniacal quest for the lush sounding echo. As for our roles in these ventures, the concepts were generally of my instigation, but it was Alex who was the musical alchemist... me never, because I was not and still am hardly a musician. I am simply a performer, a provocateur... and only play *upon* musical instruments, rather than approach such devices with any degree of musical understanding other than intuitive. On later recordings Alex twirled the knobs more or less 'fixing' everything in the mix as was his extraordinary talent to do... such talent matched only by his astonishing gifts as one of the few towering guitarists and singers of our age, among whom there is no finer. What song writing that has been done in Panther Burns came much later and was by my own hand.

BOMB: *You've made mention of theorists/poets Antonin Artaud and Louis Aragon as lyrical and 'stylistic' influences on Panther Burns as well as practitioners of 'art brut' who much like the forgotten Southern musicians toil on the margins of culture – I agree with you whole-heartedly on this.. In fact (quick aside) I dedicated the introductory section of the Spacemen book to a kind of alternative history of radiation and music that flows through the 20th century demimonde of Georges Bataille, Jean Genet, etc. but centering on the electronic experiments of Artaud contemporaneous with the invention and use of the Atomic Bomb.*

TAV: These are exciting considerations and connections you are evoking. Certainly Artaud and Aragon were influential, but more than lyrical and stylistic, it was the overriding import of their MANIFESTOS that inspired me to action and their unbridled flaying of thought from the bone meat of existence that moved me. How far their influence may have extended, outside of France and Spain, and the narrow strata of those who explore the extremes of theatre and poetry, to equally marginal Southern musicians and bluesmen is difficult to imagine. Perhaps one can relate the rants of Hasil Adkins in some sort of Artaudian context, but the derivative nature of most of these Southern musicians and bluesmen was essentially agrarian. However disenfranchised they were, however mistreated they became, however much their tolerances warped, and once transplanted to the cities, whatever complexities, anxieties, and uncertainties they underwent, they all possessed an understanding of, a thread to, an inner peace, an inner clear spot or memory of it: a pastoral numinous beatific oneness that infused the lives of those who lived or had once lived in the country.

The poetry they wrote, however dark or opining, was always composed as a measure of their inherent connection to universal mysteries, but expressed in compelling everyday, barnyard terms and metaphors. Whereas the awareness of Bataille, Genet, Artaud was self-conscious, erudite, spewing, disassociated, psychoanalytic, subversive – involving a perception of the so called natural order of things from an inverted, convoluted, and irrationally angular view... as Bataille's vision of his syphilitic father's sightless eyes transforming into chicken eyes as he was straining to piss. Even though the radiophonic experiments of Artaud were suppressed toward the end of his life as was his theatre before then, it is interesting to think that aspects of his fractured and frenzied incantations were already taking root, even in the constellated thoughts of country people. With the advent of the Bomb and the Atomic Age, for the first time men began to live with the threat of total annihilation resulting from development and deployment of their own technologies. The mandate to confront the resulting absurdity of existence, the universal fragility of life, as we know it, and the thought of life having less significance than a smear of slime mold, came into startling focus.

BOMB: *Experiments with electrical noise seem to share an historical and procedural similarity with Southern musicians of the post-War era. For example, in another interview on your influences you explained, "In the '50s when these white cats were taking up electric guitars for the first time and black cats were taking them up, this was all new. Audiences weren't educated to this kind of music. You walked out with a tiny Fender amplifier with one 12-inch speaker and one microphone on stage and it was revolutionary. And it was loud, too. They got an incredibly fine mix – an awfully hot sound."*

TAV: As referenced earlier in our discourse, the use of a cracked guitar speaker in Memphis by the incendiary electric country blues guitarist, Pat Hare, thus producing the first fuzz tone guitar sound may have been simply accidental... like many innovative discoveries. The velvet noise that floated on the razor's edge of Pat Hare's guitar sound became his signature when he played with James Cotton or whomever else. The discontent, the urgency, the RAGE heard on the recordings of his guitar are more poignant, more powerful, and more meaningful in its country blues phrasing and lyricism than a freight train load of all the million selling faux-revolutionary, ghetto hate-music one hears everywhere today. Pat Hare's origins were traced in a lineage from Robert Johnson, but instead of poisoning by a jealous female, he died in prison convicted of murdering his woman.

Personally, I have come full circle in my proclivities for aesthetic expression that I choose to wrap around myself tipping down this lonesome road. I now seek harmonious tones infused with noises... harmony in extremes, in contrasts of blacks and whites and its delicate gradations in between. I crave dissonance in its most discordant elegance; movement in its most dynamic and erotic transports and postures; body movement of the most subtle and dimensional form like two people walking through each other. Light and Shadow... and shadow *lifted* from its object. Bombardment of Noises and its attendant silence. TOUCH and the UNtouchable. THRILL and the ENthralled. Wherever I go I am searching the *doppelganger*... Mirror and reflected Image. Sound and the VOID.

BOMB: *What kind of connections did you find between the mid-century French poets and the Appalachian and Delta musicians that drew you to both? Was it purely lyrical? Or was it a connection made between these two embattled groups taking up electric equipment to incite a kind of musical violence?*

TAV: Regarding mid-century French poets, I was not particularity drawn to any as I was drawn to mid-19th century French Symbolists, until these last three and a half years spent in Paris when I discovered the actions, provocations, and antics of the Situationists and their *Führer*, Guy DeBord. With this movement, I feel kinship... as I do with the era of Happenings that occurred in New York in the 60s, and later in the 80s with such saintly art-actions as Chris Burden nailing himself to a Volkswagen. Here again I must reiterate the fact that Panther Burns do not engender or mitigate toward evocations of violence. Although once backed into a corner, we have incited to *riot*... as in the case of being retained by the Clash and their manager Cosmo Vinyl to open the first two dates on their last and abortive US tour, wherein Panther Burns were denounced on the Vanderbilt University stage and greeted with howls of derision by an audience of benighted college students.

Onstage next night in Knoxville, the band was greeted by 6000 inebriated rednecks at the University of Tennessee, whereupon fistfights were breaking out everywhere as Panther Burns attempted to entertain this assemblage of unruly music lovers, only to finally throw up our arms in pale and ashen futility, and launch into a 20-minute fuzz-toned rendition of the "Bourgeois Blues", which even *they* understood the true significance of, and which inflamed an already volatile situation beyond the threshold of riotous invective. If they'd had beer bottles, they would have killed us.

When Panther Burns at last acquitted themselves, heroic only as victims of pure desperation, and left the enormous stage with its ponderous PA monitors the size of a Ford Focus, we had departed in the defeated glory of knowing that we had been *heard* and heard well before an auditorium overstuffed with rattling puppet heads. When the Clash came out with their massive amplification stacked high and with the redundancy of three tuneless electric guitars blaring and myriad electronic processing devices running, the grinding wad of indecipherable and uncalculated *white* noise they produced had the untoward effect of *assuaging!* the lusts of the assembled. The same army of Clash fans who, when Panther Burns were onstage, had been panting and clawing the air for something even more hot and nasty, were now transformed from riotous celebrants into an appalling host of docile troglodytes.

BOMB: *I'm also curious how much of an effect the French and Beat poets had on you as a 'stylized' performance artist?*

TAV: When I first saw the Cramps on stage, I was sure then that I recognized a significant and contemporary manifestation of Artaud's *Theatre of Cruelty*... for this is a multi-faceted dramaturgy beyond hardcore. There must be lyricism, eroticism, Dionysian thrashing, masks, and the forked tongues of vipers. Groups such as Throbbing Gristle and Furo del Baus in Spain further embody this theatre in our era. Panther Burns, however, are not consciously or unconsciously adherents of the *Theatre of Cruelty*. Rather, Panther Burns are an iteration of the Orphic Vision... as celebrated by symbolist poets, and as opposed to mystical vision. Thusly it is the mission of Panther Burns to stir up the dark waters of the unconscious.

BOMB: I also really enjoyed your explanation of Panther Burns' perspective on celebrity that you espoused on the Marge Thrasher Show on WHBQ-TV: "We create an anti-environment to make visible that part of Memphis and of life that is normally overlooked…the Panther Burns are anti-stars. They're black holes where a star should be. The purpose of the Panther Burns is to forge an anti-environment to make authentic music that's all around us more visible, especially in Memphis." How much of Panther Burns' mythology do you think comes from your very definitive image and style?

TAV: It is impossible to separate Panther Burns from its mystique.

BOMB: Once again, it seems you've surrounded yourself with an admixture of classical Gothic elegance and the American hillbilly aesthetic—

TAV: Panther Burns is a Southern Gothic, backwoods ballroom musical troupe – purveyors of *Antler del Arte*. We are, however, as Eggleston would say, *gentlemen… not farmers*.

BOMB: Is this an intentional tribute to past idols or do you see it as a 'postmodern' reinterpretation of these influences?

TAV: Both, in fact. Jerry Lee Lewis has referred to himself as an interpreter of styles. Likewise in the case of Panther Burns, yet in terms of post-postmodern positioning, we would be considered as *re*-interpreters.

BOMB: In another interesting quote from the 80s, you were explaining the relationship between blues-based groups like Panther Burns and atonal musicians like Arto Lindsay on the New York scene. You said, "Groups like DNA became our friends. Whereas Arto Lindsay works from a radically different point of view, this atonal 'beyond free jazz' music, is hardly without emotional content in the conventional sense of the term and at a point in its trajectory, converges with that of Panther Burns."

TAV: Certainly Arto Lindsay impressed me as an artist and as an individual, as did Tim Wright, the bass player of DNA who in fact introduced me around New York and to Chris Stein/Glenn O'Brien's *TV Party* cable show in particular. The terse, 45-second musical implosions delivered on stage by DNA as 'songs' at Hilly Crystal's (himself a 60s icon) joint called CBGBs were the kind of extreme atonal primitivism that appealed directly to my sensibilities. Yet inherent in the yowling vocals and the fearsome electric instrumentation of DNA lurked an intellectual gradient that had sardonically turned in upon itself. Something like the image from antiquity of the snake biting its tail – the ouroboros. There was a completeness of expression in DNA that brought rampant atonal chaos around full circle with an enthralling cataclysmic dissonance… resulting in a totally luxurious sonic abstraction.

BOMB: You were quoted: "The no-wave ethos was mainly the ideas of people who turned up at the Mudd Club: the notion of a detached relationship, bloodless, under narcosis. And groups like The Cramps or Panther Burns had the kind of flame, which seemed ideal to give an antithetical direction to this type of empty engagement. There was a demand for what we did; the scene needed groups like ours, and we could work elbow to elbow with bands which, on the surface, appeared completely different."

TAV: Panther Burns originated in Memphis as an Anti-Environment affronting prevailing conditions. Arriving in New York we quickly found ourselves likewise positioned in the sense that we represented unbridled emotional frenzy and sentiment – tribal, anti-intellectual, provocative, and by any standard, reckless as only renegades from the heathen swamps can be. In New York it was not our progenitors whom we set in relief, but our esteemed, ultra-chilled, and in most cases quasi-professional colleagues. Panther Burns were not and still are not professional anything. However, we did bring with us the flourish of a suave and stylish urbanity that only certain southern cities possess. For these attributes Panther Burns were accepted on the fringes of the downtown scene, and at times celebrated by the cognoscenti. Yet for most New Yorkers we would probably be looked upon with curious condescension as hicks from Arkansas and Memphis… expressive of a lingering northern attitude toward Southerners in general, which in itself is revelatory of a benighted projection of themselves.

BOMB: *Can you explain how/why Panther Burns decided to migrate to NYC at the time? How would you compare the Memphis scene surrounding Ardent and Jim Dickinson with the New York scene of the late 1970s/early 80s? How exactly did you ingratiate yourself into the Mudd Club and the Downtown '81 scene?*

TAV: Well, despite the unfortunate term, 'ingratiate', Panther Burns were actually invited to play in New York. Before Steve Mass had even thought of the name, *Mudd Club*, he was traveling through the South, and he, in fact, dropped by my pad with Anya Phillips, later a cohort of James Chance. It was on this trip south, that the concept of the Mudd Club befell Steve Mass. This joint on White Street in NoHo with a uni-gender, no-doors bathroom evolved into a kind of social club, a *demi-monde* for puerile exuberants from all five boroughs who were responsible for its ever-mutating, artful décor and downtown philosophies. It was a democratic room like CBGBs. I mean there was a doorman, but not too discerning. A relaxed crowd, usually stoned, but ready for anything. Part of its success was owing to the eclectic nature of Steve's booking. Even Johnny Thunders went there one night to catch a doubleheader with Panther Burns and Beatster poet John Giorno holding forth on the same bill.

In Memphis, Ardent is a state-of-the-art commercial recording studio. Panther Burns were tolerated at Ardent. Once the owner, John Fry, brought us a box of cookies while we were mixing. Reckon that's righteous treatment for a group that never sold any records. Jim Dickinson is not only a formidable musician and a sensitive artist, but he is also an erudite closet gentleman. Jim made a living in the recording studios in Memphis, he has fronted the raucous and provocative Mudboy and the Neutrons, and he has been supportive of alternative and underground groups and artists... to the point of personal sacrifice. One miserable day in Midtown Memphis, Mudboy grunted and gave birth to a critter called Panther Burns.

BOMB: *How did you view the electronic/dance sub-culture that was also brewing at the time? Did you ever go to the Danceteria or the SoHo loft parties that hosted these various events? Did you see any particularly outrageous 'noise' shows around that time, like Glenn Branca's guitar orchestra, or early hip-hop shows? If so, do you think this kind of foray into experimental sound affected your own work?*

TAV: The first gig Panther Burns played in New York was organized by Jim Fouratt at Danceteria, who was in charge of booking the club during the heady, incipient phase of its existence. Maybe it was a Mafia joint, like Peppermint Lounge, but who cares. On this auspicious event at Danceteria, Panther Burns hit the stage around 2:30 in the morning as the headliner usually came on around 4:00 a.m. in New York in those days. We came out six-strong including a fellow Arkansan, Bob Palmer – then Pop & Jazz critic for the *NY Times* – wailing on a savagely dissonant clarinet. Panther Burns sawed through a brutal forty-five minute set of such cacophony that the audience seemed riveted in some swaying, yet petrified trance. Afterward, Fouratt came backstage to our dressing room and proclaimed, "That was the worst sounding crock of unadulterated *NOISE* I have ever heard... *in my life*! But there is someone outside from London who wants to talk to you about recording a record. Geoff Travis from some company called Rough Trade. Shall I let him in...?"

By the time Travis had left the room, Jim Fouratt was still undergoing a verbal flogging from Alex Chilton on the topic of Panther Burns' tone-science versus Fouratt's unsolicited opinions. Some months later when the album was released, a half page review in *Melody Maker* appeared under a block letters subheader entitled, "PURE SICK NOISE", thus corroborating the prophetic nature of Fouratt's remarks. In a subsequent show at Danceteria, Panther Burns invited performance artist and actress, the exquisite Anne Magnuson, to share the bill with us, and later I joined her onstage in one of her performances at Life Cafe on Avenue B. Diagonally across Tomkins Sq. Park from there was a tasty underground pit called the Pyramid Club where Panther Burns also delivered more than one darkly luminous concert on a bill with house favorite, John Sex.

Further uptown at Peppermint Lounge, Panther Burns shared an Anti-Nuclear Rally bill

Katy K & John Sex, *Soho News* August 20, 1980 Photo: Dean Chamberlain

with Allen Ginsberg during the period when he was playing the harmonium and backed by Parisian street musicians on electric guitars. I presented the bard with our first album entitled, *Behind the Magnolia Curtain.* Some years later when Panther Burns were in town, we dropped by Allen's pad on East 12th Street announcing our arrival by tossing a pebble up to what we suspected to be his apartment window. Miraculously, the poet appeared at the windowsill and invited us up. As we sat around his table, I asked if he'd remembered ever listening to the album

I'd once given him. Allen gave some sort of ambiguous reply. A few minutes later I was astonished when I happened to notice our very album was actually sitting on the turntable of his phonograph!

As for the Glenn Branca guitar orchestra, I did not see it. I can, however, say that I witnessed an all girls orchestra named Pullsalama, who often played Danceteria and who were outrageously noisy. The only hip-hop events that moved me were those of Afrika Bambaataa, whom I met and grooved on, along with Phast Phreddie on Avenue D. Still, the one orchestra delivering arias of melodic atonality, which had a formative influence on my own aesthetic, was Sun Ra & the Solar Myth Arkestra who enthralled me at the Squatt Theatre.

BOMB: When discussing Panther Burns' contribution to the New York No Wave scene, you had said that the rebirth of great music in the early eighties was a product of the sixties. How did you see the interrelationship between these two different eras of music? No Wave had a reputation for 'killing the idols' of music's past, whether it be in the traditional punk sound of The Ramones and The Sex Pistols or the monolithic histories of the 60s and 70s. That said, how do you connect the sounds of No Wave with the 60s? Was it more a spiritual kinship than a musical connection?

TAV: As for the No Wave ferment that emerged in New York during the 80s, what you had for example were musical groups such as the Lounge Lizards or James Chance and the Contortions working of out an often atonal bag blatantly inspired by 60s jazz titans and pioneers ranging from early Paul Bley to a spread of 'cool jazz' artists like Eric Dolphy. DNA and Arto Lindsay were perhaps the closest to outright celebration of pure noise in the sublimely exalted moments of their performance... connected, in my mind, to such experimenters from the 60s as LaMonte Young. We can distinguish No Wave in degree from its musical antecedents in terms of spirituality or absence thereof, by its supreme lack of emotion and by its bloodless attempts to adopt a posture of narcotized cool, contrasting with transports of emotional frenzy produced by thrashing instrumentation and extreme vocalizations as in the case of Arto and Chance.

No Wave was iconoclastic. I have not read any manifestos of No Wave, but its attempt to wipe the slate clean. to hatch an original genre, and to explore a completely original direction was, as always, practically impossible. Under this mandate, what artists often do is to emulate their mentors, and then once having absorbed what techniques, attributes, styles, and innovations they can manage to acquire, they destroy or try to expurgate traces of their masters' influence. The residue of what is left, combined with the contemporaneous psychology of the moment, is the kernel of that which will emerge and be heralded as a new direction.

The essential connection between the fertile scene of the early 80s in New York and San Francisco, and the era of the 60s was a sense of experimentation. The notion of the errant individual; the idea that anything is possible with or without training, resources, money; the job of breaking down barriers between art forms and between social strata were the driving forces that connected these periods. Out of this experimental scene in New York surfaced performers as diverse and supremely inventive as Ann Magnuson, Klaus Noami, Suicide, and later Antony and the Johnsons; there were artists as iconic as David McDermott and Peter McGough, Keith Haring, Kenny Scharf; visionary publishers such as Betsy Sussler and Diego Cortez, and filmmakers like Amos Poe and Eric Mitchell. All of them were experimental, individual, and defying strict categorization. As in the 60s, personalities emerged who were products of an experimental and explosive art scene and cultural movements that sprang from the underground.

The magazines got their interviews, the labels got their records, the band got its audiences, and as the end of the second decade of Panther Burns approached, and as assorted Memphis hussies were closing in on me, I had the idea to split from the Bluff City to another river town, way, way down south – to Buenos Aires on the Rio del Plata. Tav Falco had more or less matured to the point where he could handle himself onstage in the usual unreliable scenes and places. I passed some luxurious months in the Argentine capitol hanging out at *milongas* and dancing tango every night. Alas, it was the call of the Panther Burns that brought me back to the states to New York to orchestrate the formation of a traveling line-up of young turks from Gotham for an upcoming six-weeks tour of the European continent.

Memphis musicians never proved hardy enough for such protracted ventures, so their crusty Yankee brethren had to be cajoled into coming aboard. After the exit of Ron Miller from the group, an East Village gentleman scholar, humanitarian, and Avenue D wit named Kai Eric took over the bottom frequencies. He played a lavender electric bass that the Gibson office in Hamburg had soon bestowed upon him as a core member of Panther Burns. Kai was the son of a ranking official at the United Nations in New York. He seemed to know everybody on the downtown scene, and everybody knew him as a Rod Sterling spin-off, down to the same Twilight Zone dark suit and banter for which Sterling was famous. He was a roommate with John Michel Basquiat before the untoward OD of the Warhol protégé. The presence of Kai Eric was invariably stimulating, stylish, and amusing, and I pushed for his inclusion in the group. Nevertheless his tolerance for the vicissitudes of the road was limited. After a few weeks of hardship on the road, his entertaining personality morphed into that of a mutinous conspirator that almost wrecked the tour. Yet, to his credit, Kai Eric was no quitter, and inevitably he rode out the tours to the bitter end. As my high school Go-Devils football coach insisted, *a quitter never wins, and a winner never quits.*

After the last Euro tour the band decided to establish a beachhead in Paris and try to land a new record deal in the City of Light. Initially conceived by me as a memoir of sorts under the title of *The Argentine Diaries*, from the notes I'd kept in Buenos Aires, I had transformed the poems and scribbles into songs while in New York. As Falco was not such a prolific songwriter, I gave this folio of songs to the band and in a rehearsal studio in Saint Vincennes, the group constructed a roughly hewn skeleton of album demos. We solicited the demo – the first demo ever made in the career of the Panther Burns – to independent labels throughout America, Europe and Japan. Alas, the answer by A&R execs was a resounding NO. Instead, they offered up any number of "suggestions" of how to change the Panther Burns concept to make it more popular and more profitable. And the answer from Falco – ever the stubborn Calabrese – was an equally intransigent NO. Falco, in the grandiose vision he had of Panther Burns, actually thought he had something rarefied in those recordings. He informed me, *what a critic doesn't understand, he despises, and despite the rhetoric, what a label finds strange and new, it discards as rubbish.* OK, who was I to argue with hotheaded, road weary singer who'd drifted into Memphis from some nameless place in Arkansas. Eventually Falco retreated back to the Bluff City to chill, and left me in Paris to flog the demo. After a couple of years it became apparent that the demo was doing more harm than good, but at least the demo had the beneficial effect of weeding out the men from the boys on the indie record scene.

Left in Paris to my own devices was not so bad, I came to realize. I could dance tango any night of the week, and I started spending many happy hours viewing obscure films in the Cinémathèque Française on Boulevard Bonne Nouvelle, and I hung out at Café Zimmer at Place Chatelet – a café that reminded me of my days in the coffeehouses of merry and sinister Vienna when we were recording the *Shadow Dancer* album with Panther Burns, and making the short film, *Masque of Hotel Orient* with Kenneth Anger. Soon I was attending to soirées in galleries and in private salons with artists, musicians, and photographers.

Introduced to the best musicians of the city, I persuaded a promising guitarist to join the band, Grégoire Garrigues, who'd started his career at seventeen in the band of leather clad French idol, Vince Taylor. Laurent Lanouzière, a young bass player and fanatic for Panther Burns, came on board. The saucy Italian girl from Rome, whom we had met eons before in New York and brought to Memphis to play with the Hellcats, rejoined the fold on drums. Falco flew over when we booked mini-tours for the group here and there around the continent, then he'd shuttle back to Cox St. where he continued to live as a kind of stranger in his own hometown.

One evening roaming around Saint Germain-des-Prés, I ran into Julien Hohenberg and Bibi Ford in front of La Closerie des Lilas. We went inside and had a few rounds of drinks. They were newlyweds! They had gotten together when Julien had hired Bibi as legal counsel during the litigation of his estate. It became obvious that she was trying to resurrect him, but Julien was severely depressed, drooping his head at the table in Cloisere. He ended up losing all his money, basically, like he'd told Connie, *what if he lost his money*. Had only his children and stockholders had faith in Julien's speculation, his business acumen would've been vindicated and all concerned would be sitting on easy street. Julien and Bibi seemed to be in love and celebrated their union with élan, still he was a walking advertisement for solemnity of trust that's been broken. A year or so after our encounter on the *trotoir*, I heard that the droll couple had divorced, and Julien was hanging with a bevy of black girls in north Memphis who were taking him for a ride.

Then, out of nowhere, against the grain, and despite the all apparent odds, the new album, CONJURATIONS; *Séance for Deranged Lovers*, was picked up by Stag-O-Lee records in Germany. Falco caught the next plane smoking, and came sailing in on the wing to the fatherland. Concert agencies put the French/Italian version of the band out on another six-weeks tour of all the equivocal clubs, canal barges, and RnR festivals on the continent east and west. Last I heard, Tav Falco and the Unapproachable Panther Burns are still out there… touring in some god-forsaken place in the Orient.

Tav Falco in Munich Photo: Bernhardt Kümstedt c. 1996

EPILOGUE

Withdrawn, as I have from the shores of the Bluff City, the lot of a frugal and relatively carefree existence on the *rive droit* of Paris has befallen me. I dwell in an artist's garret on the Rue des Solitaires in the old quarter of Belleville where Edith Piaf was found as a baby abandoned on a doorstep, and where the *mauvais garçons* would never anywhere, anytime, remove their caps. I haunt the bistros and cabarets and run with gypsies – I loaf by day and I move by night... and I wish you *mes amis, une très bonne nuit.*

–E. Baffle

EULOGY
JIM DICKINSON

R.I.P.

I'm just dead, I'm not gone.

Jim Dickinson was the creator, muse, protector, and an esteemed member of Panther Burns. Jim was always there for me personally as a supporter and a guiding force long before I ever picked up a guitar, and he stood behind my efforts right up to the end – revealing in his taciturn, yet expansive way the mystery of what it is to be an artist. You are hardly gone, JIM. Your presence will remain eternally with us and with those who are listening to the echoes of your battle cry, *Power to the People.*

 –tav falco, 2009

 P.B.F.L.

 Panther Burns Forever Lasting

EULOGY
ALEX CHILTON

R.I.P.

Let us raise our glasses to a fallen comrade. And ask ourselves did we celebrate this man in life as we do now in death? Ah yes, we did embrace our comrade and drew him close to our hearts and minds... as close as he would allow. Sure he touched us literally and he touched us profoundly: as an artist with lyrical intensity, as a person with camaraderie granted and camaraderie rebuffed. Such are the complexities of the artist and of the person. We realize it's not so easy to be friends with an artist, especially a gifted one. His smile often twisted into a leer, even when he was amused by your bonhomie and by your adulation. Be careful of tendencies: OK we've created it; now let's deconstruct it. Godhead on the one hand, destroying angel on the other... Lord help you if you were caught in between. His tones were golden, and he knew that... better than anyone.

Was he resentful because he had given so much, and had received less than the key to the temple of abiding good fortune and fame immemorial? Was he content in his rickety 18th century cottage on the edge of the French Quarter, surrounded by his guitars and aquatints and cognoscenti of musicians who celebrated him as we do now? Did he draw all that he could take from his talents? Did he quaff draughts of indolence? The answers mean little, and the questions even less. What matters is that those whom he touched, were touched immutably. His legacy is of the mind, of the soul, of earthly pleasure, and of just and lost causes. He left us with that redeeming spark of wit and flame to keep us going when we're hovering down in the foxhole of doubt and uncertainty and dodging the adverse missives of Lady Luck... comforted in thinking that Alex would have liked that, or he would have appreciated this, or he would have been elated by this or that, or let's do it the way Alex does it. His opinion, his taste, his love is what matters in the end.

The last time I saw Alex was in Paris visiting in his posh suite at Hotel George le Cinq. He was pleased with his rooms, and we stayed up late while he merrily tutored me with the unending music lesson that had been on-going since I met him some twenty-five years before... the lesson that never seemed to quite 'take', and which I understood little better than the first time he drilled me. He would say *Tav, somebody's got to keep the rhythm*. And now I wonder, as the last grain of sand has sped through the hourglass, *who...* will keep the rhythm? Raise our glasses to console the living for the loss of a comrade fallen in the snow, which in its chill and whiteness is purifying, rather than fallen in the desert, which is barren.

–tav falco, 2009

P.B.F.L.

Panther Burns Forever Lasting

Jim Dickinson playing his Venetian drum on *Sugar Ditch Revisited* Sessions, Studio B in Sam Phillips Recording studio
photo: Eugene Baffle 1985

INDEX

(Italic numbers = illustrations)